ISRAEL

The Historical Atlas

ISRAEL
The Historical Atlas

The Story of Israel
From Ancient Times to the Modern Nation
By Correspondents of The New York Times

Joel Brinkley

Malcolm W. Browne

Peter Grose

Bernard Gwertzman

Clyde Haberman

Judith Miller

Serge Schmemann

David K. Shipler

John Noble Wilford

And a Special Biographical Section
Nation Builders
Leaders Who Shaped Israel

Macmillan USA

MACMILLAN PUBLISHING USA
A Simon & Schuster Macmillan Company
1633 Broadway
New York, NY 10019-6785

Library of Congress Cataloging-in-Publication Data

Israel : the historical atlas: from ancient times to the modern
   nation / by correspondents of the New York Times.
        p.   cm.
      Includes bibliographical references and index.

      ISBN 0-02-861987-0 (alk. paper)
        1. Israel — Historical geography — Maps.   I. New York Times
Company.
G22366.S1   I8   1997   <G&M>
9110'.5694 — DC21   97-24608
                                                         CIP
                                                         MAPS

Printed in the United States

Design, artwork and typesetting by
Arcadia Editions Limited

10 9 8 7 6 5 4 3 2 1

DESIGN: Malcolm Swanston and Jonathan Young

INDEXING: Shirley Ellis, Kate Swanston

MAPS DESIGNED AND CREATED BY: Peter Gamble, Elsa Gibert, Peter Smith, Malcolm Swanston and Jonathan Young

CORRESPONDENTS

Joel Brinkley — Jerusalem bureau chief (1988-1991); reporter and editor for *The New York Times* since 1983.

Malcolm W. Browne — Science reporter for *The New York Times*; won Pulitzer Prize in 1964 for coverage of the Vietnam War.

Peter Grose — Jerusalem bureau chief (1970-1972), formerly Moscow bureau chief and a Vietnam correspondent; former managing editor of *Foreign Affairs* magazine.

Bernard Gwertzman — Foreign editor of *The New York Times* (1989-1995), former chief diplomatic correspondent and Moscow bureau chief; editorial director of *The Times'* Electronic Media Company.

Clyde Haberman — Jerusalem bureau chief (1991-1995), former bureau chief in Tokyo and Rome; *Times* columnist.

Judith Miller — Cairo bureau chief (1983-1985); reporter and editor for *The New York Times* since 1977.

Serge Schmemann — Jerusalem bureau chief since 1995; former bureau chief in Moscow and Bonn; won the Pulitzer Prize in 1991 for international reporting.

David K. Shipler — Jerusalem bureau chief (1979-1984), former Moscow bureau chief and Washington correspondent; won the Pulitzer Prize in 1987 for his book *Arab and Jew*.

John Noble Wilford — Archaeological specialist for *The New York Times;* won the Pulitzer Prize in 1984 for science reporting.

Editors

Bernard Gwertzman
Dean Toda
Mitchel Levitas
Karen Cetinkaya, photographs

Preface

This book lies somewhere on that often disputed border where history meets journalism: an historical atlas (with magnificent maps and many vintage photographs) written by reporters. Is it History with a capital H? Hardly. Is it "just" journalism? Not quite. At the same time, this is journalism that reflects a half-century of commitment by *The New York Times* to reporting from the scene the remarkable transformation of Israel from the mere hope of a new Jewish homeland into a regional superpower.

Few places on earth are more freighted with the stones and stories that have shaped actual history; this has made reporting from Israel a uniquely formidable assignment that occasionally catches the correspondent between a time warp and a twister. For example, the period of the Ottoman Empire hardly seemed a propitious time to launch the dream. Two terrible World Wars finally made it happen and after more bloody struggles with Arab neighbors and now an edgy peace it is Islamic, secular, modern Turkey that is the closest regional military ally of the Jewish state.

The nine outstanding writers who contributed new articles for this book served as *Times* correspondents in Israel and the Middle East since the 1948 War of Independence or have written widely on their subjects. All but two are still with the paper. So this effort is by way of a professional reunion for them — along with many other correspondents, some of whom are no longer alive, whose original work is reflected in the documentary sidebars republished from *Times* files. If their reporting was history on the run, the new content may be called journalism while seated.

Mitchel Levitas
Editorial Director,
Book Development
The New York Times

Such a land, resettled by a new and Jewish nation, tilled and watered by intelligent hands, warmed by the tropic sun, producing on its soil all the plants that men find necessary or delicious, from sugar cane and bananas to the vines and grains of the temperate regions and the cedars and pines of the Alps. Such a land, I repeat, would be the Promised Land of our day if Providence were to give it a people, and the tide of world affairs peace and freedom.

ALPHONSE DE LAMARTINE
(1790-1869)
From "Voyage to the Orient" (1835)

Contents

Tracing the history from biblical times and the Roman Conquest, this chapter reviews the peoples of the Old Testament and the birth of Christianity, the Crusades through the fall of the Ottoman Empire up to the Balfour Declaration, the British Empire's reluctant promise in 1917 to create a Jewish homeland.

A report on the personalities, issues and the internal conflicts that marked the Zionist movement, beginning in the late 19th Century, and which culminated in the creation of Israel in May, 1948. The agrarian kibbutz movement of early settlers to Palestine in the period between the wars was followed by the desperate efforts of Holocaust survivors to reach the Promised Land despite a powerful British military cordon. Then, as the British mandate began to crumble under political and Jewish military attack, fighting broke out between Jewish armies for supremacy in the conclusive chapter of the drive for statehood.

United Nations partition between Jews and Arabs led to an immediate multi-pronged Arab attack and the War of Independence. The next war wasn't long in coming: the 1956 Suez invasion, and superpower involvement in the future of the state. The period was marked by shifting internal politics, huge migration from abroad and economic growth.

The war's aftermath both inspired and traumatized Israel, and has had lasting influence on shaping its domestic political culture and on international relations in the Mideast. Israel was surrounded by implacable enemies as a flourishing democracy with characteristics of a virtual garrison state, a Cold War pawn with only one reliable ally.

CHAPTER 5
FROM WAR TO PEACE   82

Bernard Gwertzman

The glory of the Six-Day War almost turned into a disaster for Israel when lands it had captured were overrun by Syria and Egypt. With U.S. emergency aid, Israel recovered and dealt its Arab foes both a military and psychological defeat. The stage was thus set for Anwar Sadat's historical journey to Jerusalem in 1977 — the first truce in 30 years of war. Two years later Egypt and Israel, under its first Likud leader, Menachem Begin, signed a peace treaty brokered at Camp David by Jimmy Carter.

MAPS

CHAPTER 6
THE WARS IN LEBANON AND AT HOME   96

Joel Brinkley

Following the Israeli invasion of Lebanon in 1982, aimed at wiping out the P.L.O. and its safe havens, world opinion turned against Israel and even Israelis questioned whether the nation's overwhelming military power had been wisely used. The division deepened with the rise of Palestinian terrorism abroad — the *Achille Lauro* hijacking and the airport massacres in Rome and Vienna, all in 1985 — and the beginning of organized Palestinian resistance, the intifada, at home. Israel harshly struck back and a renewal of the bitter standoff seemed the most likely future.

Special Report: Massacre in Beirut   103

MAPS

CHAPTER 7
BREAKTHROUGH 114

Clyde Haberman

It was precisely the standoff — and American pressure in the wake of Operation Desert Storm — that led each side to radically rethink reality. Israel realized that it was better to seek a deal with the P.L.O. than confront more terrorism from increasingly powerful Islamic fundamentalists who threatened the P.L.O. as well. For its part, the P.L.O. finally admitted that Israel was here to stay. The twin conclusions led in 1993 to a secret deal in Oslo, sealed on the White House lawn in September, 1993, with a stunning handshake between Yitzhak Rabin and Yasir Arafat. A peace treaty with Jordan followed in 1994 and tough negotiations with Syria ensued. But violence was never far off: an Israeli settler massacred 29 Arabs in a mosque in Hebron and a wave of Islamic terrorist suicide bombings killed scores of Israelis.

MAPS

CHAPTER 8
HOPES AND FEARS 126

Serge Schmemann

The peace process fitfully continued with Israeli withdrawal from portions of the West Bank and Gaza Strip, even while many Israelis had second thoughts about their future security, and since terrorist bombings did not subside, even some doves became edgy. Then, amidst increasingly angry and fearful opposition by right-wing Israelis, a young Orthodox student assassinated Prime Minister Rabin in November, 1995, just as he left a peace rally. His successor, Shimon Peres, could not allay security fears skillfully exploited by the young Likud leader, Benjamin Netanyahu. In an extremely close vote in May, 1996, the Labor government was toppled by Netanyahu.

MAPS

Chapter One:
The Ancient Land

John Noble Wilford

The Greek Orthodox monastery of St. George, with foundations dating to the early 5th century, nestled among the cliffs near Jericho.

"IN THE BEGINNING" — the familiar opening to the Book of Genesis is both irresistible and appropriate. In the beginning, a time much earlier than once imagined, there was the land, which a people would one day call the Promised Land. A small land, squeezed between the Mediterranean and the lowest place on earth, the Dead Sea, and no more than 150 miles from Dan in the north to Beersheba in the south. A small but central piece of geography between the sea and the desert, a narrow corridor linking the two great land masses of Africa and Eurasia. Through this corridor passed ancestral humans migrating out of Africa more than a million years ago.

Skeletons and stone artifacts found in caves near Mount Carmel attest to the earliest known occupation of this land, about 100,000 years ago. These cave dwellers were anatomically modern humans, *Homo sapiens sapiens* — people like us. For a long time, they must have shared the land with another kind of humans, the now-extinct Neanderthals, whose 60,000-year-old bones have been collected in neighboring caves and over by the Sea of Galilee. For all anyone knows, the Neanderthals had been there as long or longer than the modern humans. Was their co-existence peaceful, or the first contest over a land that has seldom known tranquility?

Digging at Jericho, archeologists have uncovered traces of later people who were making the transition from hunting and gathering to a more settled society that cultivated cereals. The Natufians, as they are called, were among the first to experiment in village living. Beginning around 11,000 years ago, they were building clusters of round stone-walled houses; Jericho is often referred to as the earliest town in the world.

By the time of written history, some 5,000 years ago, agriculture, the wheel, bronze metallurgy and the first cities were transforming the region now known as the Middle East. The people then living in the land-corridor were mainly simple farmers and herders, though hardly isolated from larger events. For their land lay midway between the rising civilizations along the Nile and between the Tigris and Euphrates rivers, empires that would bestride the ancient Middle East for several millennia. Time and again, whoever lived in this corridor had to contend with armies of conquest marching through, bringing war, pillage and the burden of ceaseless tribute.

Excavation of the earliest city of Jericho. The fabled walls of Jericho from the Bible were of a much earlier era and have disappeared in the ravages of nature.

It was to this imperiled place, according to the Bible, that the people of Abraham came from Ur in Mesopotamia, probably in the early second millennium B.C. In those days, the migration of families and tribes along the fringes of Mesopotamia was not uncommon. Abraham's people, after a sojourn in Egypt, settled in the hill country of the land, then occupied by people called Canaanites. Here begins the biblical history of Israel.

Abba Eban, the modern Israeli statesman and writer, described the Bible as "a body of splendid and passionate writing revered over the centuries by more people than have ever come under the spell of any other literature." Like all accounts of their histories by ancient cultures, the Bible blends fact and legend, and it is often impossible to separate the two. Scholars are always trying. From Egyptian monumental inscriptions and Babylonian clay tablets, and increasingly in archeological digs in Israel, they have extracted some corroboration of bib-

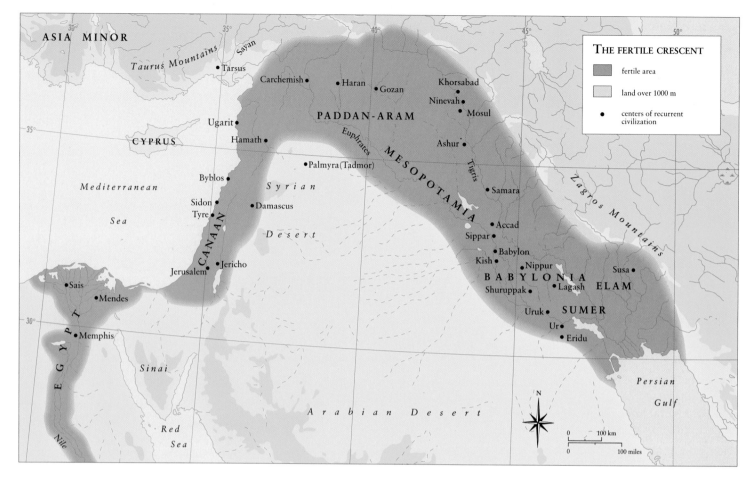

THE FERTILE CRESCENT

- fertile area
- land over 1000 m
- centers of recurrent civilization

BELIEVERS SCORE IN DEBATE OVER THE BATTLE OF JERICHO

By JOHN NOBLE WILFORD

After years of doubt among archeologists, a new analysis of excavations has yielded a wide range of evidence supporting the biblical account about the fall of Jericho. It may well be true that, in the words of the old spiritual, "Joshua fit the battle of Jericho, and the walls come tumbling down." A study of ceramic remnants, royal scarabs, carbon-14 dating, seismic activity in the region and even some ruins of tumbled walls produced what is being called impressive evidence that the fortified city was destroyed in the Late Bronze Age, about 1400 B.C.

The prevailing view among scholars has been that the city was destroyed some 150 years earlier and thus did not exist at the time of the Israelite invasion, which is believed to have occurred no earlier than 1400 B.C.

The New York Times February 22, 1990

lical characters and events. So even if the language is that of national myth, as Eban said, the story may be considered true in essence, at least true enough to serve as an outline of Israel's early history and a people's emerging sense of destiny.

In the story of Abraham, the Jews created for themselves a unifying and sustaining vision of descent from a single ancestor. It was believed that the territory "from Dan to Beersheba" was promised to him as a divine inheritance. The patriarchal line continued with Isaac and his son, Jacob (also known as Israel), who in turn had 12 sons. The descendants of these brothers formed the "tribes of Israel." They became known as the Israelites, literally "Children of Israel."

All was not harmonious among the brothers, who were especially jealous of young Joseph. They sold him to a caravan on its way to Egypt and took his fine "coat of many colors," splattered with goat's blood, to Jacob, saying that his son had been killed and eaten by a wild animal. In Egypt, Joseph was sold into slavery but after many tribulations, he assumed the role of valued adviser to Pharaoh. So successful was Joseph that Pharaoh allowed him to send for his brothers and their families to come and live in Egypt. Though they retained contact with other Israelites remaining in Canaan, this was the first extended separation of a large number of the people from the land promised to Abraham.

Over many generations in Egypt the Israelites multiplied, despite persecution and finally enslavement. It was sometime in the 13th century B.C., probably in the reign of Ramesses II, that some of them united under Moses to escape into the wilderness of Sinai. The authenticity of the biblical narrative of the Exodus has been questioned. But somehow in this period was forged the political and spiritual metal of the people's nationhood.

As the story goes, traditions of Israel's culture had their origin on a mountain in Sinai, where Moses is supposed to have received the Ten Commandments from Yahweh, the god of the Israelites. Moses placed these stone tablets in an

acacia chest, the Ark of the Covenant. The people believed they now had a special relationship, a covenant, with Yahweh and a special burden of spiritual responsibility. As long as they had the ark with them, they felt sure of divine protection.

The climax of these wanderings was the conquest of Canaan. The Bible, being the story from the victor's point of view, speaks not of a conquest by an alien people, but the return of people to their ancestral home. In the biblical account, Joshua, the successor to Moses, led an army across the Jordan into Canaan and won a decisive victory at Jericho — where with divine help, in the words of the old spiritual, he "fit the battle of Jericho, and the walls come tumbling down."

The prevailing view among scholars is that the walled city was destroyed at

Abraham's sacrifice depicted in a 6th century mosaic found at Hefzibah.

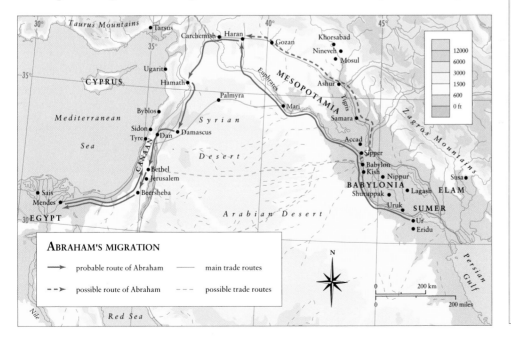

ABRAHAM'S MIGRATION

→ probable route of Abraham   main trade routes

--→ possible route of Abraham   --- possible trade routes

ARCHEOLOGISTS UNEARTH 'GOLDEN CALF' IN ISRAEL

By JOEL BRINKLEY

ASHKELON, Israel, July 24 — Harvard University archeologists excavating Canaanite ruins surrounding the site of the ancient port city of Ashkelon have unearthed a "golden calf" that was an object of worship dating from the second millennium B.C.

The tiny image of bronze and other metals was recovered almost intact, with legs, ears, tail and one of its two horns, still in place, even though the temple in which it was housed was reduced to rubble during a conquest of Ashkelon in about 1550 B.C., midway through the Bronze Age.

The earliest legends of Judaism show the religion's fathers inveighing against the worship of golden calves. In the Bible, golden calves, similar in form but considerably larger than the Ashkelon find, are referred to in the story of Aaron during the Exodus.

The New York Times July 25, 1990

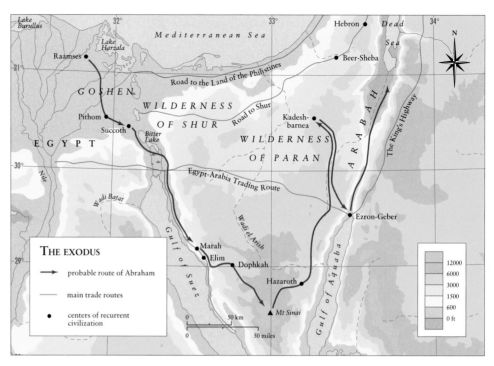

THE EXODUS

→ probable route of Abraham

— main trade routes

● centers of recurrent civilization

12000
6000
3000
1500
600
0 ft

DAVID'S KINGDOM

c. 1000-993 B.C.

Israelite territory

areas under Israelite rule

areas under vassal treaty

extent of David's kingdom

The young David being annointed, in a wall painting from a 3rd century synagogue along the Euphrates River in southern Iraq.

least a century before and thus did not exist at the time of the Israelite invasion. The entire story of military conquest may have been a literary embellishment of what probably was a gradual migration of Israelites into Canaan, where they came into sporadic conflict with the inhabitants. Strife between Israelites and Canaanites appears to have persisted for at least three centuries, during the era of the Judges who ruled after the death of Joshua. Biblical authors tended to telescope history, for their purpose was not so much to chronicle as to dramatize the past.

The invading Israelites were greatly influenced by the more advanced Canaanite civilization. Scratching through ruins, archeologists have been impressed by the superior construction techniques and pottery in Canaanite towns, compared to those of the Israelites. But the Israelites adapted. They came to speak and write a dialect of Canaanite; in the Book of Isaiah, the Hebrew language is called "the tongue of Canaan." Many Israelites, especially those who had remained in Canaan but also many of the returnees, adopted some of the indigenous religious practices. In the Bible, Israel's misfortunes at this time were blamed on this widespread religious defection.

Another threat to Israelite independence and unity came from the sea. In the

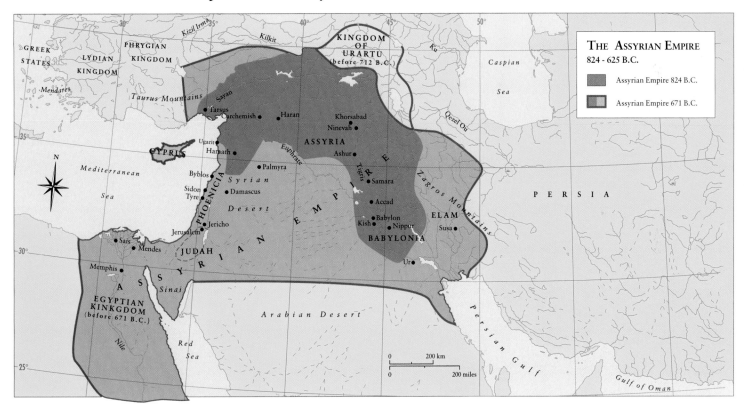

12th century B.C., a number of Aegean people, the "sea people," arrived and gained a foothold on the coast. They became known as the Philistines; it is from them that the Latinized Greek name "Palestine" is derived. These industrious people settled in and around five coastal-plain cities: Gath, Ashkelon, Gaza, Ashdod and Ekron. As arch foes of Israelites, the Philistines were scorned by biblical authors and their name in modern times has been synonymous with materialism and boorishness. But archeologists in recent years have found evidence that the Philistines were creators of fine pottery and great architecture, clever urban planners and cosmopolitan devotees of the grape. If anything, they were more cultured than the Israelites, at this time mostly shepherds and farmers living in autonomous tribes.

In their struggles with the expansive Philistines, the Israelites found greater political unity and entered their Golden Age. They chose Saul as the first king

PHILISTINES WERE CULTURED AFTER ALL

By JOHN NOBLE WILFORD

After all these centuries of calumny, the Philistines are finally having some good things said about them. They were not, it seems, deserving of that withering epithet: Philistine.

Archeologists are uncovering increasing evidence that the Philistines, arch foes of the Israelites in biblical times whose name became synonymous with barbarity and boorishness, were actually the creators of fine pottery and grand architecture, clever urban planners and cosmopolitan devotees of the grape. If anything, the Israelites, at the time mostly shepherds and farmers in the hills, were the less sophisticated and cultured folk.

In excavations this summer among the ruins of Ashkelon on Israel's Mediterranean coast, archeologists from Harvard University came upon revealing remains of the Philistine city as it was on the day of its destruction by King Nebuchadnezzar's Babylonian army in 604 B.C.

The New York Times September 29, 1992

of the lands of Israel.

A brave but tragic figure, Saul consolidated the tribes to the sound of the shofar and went into battle against the Philistines, scoring several triumphs. Fate and his own nature, however, left him little time to enjoy success. Growing opposition to his rule preyed on his melancholic mind. In a battle against Philistine forces led by Goliath, Saul lost his nerve and, as the Bible says, was "greatly afraid." This was when the boy David stepped forward and slew Goliath in single combat.

The young hero then became a fixture in the royal household. He played harp for the king, was a bosom friend of the king's son Jonathan and married one of the king's daughters. But Saul came to fear David as a potential rival to the throne, and so David had to flee into the hill country of Judah. He was there when the Philistines defeated the Israelites in battle on Mount Gilboa, leaving Saul and his three eldest sons dead.

After a struggle for succession, David became king shortly before 1000 B.C. and ruled for almost 40 years. Biblical tradition attributes to David all the qualities of royal greatness and a lifetime of passion. He had the gift of poetry and music. Many were his loves, notably his passion for Bathsheba, whose husband he sent to certain death in battle. As a courageous military leader, he drove back the Philistines and subdued rival tribes east of the Jordan. As a political leader, he managed what had heretofore been impossible: the unification of the two main bodies of Israelites, Israel in the north and Judah in the south.

Putting a seal to the unified kingdom, David led an army to seize Jerusalem, which had remained in Canaanite hands. At the outset of the first millennium B.C., David made Jerusalem his royal capital and also symbolic seat of the religion of Moses. He had the ark transferred there and made plans for a temple to house it in holy splendor. As the City of David, Jerusalem assumed its place in

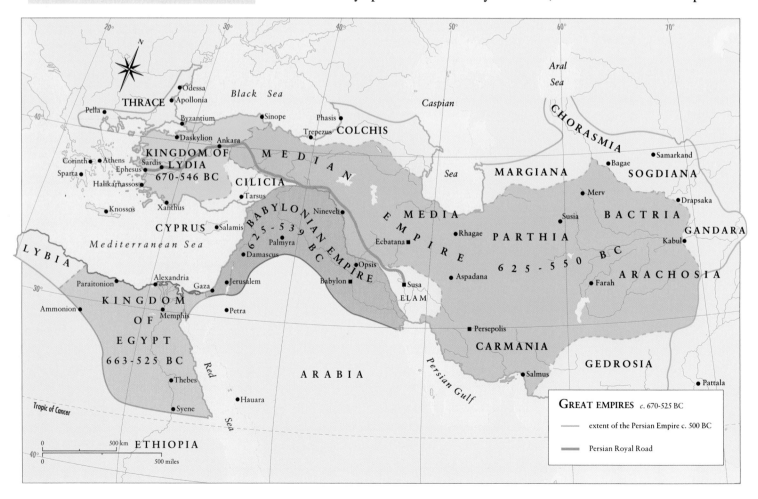

GREAT EMPIRES *c. 670-525 BC*

—— extent of the Persian Empire c. 500 BC

—— Persian Royal Road

history to this day as the spiritual center of Jews everywhere.

Under David, the kingdom emerged as a power in the region. Egypt's fortunes were in decline, and Mesopotamia was divided into several states. So when Solomon succeeded his father, he took advantage of the relative power vacuum and expanded the country's material base. He built new fortified cities and amassed a large merchant fleet, which brought back gold and ivory from distant lands. In Jerusalem, he erected opulent palaces and government buildings and, fulfilling David's plan, saw to the construction of the magnificent Temple, the House of the Lord.

At the death of Solomon in the late 10th century B.C., the united kingdom split apart. The 10 northern tribes seceded and formed their own kingdom of Israel, while the southern tribes joined as the smaller kingdom of Judah. Soon Jerusalem was plundered by the Egyptians, who seized nearly all the gold Solomon had gathered during his reign. The Golden Age was over.

Both kingdoms were vulnerable, the more so as the Assyrian empire gathered strength in Mesopotamia. It was the time of the biblical prophets, whose teachings reshaped the religion of Moses into a universal monotheism and whose voices denounced the evil ways of the people. The prophets foretold the fall of Israel, as punishment for its sins, but reassured the people that they would eventually return to the land.

The northern kingdom of Israel was the first to fall. Samaria, its capital, capitulated to the Assyrians under Sargon II in about 722 B.C. Many of the people were forced into exile and replaced by settlers from other territories. This deportation inspired the enduring legend of the 10 "lost tribes of Israel."

Judah held out for more than a century, until Jerusalem finally fell in 587 B.C. to the Babylonians of Nebuchadnezzar. Solomon's Temple was destroyed, and the king was forced to watch the execution of his sons before his own eyes were

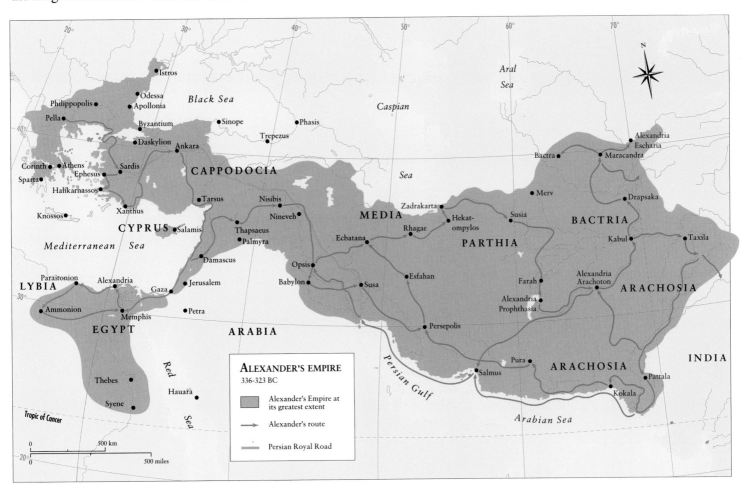

gouged out. Then the people of Judah were sent into their 50 years of Babylonian captivity, not returning until Babylonia itself was defeated by Cyrus of Persia.

Once again, Israelites claimed their homeland. As before, and since, they were not entirely welcome, for in the meantime others who had settled there had made the land their own. But under Persian protection, the returning people rebuilt the Temple on the mount where the first one had stood. Jerusalem again became Jewish. But the land would remain under foreign control for centuries to come.

In the wake of the conquests of Alexander the Great, control of Israel passed to the Greeks, who were bent on Hellenizing the Jews. Resistance to cultural assimilation and especially the forced conversion of the Temple in Jerusalem into a Greek temple culminated in the Maccabean revolt of 167 B.C. Led by a

priest and his five sons, known as the Maccabees, the Israelites regained their Temple and secured religious freedom. This triumph is commemorated in Jewish history as Hanukkah, the Feast of Lights.

The Romans assumed control of what they called Judea in the first century B.C. The most prominent of their appointed rulers was Herod, King of Judea from 37 to 4 B.C. An ambitious builder, he doubled or tripled the size of the Temple Mount in Jerusalem to accommodate an enlarged temple and other imposing buildings. Now it covered more ground than the esplanade of the Acropolis in Athens. "The whole area was paved with stones of every kind and color," observed the Jewish historian Josephus in the first century A.D. And the white-marble sanctuary itself, he added, "seemed in the distance like a mountain covered with snow; for any part not covered with gold was dazzling white."

Herod's monument would not stand a century. These were turbulent times.

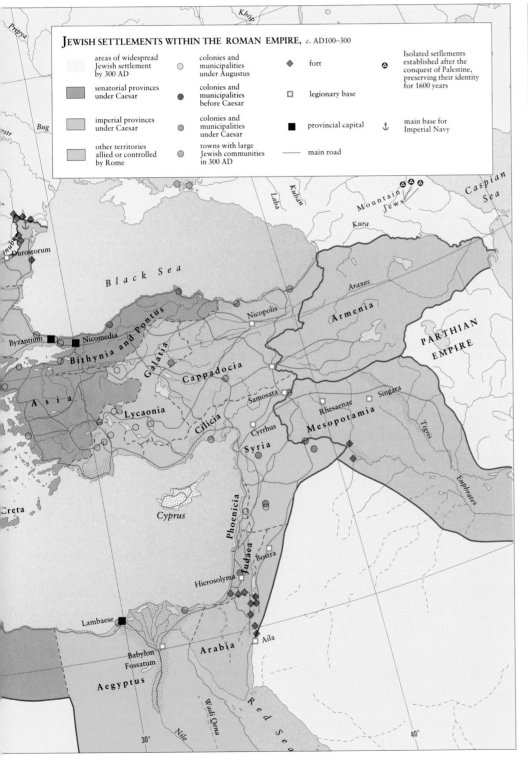

JEWISH SETTLEMENTS WITHIN THE ROMAN EMPIRE, *c.* AD100–300

- areas of widespread Jewish settlement by 300 AD
- senatorial provinces under Caesar
- imperial provinces under Caesar
- other territories allied or controlled by Rome
- ○ colonies and municipalities under Augustus
- ● colonies and municipalities before Caesar
- ◓ colonies and municipalities under Caesar
- ● towns with large Jewish communities in 300 AD
- ◆ fort
- ☐ legionary base
- ■ provincial capital
- —— main road
- ⌂ Isolated settlements established after the conquest of Palestine, preserving their identity for 1600 years
- ⚓ main base for Imperial Navy

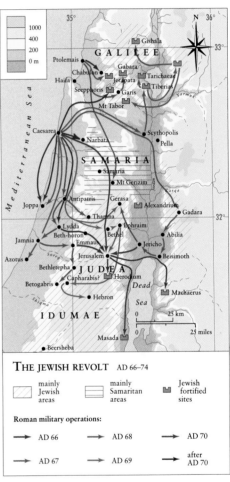

THE JEWISH REVOLT   AD 66–74

- mainly Jewish areas
- mainly Samaritan areas
- Jewish fortified sites

Roman military operations:

- → AD 66
- → AD 67
- → AD 68
- → AD 69
- → AD 70
- → after AD 70

MONOPOLY BROKEN OVER RESEARCH OF DEAD SEA SCROLLS

By JOHN NOBLE WILFORD

In a move expected to shatter the wall of secrecy surrounding much research on the Dead Sea Scrolls, a major library in California has disclosed that it has a virtually complete set of photographs of the rare documents from biblical time and has decided to make them available immediately and without restriction to all researchers.

Officials of one of the largest independent libraries in the country, the Huntington Library in San Marino, Calif., a suburb of Los Angeles, decided last week to open the collection of some 3,000 master photographic negatives of the ancient Jewish manuscripts found four decades ago in caves near the Dead Sea. They said they believed that the collection consisted of all of the known scroll texts.

Scholars who have been denied access to many of the unpublished materials hailed the decision, saying it would effectively end a tightly controlled research monopoly maintained by a coterie of editors since the discovery of the scrolls. One researcher said it was the scholarly equivalent of breaking down the Berlin Wall.

Some of the controlling editors, stunned when they were told of the library's decision, charged that the photographs of the manuscripts were stolen property. The editors questioned whether the library had the right to make the material available to scholars not approved by them.

But Dr. William A. Moffett, director of the library, said the Huntington, unlike all other institutions with photographic collections of the scrolls, was not bound by any agreement to allow the international team of editors to control access to the documents.

Dr. Moffett said that, strictly speaking, only authors retained property rights to unpublished material and so the scrolls were in the public domain.

"This move should bring an unprecedented openness into scrolls research," he said. "It will be very hard for the cartel that's controlled the scrolls to put the genie back in the bottle."

But the custodians of the scrolls insist that virtually all of the intact biblical material has always been open to reputable scholars. They say much of the material that has not been made public consists of fragments of texts that have not been pieced together.

The New York Times September 22, 1991.

A fragment from the "Manual of Discipline."

The Qumran Caves, where the Dead Sea Scrolls were found in the 1940s.

The people of Judea grew increasingly restive under the Roman yoke and were also driven by religious controversy. The country was split by two conflicting sects, the Sadducees and Pharisees. The former represented the wealthy priestly class that had favored Hellenization and continued to insist on rigid practices of Temple worship and sacrifices; the latter sect, which had wider popular support, believed in the strict application of religious law in every sphere of life, not just at the Temple. Modern rabbinic Judaism would emerge from the Pharisees. A more militant faction of the Pharisees, known as Zealots, preached open rebellion against Rome. Another faction, the Essenes, was an ascetic group that lived in isolated desert communities, awaiting a final Armageddon between the "Sons of Light" and the "Sons of Darkness." Some of the non-biblical documents among the Dead Sea Scrolls, which first came to light in the 1940s, are thought to represent Essene ideology.

Jesus of Nazareth was born in this time of political and religious turmoil, in "the days when Herod was King of Judea." Modern scholarship generally accepts the authenticity of such a historical figure who preached to the masses, attacked the hypocrisy of the religious establishment and enunciated lofty principles for human brotherhood. His teachings, described in the New Testament, must have resonated with people dissatisfied with the status quo, people who had for many reasons come to believe in the approaching end of time and the imminence of the Messiah, a savior. The popularity of Jesus and his revolutionary message unsettled authorities fearful of a Jewish revolt against Roman rule.

In recent decades, archeologists have had striking success reconstructing the social world in which Jesus lived; they have even found inscriptions naming Pontius Pilate, the governor who authorized his crucifixion.

After his death, apostles of Jesus spread the word of his character and teachings, in their zeal no doubt expanding the account beyond its historical foundations. In time, through the missionary fervor of Paul of Tarsus, the Jesus movement was transformed into Christianity with adherents among Jews and increasingly among gentiles throughout the Roman Empire. The land of Israel had given birth to its second major religion.

The war against Rome long advocated by the Zealots finally erupted in A.D. 66, but the people of Israel were no match for the Roman legions. In 70, Roman soldiers stormed Jerusalem and dismantled the Temple that Herod had so greatly enhanced. One of the only identifiable remnants of the complex is a portion of the western retaining wall, the Wailing Wall, so named because the Romans eventually relaxed their ban on Jews entering the old city and permitted them to come once a year "to wail over its stones." The last holdout in the Jewish Revolt was the fortress at Masada, near the Dead Sea, where the Zealots fought the Romans and in the end, committed mass suicide rather than surrender.

An ancient cistern from the Herodian era at Masada. Water to maintain life on the mountaintop fortress was channeled from the cliffs through a hole in the roof of the cavern.

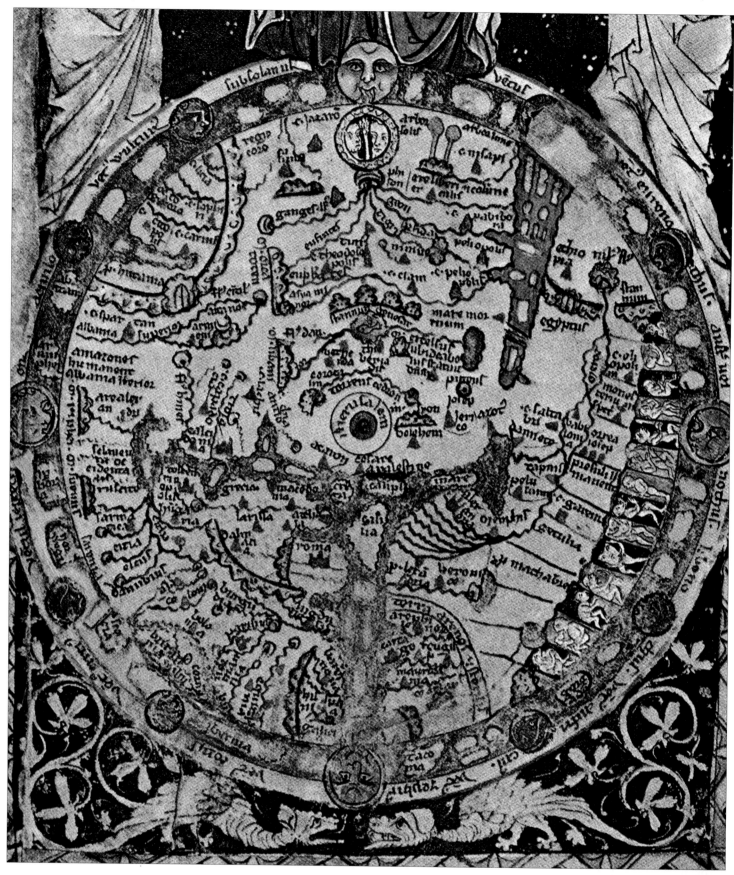

A medieval map of the world showing Jerusalem at the center.

In defeat, more Jews left Israel and settled in cities around the Mediterranean, vastly increasing the number of Jews of the Diaspora, or dispersion. The Jewish population of Alexandria already was probably greater than that of Jerusalem. Wherever they lived, though, the Jews tended to keep in touch with their co-religionists in Israel and study the Bible, though often in Greek translations. Conditions in Israel through the next 1,900 years fed the Diaspora; by the seventh century, Jews were living throughout the Middle East and in most of the

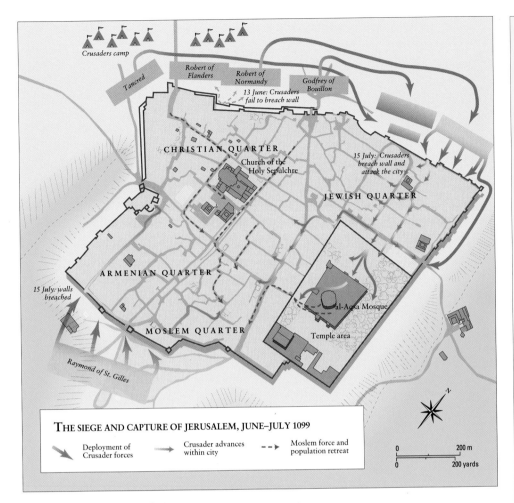

THE SIEGE AND CAPTURE OF JERUSALEM, JUNE–JULY 1099

↘ Deployment of
Crusader forces

→ Crusader advances
within city

-→ Moslem force and
population retreat

0   200 m
0   200 yards

regions of continental Europe.

Roman rule continued into the fourth century, followed by nearly three centuries of Byzantine dominance in which attempts were made to Christianize the country, with considerable success. Many non-Jews in Palestine converted, and some Jews did so to avoid losing their land. Churches and monasteries sprang up, while in certain periods the construction of synagogues was prohibited.

Next came the Arabs, who occupied the entire country by 640. In less than a decade after the Prophet Mohammed's death, in 632, Arabs swept in force through much of western Asia and northern Africa, spreading the new faith of Islam. For Palestine, the new rulers were an improvement in that they opened Jerusalem again to Jewish settlers and permitted them a good deal of local autonomy. But the Muslims put their own sacred stamp on the city. In 691, the great mosque known as the Dome of the Rock was completed on the site where Mohammed is supposed to have ascended to heaven.

Jerusalem thus became a holy city to a third major religion. Within 500 yards of one another lie the Western Wall of ancient Israel's temple, the rock believed to be Christ's tomb and the gilded shrine marking Mohammed's Night Journey. Sacred ground, but not peaceful.

This first Muslim period in Israel's history ended in 1099, when the first Crusaders from Europe marched in and seized Jerusalem and most of the country. Christians of Medieval Europe had long placed Jerusalem at the center of their world maps and their faith. Pope Urban II proclaimed the first crusade to reclaim the Holy Land from the heathen Turks. The sights of barons and knights in full armor leading armies to the East excited Europe, but also fanned a wave of ugly anti-Semitism there and more violence in Palestine. In "Jerusalem: One City, Three Faiths," Karen Armstrong described the Crusaders' brutality as a terrible profaning of the holy city, one "which permanently damaged relations

BIBLICAL PUZZLE SOLVED: TUNNEL IS A PRODUCT OF NATURE

By JOHN NOBLE WILFORD

Under the oldest part of Jerusalem, the area known as the City of David, a maze of tunnels and shafts runs through the rock and deep into biblical history. In ancient times, the people inside the city walls depended on this system to deliver water from the ever-flowing Gihon Spring outside, insuring a dependable water supply in war and peace.

But nearly everything else about the old underground waterworks, especially its recorded role in two pivotal events in the history of ancient Israel, has left scholars shaking their heads in puzzlement.

Archeologists and biblical scholars have long wondered if it was these dark, subterranean passages that enabled King David to capture Jerusalem 3,000 years ago. Biblical accounts suggest that David's general, Joab, surprised the Jebusites, or Canaanites, by sneaking in through a hidden passage.

But did any of these tunnels exist at this early time? Were the Canaanites or anyone else then capable of such excavations?

Engineers have long noted that whoever built these passages seemed to go about the task in the most curious way, with no logic in the choice of some routes, slopes and dimensions of the tunnels and many ostensible mistakes in design.

Take Hezekiah's Tunnel. According to the Bible, King Hezekiah, expecting an attack and possibly a long siege by the Assyrians in the eighth century B.C., had a tunnel built to bring water from the spring to an open reservoir within the walled city, which extends south of the Temple Mount. The siege occurred in 701 B.C., but failed, presumably in no small part because of the tunnel and its secure water supply. But why did the tunnel follow such a serpentine course, extending 1,748 feet, when a straight line of 1,050 feet would have been sufficient and easier to build?

Now, many of these questions can apparently be answered. Previous explanations had been based on the assumption that the tunnels were entirely man-made. Scholars should have consulted a geologist sooner.

A comprehensive geological study of underground Jerusalem has recently shown that the channels and shafts were formed by natural forces tens of thousands of years ago.

The New York Times August 9, 1994

between the three religions of Abraham."

After their first successes, Crusaders met growing resistance from Muslim forces, notably those led by Saladin, Sultan of Egypt and Syria. In the second half of the thirteenth century, the Crusaders were finally driven out by the Mameluke forces of Egypt.

The Mamelukes controlled the country from 1291 to 1516 and were followed by the Ottoman Turks, who were to hold power there, with brief interruptions, until World War I. At first, Turkish rule brought a period of relative stability, during which many Jews of the Diaspora, having been expelled from Spain and Portugal, found refuge there. But as the Ottoman Empire declined in the late nineteenth century, so did its power over its diverse lands, including Palestine.

By then, Palestine was an impoverished country. Visiting Europeans returned home with word of the appalling conditions of the long-neglected holy places, and this stirred new interest in Palestine by the faithful and also by archeologists. They came to clear the tombs, explore ruins and map the tunnels under Jerusalem. Their excavations called attention to the land's rich and sacred past,

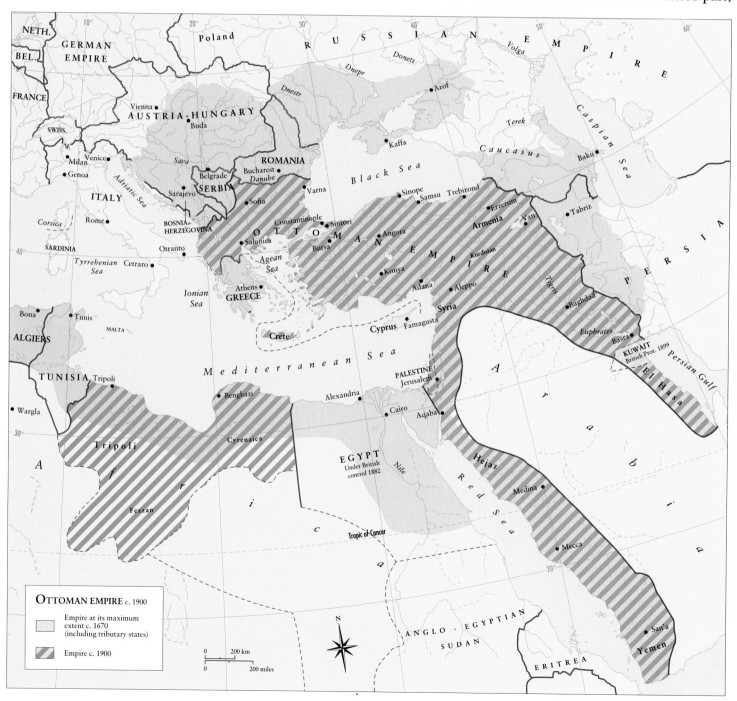

OTTOMAN EMPIRE c. 1900

Empire at its maximum extent c. 1670 (including tributary states)

Empire c. 1900

and fed a growing sentiment, indeed a movement, that would reach fruition a century later.

The idea of making Palestine a center of Jewish settlement was beginning in the 1840s to be voiced in the non-Jewish world, particularly in Britain. At that time, only 12,000 Jews lived in all of Palestine, most of them in poverty. But the Ottoman Empire rejected French and British appeals for a Jewish settlement program. It was an empire that gave shelter to 72 races or nations, and so considered nationalism of any kind inimical to its survival.

In 1882 came a turning point in the history of Palestine, as Abba Eban wrote in "My People: The Story of the Jews." In that year, the first group of Russian

The Old City of Jerusalem, holy ground for three major faiths. **From left:** *Jews at the Western Wall around 1900; the Mosque of Omar, also known as The Dome of the Rock, in 1917; Easter pilgrims at the Church of the Holy Sepulchre in the 1920s.*

Jews arrived and established farm colonies, setting an example for many others. The country's Jewish population rose to 24,000. And Jewish nationalist fervor, expressed through the new Zionist movement in Europe, would bring pressure for a more systematic settlement of Jews in Palestine.

Calling on the latent appeal of Jewish unity, Theodor Herzl, a lawyer and journalist, convened the Zionist Congress in 1897 at Basel. He unfurled a Jewish flag with two blue stripes and the Star of David and persuaded the Congress to establish the World Zionist Organization to carry on the task of Jewish immigration to Palestine. "At Basel I created the Jewish State," Herzl wrote. "In five years, perhaps, and certainly in fifty, everyone will see it." His prediction fell short by only one year.

World War I brought the diplomatic breakthrough so necessary for recognition of Jewish claims on Palestine as a homeland. Whatever the outcome of the war, France and Britain realized that the creaking Ottoman Empire was not likely to survive intact. They waged military and diplomatic campaigns with an eye to redrawing the postwar map of the Middle East, in which the fate of Palestine was up for grabs.

Even before the war, Chaim Weizmann, a young scientist in England, had won over Arthur James Balfour to the Zionist cause. Many Jewish leaders were not so sure, opposing Zionism in part out of fear that it would endanger Jewish

Copy of the Balfour declaration.

Foreign Office,
November 2nd, 1917

Dear Lord Rothschild,

        I have much pleasure in conveying to you, on behalf of His Majesty's Government, the following declaration of sympathy with Jewish Zionist aspirations which has been submitted to, and approved by, the Cabinet.

        His Majesty's Government view with favour the establishment in Palestine of a national home for the Jewish people, and will use their best endeavours to facilitate the achievement of this object, it being clearly understood that nothing shall be done which may prejudice the civil and religious rights of existing non-Jewish communities in Palestine, or the rights and political status enjoyed by Jews in any other country"

        I should oe grateful if you would bring this declaration to the knowleage of the Zionist Federation.

Arthur James Balfour, British Foreign Secretary, and the author of the 1917 Balfour Declaration.

rights in the Diaspora. But British interests coincided with Zionist aims. Britain sought a postwar role in the Middle East to secure the Suez Canal, its lifeline to India. One such role, it was proposed, would be as the protector of a Jewish Palestine. In 1917, Balfour was foreign secretary and in a position to act. After receiving support from President Woodrow Wilson, Balfour on Nov. 2, 1917, issued what has become known as the Balfour Declaration:

  "His Majesty's Government view with favor the establishment in Palestine of a national home for the Jewish people, and will use their best endeavors to facilitate the achievement of this object, it being clearly understood that nothing shall be done which may prejudice the civil and religious rights of existing non-Jewish communities in Palestine, or the rights and political status enjoyed by Jews in any other country."

  A month later, on Dec. 9, the British army led by General Edmund Allenby took Jerusalem. By the next summer, the Turks were driven out of the rest of Palestine. The children of Israel once again had reason to dream of the Promised Land.

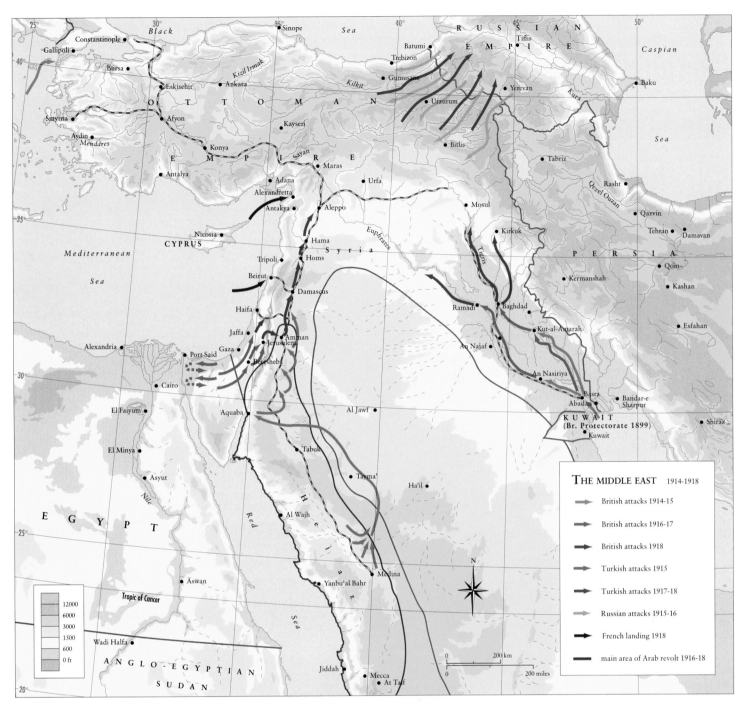

THE MIDDLE EAST 1914-1918

→ British attacks 1914-15
→ British attacks 1916-17
→ British attacks 1918
→ Turkish attacks 1915
→ Turkish attacks 1917-18
→ Russian attacks 1915-16
→ French landing 1918
— main area of Arab revolt 1916-18

General Edmund Allenby, entering Jerusalem in December 1917, established British rule in Palestine.

Chapter Two: The Struggle For Statehood

Judith Miller

Theodor Herzl in Basel, Switzerland, where he convened the first Zionist Congress in August, 1897.

THERE MIGHT NEVER HAVE BEEN a Jewish state in the Middle East — and almost surely not in 1948 — had the world's greatest Islamic empire not made a catastrophic miscalculation. By aligning itself with Germany in World War I, the Ottoman Empire tied its fate to the losing side of the great European power struggle. Weakened by debt, internal rivalries, corruption, and competition from increasingly dynamic European powers, the empire that had ruled most of the Middle East since the 16th century collapsed in 1918.

The dismantling of the empire ended Ottoman control of Palestine and gave major impetus to two competing nationalisms there — Arab (Palestinian) and Jewish. Any history of the Jewish state is primarily a chronicle of the enduring struggle between these two forces, and ultimately, the triumph in Palestine of the latter, known as Zionism. It is also the story within Zionism of fiercely competing factions — religious versus secular, socialist *vs.* conservative, pragmatic *vs.* ideological, maximalist *vs.* minimalist — and conflicting visions which exist to this day of what Israel, or a Jewish state, should be.

Until the dissolution of the Ottoman sultanate in Constantinople, however, Zionism was, in the words of historian Walter Laqueur, "a somewhat eccentric movement of young idealists who met every other year at a congress and espoused various political, financial, cultural, and colonizing activities."

First uttered in a political context at a meeting in Vienna in 1892, Zionism took shape at the turn of the century under the leadership of an extraordinary Austrian journalist, Theodor Herzl, the movement's founder.

A secular, assimilated Jew from Budapest who had admired Wagner in his youth and worshipped German culture, Herzl became increasingly preoccupied with the resurgence of anti-Semitism in Europe and a solution to the "Jewish question." A believer in radical, if impractical, solutions, Herzl originally toyed with the notion of protecting Jews through a mass conversion to Christianity. In his fantasy, Herzl would lead a procession to St. Stephen's Cathedral, where, in return for a Papal pledge of protection, the entire Jewish community, except its leaders, would become Catholic.

Dissuaded by his friends, Herzl seized upon an alternative, seemingly equally fantastic scheme three years later. Rejecting assimilation in Europe, he endorsed the restoration of a Jewish homeland. Herzl was only 36 in 1896 when "The Jewish State," his booklet arguing for such a homeland, was published in German, and had not set foot in Palestine when he wrote what was to become Zionism's manifesto. But he had no doubt about his own role in history.

"At Basel, I founded the Jewish state," Herzl confided to his diary after the opening of the First Zionist Congress, an assembly of 208 Jews from 16 countries, who met in Switzerland in frock coats and white ties in August, 1897. In the last eight years of his life, Herzl worked single-mindedly to secure a charter from a world power authorizing Jewish settlement in Palestine, exhausting his own and his wife's fortune, lobbying fellow Jews and foreign leaders and anyone else who would listen. In 1901, he even secured a meeting with Ottoman Sultan Abdul Hamid (1896-1909) to plead for a charter. While the Sultan hoped that Herzl might be able to help Turkey repay its crushing foreign debt, a dubious proposition given Herzl's perpetual shortage of cash, he was unwilling to authorize Jewish settlement in Palestine. The much coveted audience in what Herzl called "the murderers' den and the robbers' country" ended as yet another failed fantasy. And when Herzl died in 1904, at age 44, the creation of a Jewish homeland in Palestine still seemed unlikely.

Yet his movement had already begun building such a homeland, not as Herzl had envisioned, but as Chaim Weizmann, the celebrated scientist and chemistry lecturer at Manchester University who had been a Zionist leader in Russia, had advocated — with neither permission nor fanfare, but step by step, or as the strategy came to be known, by methodically acquiring "one more dunam, one more goat," year after year. By the time Herzl died, an estimated 30,000 European Jews had emigrated to Palestine in what historians call the "First Aliyah" (meaning ascent) between 1881 and 1904.

Chaim Weizmann,
"One more dunam, one more goat."

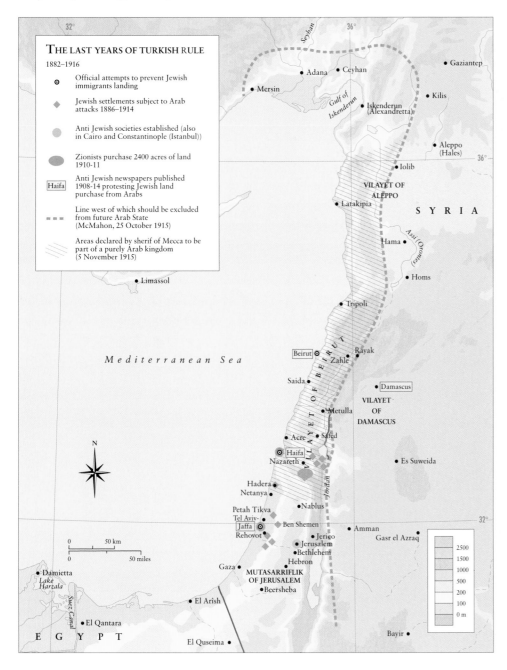

THE LAST YEARS OF TURKISH RULE
1882–1916

⊙   Official attempts to prevent Jewish immigrants landing

◆   Jewish settlements subject to Arab attacks 1886–1914

●   Anti Jewish societies established (also in Cairo and Constantinople (Istanbul))

⬭   Zionists purchase 2400 acres of land 1910-11

Haifa   Anti Jewish newspapers published 1908-14 protesting Jewish land purchase from Arabs

- - -   Line west of which should be excluded from future Arab State (McMahon, 25 October 1915)

⫽⫽   Areas declared by sherif of Mecca to be part of a purely Arab kingdom (5 November 1915)

Herzl addressing the First World Zionist Congress.

Because Herzl, like virtually all of Zionism's early leaders, was a secular thinker whose dream was not religiously but politically inspired, he failed, as did so many other Zionist pioneers, to appreciate the attachment of so many Jews to Zion. For some of these secular Europeans — and Zionism was fundamentally a European nationalist movement – the site of the initial Jewish gathering point was secondary. Herzl at one point favored what he called a "night shelter" where persecuted Jews, especially those fleeing Russian pogroms, could assemble and acquire the necessary skills for their eventual homeland in Palestine. He was eager, therefore, to establish, in effect, a *pied--terre* for his Zionist organization, a place he hoped would be sanctioned by a charter from the Sublime Porte in Istanbul. Early suggestions for such a staging ground, included, among others, Uganda, Angola, Cyprus, Asiatic Turkey, Sinai, the oil-bearing Eastern province of what is now Saudi Arabia, Tripolitania (Libya), Australia, Argentina, Mexico, Canada, and several sites in the U.S. — Arkansas, Oregon, Texas, and, of all places, Buffalo. But at the Sixth Zionist Congress in 1903, Herzl's last, a majority of delegates rejected this notion and insisted on moving immediately to what then seemed the unattainable Palestine, as opposed to a part of Uganda in East Africa, which the British had offered and which seemed more attainable at the time. Chaim Weizmann was so incensed by the proposal to accept a temporary alternative to Palestine that he threatened to stage a hunger strike at the gathering. He prevailed. The furious division over the so-called Uganda Plan revealed what became one of several key (and lasting) divisions that plagued Zionism's development. From these early conflicting visions flowed many of the most enduring feuds, schisms and quarrels among the talkative and quarrelsome Zionists, which since the Oslo peace accords in 1993, have deepened.

As a political movement, Zionism owes much to the Great War. In its search for allies against the Germans and their Ottoman ally, Britain made ambitious promises to France, the Arabs, and the Jews. In April, 1916, Britain concluded a secret agreement with France. The Sykes-Picot accord, named for its English and French authors, was a plan to divide up the Ottoman empire's Middle

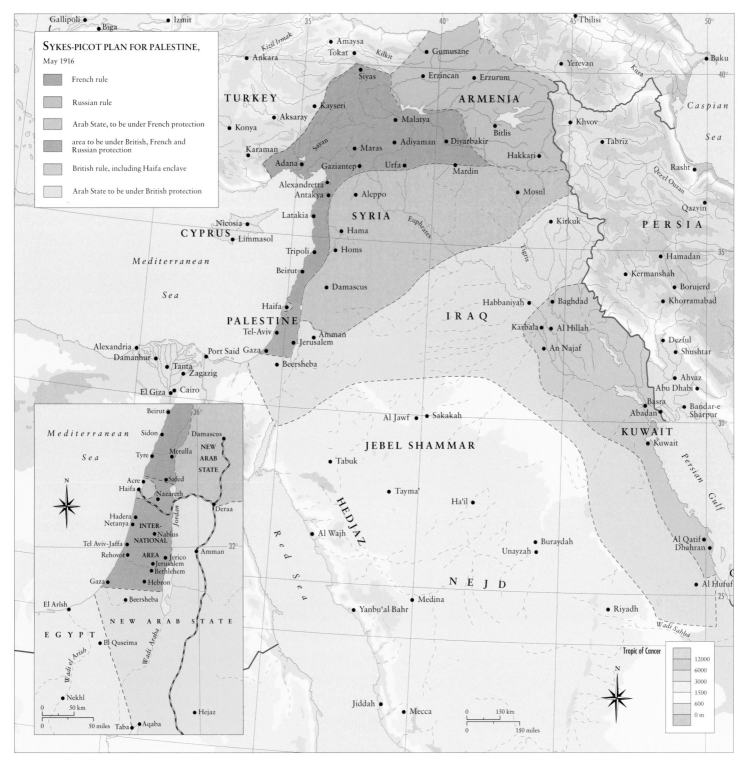

SYKES-PICOT PLAN FOR PALESTINE,
May 1916

- French rule
- Russian rule
- Arab State, to be under French protection
- area to be under British, French and Russian protection
- British rule, including Haifa enclave
- Arab State to be under British protection

Eastern territories after victory. But Britain also promised the Sherif of Mecca, King Hussein, head of a notable Gulf family, the Hashemites, and the current Jordanian ruler's great-grandfather, that Britain would support and recognize Arab independence if the Arabs helped defeat the Turks. Finally, Britain, in its Balfour Declaration made the Jews a promise that would reshape Middle Eastern history: in a one-sentence letter to Lord Rothschild, a British Zionist who had been converted by Weizmann to the Zionism he had once ferociously opposed, Britain pledged to establish a Jewish national homeland in Palestine. Almost parenthetically, it noted that "nothing shall be done which may prejudice the civil and religious rights of existing non-Jewish communities in Palestine," another pledge that would cause Britain no end of problems in the 30 years that His Majesty's Government ruled Palestine as a protectorate under a League of Nations mandate.

ARABS CONDEMN 'JEWISH PRESS' ON PALESTINE RIOTS

A group of Arab citizens and sympathizers living in and near New York met yesterday afternoon to protest against "the unfairness of the Jewish press in dealing with the present Palestine rioting." They voted to send messages to several clerical and secular leaders denying the allegation that the attacks of the Arabs on the Jews were motivated by religion.

The messages, released from the offices of Selim Totah, attorney, in the Woolworth Building, were signed by Fuad Shafars, president of the Palestine National League; Abbas M Ahushakyra, general secretary of the New Syria party, and Abd M Kateeb, secretary of the Young Mens Moslem Society of America.

After the meeting, which was held at 1170 Broadway, Mr. Abushakra said that rather than being of religious origin, the present trouble was political and economic. In 1915, he said, Great Britain told the Arabs it would give them representative government; in 1917 it told the Jews that it would cooperate in their homeland plans.

"A minority race," he said, "has been given a permanent home at the expense of the majority."

Among the messages was a cable-gram forwarded to the Permanent Mandate Commission of the League of Nations at Geneva. It said: "Present deplorable events in Palestine are the outcome of Balfour declaration. The Wailing Wall is merely an incident. We appeal for justice to the supreme source of authority on mandates."

A message to President Hoover, Senator Borah and Secretary of State Stimson read:

"We regret present situation in Palestine. Zionism is responsible for these conditions. Applications of Balfour declaration under British mandate deprives Arabs of all their rights. Abnegation of declaration is only means to insure permanent peace. Arabs world over look to American sense of freedom and justice to uphold Arabs in their struggle for national independence."

A cablegram to Pope Plus XI said:

"Present form of government deprives Arabs of all their political and national rights. Abrogation of Balfour declaration is only solution to insure permanent peace. Arabs world over look to your Holiness and the Catholic world for sympathy and support in their cause."

The New York Times August 29, 1929

Arabs rioting in Jaffa in 1933 to protest Jewish immigration to Palestine.

After the war, Britain fully honored only its promise to France. Britain and the other victors carved up the empire's Middle Eastern possessions; Britain, which took Palestine, redefined Arab borders, appointed rulers and replaced the Muslim Turks as de facto sovereigns.

Meanwhile, Jewish emigration to Palestine continued. Between 1904 and 1914 — the crucial Second Aliya — an additional 40,000 Jews arrived in Palestine, though only 4,000 of them remained in the country given economic conditions there. Still, on the eve of World War I, the Jewish community in Palestine totalled an estimated 60,000, or about 10 percent of the population of Western Palestine. The Third Aliya, between 1919 and 1923, brought some 20,000 more Jewish immigrants to Palestine. The 1922 census, the first conducted by the British Government of Palestine, found that Jews totaled 83,907, or 12.9 percent of the non-nomadic population.

The dynamic pioneers of the Second Aliya, who created many of the modern state's most enduring traditions and institutions, were an ideologically mixed bag. Second Aliya immigrants — such as Yehuda L. Magnes, Arthur Rupin, Yosef Sprinzak and Mania Shohat founded and followed Brit Shalom (or the Peace Alliance), who, to secure acceptance by and peace with the Arabs, favored renouncing the idea of a Jewish state and Jewish majority in Palestine.

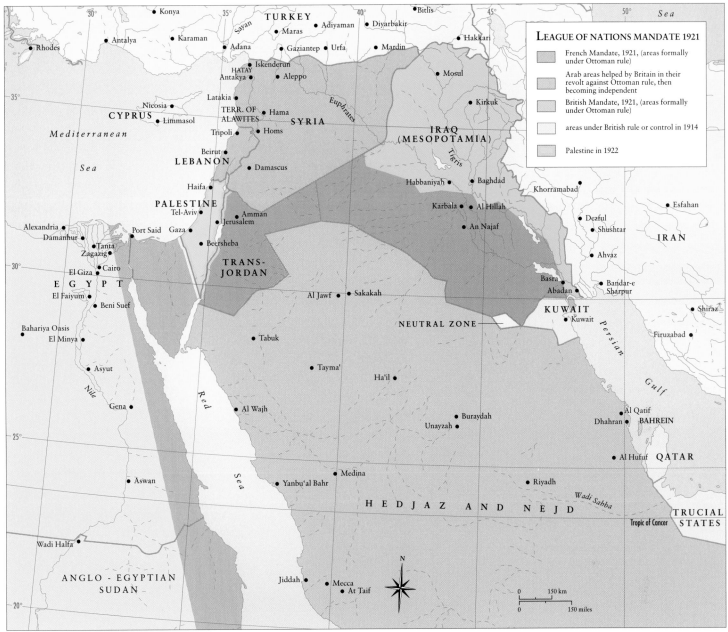

LEAGUE OF NATIONS MANDATE 1921

French Mandate, 1921, (areas formally under Ottoman rule)

Arab areas helped by Britain in their revolt against Ottoman rule, then becoming independent

British Mandate, 1921, (areas formally under Ottoman rule)

areas under British rule or control in 1914

Palestine in 1922

On the other hand, argues Anita Shapira, an Israeli historian, many Second Aliya settlers were far more combative towards the Palestinian Arabs than their predecessors had been. Veterans of anti-Jewish riots, pogroms, and the Russian revolution of 1905, these immigrants did not want to employ Arab labor in their businesses and on their farms as their predecessors had done. Keen on socialism and "self-defense," they also did not want to remain a supplicant minority in their new land.

Though before the Balfour Declaration many early Zionist pioneers hoped that Jews might settle in Palestine peacefully, Arab hostility to the Jewish settlers – and vice versa — grew steadily along with their numbers. On May 1, 1921, fighting erupted between Jewish colonists and Palestinians in Jaffa. Rioting ensued, and by the time British troops restored order, 47 Jews and 48 Arabs had been killed and several hundred others wounded.

In 1922 in the wake of the fighting, Britain, seeking to satisfy Hashemite aspirations, divided its Palestine mandate: the areas west of the Jordan were retained as Palestine and the desert east of the river was given to its Hashemite proteges to become the semi-independent emirate of Trans-Jordan. Neither Zionists nor Arabs were satisfied with this arrangement, and violence in Palestine persisted.

Amid political chaos, the Jewish settlers quietly built their political infra-

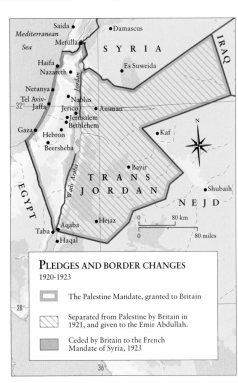

PLEDGES AND BORDER CHANGES
1920-1923

The Palestine Mandate, granted to Britain

Separated from Palestine by Britain in 1921, and given to the Emir Abdullah.

Ceded by Britain to the French Mandate of Syria, 1923

47 DEAD AFTER JERUSALEM RIOT; ARAB ATTACKS SPREAD

By THE ASSOCIATED PRESS

JERUSALEM, August 24 — With 30 dead on the Jewish side, 35 dangerously wounded, 17 Arabs reported killed and upward of 200 wounded on each side, interracial clashes in Jerusalem spread last night to the suburbs. Attacks by the Arabs began on Friday, are said by the Jews to bear all the signs of organized warfare.

Fifty British soldiers were rushed by airplane from Egypt last night, a battalion went by train and two British warships are speeding from Malta to Jaffa.

Martial law has been proclaimed in Jerusalem, a state of emergency declared throughout Palestine, all citizens are ordered off the streets by 6 p.m. and a censorship on telegraph and cable messages has been established.

A state of emergency was proclaimed to exist over all Palestine tonight, with clashes between Arabs and Jews spreading from the point of origin in Jerusalem and with a death list of nearly 50 already recorded.

Word that British warships and troops were en route to supplement the police forces was received with great joy.

The calm restored in Jerusalem this morning after two days of rioting in the streets was only temporary, and at 6 o'clock tonight the disorders were in full blast again.

The fighting had spread from the "old city" to the Jewish suburbs of Yemin Moshe, Gdud Saul, Gdud Havoda and Sephardim.

The gravest fears were expressed for the safety of Petach Tikwah, the oldest Jewish colony in Palestine and noted for its rich orange groves.

Jewish leaders appealed in their rage to cooperate with the British Administration in restoring order. They charged that the Arab attack bore every evidence of organized warfare and that the Arabs were well armed especially with daggers. It was also claimed that Communist propaganda had appeared, urging Arabs to fight the Jews and expel the English from the country.

Rioting, which broke out yesterday over the age-old religious controversy of the Wailing Wall, continued sporadically through the night and started afresh today despite the efforts of the authorities to maintain peace.

The New York Times August 25, 1929

Jewish farmers tilling the soil in 1935 at Ben Shemen, between Jerusalem and Tel Aviv.

structure, in effect, an independent government in Palestine. The Second Aliya settlers, many of the younger ones from small Jewish townships, founded various workers' parties, welfare groups, labor organizations, new forms of agricultural socialist settlements called the "kibbutz," and the "moshav," a less socialist form of the communal kibbutz, and other institutions that would later become key elements of Israeli society. It was during these crucial periods of the Second and Third Aliyas, observed politician Yossi Beilin, that Hebrew was chosen as the Jews' national language and the first Hebrew high school was founded, as well as a semi-professional watchmen organization, the Bar-Giora and the Hashomer. Second Aliya settlers also formed the Haganah, meaning "defense," the Jew's underground military organization. In 1923, Chaim Weizmann proposed at the 13th Congress of the Zionist Organization that the Zionists establish a Jewish Agency as the supreme representation in Palestine of the entire Jewish people. The Jewish Agency Executive, elected bi-annually and composed of Zionists and non-Zionists alike, was finally approved six years later. But by 1924, another wave of immigration — the Fourth Aliya — was already underway, bringing some 80,000 more Jews to Palestine by 1930, mostly from Poland, and still more tension.

The riots of August, 1929, were ignited in Jerusalem over a rumor spread by Arab leaders that Jews were going to destroy Al-Aqsa Mosque, Islam's third most holy shrine. Fighting soon spread throughout Palestine. The worst massacres were in Hebron, sacred to Jew and Muslim alike, where 67 Orthodox Jews — men, women, and children — were slaughtered by Arabs and 50 more wounded. Pierre van Paassen, a reporter, described the horror that he witnessed

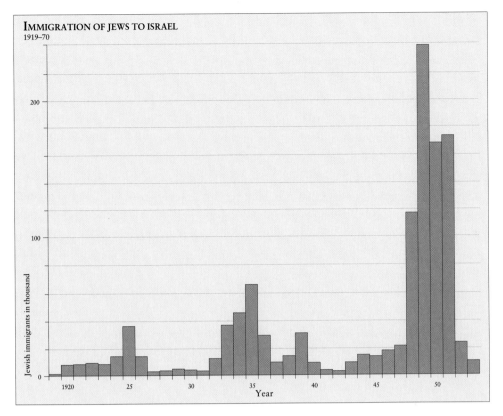

IMMIGRATION OF JEWS TO ISRAEL
1919–70

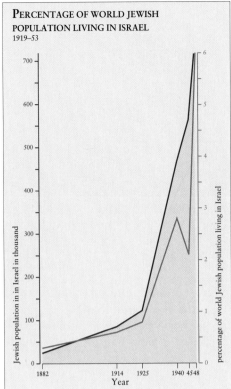

PERCENTAGE OF WORLD JEWISH
POPULATION LIVING IN ISRAEL
1919–53

by lamplight at a Jewish seminary in Hebron: "The slain students in the yard the dead men in the synagogue," slashed throats and mutilated bodies. By the time order was restored, 133 Jews had been killed, 399 wounded. The Arabs had suffered 178 casualties, including 87 deaths.

The British continued trying to reconicle the Balfour Declaration's conflicting pledges to Jews and Arabs. Commissions were formed; reports and recommendations were filed, but tensions grew. So did Jewish immigration. Some 350,000 Jews arrived in Palestine between 1930 and 1939 — the last and largest wave of immigration prior to Israel's creation — many of them from Germany after Hitler's rise to power in 1933. Much of this was due to the tireless efforts of David Ben-Gurion, the rising Zionist labor leader, and according to Israeli historian Shabtai Teveth, the only senior Zionist to warn in the early 1930s that Adolph Hitler's policies would lead to war, and that Jews throughout the world would be the targets of annihilation in the guise of this conflict. The Jewish Agency, he argued, had only four-to-five years to rescue Europe's Jews, he told a Histadrut rally in 1934. For after the outbreak of war, it would be virtually impossible to save Jews by transferring them to Palestine.

What led to the Arab Revolt of 1936 was triggered the previous year on April 19 and 20th when Arabs killed 16 Jews in Jewish neighborhoods on the outskirts of Jaffa. Riots spread amid huge property destruction and murder, once again in Hebron. A commission headed by Lord Robert Peel was convened, and in Jerusalem on January 8, 1937, the notion of a second partition was raised. The suggestion that western Palestine be further divided between an independent Jewish state and an Arab state enraged Arab Palestinians, but it excited Chaim Weizmann, who had helped extract the Balfour pledge from Britain two decades earlier. "The Jewish state," he told an aide, "was at hand."

Ben-Gurion was even more enthusiastic about the partition proposal. Because he had foreseen the destruction of European Jewry by Hitler, he was eager to accept from the British even the tiniest Jewish state — the "Tel Aviv" state, as he called it — into which he would herd as many European Jews as possible while there was still time.

Conflicting visions of Zionism. **Above,** *Vladimir Jabotinsky whose "Revisionist" movement split from the Zionist mainstream led by David Ben-Gurion,* **below**.

The Peel Commission recommended that if its proposal for partition were rejected by the British government, a limit on Jewish immigration to 12,000 a year for the next five years be imposed. But its main conclusion was that the mandate was unworkable and partition essential. Specifically, the commission proposed that the land be divided into two small states, each with a national majority, and that Jerusalem be made an international city. The British accepted the partition recommendation, but Palestine's Mufti, or chief Islamic cleric, Haj Amin al-Husseini, adamantly rejected the very notion of partition, drawing widespread Arab support. His rejection spared the Jewish community from what might have been a politically devastating split between what historians call Zionist "minimalists," those who favored the creation of a Jewish state in any part of Palestine, and "maximalists," those opposed to plans requiring them to give up most of Palestine. This divison, which cut across party lines, was to re-emerge time and again in Israeli politics.

Among the most ardent maximalists was Vladimir Jabotinsky, a Russian Zionist who during World War I had helped forge a fighting unit composed of Russian, British, American and other Jewish volunteers in Palestine. In 1923, he had resigned from the World Zionist executive to protest Weizmann's "appease-

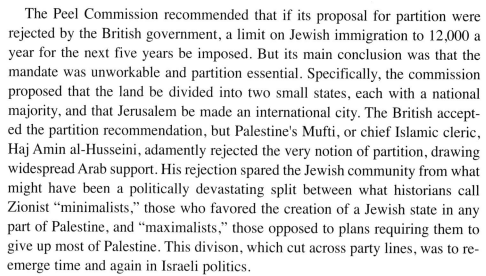

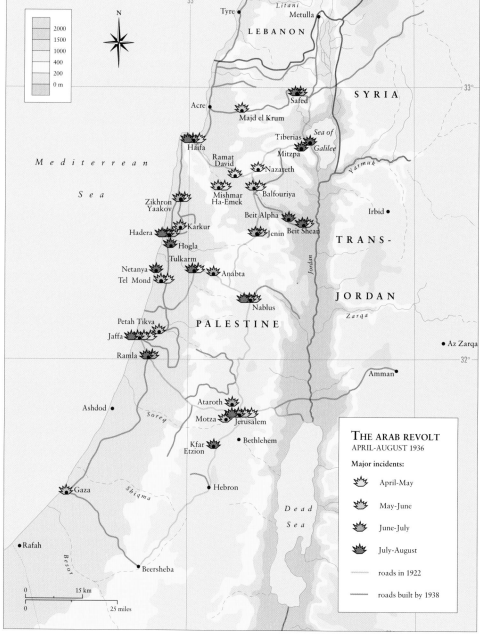

THE ARAB REVOLT
APRIL-AUGUST 1936

Major incidents:

April-May

May-June

June-July

July-August

roads in 1922

roads built by 1938

The immigration protests of the 1930s became known as the Arab Revolt. Here, British police suppress rioters in Jerusalem in 1936.

ment" of Britain, specifically, the group's recognition of Britain's creation of TransJordan, the separation of eastern Palestine from the historic, biblical "Land of Israel." There had to be an Israel on both sides of the River Jordan, he maintained. But Jabotinsky's quarrel with Chaim Weizmann and Ben-Gurion went far beyond territory. In 1925, he openly called for the creation of a Jewish state, which Weizmann, according to historian Jehuda Reinharz, had repeatedly avoided publicly advocating on tactical grounds. In 1935 his "revisionist" movement split with what became the Zionist mainstream and the left, over several other key issues. Chief among them were his belief that not just the Arabs, but also Britain were Zionism's enemies, and that a Jewish state could be established only through force. Presciently, Jabotinsky also rejected what he considered the self-deluding notion that the Arab residents of Palestine would eventually accept, if not welcome the Jews in Palestine, on the theory that Jewish immigration would mean an enhanced standard of living for all of Palestine's residents. Nor did he see an accomodation between the Yishuv (the Jewish community in Palestine) and the Arabs as an essential ingredient of Zionism's success, as the Zionist left maintained. Jewish settlement, he argued, could only take place if it were protected by an "iron wall," an armed Jewish force. While the Arabs would be granted full civic and political rights within the Jewish state, allowing even for an Arab prime minister or president, the "iron wall" of Jewish military strength would always be Israel's essential guarantor.

Fueled by Palestinian outrage over the partition plan contained in the Peel Commission report, the Arab revolt began again in 1936 and lasted until the end of 1939, with Arab turning not only against Jew, but against fel-

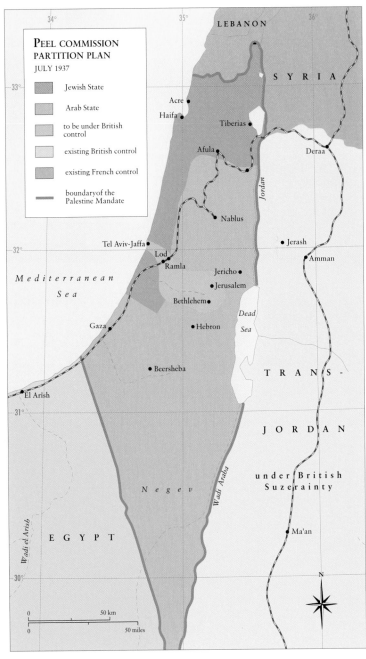

PEEL COMMISSION PARTITION PLAN
JULY 1937

- Jewish State
- Arab State
- to be under British control
- existing British control
- existing French control
- boundary of the Palestine Mandate

LEBANON
SYRIA
Acre
Haifa
Tiberias
Deraa
Afula
Jordan
Nablus
Jerash
Tel Aviv-Jaffa
Lod
Amman
Ramla
Jericho
Mediterranean Sea
Jerusalem
Bethlehem
Dead Sea
Gaza
Hebron
Beersheba
TRANS-
El Arish
JORDAN
under British Suzerainty
Negev
Wadi Araba
Ma'an
Wadi el Arish
EGYPT
0   50 km
0   50 miles
N

low Arab, killing more Arabs and British than Jews. The Mufti's Arab victims exceeded 3,000 in a bloodletting that many Palestinians, to this day, hold partly responsible for the creation of the Jewish state.

The outbreak of World War II dramatically slowed the Jewish emigration to Palestine which had swelled the Jewish population to 450,000 by 1939. Haj Amin al-Husseini allied himself openly with Hitler, while the Jewish community in Palestine volunteered in disproportionate numbers for service in an exclusively Jewish brigade and British auxillary units in Palestine. Zionists were forced to put aside many of their most intractable splits in the effort to save Jewish lives. Temporarily muted, for example, was the protracted quarrel between ultra-religious Jews — who rejected Zionism on grounds that God alone would decide whether the children of Israel would end their exile and return to the Land of Israel — and the secular Zionists, who argued that Jewish "redemption" lay in Jewish hands. Though historians still debate whether a Jewish state would have been founded if there had been no Holocaust, there seems little doubt that Hitler's genocide against the Jews sped Israel's creation.

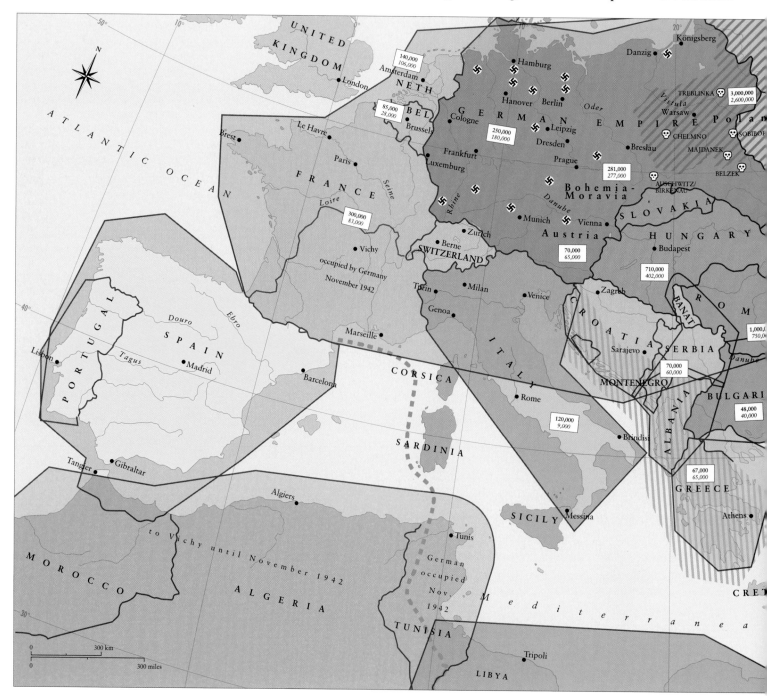

Left: *The Grand Mufti of Jerusalem meeting with Adolf Hitler in pre-war Germany.*

AMERICAN TROOPS CAPTURE DACHAU, LIBERATING 32,000

By THE ASSOCIATED PRESS

DACHAU, Germany, April 30—Dachau, Germany's most dreaded extermination camp, has been captured and its surviving 32,000 tortured inmates have been freed by outraged American troops who killed or captured its brutal garrison in a furious battle.

Dashing to the camp atop tanks, bulldozers, self-propelled guns—anything with wheels—the Forty-second and Forty-fifth Divisions hit the notorious prison northwest of Munich soon after the lunch hour yesterday. Dozens of German guards fell under withering blasts of rifle and carbine fire at the soldiers, catching glimpses of the horrors within the camp, raged through its barracks for a quick clean-up.

The troops were joined by trusty prisoners working outside the barbed-wire enclosures. Frenchmen and Russians, grabbing weapons dropped by slain guards, acted swiftly on their own to exact full revenge from their tormentors.

The sorting of the liberated prisoners was still under way today but the Americans learned from camp officials that some of the more important captives had been transferred recently to a new hideout, probably in the Tyrol. These were said to have included Premier Stalin's son Jacob, who was captured in 1941; the former Austrian Chancellor, Kurt Schuschnigg, and his wife; Prince Frederick Leopold of Prussia, Prince Xavier de Bourbon de Parme and the Rev. Martin Niemoeller, the German-Lutheran, who was arrested when he defied German attempts to control his preaching.

[Prisoners at another camp liberated by the Americans recently reported that Dr. Schuschnigg had been executed by his guards earlier this month.]

One of the prisoners remaining here said that he was the son of Leon Blum, former French Premier.

Prisoners with access to records said that 9,000 captives had died of hunger and disease or been shot in the past three months and 14,000 more had perished during the winter. Typhus was prevalent in the camp and the city's water supply was reported to have been contaminated by drainage from 6,000 graves near the prison.

The New York Times April 31, 1945

THE HOLOCAUST
1939 - 1945

Greater Germany c. 1942

occupied by Germany

occupied by Italy

Axis satellites

Allied territory

Neutral

maximum extent of Axis advance

Extermination camps

Concentration camps

Jewish Pale of settlement

| 2,500,000 | bold figure, pre-war |
| 750,000 | Jewish population, italic figure, lives lost during the Holocaust |

UNION OF SOVIET SOCIALIST REPUBLICS

Reichskommissariat Ukraine

Kiev

UKRAINE

Don

Volga

Dnieper

2,500,000 / 750,000

Rostov

Dniester

Odessa

Bucharest

Black Sea

Istanbul

TURKEY

IRAN

Izmir

Tigris

SYRIA

Euphrates

CYPRUS

IRAQ

Damascus

Sea

PALESTINE

Jerusalem

TRANS-JORDAN

SAUDI ARABIA

Even in the midst of what most Jews considered a life-and-death struggle for their people, however, some Zionist radicals refused to accept their leadership's dictates. A small group of Jewish terrorists, the Stern group (named for their leader, Abraham Stern) continued their war against Britain in Palestine; in 1944, they assassinated the British minister resident in the Middle East, Lord Moyne. The terrorism infuriated Whitehall, as well as many Zionist leaders and led Weizmann to promise the British that the Yishuv would "go to the utmost limit of its power to cut out, root and branch, this evil from its midst." But Weizmann was in London and unable to implement his pledge. That unhappy task fell to Ben-Gurion, who, defying high political risk, collaborated with the British to eradicate Jewish terror. Ben-Gurion instinctively knew that unless the authority of Jewish leadership in Palestine was buttressed there and then, a disciplined state would never emerge.

As the war raged in Europe, American Zionist leaders met with Weizmann presiding in May, 1942 at the Biltmore Hotel in New York to restate their commitment to Zionism. With only a few dissenting votes from bi-nationalists, they adopted the so-called Biltmore Program, which demanded Jewish control over immigration to Palestine and the establishment there of a Jewish Commonwealth after the war. The adoption of the Biltmore Program by the Yishuv is generally regarded as evidence that the Yishuv had at last developed into a mature national-political entity, ready to carry out its political objectives, despite the continued splits within its ranks. It was equally clear by 1946, argues

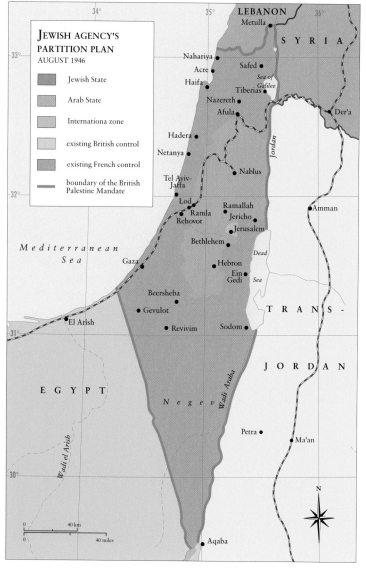

*British Police checking identification in Jerusalem in 1946. Despite such security, clandestine immigration (**below**) continued to swell the Jewish population in Palestine.*

BATTLE INTENSIFIES TO CONTROL VITAL JERUSALEM HIGHWAY

By THE ASSOCIATED PRESS

CAIRO, Egypt, May 28—Arab Legion and Israeli commanders fed armor and artillery into the mounting battle for Latrun tonight after hungry, outnumbered Israeli fighters in Jerusalem's Old City surrendered to King Abdullah's siege forces.

The victory of the Trans-Jordan troops in the Old city was not a decisive one. The battles for a bigger prize—all of Jerusalem—was being fought 14 miles west of the Holy City on the vital highway from Tel Aviv.

Israel's army announced that its troops had captured the Arab villages of Beit Jiz and Beit Susin, immediately south of the highway and little more than a mile from Latrun.

An Egyptian Defense Ministry communiqué said tonight that Egyptian bombers attacked and dispersed Israeli troop concentrations that were attempting to open the Jerusalem-Tel Aviv road at Bab el Wad, 11 miles west of the Holy City. Bab el Wad is four miles east of Latrun. The number of planes or troops involved was not given. The communiqué also said that the Egyptian reconnaisance planes observed a "large" formation of Israeli troops concentrated west of Bab el Wad. It added that Egyptian planes kept the enemy forces "under continuous attack."

The Egyptians also claimed high explosive and incendiary bombs were dropped on the settlements of Hulda, 18 miles southeast of Tel Aviv, and Abu Shusha, 17 miles southeast of Tel Aviv. Direct hits were scored and fires were started that could be seen at high altitude from Gaza and El Majdal, the communiqué said.

Without identifying any particular area, the Egyptian communiqué said:

"Our land forces made wide-scale mopping up operations, forcing the enemy out of resistance pockets and inflicting considerable casualties."

Egyptian planes also attacked the settlement of Khulda, inflicting damages, the communiqué said, and successfully strafed, six armored cars and two other vehicles near Khulda.

The New York Times May 29, 1948

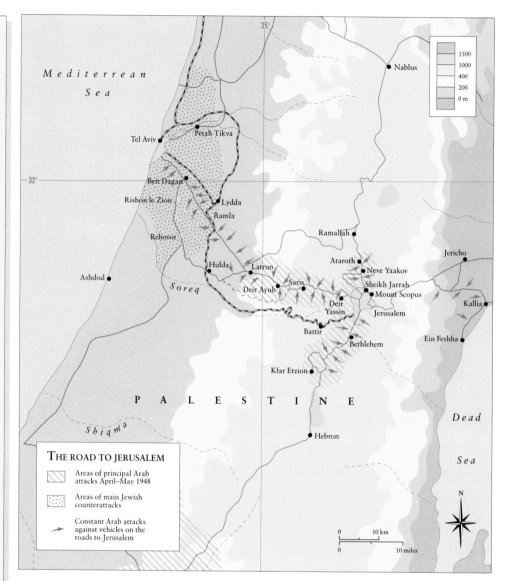

THE ROAD TO JERUSALEM

Areas of principal Arab attacks April–May 1948

Areas of main Jewish counterattacks

Constant Arab attacks against vehicles on the roads to Jerusalem

Shabtai Teveth, that Ben-Gurion had overshadowed Chaim Weizmann as Zionism's leader and main spokesman. While Weizmann thought that Britain would remain in Palestine for years and would continue to be decisive in Zionist affairs, the Biltmore Program seemed to vindicate Ben-Gurion's judgment that the United States, not Britain, would be critical in shaping developments in Palestine and throughout the Middle East.

After the war, the shock of the Holocaust caused Jewish communities everywhere, but particularly in America, to press for Palestine to be designated a refuge for what remained of European Jews. Among non-Jews, guilt about having done all too little to prevent the genocide made it unseemly for governments to openly block the creation of a Jewish state. Within Palestine, Jewish terrorism against the British was renewed.

On April 2, 1947, war-weary Britain, exasperated by the chaos and fighting in Palestine and intent on decolonization, turned the fate of its mandate over to the newly formed United Nations. On November 29th, the General Assembly voted for partition, 33 to 13. In December, rioting and fighting erupted again in Palestine and other Arab countries with Jewish communities, which further increased pressure on Britain to hasten its evacuation.

Washington, however, was still not persuaded that the creation of a Jewish state was in America's interests in the Middle East. The State Department, in particular, wanted to stall a unilateral declaration of independence by what would become the first government of Israel. As a result, the United States

Some 4,500 European Jews aboard the refugee ship "Exodus" were barred by the British from Haifa harbor in 1947 and deported to France.

Refugees from Nazi work camps in Yugoslavia arriving in Haifa via Turkey in 1944.

heavily pressured the Jewish Agency leadership to refrain from declaring independence and to accept instead a provisional U.N. trusteeship and a truce. Declaring a state, Washington warned, would trigger an invasion by neighboring Arab states that the poorly armed Yishuv would have almost no chance of repelling. Yet Ben-Gurion urged his colleagues to reject both Washington's threats and advice.

On May 12, the Jewish Agency Executive, meeting in Tel Aviv, voted on whether to accept Washington's demands or declare the creation of the Israeli state. Only 10 of the Executive's members were able to attend, as two were stranded in Jerusalem, then under siege by the Jordanians. Six voted for the state, four against. The deciding vote was cast by Moshe Sharett, a leading Zionist who had flown in from Washington to present Washington's demands. But having spent much of the night being lobbied by Ben-Gurion, he voted in favor of declaring a state.

On May 14, the British lowered the Union Jack in Jerusalem as full-scale fighting erupted throughout the country. At 4:00 P.M. that afternoon at the Tel Aviv Museum, Ben-Gurion read the Declaration of Independence of the State of Israel, extending a hand "in peace and neighborliness to all the neighboring states and their peoples," and inviting them to "cooperate with the independent Jewish nation for the common good of all." At 6:10 P.M. that day, the United States recognized the Jewish state. Arab armies entered Palestine to redeem it from the Zionists and the West. Many Palestinians were driven out of Palestine for what they assumed would be a temporary exile. Most would never see their homeland again. The War of Independence was a reality.

David Ben-Gurion, Israel's first prime minister, reading the nation's Declaration of Independence on May 14, 1948.

The New York Times Book Review February 23, 1975

Herzl

By Amos Elon.
Illustrated. 448 pp. New York:
Holt, Rinehart & Winston.

By ALFRED KAZIN

Amos Elon is a Vienna-born Israeli newspaperman whose books (in English) so precisely reflect intellectual, liberal Israeli opinion that they foreshadow changes in the political weather. "The Israelis: Founders and Sons" (1971) made it abundantly clear why the Russian-born founders of the state would soon have to yield power to the Sabras. Last year's "Between Enemies: A Compassionate Dialogue Between an Israeli and an Arab" (with Sana Hasan), revealed a desire for intellectual sympathy on the part of some Israelis and some Egyptians, a willingness to entertain *ideological* concessions, that may yet bear fruit among the politicians.

I would guess that Elan decided to write a biography of Theodor Herzl, the still ambiguous founder of political Zionism, precisely because Israel is in the worst trouble of its short life and because the Israelis have never been so painfully aware of the tragically inordinate effort to be understood and accepted that dogs the Jewish state. Herzl (1860-1904) reflects, more than any of his successors in leading the Zionist movement, the obstinate sense of unreality, that has gone, along with the most fervent self-service, into the "return to our ancient homeland."

Israelis frequently express a sense of irony about their national existence that goes unheard by their zealous supporters outside of Israel. Israelis born in Vienna, the city that nurtured Hitler and Herzl, Freud and anti-Semitic Lord Mayor Karl Lueger, Mahler and Wittgenstein, Schnitzler and Schoenberg, logical positivism and some leading murderers in the S.S., have much to be ironic about in retrospect. Vienna, Elon notes in passing, was in some respects very much like New York today. Its elaborate cultural facade did not conceal the poverty, social bitterness, the many discordant nationalities. Even the strongest and most militant among the Jewish intellectuals, like Freud, felt damaged by their constant insecurity. There was great intellectual excitement, marvellous theater and opera, but uncontrollable hatreds were already bursting through the whipped-cream surface of the rickety empire.

Herzl, the "modern Moses" who did not live to see Israel (the only *de jure* recognition of the Jews as a nation since they were dispersed by the Romans in A.D. 70), was a successful newspaperman but an embittered failure as a playwright. He was married to a psychotic woman who resented his Zionist activity (two of his children and one of his grandchildren were to commit suicide), and his deep-seated intimacy with frustration would no doubt have seemed intractable to Freud, who lived just down the block. Like so many "emancipated," uneasily Jewish middle-class Jews in Vienna, Berlin, Paris, Herzl was not emancipated from the terrors and neuroses that came from the "contradictions" of remaining a Jew in modern, "progressive" times.

Herzl came of prosperous Hungarian Jewish stock but of course preferred to live in Vienna and to regard himself as "culturally German." He even had himself naturalized as an Austrian. An only son and after the death of his young sister an only child, he kept up a relationship with his forever adoring parents that made it impossible for him to be intimate with other people. Nor did he find it easy to nurse his supposed genius in isolation and failure. He was a fluent, charming writer of "Talk of the Town" *feuilletons* for the Neue Freie Presse, an "intellectual" paper owned by assimilated Jews. They were afraid of discussing the "Jewish question," and Herzl himself was so alarmed by it that one of his early fantasies was to lead the Jews to St. Stephen's Cathedral for a mass conversion — but he would remain outside.

Herzl was Paris correspondent of the Neue Freie Presse when the mob, watching Captain Dreyfus expelled in disgrace from the French Army, shouted "Death to Jews!" One Herzl biographer reports that Herzl's account to his paper was changed to "Death to the Traitor!" In any event, as Elon abundantly shows the Dreyfus Affair showed Herzl that there was no future for the Jews in Europe. It was in Paris that he wrote the famous pamphlet, "The Jewish State: An Attempt at a Modern Solution of the Jewish Question," that founded modern political Zionism and the Zionist organization.

Herzl was extremely quick, intensely proud and ambitious, and as the delegates discovered when he called together the first Zionist congress at Basel in 1897, a man of extraordinary presence. His sense of theater was more effective in congress halls and European chancelleries than on the stage. He looked the part of a "modern Moses" as no one else did. With his full dark beard, his suitably sad eyes, but marvellous voice, his ostentatiously aristocratic manners, he even got the other delegates to wear full evening dress. The Jews were going to have some dignity at last! He somehow united normally fractious Jews by the regality of his appearance. Desperate Russian Jews, looking for relief from unwearying oppression, blissfully acclaimed Herzl as the returned Jewish King.

Ultra-rich Jews like the Rothchilds and Baron de Hirsch were less impressed. But Herzl, who wrote a bad utopian novel about the future Jewish state ("Old-New Land"), began negotiations for a charter to Palestine by meeting with the Sultan of Turkey, Pius X, Wilhelm II, the Grand Duke of Baden, the Rt. Hon. Joseph Chamberlain, Lord Cromer the English boss of Egypt, Prime Minister Plehve and Finance Minister Witte of Russia. Herzl was indefatigable, seductive and a tremendous bluff — with hardly any money, he offered to buy up the national debt of Turkey in exchange for Jewish rights in Palestine! Moses wheedling with Pharaoh had nothing on this majestic figure (always in full evening dress) who had to bribe every official at the Turkish court even to get the promise of an appointment with the "Sick Man of Europe."

Herzl had in full measure the chutzpah that in small matters gets some people disliked, but in the largest possible matters makes others "world figures." Although he was hardly impressed by his own sight of neglected, disease ridden Palestine, and at one time angered his fellow-Zionists by a proposal to settle the Jews in Uganda, the fate of the Jews had become his life, his destiny. The glib journalist of the Viennese boulevards had somehow become a prophet-figure. Something ancient, world-shaking in its unconscious truth, yet vaguely ominous, spoke through Herzl. Even the violently anti-Semetic leaders of Russia, fomenting pogoms against the helpless Pale, were vaguely impressed by him. Christian cranks joined him in justifying the restoration of the Jews to Palestine, Polish adventurers, an Anglo-Jewish professional soldier. The professional literary philistine Max Nordan, who steadily denounced everything "advanced" in modern literature and art, became Herzl's second-in-command. But most important were the Jews from "the house of bondage," imperial Russia. Unlike Herzl, they had never had to "discover" their Jewish-ness; unlike Herzl, they were cultural and spiritual Hebraists who had founded the "Love of Zion" groups long before the Zionist movement.

Herzl did not invent Zionism, but he alone was able to get it off the ground as a political movement. Despite his overbearing ways, his bold naivete in trying to get the great powers to create for the Jews that return to the Promised Land that is inseparable from their liturgy, he made the "idea" of it respectable and practical. Before his death, in 1904, he said that the state would come into being within 50 years of his death.

On the other hand, it is not so much Zionism as the Holocaust that sustains the State of Israel. Herzl's Viennese pessimism did not anticipate the destruction of European Jewry by his beloved "German culture," and like so many 19th-century prophets, his vision of the future has been realized in bizarre ways. Herzl's Jewish state rests not on his utopian illusions of a world made peacefully co-operative by technology but on the desperate military power that was the last thing the Zionists anticipated or wanted. It has been easier for the "outside world" to accept Israel than for it to *understand* the Jewish idea of the Promised Land. And now even the "acceptance" is grudging and dwindling - where it exists.

So Herzl's story is full of irony, as Israel is today. Elon does not stress the irony. His book is a full, dramatic biography, rich in "big scenes." There is little interpretation added to the facts. In this book Herzl's life mysteriously speaks for itself. As Israelis do by living where they do.

Chapter Three: The Young Nation

Peter Grose

THE MODERN JEWISH STATE came into being upon the "stored up anguish of 2,000 years," in the words of Israel's first professional diplomat, Walter Eytan, Like its predecessor of Biblical and Roman times, the Jewish homeland was ill-defined in its frontiers, fractious in its population, and surrounded by anxious, hostile neighbors. Jerusalem, the once and future capital, was blockaded by Arab forces, the longest siege in the life of the Holy City since the medieval Crusades. Aircraft from Egypt bombed Tel Aviv during the night of May 14-15, 1948, and regular Arab armies moved against the Jewish settlements from three sides within hours of their state proclamation.

Not for over a year would the citizens of Israel know the actual size and shape of their state. In area, their new homeland amounted to some 8,000 square miles (about the size of New Jersey). Half was a lush and muggy coastal strip along the eastern edge of the Mediterranean; the other half was venerated but forbidding desert of hills and mountains.

On this uncomely terrain lived 655,000 Jews and 69,000 Arabs, the latter a minuscule fragment of the throbbing Arab Palestinian population that had previously — and uneasily — shared the land with the Zionist settlers.

Of all the birth pangs, looming large from the first hours of statehood was the quest for international recognition. The United States was the first government to recognize the Jewish state, just 11 minutes after its proclamation. The Soviet Union, at that time hopeful of comradely relations with socialist Zionism, came third. (Guatemala squeaked in as second, thanks to an eager foreign minister who had been active on the side of the Zionists at the United Nations.)

For months to come, harassed Israelis struggling to put together their daily lives rejoiced in bold newspaper headlines announcing that yet another small and faraway state of, say, Central America had offered diplomatic relations. In the early archives of the Foreign Ministry is found a somber diplomatic analysis of the prospects for recognition by Liechtenstein. Deep within the diplomatic traditions of the United States had long lurked a skepticism about the viability of a restored Jewish state; American recognition and support came from President Harry S Truman, not his Department of State. As far back as 1891, the American consul in Jerusalem had dispatched a dismal prognosis to Washington:

"When and where have [Jews] learned the art of self-government? The quickest way to annihilate them would be to place them in Palestine with no restrictions or influences from any civilized government, and allow them to govern themselves; they would very soon destroy each other." Across the first half of the twentieth century, American diplomats showed little interest in revising that primitive assessment.

Prime Minister David Ben-Gurion in 1950.

The New York Times.

"All the News That's Fit to Print"

LATE CITY EDITION
Fair and warmer today and tomorrow.
Temperature Range Today—Max., 65; Min., 46
Temperature Yesterday—Max., 53; Min., 46
Full Weather Bureau Report, Page 21

Copyright, 1948, by The New York Times Company.

VOL. XCVII..No. 32,984.

Entered as Second-Class Matter,
Postoffice, New York, N. Y.

NEW YORK, SATURDAY, MAY 15, 1948.

Times Square, New York 18, N. Y.
Telephone LAckawanna 4-1000

THREE CENTS NEW YORK CITY

ZIONISTS PROCLAIM NEW STATE OF ISRAEL; TRUMAN RECOGNIZES IT AND HOPES FOR PEACE; TEL AVIV IS BOMBED, EGYPT ORDERS INVASION

NAVY PUSHES PLAN FOR CONSTRUCTION OF MISSILE VESSELS

Sullivan Asks House Committee to Approve Halting Work on Battleship, Destroyer Types

WANTS 65,000-TON CARRIER

Floating 'Submarine Killers' Are Also Stressed in Plea for Diverting $300,000,000 Fund

By C. P. TRUSSELL
Special to The New York Times.

WASHINGTON, May 14—The Navy asked Congress today for authority to shift sharply its construction of fighting craft from battleship, cruiser and destroyer types to guided missile vessels, a 65,000-ton carrier able to base, far at sea, planes with an operating radius of 1,700 miles, better submarines and floating "enemy submarine killers."

Such new ships, John L. Sullivan, Secretary of the Navy, told the House Armed Services Committee, must have a higher priority "because of the more immediate need for them in the event of an emergency." The immediate reaction of the committee appeared to favor prompt action.

For such a shift in construction, Secretary Sullivan brought out, the Navy wanted to halt the building of thirteen naval vessels, including the battleship Kentucky, the large cruiser Hawaii, seven destroyers, two destroyer escorts and two submarines. To date about $197,000,000 has been spent on them.

However, this money was not to be abandoned, Mr. Sullivan emphasized. These craft could be converted now to the new program, he explained, or be put aside for a fitting-out later as new weapons were developed.

New Aims for $390,000,000 Fund

What the Navy wanted, Secretary Sullivan asserted, was Congressional permission to divert some $300,000,000 remaining in the present ship construction account for these purposes:

Starting the 65,000-ton aircraft carrier (the biggest ones now are the two of the Midway class, at 45,000 tons), which might cost around $124,000,000.

Building, for reproduction later, of a "submarine killer." (Hearings on the defense program have indicated that Russia has made great progress in the submarine field.) A "killer" machine, it is indicated, is developing in new work on the cruiser type of seacraft.

The construction of four submarines of types advanced beyond those now building.

In addition, there was under plan a conversion in an unidentified way of a carrier and two submarines.

Secretary Sullivan told the committee that the Kentucky and the Hawaii would not have to stand by for the development of new weapons. It is planned, he disclosed, that they be converted into guided missile ships. Apparently to allay fears in Congress that larger aircraft carriers make easier targets for enemy bombers, Mr. Sullivan drew upon experience in the second World War and the results of atom-bomb tests at Bikini.

Speed Held Bomb Defense

"The experiments at Bikini," Mr. Sullivan said, "have proved that a fast-moving fleet is an unprofitable target for an atomic bomb."

Members of the committee interpreted this as a Navy Department conclusion that even though a potential enemy might acquire the atomic bomb, the revised construction program proposed today promised a maximum of safety. Mr. Sullivan recalled that the Navy lost three large and two light carriers in the Pacific, but none was sunk by aircraft landbased. He indicated that mobility of a fleet, equipped to latest model, would discourage the spotting of atomic bombs, even if an enemy had some.

Today, the Senate Republican

Continued on Page 7, Column 4

Heaviest Trading in 8 Years Marks Stock Market Spurt

3,840,000 Shares Change Hands as Wave of Bullish Enthusiasm Increases Securities 1 to 7 Points

The hectic days of the Nineteen Twenties were re-enacted yesterday on the floor of the New York Stock Exchange when the most turbulent session in recent years produced increases of 1 to 7 points in the share list. Accompanied by a burst of bullish enthusiasm not witnessed in almost a decade, the deluge of buying orders so taxed the facilities of the Exchange that the reporting ticker tape lagged behind floor transactions by five minutes.

The cracking of the 1947 high level at the approach of mid-day rush. Public participation suddenly enlarged and buying orders pressed floor traders to the utmost. This condition existed for forty-five minutes in the final hour when 1,350,000 shares were traded. Accompanied by the broadest market on record with a total of 1,151 issues dealt in, volume on the Stock Exchange spiraled to 3,840,000 shares, the largest since May 21, 1940, in contrast to the Thursday turnover of 2,030,000 shares.

Brokers termed it the "wildest" bull market in twenty years on the premise that at no time in the interval had the industrials and rails advanced with such a unity of force.

While the ground had been well laid for a movement of such scope earlier this week, it was the piercing of the 1947 resistance point that confirmed the presence of a bull market to those who act by the charts, or averages. Early in the day, telegrams were sent by several advisory services to their clients urging the purchase of securities. The response to this advice showed primarily in the bid

Continued on Page 23, Column 5

Truman Sees His Election; Calls GOP 'Obstructionist'

By ANTHONY LEVIERO
Special to The New York Times.

WASHINGTON, May 14—President Truman asserted tonight that there would be a Democrat in the White House during the next four years and that he would be the man. He made the statement to a cheering audience of 1,000 young Democrats at their meeting here.

The President's speech was a fighting one in the new Truman manner. He spoke extemporaneously, resorting to whimsy and irony and using forceful gestures of his arms to underscore his points.

Mr. Truman accused the Republican party of stealing Democratic platform planks. "You know," he said, "it has been their habit since 1936 of taking a few planks out of the old Democratic platforms and building a platform and then saying, 'Me, too.'"

[The text of President Truman's speech is on Page 7.]

"What have the Republicans done in the last fifteen and a half years?" Mr. Truman asked, then said:

"They have been obstructionists. They spent most of their time while I was in the Senate—and I was there for ten years—in obstructing progressive legislation that was for the welfare of the common man, and throwing bricks and mud at the greatest President that ever sat in the White House."

Mr. Truman was interrupted by applause at this obvious allusion to President Roosevelt.

"That has been their record," he continued, "and they haven't changed a bit. They were against Social Security. They were against TVA. They were against wages

Continued on Page 16, Column 3

MINNESOTA'S GUARD OUT IN MEAT STRIKE

Governor Acts After 200 Raid Cudahy Newport Plant, Attack 60 Workers and Abduct 25

Special to The New York Times.

ST. PAUL, Minn., May 14—National Guard troops were ordered to South St. Paul and Newport, towns on opposite banks of the Mississippi River near here, by Governor Luther Youngdahl today following violent disorders at strike-bound packing plants in the area and the statement of the local sheriffs that their forces could not maintain law and order.

The Governor did not proclaim martial law but said the troops would take their orders from the civil authorities.

The Governor's action followed a serious outbreak at the Cudahy packing plant in Newport shortly before last midnight in which a group of about 200 men charged the plant with clubs, knives and hammers. In South St. Paul on Thursday strikers forced back police who tried to open a way through picket lines at the Swift & Co. plant in

Continued on Page 16, Column 3

Princess Elizabeth, in Paris Talk, Asks Common Effort of 2 Nations

By LANSING WARREN
Special to The New York Times.

PARIS, May 14—Speaking in faultless French with just the touch of a British accent to delight French ears, Princess Elizabeth today asked France and Britain to make a common effort to lead Europe to moral and intellectual as well as economic reconstruction.

Her well-worded and discerning speech was cheered, but she went straight to the hearts of the Parisian throng when, with charming frankness, she avowed her joy that her first foreign trip since her marriage had brought her here to Paris.

"For a long time," she said, "I have wanted to come to France. More fortunate than I, my husband already knew your admirable capital and he is all the happier to return. This trip is all the more important and agreeable for the warmth of your welcome which has touched us both." From the time they stepped down from the train at the Gare du Nord early today, Princess Elizabeth and Prince Philip, Duke of Edinburgh, were the center of admiring attention from the throngs that lined the streets and from all the French officials who received them throughout the day. President Vincent Auriol voiced the general feeling when in a statement issued tonight he said:

"I have been personally struck by her grace, her charm, her modesty and her nobility. I feel sure that the sentiments that she has expressed went straight to the hearts of all the French."

Elizabeth's address, broadcast to the French nation, was delivered from the top of the monumental entry to the Galliera Museum, where she came to open the British Government's exhibition of relics and souvenirs of famous British

Continued on Page 6, Column 3

AIR ATTACK OPENS

Planes Cause Fires at Port—Defense Fliers Go Into Action

BORDER IS BREACHED

Cairo Vanguard Takes Colony—Trans-Jordan Reports a Movement

By The Associated Press.

TEL AVIV, Palestine, Saturday, May 15—Air raiders bombed this all-Jewish city at about dawn today.

First reports said there were "some casualties 'near the power and light station.

[Cairo reported that Egyptian armed forces had been ordered to enter Palestine. Arab armies moved from Trans-Jordan at 12:01 A. M. Saturday to "liberate the Holy Land from Zionism," said a Trans-Jordan communiqué reported by The United Press from Amman.]

Tel Aviv was under complete blackout all night but no sirens were sounded during the raid. Civil guards were alerted and fifteen to twenty ships in the port area moved out to sea.

The planes swooped over Tel Aviv little more than twelve hours after Jewish leaders had proclaimed the existence of a new Hebrew state of Israel.

Some bombs fell in the vicinity of the power station along the Yarkum River near Tel Aviv.

Persons at the scene said there was one hit on or near the power station, causing "some casualties."

TEL AVIV, Saturday, May 15 (UP) — Some ten bombs were dropped on Tel Aviv by two aircraft described as twin bombers and accompanied by two small fighters. One Jew was killed and three were hospitalized. Jewish Army aircraft took to the skies a few minutes after the enemy planes whizzed over rooftops at an estimated altitude of 300 feet.

Several fires could be seen north

Continued on Page 2, Column 3

U. S. MOVES QUICKLY

President Acknowledges de Facto Authority of Israel Immediately

TRUCE AIM STRESSED

Soviet Gesture to New Nation Anticipated— Others Due to Act

By BERTRAM D. HULEN
Special to The New York Times.

WASHINGTON, May 14—President Truman announced early tonight recognition by the United States of the new Jewish State of Israel. The President acted instantly upon being informed that the new nation had been proclaimed.

"This Government," he announced, "has been informed that a Jewish state has been proclaimed in Palestine and recognition has been requested by the provisional government thereof.

"The United States recognizes the provisional government as the de facto authority of the new State of Israel."

These two paragraphs constituted the text of the President's statement.

Coupled with the announcement was an expression of hope for peace in Palestine. This was made known through a separate White House statement issued by Charles G. Ross, Presidential press secretary.

"The desire of the United States to obtain a truce in Palestine," this said, "will in no way be lessened by the proclamation of a Jewish state.

"We hope that the new Jewish state will join with the Security Council Truce Commission in redoubled efforts to bring an end to the fighting—which has been throughout the United Nations' consideration of Palestine a principal objective of this Government."

[Pending stabilization of the Palestine situation and indications that the State of Israel

Continued on Page 3, Column 2

Continued on Page 2, Column 3

World News Summarized

SATURDAY, MAY 15, 1948

Several hours after the state of Israel, the first Hebrew nation in 2,000 years, had been proclaimed in a Zionist declaration of independence in Tel Aviv, [1:8.], President Truman announced that the United States recognized the "provisional government" of Israel as "the de facto authority of the new state." A second White House statement expressed the hope that the new regime would cooperate with United Nations efforts to bring about peace in Palestine. [3:5.] The British High Commissioner departed from Palestine and boarded a cruiser at Haifa as Britain's rule over the Holy Land formally ended. [1:7.]

The special session of the United Nations General Assembly ended last night after it had agreed to send a mediator to Palestine to try to arrange a truce. [1:6-7.] The trusteeship plan for Jerusalem sponsored by the United States was rejected by the Assembly, with the Arab states and the Soviet opposed to the measure. [1:6-7.]

Tel Aviv was bombed at dawn. Egypt ordered her troops to invade Palestine. Trans-Jordan reported her army on the move also. [1:4.] Haganah claimed that its forces captured Acre in the north. [2:8.]

In Moscow the newspaper Pravda, in the first editorial comment on the recent exchange between Washington and Moscow, accused the United States of double-dealing. [4:8.]

Paris crowds gave an enthusiastic welcome to Princess Elizabeth and the Duke of Edinburgh when they arrived for a visit. [1:2-3.]

Congress received a request from the Navy for authority to shift the emphasis in its construction of fighting craft to guided-missile vessels. [1:1.] President Truman predicted that he would be re-elected next November. [1:7.]

Minnesota National Guard troops were rushed to South St. Paul and Newport after 200 persons had raided the Cudahy meat packing plant at Newport, where a strike is in progress attacking about sixty workers and abducting twenty-five of them. [1:2.]

The New York Stock Exchange enjoyed one of its biggest days in recent years as an avalanche of buying orders sent stocks up from 1 to 7 points. Trading reached a total of 3,840,000 shares, the largest since May 21, 1940. [1:2-3.]

Winston Churchill's War Memoirs

See Page 17 for today's installment, in which Mr. Churchill describes the invasion of Norway and the clash of the British and German fleets.

AT HELM OF THE JEWISH STATE

David Ben-Gurion
Premier

Moshe Shertok
Foreign Minister
The New York Times

U. N. Votes for a Mediator; Special Assembly Is Ended

By THOMAS J. HAMILTON

After hearing both the Soviet Union and the Arab delegates denounce the United States for its sudden recognition of the new Jewish state in Palestine, the United Nations General Assembly decided last night to send a Mediator to the Holy Land to do what he could to arrange a truce and carry on public services.

The vote was 31 to 7, with sixteen abstentions and four delegates absent, and the General Assembly, which was called into special session at Flushing Meadow on April 16 at the request of the United States, adjourned for good at 8:32 P. M.

The failure of the General Assembly either to repeal the partition resolution of last November or to provide military force to keep the peace means that the fate of Palestine will be decided by the impending war between Jews and Arabs, not by any United Nations action.

The mediation resolution conforms substantially with a United States proposal announced last Wednesday, after it had become obvious that the General Assembly would not accept the original United States plan for a temporary trusteeship.

However, the General Assembly refused to accept a United States plan for a temporary trusteeship over Jerusalem, which was rejected earlier in the evening by a vote of 19 to 15, less than the necessary two-thirds majority.

Two other proposals regarding Jerusalem were rejected, but presumably the provisions of the partition resolution to protect the Holy City and its holy places failed to obtain the necessary two-thirds majority at the closing session at Flushing Meadow.

The vote, which came just after the bombshell of the United States recognition of the new Jewish State had burst in the Assembly, was 20 in favor, 15 against and 19 abstentions. The balance was turned by the hostility of Britain and most of the Dominions.

The United States fought hard all day, first in the Political and Security Committee of the Assembly, sitting at Lake Success, and then in the evening session of the Assembly, to get the trusteeship plan adopted before the end of the

Continued on Page 4, Column 4

CUNNINGHAM GOES AS MANDATE ENDS

British Commissioner Boards Cruiser Off Haifa—Jews Take Down Union Jack

By The Associated Press.

HAIFA, Palestine, Saturday, May 15—Britain ended her mandate over the Holy Land last midnight. Lieut. Gen. Sir Alan Cunningham, the last British High Commissioner, sailed from Haifa port, finishing British mandate guidance.

Sir Alan's departure from Palestine's richest port caused little excitement among the Jews, who control most of the city.

The British fired a few rockets and searchlights spotlighted the cruiser as it steamed from the harbor.

Wearing the uniform of a British Army general, Sir Alan walked down a few steps of dock into a launch that took him to the cruiser Euryalus.

Upon getting onto the launch, he turned and looked soberly up across the docks. There stood an honor guard of the King's Company of Grenadier Guards and Royal Marine commandos.

The launch pulled away amid the

Continued on Page 2, Column 7

U. N. Bars Jerusalem Trusteeship; Vote Follows Mandate Deadline

By MALLORY BROWNE

The United Nations General Assembly rejected yesterday the United States plan for a temporary trusteeship regime in Jerusalem.

Solidly opposed by the Arab States and the Russian bloc, the plan to set up a United Nations Commissioner authorized to protect the Holy City and its holy places failed to obtain the necessary two-thirds majority at the closing session at Flushing Meadow.

The vote, which came just after the bombshell of the United States recognition of the new Jewish State had burst in the Assembly, was 20 in favor, 15 against and 19 abstentions. The balance was turned by the hostility of Britain and most of the Dominions.

The United States fought hard all day, first in the Political and Security Committee of the Assembly, sitting at Lake Success, and then in the evening session of the Assembly, to get the trusteeship plan adopted before the end of the mandate at 6:01 P. M., New York time.

An Arab filibuster, aided by the Soviet bloc, defeated this effort. It was well past the zero hour when a roll-call vote showed that the Assembly preferred to leave Harold Evans, newly appointed Jerusalem municipal Commissioner, in sole charge of the Holy City and its treasures.

As one Arab after another filed up to the tribune and took up the maximum five-minute period allowed in repeating the arguments against a trusteeship plan, 6:01 o'clock came by.

At once Awni Khalidy of Iraq, who had led the Arab fight against the trusteeship plan, rushed up to the tribune and exultantly proclaimed that the time had passed; that the mandate was at an end, and that, since, as Francis B. Sayre of the United States had said, the measure must

Continued on Page 3, Column 5

THE JEWS REJOICE

Some Weep as Quest for Statehood Ends —White Paper Dies

HELP OF U. N. ASKED

New Regime Holds Out Hand to Arabs—U. S. Gesture Acclaimed

Text of declaration setting up new Jewish state, Page 2.

By GENE CURRIVAN
Special to The New York Times.

TEL AVIV, Palestine, Saturday, May 15—The Jewish state, the world's newest sovereignty, to be known as the State of Israel, came into being in Palestine at midnight upon termination of the British mandate.

Recognition of the state by the United States, which had opposed its establishment at this time, came as a complete surprise to the people, who were tense and ready for the threatened invasion by Arab forces and appealed for help by the United Nations.

In one of the most hopeful periods of their troubled history the Jewish people here gave a sigh of relief and took a new hold on life when they learned that the greatest national power had accepted them into the international fraternity.

Ceremony Simple and Solemn

The declaration of the new state by David Ben-Gurion, chairman of the National Council and the first Premier of reborn Israel, was delivered during a simple and solemn ceremony at 4 P. M., and new life was instilled into his people, but from without there was the rumbling of guns, a flashback to other declarations of independence that had not been easily achieved.

The first action of the new Government was to revoke the Palestine White Paper of 1939, which restricted Jewish immigration and land purchase.

In the proclamation of the new state the Government appealed to the United Nations "to assist the Jewish people in the building of its state and to admit Israel into the family of nations."

The proclamation added:

"We offer peace and amity to all neighboring states and their peoples, and invite them to cooperate with the independent Jewish nation for the common good of all. The State of Israel is ready to contribute its full share to the peaceful progress and reconstitution of the Middle East."

World Jewry Asked to Aid

The statement appealed to Jews throughout the world to assist in the task of immigration and development and in the "struggle for the fulfillment of the dream of Israel."

Plans for the ceremony had been laid with great secrecy. None but the hundred or more invited guests and journalists was aware of the meeting until it was started, and even the guests learned of the site only ten minutes before. It was held in the Tel Aviv Museum of Art, a white, modern-design two-story building. Above it flew the Star of David, which is the state's flag, and below, on the sidewalk, was a guard of honor of the Haganah, the army of the Jewish Agency for Palestine.

As photographers' bulbs flashed and movie cameras ground out reels of the scene, great crowds gathered and cheered the Ministers and other members of the Government as they entered the building. The security arrangements were perfect. Stee guns were brandished and one could hear the safeties on the roofs bristled with them.

The setting for the reading of the proclamation was a dropped gallery whose hall held paintings by prominent Jewish artists. Many of them were directed at the proclamation and -aces of the people of the Diaspora, the dispersal of the Jews.

The thirteen Ministers of the

Continued on Page 2, Column 6

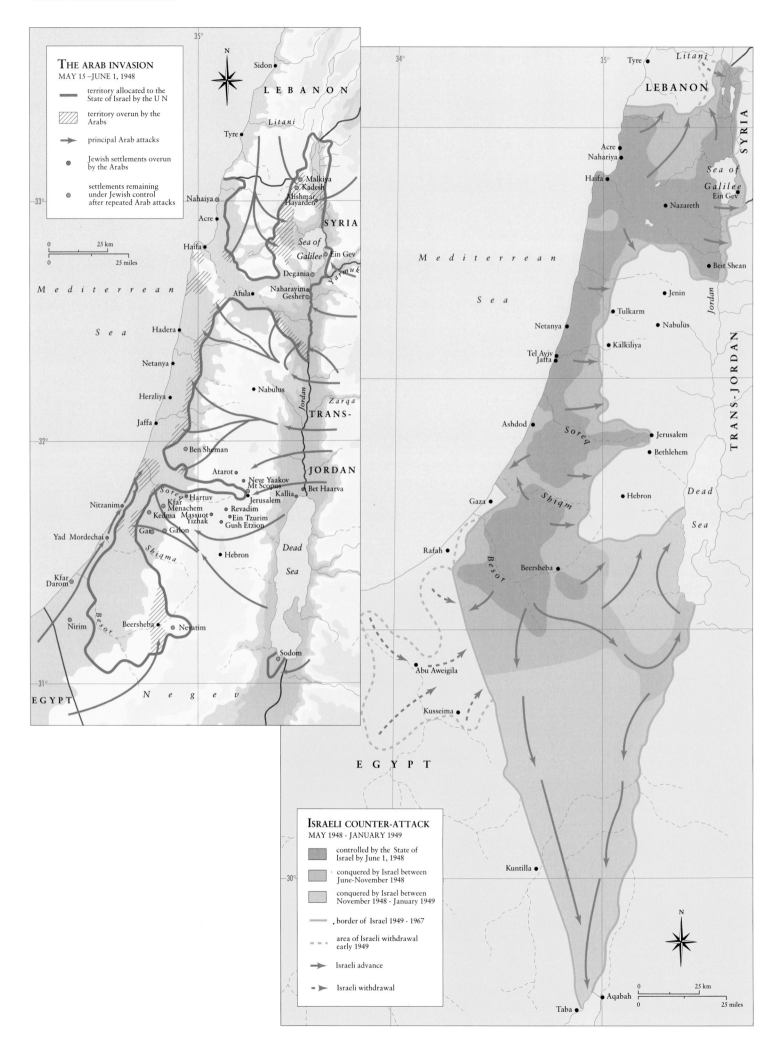

THE ARAB INVASION
MAY 15 – JUNE 1, 1948

territory allocated to the State of Israel by the U N

territory overun by the Arabs

principal Arab attacks

● Jewish settlements overun by the Arabs

● settlements remaining under Jewish control after repeated Arab attacks

0   25 km
0   25 miles

Mediterrean Sea

LEBANON

Litani

Sidon

Tyre

Malkiya
Kadesh
Mishmar
Hayarden

Nahaiya

Acre

Haifa

SYRIA

Sea of Galilee

Ein Gev

Degania

Yarmuk

Afula

Naharayim
Gesher

Hadera

Netanya

Herzliya

Nabulus

Jordan

Zarqa

TRANS-

Jaffa

Ben Sheman

JORDAN

Atarot

Neye Yaakov
Mt Scopus
Jerusalem

Kallia

Bet Haarva

Nitzanim

Soreq

Hartuv
Kfar
Menachem
Kedma
Massuot
Yizhak

Revadim
Ein Tzurim
Gush Etzion

Gat
Galon

Hebron

Dead Sea

Yad Mordechai

Shiqma

Kfar
Darom

Nirim

Besor

Beersheba

Neyatim

Sodom

EGYPT

N e g e v

ISRAELI COUNTER-ATTACK
MAY 1948 - JANUARY 1949

controlled by the State of Israel by June 1, 1948

conquered by Israel between June-November 1948

conquered by Israel between November 1948 - January 1949

border of Israel 1949 - 1967

area of Israeli withdrawal early 1949

→ Israeli advance

⇢ Israeli withdrawal

LEBANON

Litani

Tyre

SYRIA

Acre

Nahariya

Haifa

Sea of Galilee

Ein Gev

Nazareth

Beit Shean

Mediterrean Sea

Jenin

Netanya

Tulkarm

Nabulus

Tel Aviv
Jaffa

Kalkiliya

TRANS-JORDAN

Jordan

Ashdod

Soreq

Jerusalem

Bethlehem

Shiqm

Gaza

Hebron

Dead Sea

Rafah

Besor

Beersheba

Abu Aweigila

Kusseima

EGYPT

Kuntilla

Aqabah

Taba

0   25 km
0   25 miles

David Ben-Gurion, aged 62, a resident of Palestine since 1906, was confirmed as the founding prime minister of Israel in the first national elections of January 25, 1949. His Labor Party had won 57 of the 120 seats in the Knesset, or parliament. Labor had been the dominant force in Zionist politics through the struggle for statehood, speaking with eloquence and conviction in the chanceries of western Europe and America.

But arrayed against the Labor movement were always other forces within Zionism, most notably the so-called Revisionists, more ambitious and militant in their vision for the homeland restored. Led from the 1920s by the Russian-born ideologue Vladimir Jabotinsky, Revisionist Zionism had gained wide support among the Jews of Poland and eastern Europe. Impatient and fiery, Jabotinsky ridiculed the diplomatic strategies of the Labor mainstream. Then came the Nazis, the Holocaust; the Jewish masses that gave Revisionism its muscle were no more.

Under Jabotinsky's successor, a Polish intellectual named Menachem Begin, Revisionist cadres mobilized surviving remnants of Zionist militancy in the Displaced Persons camps of postwar Europe, even as Ben-Gurion pursued the diplomatic track at the United Nations. Hardened Jewish soldiers were chosen to emigrate to Palestine, to fight alongside the official Zionist militias of the mid-1940s.

Barely a month after statehood, Begin and his irregulars confronted Ben-Gurion's leadership. They sought to land a rickety transport vessel, the *Altalena*, bringing Jewish refugees from Europe, but also carrying arms and munitions to supply their own partisan units. On June 22 and 23, as Arab armies attacked the presumptuous Jewish state on all sides, the new army of Israel opened fire on fellow Jews of the *Altalena* off the beach at Tel Aviv.

The Revisionists won 14 seats in the first Knesset under the party label Herut. Manners of a parliamentary opposition, however, proved incompatible with the ideology of militancy. Herut leaders faded in popular stature as Israel's Labor-dominated political institutions took hold. Loser in election after election,

In June, 1948, Israeli government troops attacked and sunk the Altalena *off the coast of Tel Aviv. The ship was carrying weapons to the Irgun, the Jewish underground army led by Menachem Begin.*

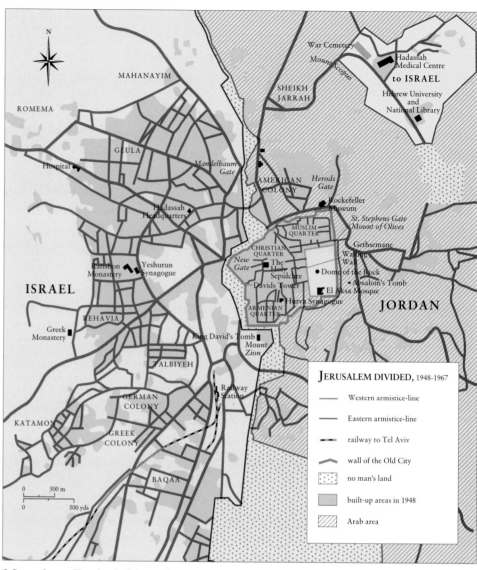

JERUSALEM DIVIDED, 1948-1967

—— Western armistice-line

—— Eastern armistice-line

■—■ railway to Tel Aviv

⌒ wall of the Old City

no man's land

built-up areas in 1948

Arab area

A Haganah fighter receiving first aid in the Old City of Jerusalem in 1948.

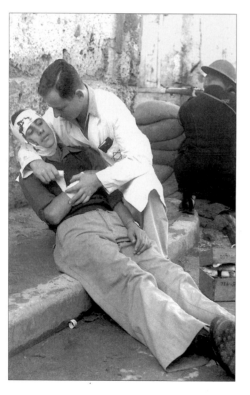

Menachem Begin held on for the next two decades, a lonely voice of opposition, subject of scorn and ridicule from the mainstream, a prophet, as he saw himself, without honor in his own land.

If the dominant Labor factions considered Begin and his Revisionists beyond the pale of responsible politics, they could not as easily dismiss other Knesset factions who held the numerical balance of parliamentary power, capable of granting or preventing a working majority for the Labor government.

When Ben-Gurion first fell from power in 1951 (it would happen repeatedly through his long and stormy tenure), it was not Begin's Herut that brought the government down, but rather the minority parties of ultra-Orthodox religious Jews, whose 16 Knesset seats gave Labor its security in office. Ever suspicious of secular influences, the religious factions determined to extract maximum concessions from a state they had scarcely sanctioned, to strengthen their own parochial institutions and practices.

To build successive parliamentary majorities, Ben-Gurion conceded demand after demand to the religious bloc: to rabbinical courts was assigned jurisdiction over marriage, divorce and burial; since Orthodox Jews would not travel on the Sabbath, public transportation across Israel was closed down from sundown every Friday; yeshiva students were exempted from military service, but army mess halls were nevertheless ordered to serve only kosher food. Above all, taxes paid by the secular majority were diverted into the operations of religious schools and welfare facilities under rabbinical, not government, direction.

Ben-Gurion and his Labor Party successors judged these concessions a price worth paying to secure the government on matters of defense and economic development considered more important. For tactical parliamentary reasons, a narrow interpretation of Jewish law came to dominate the daily routines of even secular Israelis.

Thus, from the first years of the state was established the political landscape of Israel. Politics became a national passion, argued out just as endlessly in Tel Aviv as in the coffee houses of central Europe, or the bazaars of the Middle East where Jewish life had developed before the state came into being.

For all the preoccupation with talk, the first Israelis faced a daunting human task: they called it *aliyah*, literally, "going up," the ingathering and absorption of hundreds of thousands of Jews who wanted to come, as they saw it, home.

The immediate impetus for the establishment of the restored Jewish state was the restive population of Displaced Persons in postwar Europe, survivors of the Holocaust, pathetic remnants of the once teeming Jewish society of eastern and central Europe.

Within hours after the withdrawal of British rule and its immigration restrictions, refugees started arriving after harrowing cross-Mediterranean journeys in troop ships and freighters, many scarcely seaworthy but the best that could be assembled. From Hungary and Romania they came, before the Communist regimes of those satellites closed their borders, from Czechoslovakia, Bulgaria and Yugoslavia, until there were few Jews left in those countries.

By the end of 1948 the DP camps of Germany, Austria and Italy were emptied of their Jewish population; the controversial 100,000 Jews had arrived in their new homeland, and in 1949 another 240,000 settled into Israel. On November 20, 1949, a routine airlift of 663 Jews arrived from Tripoli; with accumulated immigrants and 22,600 babies born since the state was proclamed, the Jewish population of Israel passed the one-million mark.

But there were many Jews in Europe not receptive to Aliyah, for they lived under a harsh government that barred emigration. In September, 1948, Israel sent a diplomat to Moscow: Golda Meir, a 50-year-old Russian-born but American-schooled Zionist on her way to a notable career in government. The new minister's job was to present official state credentials, and confirm recognition by the

ISRAEL'S JEWISH POPULATION CLIMBS OVER 1,000,000

TEL AVIV, Israel, November 20 — The Jewish population of Israel passed the 1,000,000 mark today with the debarkation of 663 immigrants from Tripoli.

When the state was proclaimed May 14, 1948, the Jewish population was 655,000. From then until last night, 321,991 immigrants had arrived and the natural increase in population had totaled 22,600.

In early days most of the immigrants came from the Soviet satellite states. But now Hungary and Rumania have virtually sealed their exits and only a few thousand Jews remain in Czechoslovakia, Bulgaria and Yugoslavia, whence immigration has been unrestricted.

The Soviet Union does not allow emigration to Israel and only four Russian Jews have arrived here.

Currently the largest influx comes from the Near East, including Armenia, Turkey and North Africa.

The New York Times November 21, 1949

Civilians fleeing an Arab bombardment of Jerusalem during the War of Independence.

Tent cities were the first homes for new arrivals; more than 300,000 immigrants arrived in 1948 and 1949.

Soviet Union of the new Jewish state.

Mrs. Meir performed another function as well; she brought in herself a symbol of Jewish pride, to be seen in full view by Soviet Jewry, long cowed and uneasy in their identity under Communist rule. When this envoy from Israel attended Sabbath services at the Moscow synagogue, she was greeted by teeming throngs of Jews, dancing the Hora in the dingy street outside, asserting their Jewishness against the monochrome of the Soviet capital. Aliyah for these Jews would be many years in the future.

In those first harrowing months of statehood, less familiar Jewish communities started finding their way to the restored homeland. Most surprising were the isolated Jews of Yemen, who had travelled by foot to their coast on the Arabian peninsula, near Aden, hoping for evacuation. For months an airlift of chartered American DC4s flew 47,000 Yemenite Jews to Israel, where they required — and received — immediate succor and support in an unfamiliar, European-based culture and heritage.

Others came from Syria and Iraq, homes of venerable Jewish communities dating from biblical times but fallen into destitution under the Arab nationalist regimes. From Iraq in 1950-51 came 113,000 Jews; smaller numbers came by sea and overland from Libya and Lebanon.

Though proud in their Jewish heritage, these Near Eastern immigrants were Sephardim, relatively unfamiliar in their cultures to the Ashkenazi (European) Zionists. Except for a few from Egypt and Iran, they had to leave all worldly goods behind; they arrived without savings or goods. Shelter, meals, medical attention were resources in short supply. "It was an 'Open Door' from which older and vastly wealthier nations would have recoiled in dismay," wrote historian Howard M. Sachar. In 1953, the Ford Foundation organized a social science research project at impoverished Israeli academic institutions, granting $410,000 for "the first systematic attempt to exploit the vast sociological laboratory represented by the influx of more than 700,000 immigrants from half the world in about four years."

The "ingathering of the exiles" was a dream of Zionism from the beginning; among the new state's first basic legislative acts was the "Law of Return," enacted in 1950, to guarantee citizenship and settlement to any Jew seeking to immigrate. Straightforward and welcoming as it seemed, the right of return was fraught with problems which came to light and mounted over the coming decades.

Aside from realizing the Zionist dream, Ben-Gurion saw a more practical benefit in encouraging immigration: vast new cadres of man- (and woman-) power for national defense, settlers to pre-empt vacant lands with agricultural colonies and border settlements, workers to realize the economic and industrial potential of the state.

From the start, the Arab states imposed a sweeping economic boycott on Israel, expecting thereby to starve the Zionist settlers out of their aspirations. Trade between Israel and the Arab world was forbidden; third countries, including major trading powers, were put on notice that any government engaged in economic relations with "the Jewish entity" would lose access to the much larger Arab economies. Border crossings were barred, as were postal and telephone links between Israel and its neighbors; Arab air space was closed to aircraft connecting with Israel. This communications siege lasted for four decades.

Against the crippling effects of the boycott, the new Israeli government embarked in 1950 on a four-year plan for agricultural self-sufficiency. The winter of 1950-51 brought Israelis to the edge of a subsistence economy, with

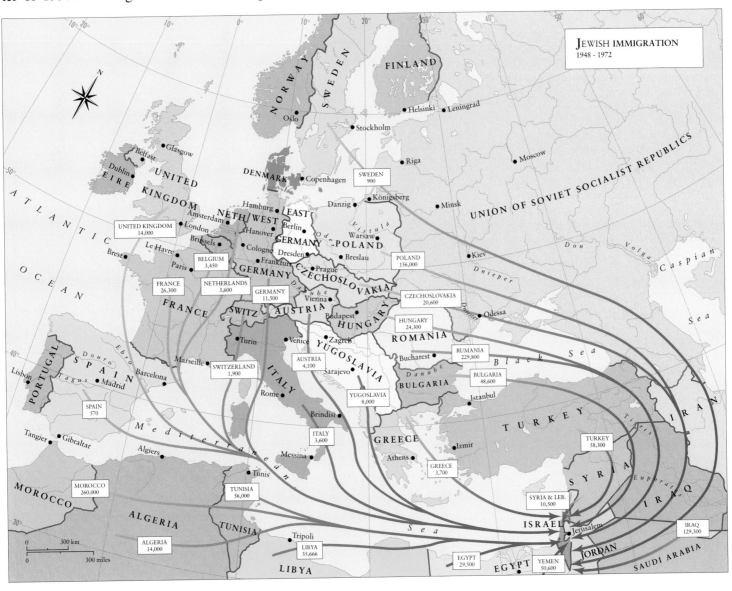

BERNADOTTE SLAIN IN JERUSALEM BY 'JEWISH IRREGULARS'

By JULIAN LOUIS MELTZER

TEL AVIV, Israel, September 17—Count Folke Bernadotte, United Nations Mediator for Palestine, and another United Nations official, detached from the French Air Force, were assassinated this afternoon within the Israeli-held area of Jerusalem.

Count Bernadotte was on his way from the former British High Commissioner's residence in southern Jerusalem and war passing through the Katamon suburb when "Jewish irregulars" held up the Mediator's car.

John J. MacDonald, United States Consul General in Jerusalem, reported to the State Department that Count Bernadotte and Col. Andre Pierre Serot had been ambushed, "presumably by the Stern Gang."

Reuters quoted a Stern Group spokesman in Tel Aviv as having said: "I am satisfied that it has happened," but added that the spokesman was unaware whether members of the group were responsible for the killing.

A Jerusalem dispatch quoted Dr. Bernard Joseph, Military Governor for the Israeli part of Jerusalem, as saying that all possible measures had been taken to apprehend the assassin.

A United Nations truce staff announcement here said: "Colonel Bernadotte killed by two Jewish irregulars in hold-up 1700 hours today on way to New City of Jerusalem. In same hold-up United Nations senior observer Col. Andre Serot of French Air Force killed.

"Mediator was on tour of Middle Eastern capitals to bring security and peace to Palestine.

"Arrangements made bring bodies in Red Cross ambulance from Jerusalem to Haifa."

Dr. Paul Mohn, acting chief of staff and legal adviser to the central truce supervision board at Haifa, ordered that all United Nations flags over the buildings that it occupies be lowered to half staff.

The Israeli-controlled "Voice of Jerusalem" radio gave the following account of the assassination of Count Bernadotte:

"He was traveling in a car from Government House to Katamon. A jeep with three armed men approached the vehicle and automatic fire opened at the Mediator's car. Count Bernadotte was seriously injured and the French colonel was killed outright. The Count died shortly afterward."

The New York Times September 18, 1948

Israeli veterans outside a Jerusalem movie theater in 1949.

rationing of essential foods and goods; as the quality of daily life deteriorated, more than a few of the idealistic immigrants reconsidered their move and left the country, warning others about the perils that lay in store. At the same time, hopes for industrial development foundered on the low productivity of an ill-educated work force and welfare policies of a socialistic government which seemed to discourage capital investments.

It was not until 1953 that an economic austerity program managed to halt a ruinous inflation and return basic goods to store shelves. Foreign capital, largely from Jewish communities in the United States and western Europe, began trickling in and the economy started to grow. Immigration resumed as the economic prospects brightened: the mid-1950s saw a new wave of Jewish immigrants from the Mahgreb, from Tunisia and Morocco — 160,000 of these so-called "Oriental" Jews by 1958, a new work force in town and farm.

If the Arabs' economic siege failed in its attempt to smother the Jewish state in infancy, continuing military threats kept Israelis and Arabs alike on edge. The Zionist settlers had suffered the onslaughts of Arab Palestinian irregulars for a decade or more before the proclamation of their state — and they had fought back with a vengeance pent up over the millennia of the Jewish dispersion. Among extremists on both sides, terrorism became a way of life.

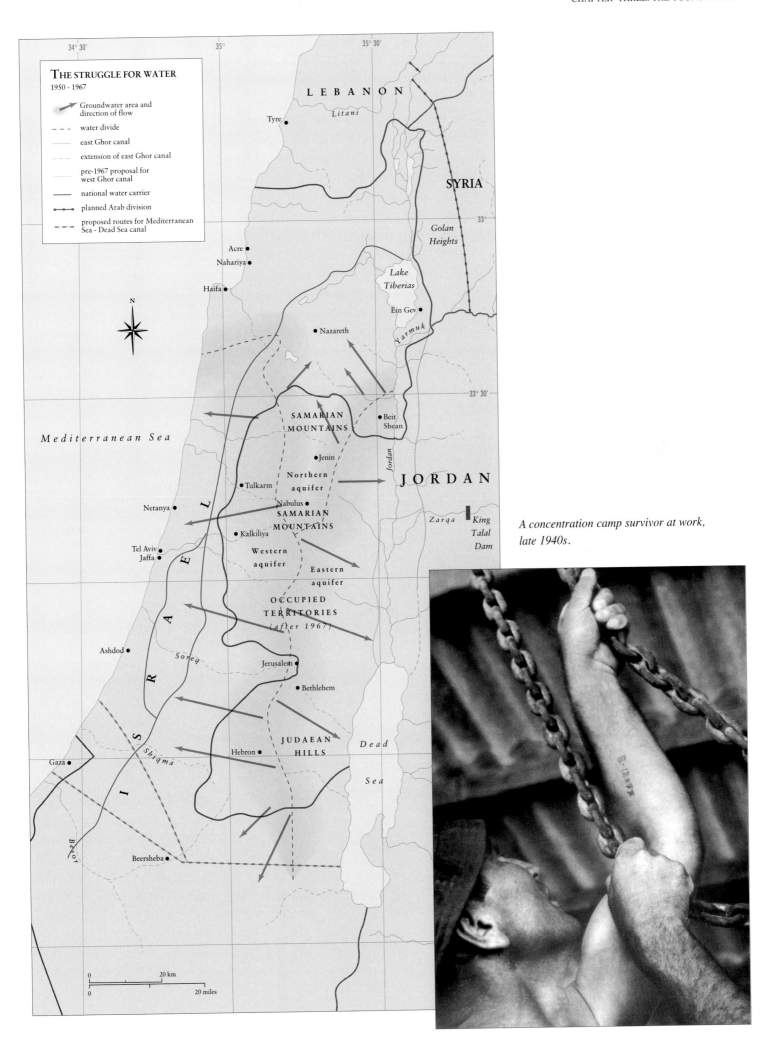

THE STRUGGLE FOR WATER
1950 - 1967

- Groundwater area and direction of flow
- - - water divide
— east Ghor canal
- - - extension of east Ghor canal
— pre-1967 proposal for west Ghor canal
— national water carrier
●-●-● planned Arab division
- - - proposed routes for Mediterranean Sea - Dead Sea canal

LEBANON

Litani

Tyre ●

SYRIA

Golan Heights

Acre ●

Nahariya ●

Lake Tiberias

Haifa ●

Ein Gev ●

N

● Nazareth

Yarmuk

Mediterranean Sea

SAMARIAN MOUNTAINS

● Beit Shean

● Jenin

Northern aquifer

Jordan

JORDAN

● Tulkarm

Netanya ●

Nabulus ●

SAMARIAN MOUNTAINS

Zarqa

King Talal Dam

● Kalkiliya

Tel Aviv ●
Jaffa ●

Western aquifer

Eastern aquifer

OCCUPIED TERRITORIES
(after 1967)

Ashdod ●

Soreq

Jerusalem ●

● Bethlehem

JUDAEAN HILLS

Dead

Hebron ●

Sea

Gaza ●

Shiqma

I S R A E L

Besor

Beersheba ●

0 _____ 20 km

0 _____ 20 miles

A concentration camp survivor at work, late 1940s.

In September, 1948, Jewish radicals assassinated the United Nations mediator, Count Folke Bernadotte of Sweden, fearing that he would order Israel to surrender territories captured in their first months of combat. Arab extremists assassinated Jordan's King Abdullah in July, 1951, as he secretly attempted to reach a diplomatic settlement with the Jewish state.

What passed for official relations between Israel and the Arab states were defined on the Mediterranean island of Rhodes in January, 1949, at a strange conference convened by the U.N. Billetted in the same elegant resort hotel, sitting together in the same meeting rooms, the Arab delegates refused to speak to Israelis; all exchanges were passed through the ingenious person of the U.N. mediator, Ralph Bunche of the United States.

Unflappable and persistent through weeks of surreal encounters, Bunche tested the contrivances and little personal tricks that became familiar tactics for future diplomats. Early in the conference, for instance, he secretly ordered a special consignment of the famous Rhodes ceramics, commemorative plates inscribed "Rhodes Armistice Talks, 1949." As the indirect negotiations threatened to break down over some arcane difficulty, the quiet American solemnly invited the contending delegations than his suite in the hotel, opened the doors of a cabinet to reveal the splendid ceramic collection. "Have a look at these lovely plates," he told the puzzled envoys. "If you reach agreement, each of you will get one to take home. If you don't, I'll break them over your heads!"

The frontiers and truce arrangements finally agreed upon at Rhodes were considered provisional and temporary; in fact they endured for the next 18 years.

Truce was far from peace. Building a viable economy and absorbing a huge immigrant population were tasks that often assumed lower priority in the first decades to the task of defending the state against continuing border raids, from the Syrian Golan Heights above the Sea of Galilee, along the 382-mile west bank border with Jordan just a few miles from Tel Aviv and the other major Jewish population centers.

One of the early architects of the Israeli defense forces, Yigal Yadin, said his army of conscript soldiers merely "happened to be on leave eleven months of the year." Self-sufficiency may have seemed a realistic aspiration in agriculture, but no such expectations were held for armaments, the weapons, ammunition and materiel to supply this citizens' army.

Major arms suppliers of the world had imposed an embargo across the entire Middle East in the years of pre-

A sugar refinery at Kiryat Gat financed with funds from Mexican Jews in the 1950s. Support from the diaspora was critical to economic growth in the early years of the new nation.

state tension. That forebearance could not be sustained after the Rhodes truce, and the ensuing need on all sides for self-defense forces. In May 1950, Britain, France and the United States reached a Tripartite Agreement to supply military materiel to both sides in the Middle East while maintaining a balance of military strength.

Supportive though private Americans had been in the pre-state military buildups, in violation of the official embargo, Israelis were not confident that the United States would serve as a reliable source of supply. They had good reason for their doubts: in October, 1953, Secretary of State John Foster Dulles abruptly suspended American aid to Israel, in punishment for Israeli raids on Arab border villages (the Israelis considered these retaliatory for previous Arab incursions). The amount involved was small, but the precedent lingered in Israeli sensitivities for decades to come.

Ben-Gurion sought an alternative alliance for military supply, with France. As fears of renewed full-scale warfare reached an ominous peak in the autumn of 1956, the Israeli prime minister flew in tightest secrecy to an obscure military airfield southwest of Paris, near the town of Sèvres, for a meeting in a nearby safe house with the French prime minister, Guy Mollet. With him he took his army chief of staff, Moshe Dayan, and a bright up-and-coming young administrator from his Defense Ministry, Shimon Peres.

The meeting at Sèvres on October 23, 1956, when British Foreign Secretary Selwyn Lloyd joined the group during the afternoon, was one of the tightest diplomatic secrets of the modern Middle East. None of the three parties judged it necessary to inform Washington at any level of their discussion; when the American archives were opened to public scrutiny four decades later, it appears that even the CIA did not know that the Sèvres conference had taken place, to say nothing of what had been decided in that remote little French farm house.

For at this meeting, the governments of France, Britain and Israel committed to an audacious invasion plan to wrest control of the Suez Canal and the Sinai peninsula from Egypt. Ostensibly as an afterthought, the young Peres also proposed a toast at Sèvres to the emerging cooperation between France and Israel for the construction of an Israel nuclear capacity.

Israel's march into the Sinai, and the subsequent British and French occupation of the Suez Canal, brought crisis to United States' relations with its closest European allies. Neither Secretary of State John Foster Dulles nor President

KING ABDULLAH OF JORDAN SLAIN BY ARAB GUNMAN

By ALBION ROSS

BEIRUT, Lebanon, July 20 — King Abdullah of Jordan was shot dead today by an assassin as he was entering the Mosque of Omar in Jerusalem. The assassin was immediately killed near the gate of the mosque by the King's guards, one of whom was reported to have been killed.

According to an official report received here, the assassin was a 21-year-old Arab Moslem tailor named Mustafa Ashu, whose home was in Dabbagha Street, in Old Jerusalem. That part of the city is now part of the Kingdom of Jordan.

Jerusalem reported local disturbances after the assassination of the 69-year-old monarch, but it is not known how serious they may have been. Martial law was immediately imposed, and the Cabinet, under Premier Samir Pasha Rifai, met and called on Prince Naif, the dead King's second son, to assume the Regency until his brother, Prince Tallal, could return from Switzerland, where he was being treated for a nervous breakdown.

Movement within the kingdom apparently had become impossible. Full curfew was imposed in Amman, Jordan's capital, as well as in Jerusalem, beginning at sun-down tonight. Arab Legion troops, armored cars and police patrolled the streets and roads of the kingdom, and road blocks were set up at all strategic points.

Arab news agency reports from Amman said that the assassin was a member of the organization known as Jihad Mukadess, or The Sanctuary of Struggle. According to one report, Ashu was attached to the so-called sabotage section of this organization.

The Sanctuary of Struggle organization was formed in Jaffa and Jerusalem under the leadership of the Husseini family. The principal figure in the Husseini clan is the Mufet of Jerusalem, Haj Amin el Husseini, who founded the Arab Higher Committee and who has headed the bitter opposition to King Abdullah for many years.

The New York Times July 21, 1951

Ben-Gurion and Foreign Minister Abba Eban conferring with President Harry Truman during a visit to Washington in 1951.

ISRAELIS INVADE SINAI; SWIFT DRIVE ALMOST REACHES SUEZ CANAL

By MOSHE BRILLIANT

TEL AVIV, Israel, October 29 — An Israeli military force thrust into the Sinai Peninsula of Egypt today. It was reported to have reached within twenty miles of the Suez Canal.

Army sources said the Israelis were west of the crossroads where the road to Kuntilla branches off from the Suez-Quseima highway.

The Israelis were said to have halted there and to have dug in.

A Foreign Ministry statement said the operation had been started "to eliminate the Egyptian fedayeen [commando squad] bases in the Sinai Peninsula."

Army sources said the Israelis had smashed the Egyptian position at Kuntilla and Ras el Naqb at the southern end of the international border. The forces then advanced more than seventy-five miles.

No fighting was reported on the northern end of the border or in the Gaza Strip, which is heavily populated.

Reports from the Sinai area described the fighting as "too big for a reprisal and too small for a war." Details of the fighting were not available tonight, but reliable sources said there had been no aerial bombardment of Egyptian positions.

It was not clear tonight whether the Israelis proposed to push on to the Suez Canal or withdraw to Israeli territory, as they have done after reprisal raids. A high official said: "I do not know. It depends on developments."

Yesterday the Israeli Government attributed its decision to call up reserves to what it said was renewal of commando activities, and to the Egyptian-Jordanian-Syrian military alliance negotiated last Wednesday, to Arab declarations that "their principal concern in a war of destruction against Israel" and to the movement of Iraqi forces to Jordan's border.

The New York Times October 30, 1956

Eisenhower had the slightest sympathy for Israel's vulnerabilities, and in March, 1957, American pressures forced Israel to withdraw from the Sinai, back to the "provisional" armistice borders drawn at Rhodes.

A remarkable sense of normalcy, not altogether unpleasant, settled upon Israel after the eruption in the Sinai. Communist eastern European regimes began lifting barriers to Jewish emigration following the Hungarian uprising (coincident in time with the Sinai War), and in 1957 some 40,000 new immigrants arrived, mainly from Hungary and Poland. Moroccan Jews continued to pour in, coalescing into an increasingly self-conscious ethnic bloc to contest the unquestioned elitism of the Ashkenazi European-inclined Labor Party establishment.

The economy reached what development economists call the Point of Takeoff. Austerity in daily life faded into abundance, at least for members of the secular, military/industrial elite. Per capita GNP started growing each year by 6 percent, moving Israel toward the ranks of the world's more affluent nations. Alongside the improved education and skills of a growing work force was the crucial role of foreign capital investment the most significant of it from world Jewry, but a less likely source as well: the Federal Republic of Germany.

Relations with Germany had been a source of anguish for the early citizens of Israel. Ben-Gurion took the psychological plunge and sought working relations with the post-Nazi generations. Others in Israel held back in bitterness, or in fear and the desire for vengeance. Menachem Begin, for one, denounced the Labor government on this matter in such explosive rhetoric that he was sus-

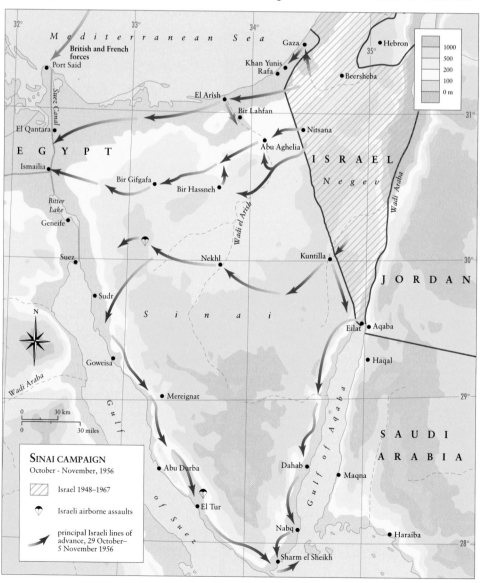

SINAI CAMPAIGN
October - November, 1956

Israel 1948–1967

Israeli airborne assaults

principal Israeli lines of advance, 29 October– 5 November 1956

pended from the Knesset for a term.

Ben-Gurion persisted and the West German Chancellor Konrad Adenauer responded in a sense of historical obligation. Agreement was reached in September, 1952, for Germany to pay the state of Israel compensation for European Jewish properties siezed under the Nazis, hundreds of millions of marks, dollars and gold. Begin called it blood money; other Israelis began reluctantly to accept the spirit and the cash. In March, 1960, the chancellor of the German Federal Republic and the prime minister of Israel met face to face for the first time; they shook hands. Over the years 1953 to 1966, Germany provided 20 percent of Israel's state development budget.

On May 23, 1960, Ben-Gurion sought recognition in the Knesset to make an extraordinary announcement. He told hushed legislators that Israeli commandos had apprehended the man named Adolf Eichmann. Tracked down to an obscure exile in Argentina, where he had lived under assumed identity since escaping from Europe in 1950, Eichmann had been kidnapped by an undercover shock force. Under challenge he admitted his true identity. He was flown in the tightest secrecy to Tel Aviv and, as Ben-Gurion spoke, was arraigned and confined to captivity in the homeland of the Jews.

Eichmann had been a Lieutenant Colonel of the Nazi S.S., chief of operations for implementing what Hitler had called the Final Solution, the extermination of the Jews of Europe. His was a name that resonated as the still living symbol of the Holocaust.

The Egyptian city of Port Said in ruins after an Anglo-French attack in support of Israel during the 1956 war.

BEN-GURION ANNOUNCES ADOLF EICHMANN SEIZED BY ISRAELI AGENTS

By LAWRENCE FELLOWS

JERUSALEM (Israeli Sector), May 23 — Premier David Ben-Gurion announced today that Adolf Eichmann, the S.S. colonel who headed the Gestapo's Jewish Section, was under arrest in Israel and would stand trial for his life.

The Premier made the announcement in the Knesset (Parliament) this afternoon with dramatic understatement. Members were startled by the news.

Mr. Ben-Gurion gave little additional information, nor could much be learned afterward of the circumstances under which Eichmann had been apprehended and where he was being held.

"I have to inform the Knesset," Mr. Ben-Gurion said, "that a short time ago one of the greatest of the Nazi war criminals, Adolf Eichmann, who was responsible together with the Nazi leaders for what they called the final solution of the Jewish question, that is the extermination of 6,000,000 of the Jews of Europe, was discovered by the Israel security services."

"Adolf Eichmann is already under arrest in Israel and will shortly be placed on trial in Israel under the terms of the law for the trial of Nazis and their collaborators," he added.

Pinhas Rosen, the Minister of Justice, held a news conference after the Knesset meeting together with Josef Nahmias, Inspector General of the police.

They declined to say where or when Eichmann had been found, or whether any other country had assisted in his capture. [According to The Associated Press, it was learned that Eichmann had not been extradited from another country.]

Mr. Rosen said Eichmann was held without charge under a magistrate's warrant issued today in Jaffa.

Eichmann disappeared in 1945 in central Europe ahead of advancing United States and Soviet troops. Jewish units had been searching for him with the help of former S.S. officers since the end of the war.

The New York Times May 24, 1960

Adolf Eichmann on trial for Nazi war crimes in 1961. He was executed on May 31, 1962.

The shock announcement electrified Israel–indeed, Jews and Gentiles of historical mind the world over. Suddenly the most painful of Holocaust memories came to life again, including among a new generation of Israelis whose daily lives had been too consumed with their own survival to dwell on the ordeal of their parents and forebears.

The trial in Jerusalem of Adolf Eichmann through six months of 1961 turned into a profound experience of memory and education for the entire world. Reported daily by press and television the world over, coverage educated both Jews and non-Jews anew about the attempted genocide at the hands of efficient, orderly Nazi fanatics.

Eichmann, an otherwise bland and unremarkable bureaucrat, had become obsessed with Jews in the early Hitler years. In the mid-1930s he actually visited the Zionist settlement in Palestine, to enhance his expertise.

The 55-year-old Eichmann was sentenced to death on December 15, after a trial marked by elaborate legal safeguards. After last rounds of appeals, he was executed on May 31, 1962, his ashes dumped into the Mediterranean. It was the first and only sentence of capital punishment carried out in Israel.

At the core of the restored Jewish homeland lurked an existential question that has gone unresolved for half a century. Who, actually, is a Jew? The matter scarcely troubled earlier generations, surviving in alien societies which imposed their own standards for defining a Jewish identity. Once restored into a state and national culture of their own, the problem of definition became crucial.

Ben-Gurion and West German Chancellor Konrad Adenauer meeting for the first time in New York in 1960. Their handshake symbolized the rapprochement reached in 1952 when West Germany agreed to pay Israel compensation for Jewish assets seized by the Nazis.

The civil rights enshrined in the 1950 Law of Return gradually became a point of contention through the 1960s, as a politically powerful rabbinical establishment sought to impose its own definition of Jewish law, recognizing as a Jew only those born of Jewish mothers or converted by Orthodox process. There was no room in the definition for Jews of Conservative or Reform traditions. Obscure communities around the world — in Ethiopia and India, for example — who had held on for many generations estranged from rabbinical institutions may have considered themselves Jews but, Israeli rabbis asked, were they really? What of the children of Jewish fathers who had married non-Jews? Though raised as Jews and never doubting who they were, were they now to be told by the government of Israel that they were not Jews at all?

The secular Labor leadership professed no interest in theological complaints which seemed only to weaken the sense of national identity. But, as from the first years of the state, Labor needed the parliamentary support of the Orthodox religious parties to stay in office; in 1958 the Labor cabinet almost fell from power as the religious bloc threatened to pull out.

Pragmatic politicians succumbed to the Orthodox, and in 1960 the government of Israel accepted the rabbinical definition, with all its strictures against Israelis of different Jewish traditions. A decade later, the Supreme Court ruled that the child of a mixed marriage could be registered as a "Jew by nationality"; the measure was promptly overturned by the Knesset under pressure from the militant religious parties. The issue continues to fester as the growing society of Israel considers the threat of a *kulturkampf* between the religious and secular citizenry.

These controversies of the early years faded from national attention upon a rush of events unleashed in June, 1967. In one dramatic week, Israel arrived at a defining moment, which engaged the passions of Jews and non-Jews around the world, even as it transformed the political and military landscape of the modern Middle East.

Chapter Four:
The Six-Day War

David K. Shipler

ON THE SEVENTH DAY, when Israel basked in exhausted euphoria, only the most prescient could have imagined how corrosive the victory would eventually become. The stunning six–day conquest over Arab armies would burden Israel with hundreds of thousands of Palestinian Arabs, in captured territories, who would spend the coming years in violent struggle for independence. It would draw young Israeli soldiers into moral compromise as they used their rifles against stone-throwing Arab children. It would unleash religio-nationalist zealotry on both sides — Muslim and Jewish — that would, decades later, introduce the suicide bomber into Arab terrorism and the assassin into Israeli politics. Indeed, while Israel acquired new lands as bargaining chips, deep arguments over whether to put those chips on the table soon divided the Jewish state

Israeli paratroopers at the Western Wall in June, 1967, after capturing the Old City of Jerusalem.

poisonously against itself. Thirty years hence, the most hopeful moves toward peace with the Palestinians were to be stalked by ominous talk of civil war if militant Israeli settlers, committed to the land as a biblical birthright, chose to resist a government that wished to give it up.

None of that grim future tainted the mood of the Israelis who awoke Sunday, June 11, 1967, to find the boundaries of their tiny state dramatically revised. The only pall that hung over the country came from the smouldering ruins of the last Syrian tanks to be destroyed. It had taken no more than Monday through Saturday for the tiny David to slay the Arab Goliath, to capture the admiring fascination of the Western world, and to feel the fervent sensation of rebirth. Not only had Israel survived Arab threats of annihilation, but it had freed itself from the claustrophobic crowding that its pre-1967 borders had imposed. Breathing room had suddenly been won. The horizon lay at a more comfortable distance: beyond Sinai at the Suez Canal, across the strategic Golan Heights that overlooked the Sea of Galilee, and past the rocky hills of the West Bank that plunged through the Judean Desert to the River Jordan. Israeli control now extended from tributaries of the Jordan, a critical source of water which Syria had sought to divert, to the vital oil fields at the Gulf of Suez, which could provide most of Israel's energy needs. Moreover, the most precious spiritual jewel of all, the Old City of Jerusalem, the site of the First Temple of Solomon and the Second Temple of Herod, was again in Jewish hands, as in the sanctity of ancient times. Who can ever forget the pictures of Israeli soldiers reverently touching the Herodian stones of the Western Wall, tears glistening through the grime and weariness of battle?

Israel alone could not have avoided this war. Every step the Arabs took, and every step that the great powers failed to take, narrowed the options of history.

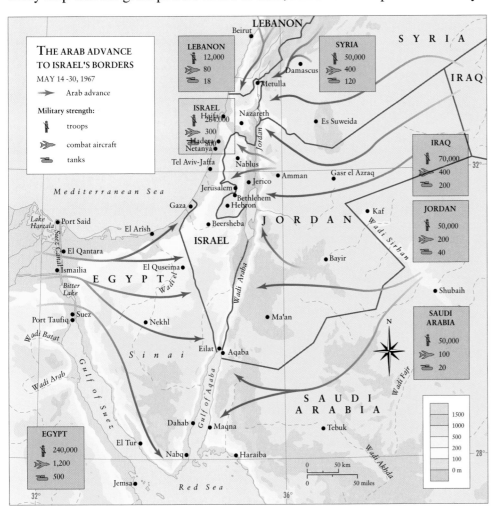

CAIRO CALLING UP 100,000 RESERVES; IRAQ TO SEND AID

By ERIC PACE

CAIRO, Monday, May 22—The United Arab Republic ordered total mobilization of its 100,000-man army reserve yesterday and reported today that Iraqi army and air force units were to be sent here to buttress the military build-up against Israel.

The Cairo-backed Palestine Liberation Organization announced that it was going ahead with plans to step up terrorist attacks on Israeli soil.

Terrorist raids from Syria and Israeli threats of retaliation started the spiral of military preparations by Arabs and Israelis of the last week.

Besides the call-up of reserves other warlike preparations continued. Air-raid sirens were tested. More than forty truckloads of troops moved through the outskirts of Cairo, apparently headed for Suez.

Travelers found the road to Suez closed to civilian traffic.

Reliable witnesses have reported seeing an Egyptian cruiser, four torpedo boats and two submarines moving south through the Suez Canal in the last few days.

The naval movements were considered here to be a key element in the Egyptian build-up against Israel.

The war-ships could be used to block Israeli shipping to and from Elath, on the Gulf of Aqaba, the only Israeli outlet to the Red Sea and the Indian Ocean, Egyptians do not permit Israel's ships to go through the Suez Canal.

Ground forces could be almost doubled by the mobilization of Egypt's reserves, which was decreed by Field Marshal Abdel Hakim Amer, deputy commander of armed forces. President Gamal Abdel Nasser is commander in chief.

Cairo's populace, hitherto unmoved by the mounting threat of war, began gathering around radios to hear news last night after the announcement of the call-up decree.

Some reservists had been quietly called up earlier, Israel has been mobilizing her reserves, estimated here at 230,000 all told.

The New York Times May 23, 1967

Month by month, week by week, day by day, the storm gathered inexorably. Like so many other wars, this one began well beyond the context of the parties' particular dispute.

The United States was shackled to its grinding war in Vietnam. For months, China had been urging the Soviet Union to heat up the Middle East as a way of pressing Washington to reduce the bombing of North Vietnam and seek a settlement, James Reston reported in *The Times* at the end of May. Calculating that the Americans could not easily pursue their interests in two crisis-ridden regions simultaneously, Moscow deftly applied a small flame to the tinder of the Arab-Israeli conflict. Soviet prospects in the Middle East had been brightened in 1966 by Britain's announcement of its plan to withdraw from Aden, and by the installation of a pro-Soviet regime in Syria. Soviet weaponry poured into Egypt and Syria. On May 12, 1967, the Soviet Ambassador in Cairo provided Gamal Abdel Nasser's government with fabricated intelligence on Israeli troops supposedly massed at their northern border for an attack on Syria. The ambassador cabled Moscow "We have advised the [Egyptian] government to take the necessary steps," Howard M. Sachar writes in *A History of Israel*.

Nasser needed little prodding. His preeminence as leader of the Arab world was being eroded by derision from abroad and economic unrest at home. He faced jeers from both Jordan and Saudi Arabia for reducing tension on his fron-

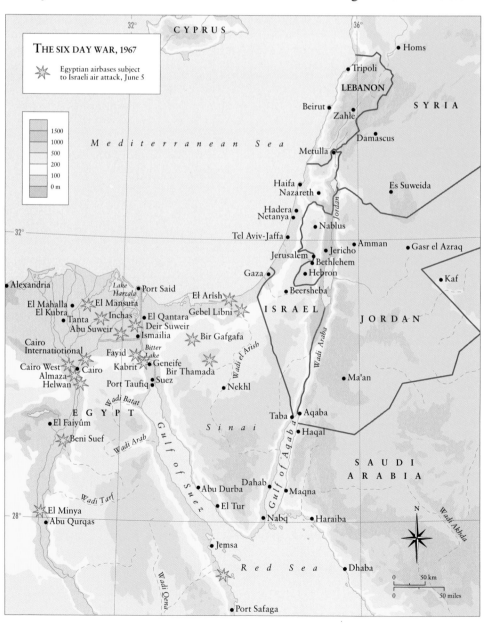

THE SIX DAY WAR, 1967

Egyptian airbases subject to Israeli air attack, June 5

tier with Israel and for permitting United Nations peacekeepers to remain stationed in Sinai. In 1966, the United States had made good on a threat to end wheat shipments if Egypt continued its military build-up; Western financial institutions followed suit by suspending loans, causing unemployment and food shortages that stirred rising discontent among Egyptians. To galvanize his own people, to please the Russians, to reinforce his stature in the Arab world, Nasser sought — and found — confrontation with Israel.

Left: *Preemptive airstrikes by the Israelis wiped out the Egyptian air force, leaving troops exposed on the ground.* **Above:** *Smoldering tanks and trucks littered the Mitla Pass in the Sinai Desert.*

There were, in fact, verbal threats against Syria by Israel. All spring, infiltrators from Syria, Lebanon, and Jordan had conducted terrorist raids in Israel, and Syrian guns on the Golan Heights had repeatedly shelled Israeli towns and kibbutzim. In response, both Prime Minister Levi Eshkol and the Chief of Staff, General Yitzhak Rabin, warned of possible retaliation. On April 7, in the third shooting incident in a week, Syrian gunners targeted an Israeli tractor working a field east of the Sea of Galilee, and French-built Israeli Mystère jets took to the air. Soviet-made MiGs intercepted, a dogfight ensued, and the Israelis downed six Syrian planes. Nasser sent a military delegation to Syria to pledge mutual support.

On May 14, two days after the Soviet ambassador's message on Israeli troop concentrations, Nasser paraded Egyptian troops and artillery through the streets of Cairo, put the country on a war footing, and sent units across the Suez Canal into Sinai. Israel began quietly calling up reservists. On May 17, Nasser demanded the withdrawal of U.N. troops, and Secretary General U Thant complied. The buffer separating Israeli and Egyptian forces was gone.

On May 22, Nasser dispatched torpedo boats and submarines into the Gulf of Aqaba and closed the strait of Tiran to Israeli shipping, thereby cutting off the port of Eilat, Israel's main reception point for oil. This was as close to an act of war as Egypt could get without firing a shot, and it rankled even Moscow, for it violated the 1957 undertaking by maritime nations, following the Sinai campaign, to guarantee the accessibility of the waterway. The closure also set off a flurry of diplomatic activity that betrayed the fragility of Israel's ties with France and the immobility of a United States that was entangled in Vietnam.

At the time, France provided most of Israel's sophisticated arms. Indeed, throughout the tense spring of 1967, a French airlift of weaponry kept Israel

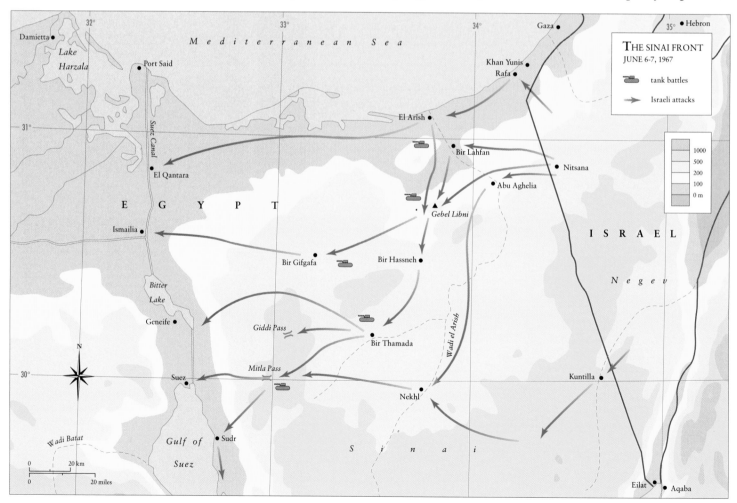

well supplied. But no French statements of objection had greeted Nasser's moves, and when Abba Eban, Israel's eloquent foreign minister, entered the Elysée palace seeking France's support, President Charles de Gaulle met him with a grave admonition, Eban reports in his memoirs. "Do not make war," de Gaulle warned even before Eban had a chance to take a seat. "At any rate, don't shoot first. It would be catastrophic if Israel were to attack. The Four Powers must be left to resolve the dispute. France will influence the Soviet Union toward an attitude favorable to peace."

In the end, however, the Soviet Union rejected French appeals for joint Four-Power action, and nine days after their meeting, de Gaulle, anxious to enhance French influence in the Muslim world, halted the emergency airlift to Israel. The French-Israeli alignment was broken irreparably.

Eban received more sympathetic hearings in London and Washington, but ultimately they translated into empty promises. Prime Minister Harold Wilson told him that Britain would not allow the blockade of the straits to stand; President Lyndon Johnson agreed that the maritime powers should open the waterway by force, if necessary. Consumed by Vietnam, however, Johnson felt unable to act without the blessing of Congress and the United Nations. Nor did he feel pressure from Eban, of whom he later remarked: "I was ready for heavy bargaining, but I found myself up against a lightweight, and could get away with niceties."

As Washington dithered, events on the ground rushed ahead. Iraq, Kuwait, and Algeria sent troops to Jordan and Egypt, and statements from Arab leaders grew increasingly bellicose. King Hussein of Jordan, under public threats of assassination from both Syria and Egypt, flew to Cairo and signed a mutual defense pact with Nasser; an Egyptian general was assigned as joint commander of Jordanian troops.

Inside Israel, pressure built for preemptive action. The country could not remain fully mobilized for long without severe economic consequences, and the stress was wearing at the leadership. Rabin had collapsed the day after the Strait of Tiran was closed, suffering either a nervous breakdown or, in the official version, "nicotine poisoning," and had to be replaced for several days by Major General Ezer Weizman. Senior military officers argued urgently that time had become an enemy.

But Eban prudently persuaded the Cabinet to wait, for if Israel were seen to be acting precipitously, he figured, it might win militarily and lose politically. For this he was criticized for dovishness, but his calculation proved accurate; Israel's patience at the edge of oblivion aroused a clamor of sympathy in Europe and the United States. Some Israelis thought cynically that Jews were always most popular as victims. Yet the admiration was also generated by Israel's sinewy resilience, and the acclaim reached a crescendo when the battle was joined and quickly won.

By June 4, Eban agreed that further delay was pointless. The French supply line had been broken, the Soviet pipeline to the Arabs remained open. The diplomatic possibilities had been exhausted, the western powers had reneged on their 1957 commitment to keep open the Strait of Tiran. He threw his support behind the new Defense Minister, Moshe Dayan, and others who wished to go ahead, and the cabinet voted secretly to attack. Dayan had no illusions, however. The day before, answering a reporter's question on whether a war might end the Arab threat once and for all, he had declared, "I don't think in war there is any such thing as once and for all."

At 7:45 A.M. Monday, June 5, Israeli planes swept across Egypt, many coming

NASSER ASSUMES RESPONSIBILITY FOR 'GRAVE SETBACK'

By ERIC PACE

CAIRO, Saturday, June 10 — Gamal Abdel Nasser said last night that he had decided to resign as President of the United Arab Republic and "return to the ranks of the public."

However, the National Assembly met later and voted not to accept the resignation. [The Cabinet also met and voted not to accept the resignation, Reuters reported.]

Mr. Nasser is to appear before the Assembly this morning to discuss his resignation.

In his televised resignation speech, which was also carried over the Cairo radio, Mr. Nasser said he took "entire responsibility" for Egypt's "grave setback" on the field of battle this week. He said he had asked Zakariya Mohieddine, a Vice President to take over as President.

Less than an hour after Mr. Nasser spoke, crowds surged through Cairo's streets, darkened in a blackout, chanting: "Nasser! Nasser!" and "We Want Nasser!"

[The police and soldiers fired grenades into the air Friday night to drive back demonstrators marching on downtown Cairo and an anti-aircraft barrage lit up the sky, the Associated Press reported. The Ministry of Information said an air raid was in progress but there were no signs of planes and no bombs had been dropped up to 11:30 P.M.]

In his speech Mr. Nasser said "I have decided to give up completely and finally every official post and every political role and to return to the ranks of the public to do my duty with them like every other citizen."

President Nasser's declaration, which was thought to have been recorded in advance at a Cairo studio, stunned the Egyptian populace. In Cairo people sobbed and wept openly.

Mr. Nasser wore a business suit and his manner was solemn during the broadcast. He looked tired as he said:

"We cannot hide from ourselves the fact that we have met with a grave setback in the last few days."

The New York Times June 11, 1967

in low from the Mediterranean to avoid radar detection, and found most Egyptian planes and pilots on the ground, just as intelligence information had said they would be at that hour. In 500 sorties, Israel destroyed 309 of Egypt's 340 aircraft, Chaim Herzog reports in *The Arab-Israeli Wars*. The largest air force in the Middle East was gone.

Dayan had ordered Jordan and Syria left untouched. But events outran his caution. Enticed by false Egyptian reports of impressive Arab victories, Jordan, Syria, and Iraq conducted air strikes on oil refineries in Haifa, an airfield at Megiddo, the Mediterranean town of Natanya, and other Israeli targets. Israel promptly destroyed virtually the entire Jordanian, and two-thirds of the Syrian, air force that first day, and hit an Iraqi air force base. By the end of the second day, June 6, Israeli officials believed the war had already been won. As of that evening, Herzog writes, "416 Arab aircraft had been destroyed, 393 of which were destroyed on the ground; 26 Israeli aircraft had been lost in action. Of the total number of Arab aircraft lost in the war, 58 were downed in aerial dog-fights."

Without protection from the air, Arab troops were completely vulnerable, and Israel immediately pursued the advantage. As Israeli planes pounded Egyptian bases, Israeli ground forces went into action across the border in northern Sinai. Once the Israeli Air Force was finished with Egyptian aircraft, Israeli armor and infantry got unchallenged air support as they rolled over the heavy Egyptian fortifications. Israeli tanks out-dueled their Egyptian counterparts, and in the coming days, as the Egyptians withdrew toward the Suez Canal, Israeli planes flew unhindered over Sinai, attacking convoys of retreating tanks and trucks. On Wednesday, June 7, Israeli paratroopers were dropped into Sharm el-Sheikh,

Egyptian prisoners from the Sinai campaign.

overlooking the Strait of Tiran, to find the Egyptian fortress already abandoned. By dusk, a contingent of Israeli forces had reached Rumani, about ten miles from the canal. Thinking of world opinion, Dayan did not want the canal captured, but again, the momentum of battle carried beyond policy, and his troops reached the waterway the following day, June 8.

Nasser did not immediately know the scope of the debacle. During most of the first day, his commanders reported victories to him, and those fictitious claims, broadcast throughout the Arab world, induced King Hussein to throw Jordanian forces into the fighting — a fateful error, as it emerged. "On the morning of June 5," Sachar reports, "Cairo informed Amman that 75 percent of Israel's planes had been destroyed and that Egyptian armored units were fighting deep inside Israeli territory." The impression of Egyptian victories also prompted Moscow to delay a U.N. call for a cease-fire; the Russians realized the truth too late for diplomacy to save Egypt.

When Nasser learned that his air force had been virtually demolished, he thought up an excuse and called Hussein to coordinate. Together, they concocted an assertion that American and British planes had participated in the attack on Egypt. The story collapsed when Israel released a tape of the intercepted conversation, which had occurred at 4:50 A.M. June 6. "Shall we include also the United States?" Nasser asked the King, "Will we say the U.S. and England or just the U.S.?"

"The U.S. and England," Hussein replied.

The King had hesitated when the war began, but not for long. Drawn toward the mirage of victory, he turned his artillery on Israel at midday on June 5, shelling Tel Aviv and various Israeli towns and kibbutzim near the border. He

Searching for enemy troops in the West Bank.

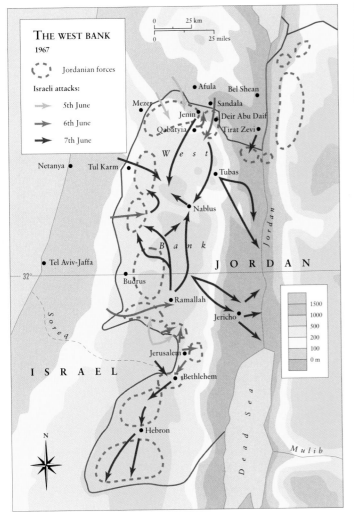

ISRAELI TROOPS VOW NEVER TO DEPART 'HOLIEST OF PLACES'

By TERRENCE SMITH

JERUSALEM, June 7 — Israeli troops wept and prayed today at the foot of the wailing wall—the last remnant of Solomon's Second Temple and the object of pilgrimage by Jews through the centuries.

In battle dress and still carrying their weapons, they gathered at the base of the sand-colored wall and sang Hallel, a series of prayers reserved for occasions of great joy.

They were repeating a tradition that goes back 2,000 years but has been denied Israeli Jews since 1948. When the first of three wars with the Arabs ended in this area.

The wall is all that remains of the Second Temple, built in the 10th century before Christ and destroyed by the Romans in A.D. 70.

The Israelis, trembling with emotion, bowed vigorously from the waist as they chanted psalms in a lusty chorus. Most had submachine guns slung over their shoulders and several held bazookas as they prayed.

Among the leaders to pray at the wall was Maj. Gen. Moshe Dayan, the new Defense Minister. He told the troops:

"We have returned to the holiest of places, never to depart from it again."

General Dayan, who was appointed only last week, drove out in a military truck and was almost engulfed by the crowds. He wore a bunch of violet wild-flowers that added a dashing touch.

The soldiers arrived at the wall minutes after sweeping unopposed into the Old City, where 21 of the most revered sites of the three great western religions are situated.

They were joined quickly by the military chaplain, Rabbi Shlomo Goren, and the deputy Mayor of Israeli Jerusalem, Rabbi Shear Yashuv Cohen. Rabbi Cohen came as an envoy of the people of the city and because he was the last Israeli soldier to be evacuated from the Old City in 1948.

Rabbi Goren carried with him a shofar, or ram's horn, and a Torah, the parchment scroll on which are written the first five books of the Bible.

The New York Times June 8, 1967

then sent a unit into Jerusalem's demilitarized zone to take the United Nations observers' headquarters at Government House on the Hill of Evil Counsel. From that point, Jordan could shell West Jerusalem, the Israeli side of the city that had been divided since the War of Independence.

Unlike the empty reaches of the Sinai Desert, the Jordanian front snaked through a complex landscape peopled with civilians from both sides and laced with ancient monuments sacred to Islam, Judaism, and Christianity. The battle was hard, and Israeli casualties exceeded those endured against the Egyptians in Sinai. Moving into the area dubbed the West Bank of the Jordan River, Israel seized the key mountain ridge and road from Jerusalem to Ramallah. Here, every soldier followed in the footsteps of his predecessors long gone. As Herzog notes, this spine of Judean hills was Joshua's initial objective when he crossed the Jordan, "and it was also the area that the British 90th Division in the First World War occupied before Allenby took Jerusalem." Its strategic importance still haunts Israeli debate over what land to relinquish in exchange for the hope of peace.

Israeli forces fought for control of the other critical routes through the West Bank, capturing the two-lane roads that ran southwest from Jerusalem to Latrun, north to Nablus and Jenin, and south through Bethlehem and Hebron.

Israeli troops advancing on the Dome of the Rock.

Significantly, Israeli planes were said to have hit Palestinian refugee camps near Jericho. From Amman, Dana Adams Schmidt in *The Times* quoted U.N. and Jordanian officials as saying that that some 100,000 Palestinian civilians, ordered out by Israeli troops, had fled eastward across the Jordan; many were able to return after the fighting and settle elsewhere in the West Bank. The camps near Jericho remained ghost towns. The Israelis also cut the main road from Jericho to Jerusalem and hit Jordanian reinforcements with air strikes before they could climb through the desert hills to the holy city, the site of the most emotional battle of all.

Judaism and Islam intersect on a man-made plateau that dominates the walled Old City of Jerusalem. At the center of the plateau, known to Jews as the Temple Mount, there rises an outcropping of bedrock believed, in ancient Jewish tradition, to be the stone around which God created the earth. Here is where the Temples of Solomon and Herod stood, the latter destroyed in 70 A.D. All that remains of the Temple is the great retaining wall of the plateau, known to Jews as the Wailing Wall or the Western Wall. Muslims, for their part, believe that the bedrock, now surrounded by a mosque with a golden dome, the Dome of the Rock, was the point from which the Prophet Muhammad made a night journey on horseback to heaven.

Defense Minister Moshe Dayan entering the Old City, flanked by Yitzhak Rabin, right, and Uzi Narkis.

The Old City had been in Jordanian hands since the war of 1948, but King Hussein's rash attacks in 1967 opened a door of rare opportunity for Israel. On June 7, at the climax of a fierce battle for the Old City that lasted 47 hours (without artillery or air support for fear of damaging the holy places), Israeli troops broke through St. Stephen's Gate, moved quickly along the Via Dolorosa, took out snipers on the Western Wall, and secured the heart of Jerusalem. Israelis are still stirred by the old photographs of Moshe Dayan in battle fatigues, the famous black patch over his left eye, striding through the Old City. Mindful of its place in religious emotions, he had wished merely to surround it, not enter. But with a U.N. call for a cease-fire on the horizon, Eshkol and other ministers prevailed, and now, as the conqueror, Dayan made a ringing declaration: "We have returned to the holiest of our holy places, never to depart from it again."

Three days had passed, and Syria had been spared. This galled most of Israel's cabinet ministers and senior army officers, for of all the Arab nations, Syria had been a major font of hateful rhetoric and military friction. From the Golan Heights, a plateau 400 to 1,700 feet above the Chula Valley, Syrian artillery had been showering shells onto Israeli villages, but Israel had mounted no offensive. Dayan, fearing Soviet intervention, urged caution. Then, on June 8, after the fighting had subsided on the Egyptian and Jordanian fronts, Eshkol brought a delegation from Galilee villages into a cabinet meeting to hear their pleas for an attack on Syria. The assault was approved, and the hellish battles up the boulder-strewn heights began the following day. By Saturday, June 10, the Israelis were in control of Golan and held the road to Damascus. The war was over.

The defeat shattered the taboos on self-criticism in much of the Arab world.

Palestinian refugees from the West Bank in a camp north of Amman, Jordan, in 1969, more than two years after the war.

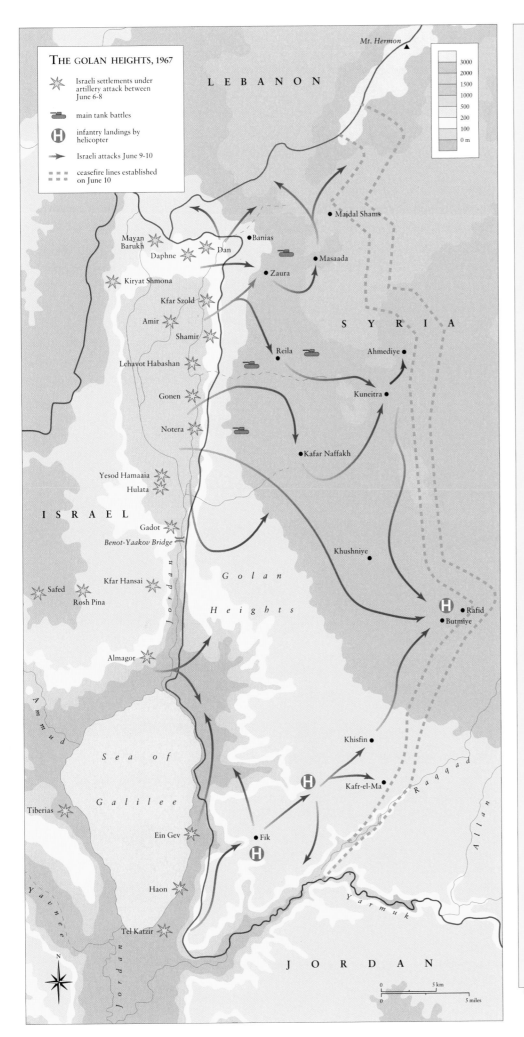

THE GOLAN HEIGHTS, 1967

✳ Israeli settlements under artillery attack between June 6-8

🛢 main tank battles

Ⓗ infantry landings by helicopter

➤ Israeli attacks June 9-10

▪▪▪ ceasefire lines established on June 10

3000
2000
1500
1000
500
200
100
0 m

Mt. Hermon ▲

LEBANON

• Majdal Shams

Mayan Barukh ✳
Daphne ✳ — Dan — • Banias
Kiryat Shmona ✳ — • Zaura — • Masaada
Kfar Szold ✳
Amir ✳
Shamir ✳
Lehavot Habashan ✳ — • Reila — Ahmediye •
Gonen ✳ — Kuneitra •
Notera ✳
• Kafar Naffakh

S Y R I A

Yesod Hamaaia ✳
Hulata ✳

I S R A E L
Gadot ✳
Benot-Yaakov Bridge

Jordan

Kfar Hansai ✳
✳ Safed
Rosh Pina ✳

Golan

Heights

• Khushniye

Ⓗ • Rafid
• Butmiye

Almagor ✳

A m m u d

Sea of

Galilee

• Khisfin

Ⓗ

Tiberias ✳

Ein Gev ✳

Ⓗ • Fik

Kafr-el-Ma •

R a q q a d

A l l a n

Ⓗ

Haon ✳

Y a v n e e l

Tel Katzir ✳

Y a r m u k

Jordan

J O R D A N

N

0 ——— 5 km
0 ——— 5 miles

ISRAELI TANK COLUMN 35 MILES FROM DAMASCUS

By SYDNEY GRUSON

TEL AVIV, June 22 – Israeli armored and infantry forces smashed deep into Syria today after the Syrians, according to Israel, had broken the cease-fire on the northern front and shelled 16 settlements along the 48-mile front.

At 7 P.M. (1 P.M. New York Time), there were unofficial reports that the leading Israeli tanks were only 30 or 35 miles from Damascus, Syria's capital.

There was no official confirmation, and no one here expected the Israelis to try to take the capital, although one Israeli' Army officer remarked that it would not be a very hard task.

(The Syrian Defence Ministry said that Israeli tanks and artillery resumed shelling Syrian positions Saturday, according to a Damascus radio broadcast, Reuters reported from Beirut. The Ministry said Syrian forces were "fiercely fighting on all fronts.")

Earlier, another unofficial report said an Israeli column had broken through the Syrian lines and captured El Quneitra, a key road junction 12 miles east of Gadot, midway along the Syrian border. El Quneitra is on a major highway 40 miles southwest of Damascus.

Gadot was presumed to have been an Israeli jumping-off point for the three-pronged assault on the Syrians.

At El Quneitra, the Israelis would be beyond the hill region from which the Syrians, deeply dug into the rocks, have pounded Israeli settlements since Monday morning when the war broke out between Israel and the Arab States.

All day every available plane of the Israeli Air Force, which established total air superiority in the first hours of the war, poured rockets and bombs on Syrian gun emplacements and on the roads ahead of the advancing troops.

The fighting in the north, taking the war into Syria for the first time, was the only meaningful military action of the day, according to the Israelis.

Only occasional sniping in the Old City of Jerusalem disturbed the cease-fire on the front with Jordan, where the Israelis are in control up to the west bank of the Jordan River.

The New York Times June 23, 1967

It broke Nasser's mythical stature, at least until after his death three years later. It forced "an audit during a moment of great stress and clarity," Fouad Ajami writes in *The Arab Predicament*. It gave the lie to the assumption that Arab socialism, instituted after the 1948 defeat, constituted a revolution from feudalism to modernity. "Arab socialist states turned out to be traditional orders," Ajami observes. More significantly for Israel, it led to the spin-off of an independent Palestinian nationalist movement that the Jewish state would ultimately have to reckon with. On the Israeli side, the victories of the Six-Day War stimulated a new messianism, mainly in the form of Orthodox Jewish settlers who used the Bible as a deed to captured lands. Surreptitiously at first, then with the blessing of the government, they planted the Israeli flag in the Arab city of Hebron and on stony hilltops throughout the West Bank and Gaza, putting down the roots of an invigorated Jewish fundamentalism. The revised geography set the stage for the next wars, and the first peace.

A sentry keeping watch along the Syrian border in 1968 from an outpost on the Golan Heights.

The War of Attrition, 1967–1970

Those outside the Middle East who keep track of Arab-Israeli wars usually count five: the War of Independence in 1948, the Sinai Campaign of 1956, the Six-Day War of 1967, the Yom Kippur War of 1973, and the Lebanon War of 1982. But for Israelis and Arabs themselves, a sixth war figures in the calculation of hardship. It is known as the War of Attrition, named after Nasser's drive to grind away at Israel's military and emotional readiness.

Although territory did not change hands, the battles summoned the full range of conventional forces on land and sea, and particularly in the air, where Israeli planes tangled with Egyptian and Soviet pilots in dramatic dogfights. Across the Jordan River, Jordanian, Iraqi, and P.L.O. forces staged hundreds of attacks on Israel, and Israel responded with raids into Jordan, driving the P.L.O. into the mountains. For three years, the sporadic conflict on the two fronts served as a deadly laboratory for American and Soviet weapons systems, presenting each side with valuable data about the capabilities of the other's hardware.

It began just three weeks after the end of the Six-Day War, which had left Israeli units ensconced on the eastern bank of the Suez canal. On July 1, 1967, Egyptian troops crossed the narrow waterway and set up an ambush ten miles south of Port Said. When an Isralei company of tanks moved northward along a dike to engage the intruders, Chaim Herzog recounts in *The Arab-Israeli Wars*, Egyptian artillery and machine-gun fire opened up from the western side of the canal. The conflagration spread like wildfire. Israeli aircraft went into action, pummelling Egyptian artillery emplacements. About 120 Egyptian soldiers tried to cross the canal in rubber boats. Off the Sinai coast, Egyptian torpedo boats were sunk while attacking three Israeli ships, including a destroyer.

A lull ensued. Then another battle erupted in mid-July, followed by three months of relative quiet. And so the pattern was set, with Egypt using extensive resupplies from Moscow to build up a formidable array of artillery, which periodically pounded Israeli positions. On October 21, an Egyptian missile boat anchored at Port Said fired three Styx missiles and sank the Israeli destroyer Eilat fourteen miles offshore. Israel retaliated by shelling the oil refineries at Suez, setting them ablaze and further damaging Egypt's economy.

A year later, after a well-coordinated Egyptian assault, Israel chose a more aggressive defense, sending planes and commandos deep into Egypt to blow up bridges and an electric power station in the Nile valley. Much to Moscow's embarrassment, Egypt's Soviet-made air defense system performed so poorly that Israeli planes were able to roam over Egyptian territory with virtual impunity. In 1969, an Israeli force crossed the Gulf of Suez to capture an entire Soviet-built radar station, using helicopters to airlift out seven tons of equipment for analysis by Western specialists.

The strategy did not deter Nasser from his attacks, however. It merely provoked Moscow in 1970 to provide more sophisticated missile systems and the personnel to man them and design their deployment. Soviet pilots flew MiGs in defense of Egyptian territory, deterring some Israeli air action, but also getting into several unpublicized dogfights. On July 30, 1970, Herzog reports, five Soviet pilots were shot down; no Israelis were lost. On August 8, an American-brokered ceasefire took effect.

By DAVID K. SHIPLER

Special Report: Israel and The Bomb

Malcolm W. Browne

SINCE ITS ESTABLISHMENT AS A STATE IN **1948**, Israel, a nation at bay among hostile Arab neighbors, has fought five major wars and many smaller campaigns punctuated by raids, skirmishes and terrorist attacks.

To prevail against the numerical superiority of its adversaries Israel has developed one of the most advanced arms industries in the world — an industrial base capable of producing weapons as diverse as Uzi submachine guns, advanced combat aircraft, missiles and nuclear weapons.

Although many in Israel initially opposed the development of nuclear weapons, some of its most influential leaders, including the nation's first premier, David Ben-Gurion, believed that the country's very survival might one day depend on the deterrent threat of nuclear counterattack.

Experts at the London-based International Institute for Strategic Studies and other analysts believe that over the years Israel has built at least 100 and possibly as many as 200 nuclear warheads. It has also developed a line of intermediate-range ballistic missiles capable of carrying nuclear destruction to any Arab capital.

Although Israel and other nations possessing nuclear capability have been under pressure from the United States and other major powers to support the doctrine of non-proliferation, Israel has refused to sign the Nuclear Non-proliferation Treaty. Jerusalem has tacitly agreed never to use nuclear weapons unless facing outright annihilation, but this position is understood to be contingent on assurances that the United States would come to Israel's aid if worse came to worst; otherwise, many arms experts believe, Israel might unleash devastating nuclear blows against her attackers, using both thermonuclear warheads and low-yield neutron bombs intended to kill people without causing much material destruction.

American protection of Israel was reaffirmed by Washington during the Persian Gulf War in 1991, and American Patriot missiles were provided to defend Israel against Iraqi Scud missiles. Although some Scuds penetrated the shield and caused casualties and damage, Israel refrained from the massive retaliation some had feared, which might have included a nuclear attack. Washington praised Israel for its restraint.

Israel has never acknowledged membership in the nuclear club, which includes the United States, Great Britain, France, the former Soviet states, China and India. Nevertheless, experts in nuclear arms estimate that Israel not only possesses many nuclear warheads but can deliver them either by artillery shells or its Jericho missiles, which can reach targets 1,000 miles away.

Israel's first nuclear warhead was probably completed in 1968 after more than a decade of intensive development, benefiting not only from the talents of Israeli scientists and engineers, but from the help of France, the United States and South Africa.

Israel's Atomic Energy Commission was established in 1952, initially under the scientific direction of a brilliant German-born chemist, Ernst David Bergmann, who enjoyed the confidence of Ben-Gurion. Bergmann has been compared with J. Robert Oppenheimer, leader of America's Manhattan Project, which created the first atomic bombs.

Major support by France for Israel's nuclear program had begun in 1949, when Israeli scientists were invited to work alongside French counterparts at the Saclay research reactor near Versailles.

The United States also helped. In 1955, Israel approved an "atoms for peace" agreement with the Eisenhower administration, by which the United States financed and supplied fuel for the Nahal Soreq research reactor south of Tel Aviv. By the mid-1950s Israel had developed an ion-exchange system for separating deuterium oxide (heavy water) from ordinary water — an important technological step on the road to nuclear weapons.

Israel supported French policies in North Africa, and the two nations developed close diplomatic, military and scientific ties. When France detonated its first nuclear bomb in the South Pacific in 1960, Israeli experts were present as observers.

In 1957, following the Suez-Sinai War, in which Israel, Britain and France were pitted against a combined Arab army, Israel began construction of a new nuclear research facility at Dimona near Beersheba in the Negev Desert. Much of the plant was built out of sight underground but most Israeli citizens were at least vaguely aware of the plant's probable purpose: to develop nuclear weapons.

Dimona is presumed to have remained Israel's main nuclear weapons plant ever since, according to foreign experts and Israeli defectors.

In 1958, French technicians and scientific advisers began pouring into Dimona. Before long, according to Seymour M. Hersh, a reporter who extensively investigated Israel's nuclear program, these foreign advisers had "turned Dimona into a French boom town."

Israeli scientists decided against basing their nuclear explosives primarily on uranium-235, the fuel used in America's "Little Boy" bomb that destroyed Hiroshima. All processes required for separating bomb-grade uranium-235 from the mixture of uranium isotopes found in nature are enormously expensive and time-consuming. Instead, Israel opted to produce plutonium, the fuel of the "Fat Man" bomb that destroyed Nagasaki.

Plutonium does not exist in nature in appreciable amounts. But nuclear reactors that use enriched uranium as fuel create a certain amount of plutonium by joining protons to the nuclei of uranium atoms. Since plutonium is a different chemical element than uranium, it can be separated from uranium using relatively simple chemical processes.

A chemical separation plant for extracting plutonium from spent uranium reactor fuel is believed to be one of the key features of Dimona, and the plant has steadily increased its capacity.

When Dimona began operating, American experts estimated that the secret plant could produce enough plutonium to make about two low-yield weapons per year. But this rate — and American estimates — increased rapidly.

Dimona's technical features and chemical separation system are widely believed to have been modeled on those of France's Marcoule reactor. But to produce the amount of plutonium needed for a nuclear arsenal, Israel needed natural uranium to run its heavy-water reactor — uranium that South Africa's mines could produce in abundance.

Israel's already cordial relations with South Africa broadened into a nuclear partnership. Jerusalem shared its growing nuclear expertise with Pretoria in exchange for South African uranium, and the two nations' nuclear programs developed in parallel.

No new nuclear power can be entirely confident about the reliability of its arsenal until it has tested at least one weapon. Despite denials by Israel, many foreign experts believe that one of its devices was exploded at sea.

On Sept. 22, 1979, an American Vela satellite spotted something that caused an international sensation. Some 1,500 miles southeast of the Cape of Good Hope in the southern Indian Ocean the aging and somewhat unreliable satellite saw something that looked a lot like a nuclear explosion.

A characteristic flash had appeared on the ocean surface — a double flash, typical of nuclear explosions, in which the flash of the initial burst is followed a fraction of a second later by a flash created by the shock wave.

But while some experts declared the flash to be a nuclear test by Israel, other experts were doubtful, saying that under certain circumstances, the reflection of sunlight from a pair of waves could produce a visual effect easily confused with a nuclear blast.

Israel never acknowledged participation in a nuclear bomb test, but in April, 1997, a senior South African official, Deputy Foreign Minister Azis Pahad, told reporters in Israel that the flash seen by the Vela satellite was indeed caused by a nuclear bomb test. He said the test was carried out by South Africa, and that although he did not know whether Israel had participated in the test, the former South African government of P. W. de Klerk had received much technical help from Israel in the development of nuclear weapons.

Prior to Mr. Pahad's statement, neither Israel nor South Africa had ever acknowledged conducting a nuclear test, and no fallout or other physical evidence of a nuclear explosion was ever detected. Sidney Drell, a nuclear arms expert at the Stanford Linear Accelerator Center in California, said recently that he "wouldn't bet the farm either way. It might or might not have been a nuclear test."

According to some accounts, South African nuclear physicists and experts participated in planning for the test and were aboard the Israeli ship that controlled the explosion.

In any case, South Africa announced a decade later that it had abandoned its nuclear program, and in 1992, Pretoria signed the treaty to prevent the spread of nuclear weapons. Since 1995 it has led an international effort to recruit other signers of the treaty, especially among third-world nations.

Meanwhile, Israel refuses to sign the 1969 Nuclear Non-Proliferation Treaty. The existence of Israel's nuclear stockpile remains unacknowledged, and Israeli officials seem satisfied by keeping the world guessing.

But whether Israel possesses ten nuclear warheads or 1,000, none of its adversaries are eager to provoke a demonstration of their lethal capability.

Chapter Five: From War to Peace

Bernard Gwertzman

In the 1970s, terrorism became a frequent instrument of Palestinian nationalism. Palestinian guerrillas training in Jordan.

AFTER ITS QUICK VICTORY in the Six–Day War of 1967, Israel found itself in the unfamiliar role of a Goliath in the Middle East, after regarding itself for so many years as a David. This change took considerable getting used to in Israel. And the new situation caused by its easy defeat of Egyptian, Syrian and Jordanian forces produced a number of serious problems for the Israeli state.

Over time, the greatest was to be the rise in Palestinian nationalism fanned by local resentment of Israeli military rule in the West Bank and Gaza Strip, and the creation of thousands of new Palestinian refugees forced into camps and exile around the Middle East. When they were in control of the West Bank and Gaza respectively, Jordan and Egypt did not encourage Palestinian nationalist strivings, but once those lands were lost to the Israelis, Palestinian statehood became a general rallying cry for the Arab world and its supporters. The Israeli occupation gave prominence to Yasir Arafat, who until then had been the relatively obscure leader of Al Fatah, one of many Palestinian groups. Under Arafat, the Palestine Liberation Organization became the main conduit for Palestinian nationalism.

Acts of terrorism, some carried out by Al Fatah but many others the work of more radical groups, became almost commonplace. Some were spectacular, such as the hostage-taking of Israeli athletes at the Munich Olympic Games in 1972, which left 11 Israelis dead and nearly destroyed the Olympic movement. Israel's nervousness produced such actions as the deaths of 106 people in 1973 in the shooting down of a Libyan airliner that crossed into closely monitored Israeli airspace.

Israelis, yearning for international acceptance, found it galling that much of

Terrorists stormed the Olympic village at the 1972 Summer Games in Munich. **Below:** *The 11 Israeli victims.*

the world shunned them while lionizing Palestinian terrorists and the Arab neighbors who had pledged to drive Israel's Jews into the Mediterranean.

Golda Meir, who became Prime Minister in 1969 after the death of Levi Eshkol, recalled the publication in Israel of the satirical book, *So Sorry We Won,* which epitomized the bitterness of many Israelis toward the pressures mounting on Israel to yield to Arab demands.

"Our crime," she wrote, "appeared to be that we kept saying to the Arabs, 'Let's negotiate.' Not as we were entitled to do, 'This is the new map; sign on the dotted line,' but 'Let's negotiate.' "

"In some mysterious way, this made us the villains," she continued. "I couldn't for the life of me ever grasp, for instance, why Willy Brandt, when he recognized the Oder-Neisse border because the time had come to put right the wrong that Germany had done to Poland in World War II, got (and richly deserved) the Nobel Prize for it and was hailed as a great statesman and man of peace, while Eshkol and later I were branded as expansionists for wanting exactly the same kind of border adjustments between Israel and its Arab neighbors."

Ironically, however, it was the territories acquired in 1967 that ultimately formed the basis for what, 30 years later, appears to be moving toward the eventual partition of Palestine into Jewish and Palestinian states, at long last turning the designs of the United Nations partition plan into reality. If Jordan had hung on to the West Bank, and Egypt had kept the Gaza Strip, there may never have been any possibility for Palestinian nationalist aspirations to be rewarded.

But of far more immediate concern to the Israelis was the resolve for revenge of the Arab nations that had been humiliated in the 1967 war. In a

ARAB TERRORISTS KILL 11 ISRAELIS ON OLYMPIC TEAM

By DAVID BINDER

MUNICH, West Germany, September 6— Eleven members of Israel's Olympic team and four Arab terrorists were killed yesterday in a 23-hour drama that began with an invasion of the Olympic Village by the Arabs. It ended with a shootout at a military airport some 15 miles away as the Arabs were preparing to fly to Cairo with their Israeli hostages.

The first two Israelis were killed early yesterday morning when Arab commandos, armed with automatic rifles, broke into the quarters of the Israeli team and seized nine others as hostages. The hostages were killed in the airport shootout between the Arabs and German policemen and soldiers.

The bloodshed brought the suspension of the Olympic Games and there was doubt if they would be resumed. Willi Daume, president of the West German Organizing Committee, announced early today that he would ask the International Olympic Committee to meet tomorrow to decide whether they should continue.

In addition to the slain Israelis and Arabs, a German policeman was killed and a helicopter pilot was critically wounded. Three Arabs were wounded.

There were some reports that two of the hostages said to have been killed might still be alive. "It is a dim hope," said Dr. Bruno Merk, the Interior Minister of Bavaria, "but I am skeptical on this point."

The New York Times September 6, 1972

Girls in military training at a Fatah youth camp near Damascus in 1975. The Arabic sign reads, "The blood of the Palestinians who were murdered will be avenged."

conference in Khartoum in August-September 1967, 11 Arab states and the P.L.O. adopted the famous "four no's": no peace with Israel, no recognition of Israel, no negotiations with Israel and no concessions on the question of Palestinian national rights. And with the help of the Soviet Union, which was eager to expand its influence in the region, they set about rebuilding Arab military strength to press their demands by force.

Right after the war, Israel had said that if the Arabs would make peace with Israel they could get back most if not all of the lands captured in 1967 except East Jerusalem. But an increasingly bitter debate in Israel — a revival of the "minimalist-maximalist" split that had dogged Zionism since its infancy — made it clear that this offer would not remain on the table without fierce internal debate.

The rightist political opposition, led by the Herut Party leader Menachem Begin, opposed withdrawal from the West Bank, arguing that it was part of Israel dating to biblical times. In Begin's mind, Israel had liberated Judea and Samaria, and had no reason to return any of it. The Labor Party, which had ruled Israel since independence, was divided. Some, such as Foreign Minister Abba Eban, wanted to pursue negotiations actively to see if peace could be achieved; others, such as Yigal Allon, a former major general who was deputy premier and who had been passed over for the party leadership after Eshkol's death, wanted to make sure Israel kept a security strip in the West Bank but were willing to return the rest.

Meanwhile, tensions along the Suez Canal continued unabated, even after the death of Nasser in 1971 and the coming to power of Anwar el-Sadat. Unlike Nasser, who was driven to be the leader of the Arab world, and who fluctuated back and forth between pragmatism and ideology, and who depended heavily on the Soviet Union for support, Sadat was a pragmatist through and through. He quickly decided to mend fences as best he could with the United States, and ended Egypt's heavy reliance on Moscow. Sadat's goal, repeated over and over again, was the recovery of the Sinai Peninsula from Israel, and he frequently warned that he would go to war to regain the territory if diplomacy was barren. He launched several military moves to test Israel's defenses in the early 1970s. And he secretly built up his armed forces to a level far more impressive than ever attained under Nasser.

But Sadat concluded that Israel on its own would never cede the Sinai, and that Washington, the only third party that could force a resolution, was paying little attention to the issue, preoccupied as it was with Vietnam and the Soviet Union. This led Sadat to a dangerous calculation. He decided that only by launching a credible war against Israel could he get Washington's involvement in the crisis.

In early 1973, Israeli intelligence began noticing increased Egyptian military activity and went on alert for a war in the spring that did not materialize. In late September, warning signs again appeared, but the Israeli military establishment was divided on whether the increased military movements presaged war. Finally early in the morning of Oct. 6, Yom Kippur, the Day of Atonement for Jews, definitive word was received by Israeli intelligence of an impending Egyptian and Syrian attack before dusk that day.

The Israeli Air Force was prepared to launch pre-emptive air strikes against Egypt and Syria, as it had done against Egypt in 1967, but Washington warned and Moshe Dayan, the Defense Minister, and Meir, the Prime Minister, agreed that Israel should not fire the first shot since that would make it diplomatical-

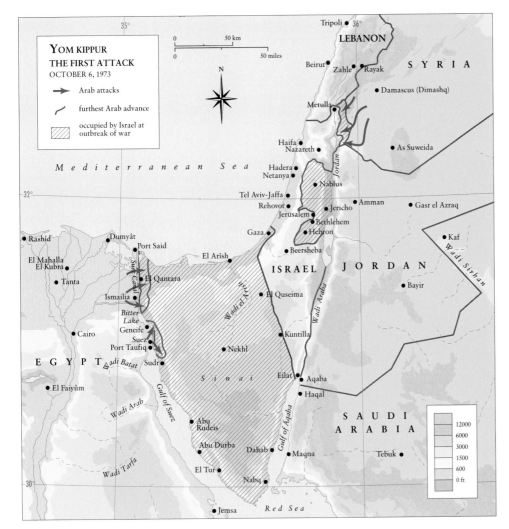

ly difficult for the United States to provide much help if such help proved to be necessary.

The Arab offensive began shortly before 2 P.M. But with such little warning, and constrained from striking the first blow, Israel suffered heavy casualties in lives and materiel — 2,500 killed in a month of fighting, most of them in the first week — and was forced to seek a major military resupply from the United States.

Dayan wrote that although "the Sinai Campaign of 1956 and the Six- Day War of 1967 were not difficult wars...the Yom Kippur War was different.

"It was not only a hard war to fight, but also a hard atmosphere to fight in. We had to tackle mass forces equipped with large quantities of powerful armor, guns and surface-to-air missiles, and when we succeeded in knocking out hundreds of tanks, no one made merry. But when one of our front-line strongholds fell, or when we lost 30 tanks in a single action, the nation was

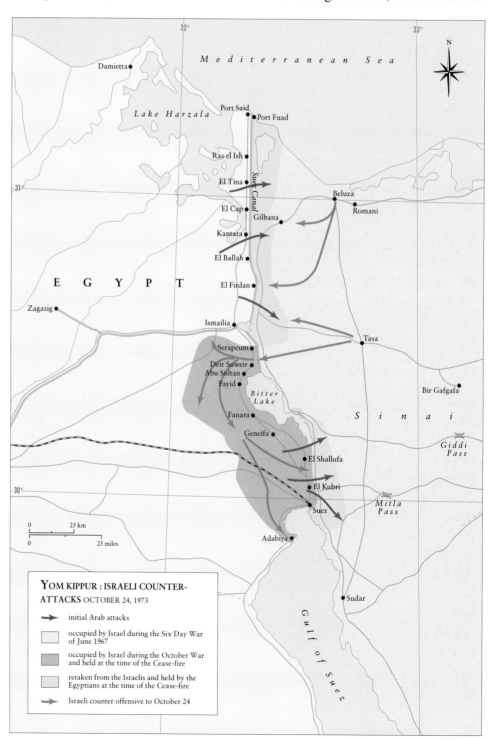

Egyptian troops crossing the Suez Canal during the Yom Kippur War.

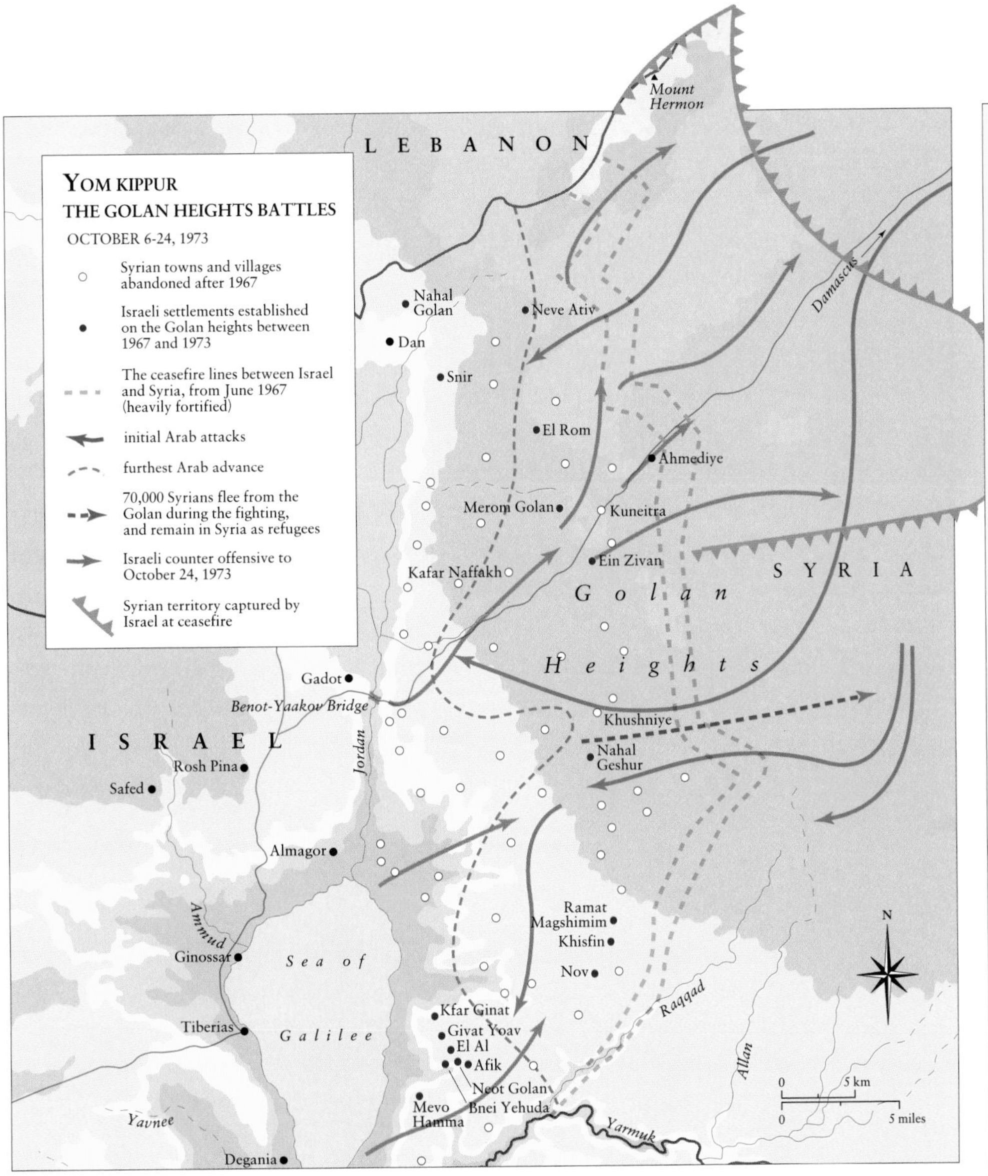

YOM KIPPUR
THE GOLAN HEIGHTS BATTLES
OCTOBER 6-24, 1973
Syrian towns and villages abandoned after 1967
Israeli settlements established on the Golan heights between 1967 and 1973
The ceasefire lines between Israel and Syria, from June 1967 (heavily fortified)
initial Arab attacks
furthest Arab advance
70,000 Syrians flee from the Golan during the fighting, and remain in Syria as refugees
Israeli counter offensive to October 24, 1973
Syrian territory captured by Israel at ceasefire
Mount Hermon
LEBANON
Nahal Golan
Dan
Neve Ativ
Snir
El Rom
Ahmediye
Merom Golan
Kuneitra
Ein Zivan
Kafar Naffakh
SYRIA
Golan Heights
Damascus
Gadot
Benot-Yaakov Bridge
ISRAEL
Rosh Pina
Safed
Jordan
Khushniye
Nahal Geshur
Almagor
Ramat Magshimim
Khisfin
Amnud
Ginossar
Sea of Galilee
Nov
Tiberias
Kfar Ginat
Givat Yoav
El Al
Afik
Raqqad
Allan
Neot Golan
Mevo Hamma
Bnei Yehuda
Yavnee
Yarmuk
Degania
N
0 5 km
0 5 miles

plunged into gloom," Dayan wrote.

Even though, in the end, Israel defeated Egypt and Syria, most Israelis were angered at the seeming unpreparedness, and at the heavy casualties. "Each day, each hour brought news of tragedy," Dayan wrote. "Our people did not want to remember what other wars had been like or what had happened in Europe."

At the end of the war, Israeli troops were clearly in a superior position militarily. In the north, Israeli forces had slashed their way deep into Syria. On the Suez front, Egyptian forces had beachheads on the eastern side of the canal, but Israeli troops were entrenched on the western side, where they had the Egyptian Third Army surrounded.

Thus the cease-fire lines at the end of October were unstable, and the United States, seeing the danger of renewed war, plunged into the effort to secure a lasting disengagement. The involvement of the United States led to the start of the first serious, prolonged diplomatic negotiations in the Middle East since 1948.

Although America had long been involved in the Middle East, this new active diplomacy was unprecedented for the United States. The decision to get involved was based, of course, primarily on American self-interest. It was a way to protect American interests in the Arab world, the importance of which had been driven home by the economic pain caused by an oil embargo imposed by the Arab oil producers at the start of the war. It was also a way to reduce the Soviet influence in the region, and to avoid yet another war, which always ran the risk of a direct big-power confrontation.

BATTLES RAGE IN GOLAN AND ALONG THE SUEZ CANAL

By ROBERT D. McFADDEN

The heaviest fighting in the Middle East since the 1967 war erupted yesterday on Israel's front lines with Egypt along the Suez Canal and Syria in the Golan heights.

Official announcements by Israel and Egypt agreed that Egyptian forces had crossed the Suez Canal and established footholds in the Israeli-occupied Sinai Peninsula.

A military communiqué issued in Cairo asserted that Egyptian forces had captured most of the eastern bank of the 100-mile canal. An Israeli military communiqué said the Egyptians had attempted to cross the canal at several points by helicopters and small boats and had succeeded in laying down pontoon bridges at two points. Armored forces were poring across them into Sinai, it said.

A communiqué issued early today in Tel Aviv said fighting had raged all night along the canal's eastern bank and along the entire cease-fire line with Syria.

Each side accused the other of having started the fighting. But military observers posted by the United Nations reported crossings by Egyptian forces at five points along the Suez, and said Syrians had attacked in the Golan Heights at two points.

Israeli and Syrian artillery dueled in the Golan Heights, and on both battlefronts there were air clashes. The Cairo radio said Egyptian forces had shot down 11 Israeli planes and lost 10 of their own in battles over the Sinai and the Gulf of Suez. The Israeli spokesman did not comment on losses but said Israeli planes had shot down 10 Egyptian helicopters carrying troops into the southern Sinai.

In Damascus, the military command said that Syrian pilots and ground fire had shot down 10 Israeli aircraft in renewed action over the Golan Heights this morning.

Syrian artillery was reported by the Israelis to have shelled a number of settlements in the occupied Golan Heights and the Hula Valley area.

The Damascus radio said that Syrian forces had reoccupied Mount Hermon in the Golan Heights for the first time since 1967, and said Syrian troops were fighting on the ground with Israeli forces along the entire cease-fire line.

The New York Times October 7, 1973

REPORTER'S NOTEBOOK: ALL ABOARD FOR THE KISSINGER SHUTTLE

By BERNARD GWERTZMAN

JERUSALEM, January 15—A few minutes before take-off from Aswan last night Joseph J. Sisco stood in the aisle of the Air Force jet and cried out to no one in particular, "Welcome aboard the Egyptian-Israeli shuttle!"

After hopping between Aswan and Tel Aviv for four consecutive days in search of a disengagement agreement, Mr. Sisco who has been nominated as Under Secretary of State for Political affairs was reflecting the feeling of most members of the party traveling with Secretary of State Kissinger that the shuttle had somehow become a permanent fixture in Middle Eastern diplomacy. Not only were Secretary of State Kissinger and his aides carrying proposals back and forth between the Egyptians and the Israelis, but the other members of the party, including the press, were reporting the mood on each side to the other, something that in purely human terms may be more important than the detailed ideas on disengagement of forces on the Suez front.

At the press center in the Old Cataract Hotel in Aswan on Sunday night, a senior Egyptian editor drew an American newsman aside.

"Kissinger says that the Israelis can be trusted" the editor said. "You've just been to Israel. Do you think a real peace is possible after disengagement?"

The next night in the press center at the King David Hotel here the same newsman was approached by three Israeli journalists. "Tell us" they asked "What are the Egyptians really like?"

At another point an Israeli said: "Aswan is a hundred miles from here, but as far as we're concerned it could as well be on the moon."

The New York Times January 16, 1974

"From the outset, I was determined to use the war to start a peace process," Henry Kissinger, the American Secretary of State whose name will be forever linked to the phrase "Middle East peace process," wrote in his memoirs. He reported that he told his staff, "After we get the fighting stopped, we should use this as a vehicle to get the diplomacy started."

The negotiations between Israel and its neighbors, brokered first by Kissinger and then by President Jimmy Carter and his Secretary of State, Cyrus Vance, would lead to a succession of U.S.-sponsored accords, climaxing first in the Camp David accords of September, 1978, and then in the Israeli-Egyptian peace treaty of March, 1979.

For Kissinger, the atmosphere for negotiations was good. Israelis were in a state of shock. Sadat had made it clear from the start that he never harbored any real hopes of driving the Israelis out of the Sinai, but he wanted negotiations to achieve that goal for him. And the Syrians, who had Israeli forces virtually on the outskirts of Damascus, were eager for American diplomatic muscle to help them out. Kissinger's immediate diplomatic problem was to disengage the troops of Israel from both Egyptian and Syrian forces in a way that

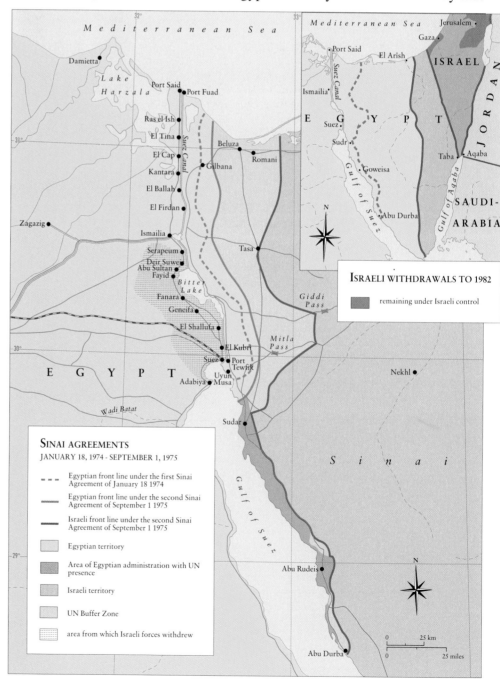

ISRAELI WITHDRAWALS TO 1982

remaining under Israeli control

SINAI AGREEMENTS

JANUARY 18, 1974 - SEPTEMBER 1, 1975

- - - Egyptian front line under the first Sinai Agreement of January 18 1974

—— Egyptian front line under the second Sinai Agreement of September 1 1975

—— Israeli front line under the second Sinai Agreement of September 1 1975

Egyptian territory

Area of Egyptian administration with UN presence

Israeli territory

UN Buffer Zone

area from which Israeli forces withdrew

U.S. Secretary of State Henry Kissinger in his airborne office, shuttling between Middle East adversaries in 1974.

might launch a true exchange leading to longer-range agreements.

For the Israelis, beset at home with recriminations over who was responsible for the unreadiness for the war, the initial diplomatic contact with the Egyptians was a mixed blessing. While many Israelis welcomed the chance to end their country's international ostracism, there was concern among many about appearing to reward Arabs for starting a war, and about giving back territory to Arabs for anything less than full peace. Many Israelis feared that the Arabs could not be trusted and that any reduction in Israel's security buffer could be disastrous. Every call for an Israeli withdrawal was matched by an Israeli concern that its security was being jeopardized.

The first agreement between Israel and Egypt was achieved in January, 1974, after Kissinger carried out an intensive diplomatic effort, flying between Jerusalem and the Egyptian city of Aswan to work out the details. As a result of that first shuttle diplomacy agreement, Egypt was ceded a narrow belt on the eastern bank of the Suez Canal, and the Israelis pulled back beyond a U.N. buffer zone in the Sinai.

Kissinger then turned his attention to the Syrian front, and spent 33 days flying between Jerusalem and Damascus in May, 1974, in search of an agreement. But the Egyptian-Israeli accord was a snap compared to the Israeli-Syrian one.

Part of the problem was that by May, the Israeli Government had in effect collapsed. Meir resigned that month, worn out by the war and the recriminations that followed, to be succeeded by Yitzhak Rabin, the former Defense Minister.

Moreover the Syrian President, Hafez al-Assad, lacked Sadat's vision of

ISRAEL'S LABOR PARTY LOSES TO RIGHTIST BLOC

By WILLIAM E. FARRELL

TEL AVIV, May 18 — Israel's governing Labor Party was defeated today in national parlimentary elections, bringing to an end the party's 29-year domination of the nation's political life.

The Likud, a right-of-center alignment and long the Labor Party's chief opposition, emerged as Israel's major political force, although, based on incomplete returns, it did not appear that the Likud would get anywhere near enough seats to command a majority in the 120–member Parliament.

Based on projections by Israeli television, it appeared that the Likud, which won 39 seats in the 1973 election, would obtain 40 to 44 seats.

The same projection showed that the Labor Party, which won 51 seats in 1973, would receive 30 to 32 seats.

A new political party, the Democratic Movement for Change, appeared, according to the projections, to be assured of as many as 13 seats. It was clear that the movement, which is headed by Yigael Yadin, an archeologist, had siphoned strength from the Labor Party.

The Likud is headed by Menahem Begin, a hard-line 64-year-old politician who has been a Labor Party critic for years.

Early this morning, Mr. Begin said that he expected Israel's President, Ephraim Katzir, to ask him to form a new majority coalition government.

A majority government needs at least 61 seats in Parliament and Mr. Begin, in a gesture of amity, said that he hoped to be able to form a national unity government.

While he did not specifically mention the Labor Party, his remarks were construed here as an invitation to the Labor Party to join with the Likud.

Forming a majority government has taken weeks, even months, in the past and it was not known early today what the prospects were for quickly obtaining a new one. The Labor Party was in disarray at its toppling from the predominance it has enjoyed since Israel was founded in 1948.

The New York Times May 18, 1977

using the talks to cement ties with the United States and gain back all his territory. The Syrians knew they were not going to get back the entire Golan Heights, which in fact was later annexed by Israel in 1981.

"Israel without faith and with much hope, Egypt with much faith but less hope, were both feeling their way toward a state of peace," Kissinger later wrote. "Neither the compulsions nor the convictions existed on the Syrian front.... Assad was claiming in the negotiation what he had not achieved in the battlefield. To the Israelis, a Golan disengagement looked suspiciously like a unilateral withdrawal to enable Assad to proclaim that Syria had not fought in vain — not a compelling goal for the victim of surprise attack."

Assad wanted not only the withdrawal of Israeli forces from deep inside

Golda Meir, shortly after her resignation as Prime Minister in 1974.

Syria, their point reached during the October war, but the return of Kuneitra, a town occupied by Israel in the 1967 war. And Israel saw no point in giving back something to Syria, even the sliver Assad wanted as a symbol, since Syria had achieved none of the military accomplishments of Egypt.

Despite these obstacles, in May, 1974, both sides accepted an agreement establishing a buffer zone between Israeli and Syrian forces and a cease-fire line roughly that of 1967, but with Israel giving up a bit of land including Kuneitra. Israel would be permitted to use force in case of a guerrilla attack launched from Syria. And both sides agreed to limit their forces near their mutual border.

But the real importance of the accord was that "if radical Syria could sign an agreement with Israel, there were no ideological obstacles to peace talks with any other Arab state," Kissinger later wrote.

Further diplomatic initiatives quickly petered out, however. It was not until 1977, with new hands at the helm in Washington and Jerusalem, that the peace process received a new infusion of energy.

The new American President, Jimmy Carter, was convinced that the time had come to seek a comprehensive peace, not just another round of modifications of the cease-fire. And the new Israeli Prime Minister, Menachem Begin,

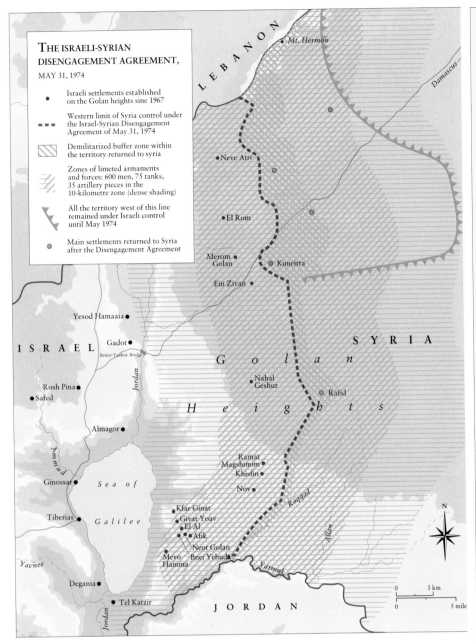

THE ISRAELI-SYRIAN
DISENGAGEMENT AGREEMENT,
MAY 31, 1974

- Israeli settlements established
  on the Golan heights sine 1967

- - - Western limit of Syria control under
  the Israel-Syrian Disengagement
  Agreement of May 31, 1974

Demilitarized buffer zone within
the territory returned to syria

Zones of limeted armaments
and forces: 600 men, 75 tanks,
35 artillery pieces in the
10-kilometre zone (dense shading)

All the territory west of this line
remained under Israeli control
until May 1974

Main settlements returned to Syria
after the Disengagement Agreement

105 HOSTAGES FREED IN DARING RAID ON UGANDA AIRPORT

By TERENCE SMITH

JERUSALEM, July 4 — Israeli airborne commandos staged a daring night time raid on Entebbe airport in Uganda last night, freeing the 105 mainly Israeli hostages and Air France crew members held by pro-Palestinian hijackers and flying them back to Israel aboard three Israeli planes.

The hostages and their rescuers were due back in Israel this morning after a brief stopover at Kenya's International Airport in Nairobi, where at least two persons were given medical treatment in a field hospital on the runway. No details of the extent of the casualties were available here pending notification of the families.

Only fragmentary reports of the raid were immediately available here. An unspecified number of commandos apparently flew the 2,300 miles from Israel to Entebbe Airport and surprised the hijackers on the ground.

The hijackers were spending the night with their hostages in the old passenger terminal at Entebbe, where they have been confined all week. They had commandeered an Air France airliner last Sunday shortly after it had left Athens on its way to Paris.

News agency reports from Entebbe said that a number of large explosions — perhaps bombs — were set off at a distant point on the airport, apparently to divert the ring of Ugandan troops that had surrounded the old terminal all week.

The commandos reportedly broke into the old terminal and fought a gun battle with the heavily armed hijackers. Reports from the scene said that the terrorists had been killed in the skirmish, but military sources here declined to confirm or deny this.

The hostages apparently were then rushed to the waiting Israeli planes and flown away before Ugandan forces could intervene.

An Israeli radio report said that the raiders were infantrymen and paratroopers dressed in civilian clothes.

Government sources here said that the decision to stage the military operation was approved unanimously by a special Cabinet meeting in Tel Aviv yesterday.

The New York Times July 4, 1976

was unencumbered by the political baggage of his predecessor, Rabin.

The weakness of the Labor Party government, whose management of the economy had been severely criticized, produced a startling result in the elections of May 17, 1977. Begin, the onetime leader of the Irgun terrorist group, was elected with his Likud bloc to power, breaking the Labor Party's lock on the office of Prime Minister of Israel.

Begin had been a member of a national unity government in Israel following the 1967 war, but resigned when the government accepted the American-brokered U.N. Security Council Resolution 242 of November 1967, which obliged Israel to return occupied land for peace. Begin, as a follower of the Polish Zionist Vladimir Jabotinsky, felt strongly that Israel had the right to retain control over Judea and Samaria, as he always called the West Bank. For the same historical reason, Begin argued that Jews had the right to settle in those lands. He contended that while Resolution 242 obliged Israel to withdraw from occupied territories, it did not say on all fronts, and that therefore any Israeli withdrawals in Sinai would be sufficient compliance.

"Begin was a puzzle to the Americans who met him," wrote William B. Quandt, the White House national security adviser on the Middle East. "His Polish origin showed through in his courtly manner, his formal dress, and his

SADAT, MAKING MIDDLE EAST HISTORY, ARRIVES IN ISRAEL

By WILLIAM E. FARRELL

JERUSALEM, November 19—The leaders of Egypt and Israel, two nations that have fought four wars in 29 years, met on Israeli soil tonight.

At 8.03 P.M. [1.03 P.M.. New York time], President Anwar el-Sadat of Egypt stepped aground at Ben-Gurion International Airport, creating Middle East history as the first Arab leader to visit Israel since its founding in 1948.

He was greeted by Prime Minister Menachem Begin and President Ephraim Katzir, who have lauded Mr. Sadat in recent days for his bold move in deciding to come to Israel despite growing antipathy and violence in the Arab world caused by his tacit recognition of Israel's existence.

Mr. Sadat greeted Mr. Begin by saying "Thank you" Mr. Begin responded, "It's wonderful to have you. Thank you for coming."

Then as Mr. Sadat walked from his airliner to a waiting limousine, he shook hands with people whose very names recalled the years of conflict that have marked relations between Israel and the Arab world, among them Moshe Dayan, Golda Meir, former Prime Minister Yitzhak Rabin and Gen. Ariel Sharon.

After his arrival at the King David Hotel, President Sadat met for a half-hour with Mr. Begin, Mr. Dayan and Deputy Prime Minister Yigael Yadin for what was described as a courtesy call.

"I have already had private discussion with him," Mr. Begin said to reporters, referring to the Egyptian leader, "and I can say that we like each other."

Mr. Sadat and an entourage of Egyptian officials and reporters had flown from the Abu Suweir airbase in Egypt, directly to Ben-Gurion International Airport. The plane, emblazoned with Egypt's flag and the words "Arab Republic of Egypt," taxied up to a red carpet on the tarmac. Three minutes later the Egyptian leader emerged onto an airport ramp of El Al, Israel's airline, and was greeted by a fanfare of trumpets.

Mr. Sadat was visibly moved as he stood on the platform, his eyes moist, his mouth tight.

The New York Times November 20, 1977

Menachem Begin and Anwar el-Sadat during the Egyptian President's historic visit to Jerusalem.

historical frame of reference. His terrible personal trauma as a Jew in central Europe at the time of Hitler's rise to power seemed never far from his mind. Nearly all his immediate family had been killed in the Holocaust. The depth of his feelings about the tragedy that had befallen his people seemed to make him incapable of having much empathy for others with grievances, especially for Palestinians who expressed their anger and frustration in attacks on Jews."

But the decisive move was not Begin's or Carter's, but Sadat's. Speaking to his Parliament on November 9, 1977, he said he was ready to go "to the ends of the world" in search of peace. Then he added: "Israel will be astonished when it hears me saying now before you that I am ready to go to their house, to the Knesset itself, and to talk to them."

At first the remark was regarded as a rhetorical flourish, but Begin, who had always sought a direct dialogue with Sadat, seized upon it, and indicated he would be willing to receive him. Five days later Sadat repeated his willingness to address the Knesset, and Begin said an invitation would come.

Courageously defying Arab refusal to recognize the Jewish state, Sadat arrived in Israel on November 19 and spoke to the Knesset the next day. It was the first visit to Israel by any Arab leader, and that alone marked a major moment in Middle East history.

But the actual substance of the talks did not advance the negotiations significantly. Sadat still was holding out for a grand gesture from Begin, to agree to pull back from all occupied lands, and to grant the Palestinians the right to self-determination. For that, he would urge all Arabs to make peace with Israel. But Sadat also seemed to be leaving open the possibility of a separate peace with Israel if he could get back the whole Sinai, including the evacuation of Jewish settlers living there.

The Israelis were interested in a peace treaty with Egypt, but the sides were far from agreement. Ezer Weizman, who was Begin's Defense Minister and later became President, summed up the differences between Begin and Sadat this way:

"Anyone observing the two men could not have overlooked the profound divergence in their attitudes. Both desired peace. But whereas Sadat wanted to take it by storm, capitalizing on the momentum from his visit to Jerusalem to reach his final objective, Begin preferred to creep forward inch by inch. He took the dream of peace and ground it down into the fine, dry powder of details, legal clauses and quotes from international law."

Through much of 1978, the United States sought to mediate between the two sides. Clearly irritated with Begin's recalcitrance, Carter at first decided on a policy of siding with Sadat and trying to pressure concessions from Begin. But as meeting after meeting failed to bring the sides closer to agreement, and with Sadat regularly threatening to break off talks, Carter decided to set up a three-way summit meeting at the presidential retreat at Camp David, Maryland.

This was an act of desperation by Carter. He knew that if he were to take

Israelis watching Sadat speak on state television.

President Jimmy Carter with Sadat and Begin at Camp David in September, 1978. The negotiations eventually led to the handshake that sealed the Egyptian-Israeli peace treaty in March, 1979.

advantage of Sadat's trip to Israel, time was running out.

The talks lasted from September 5 to 17, and were held in extreme secrecy, with the vast press corps kept away. Officials later said that the talks came close to collapse several times because Sadat and Begin could not talk to each other without blowing up. In fact, two days before the talks ended, Sadat told Carter he was going home without an accord. But in the end, Sadat, eager to get back the Sinai, made most of the concessions, accepting a rather general outline for West Bank and Gaza autonomy, in return for the return of the Sinai as part of a peace agreement whose details were to be worked out later. In effect, Sadat was dropping his previous insistence on something concrete for the Palestinians. Israel agreed at virtually the last minute to drop its demand that settlers could remain in the Sinai, which made it possible for Sadat to accept. Summing up the talks, Quandt said that the Israeli Prime Minister "was no doubt the most able negotiator at Camp David."

"He understood best how to play the cards in his hand, he was meticulous in turning words to his advantage, and he credibly used the threat to break off the talks to extract concessions at crucial moments. He kept his eye on specific issues, sometimes giving in on a symbolically important but intangible point to obtain something more concrete. He knew how to play the game of brinkmanship, holding back on his final concessions until everyone else had put his cards face up on the table."

In particular, Begin seemed to stare down Carter in a dispute over what they had agreed to in the talks. Carter insisted that Begin had assured him that no new Jewish settlements would be built in the West Bank for the duration of the negotiations on self-government in the West Bank. Begin insisted that all he had agreed to was a three-month freeze. Carter eventually dropped the

issue.

But even the resolution of Camp David did not presage a quick signing of a peace treaty. Although the Camp David agreement set a goal of three months to negotiate the peace treaty, it took the parties until March, 1979, when Carter himself flew to Egypt and Israel to nail it down. The differences that delayed the accord were so minor as to be truly historical footnotes.

Finally on March 26, 1979, a chilly early spring day in Washington, Begin, Sadat and Carter assembled on the White House lawn to put their signatures on the first peace treaty between Israel and an Arab state.

Signing as a witness for the United States, Carter said, "We have won, at last, the first step of peace — a first step on a long and difficult road."

In their speeches, all three men offered prayers that the treaty would bring true peace to the Middle East. By coincidence, they all referred to the words of the Prophet Isaiah.

"Let us work together until the day comes when they beat their swords into plowshares and their spears into pruning hooks," Sadat said. Begin exclaimed: "No more war, no more bloodshed, no more bereavement. Peace unto you, shalom, salaam, forever."

TREATY ENDS A STATE OF WAR AFTER 30 YEARS

By BERNARD GWERTZMAN

WASHINGTON, March 26 — After confronting each other for nearly 31 years as hostile neighbors, Egypt and Israel signed a formal treaty at the White House today to establish peace and "normal and friendly relations."

On this chilly early spring day, about 1,500 guests and millions more watching television saw President Anwar el-Sadat of Egypt and Prime Minister Menachem Begin of Israel put their signatures on the Arabic, Hebrew and English versions of the first peace treaty between Israel and an Arab country.

President Carter, who was credited by both leaders for having made the agreement possible, signed as a witness for the United States. In a somber speech he said, "Peace has come."

"We have won, at last, the first step of peace—a first step on a long and difficult road," he added.

Later, at a state dinner, Mr. Begin suggested that Mr. Carter be given the Nobel Peace Prize, and Mr. Sadat agreed.

At the signing ceremony, all three leaders offered prayers that the treaty would bring true peace to the Middle East and the enmity that has erupted into war four times since Israel declared its independence on May 14, 1948.

Mr. Begin, who gave the longest and most emotional of the addresses, exclaimed: "No more war, no more bloodshed, no more bereavement, peace unto you, shalom, salaam, forever."

"Shalom" and "salaam" are the Hebrew and Arabic words for "peace."

The Israeli leader, noted for oratorical skill, provided a dash of humor when in the course of his speech he seconded Mr. Sadat's remark that Mr. Carter was "the unknown soldier of the peacemaking effort."

Mr. Begin said, pausing, "I agree, but as usual with an amendment"—that Mr. Carter was not completely unknown and that his peace effort would "be remembered and recorded by generations to come."

The New York Times March 27, 1979

Chapter Six: The Wars In Lebanon And at Home

Joel Brinkley

Birthplace of the intifada: Rioting that began in Gaza in December, 1987, exploded into a five-year-long uprising by the Palestinians.

AS THE 1980S DAWNED, many Israelis hoped that the peace made with Egypt would be re-enacted with their other Arab neighbors, bringing a new era of security and prosperity to Israel and the region. But the Camp David accords had no coattails; indeed, they had little effect on day-to-day relations between Israel and Egypt. The two nations quickly settled into what came to be known as the "cold peace."

Egyptians clearly had no intention of welcoming the Israelis. When Eliahu Ben-Elissar, the new Israeli Ambassador to Egypt, took up residence in Cairo, for several months no Egyptian would agree to lease him space for an embassy or a personal residence. Egyptians never invited him to diplomatic receptions or other social gatherings, and Egyptian officials refused to attend dinners or receptions if they knew Ben-Elissar would be present.

While thousands of Israelis eagerly signed up for organized tours of Egypt, only a handful of Egyptians chose to visit Israel. And when a cruise ship sailed from Haifa to Alexandria in 1980, several dozen Israeli tourists aboard were not allowed to disembark with the other sightseers.

"The Egyptians don't want to implement the normalization and turn it into a reality," former Foreign Minister Moshe Dayan complained a year after the peace treaty was signed. "They also make it difficult for every Egyptian who is willing to do commercial business with Israel."

But while the Israelis did not find the warm acceptance they craved, at least they no longer feared that their largest and most powerful neighbor might attack them at any time. And as their preoccupation with survival began to ebb a bit, many Israelis began noticing problems in the nation's social structure that had

been pushed into the background of the public consciousness by questions of war and peace.

The nation's socialist fiscal policies — the Government owned most of the largest businesses and had its hand in almost every sector of the economy — helped produce an inflation rate that approached 100 percent a year. That created an economic structure that heavily favored Israelis who could afford to maintain holdings of foreign currencies.

As a result, the nation grew more and more stratified. The upper middle class, largely the Ashkenazi Jews of Northern European origin, grew wealthier, while the rest of the population, principally the Sephardics of Mediterranean or eastern origin, lagged farther behind. That encouraged resentment that had been festering for years.

To get control of the economy, the Begin Government periodically cut food subsidies, and by 1981 the number of Israelis living below the poverty line rose above 100,000. The stratification, and anger, grew worse.

Newspaper opinion polls began showing that Israelis viewed the Begin Government as the worst in the nation's history, and 1981 was an election year. In response, the government slashed import tariffs on a wide variety of consumer goods, sending thousands of Israelis into stores to buy TVs, microwave ovens and other foreign-made goods.

Preparing to invade Lebanon, Israeli armor assembled along the coastal highway leading to Beirut in July, 1982.

Simultaneously the Government began spending its scarce foreign currency reserves to shore up the value of the shekel. Food, housing and educational subsidies were restored, and the government's popularity began to recover. But economists and opposition politicians warned that the Begin government was committing economic suicide for short-term political expediency.

Certainly the populist, election-year economic policies helped Begin regain lost support. But among Israelis nothing was more likely to rally voters than a bold, successful military strike. And in June, 1981, weeks before voters went to the polls, the Israeli Air Force pulled off a stunning military accomplishment.

For years, Israel had been warning that Iraq was building a nuclear reactor with the aim of producing nuclear weapons, with Israel the presumptive target. The French government, Iraq's patron in their nuclear venture, was working to be sure the reactor was used only to produce energy. But in 1981 the Israeli government seemed to believe that Iraq was just months away from acquiring enough weapons-grade plutonium to produce a bomb. In strict secrecy, the Israeli military prepared to act.

Late in the afternoon of June 7, six F-16 fighters, the sophisticated American-made aircraft that were the Israeli Air Force's most potent weapon, took off from a base in the Sinai. The planes flew low over the Jordan-Saudi Arabia border, along a path that the Israelis had determined to have spotty radar coverage. They swooped in over the reactor and dropped their 2,000-pound bombs with precision, destroying the reactor, then reversed course, returning safely to Israel, evidently undetected by the Iraqi, Jordanian and Saudi defense systems.

Israelis rejoiced at the daring raid. But the rest of the world reacted with disapproval. The United States called the attack "a source of utmost concern," and in Washington there was talk of imposing sanctions on Israel for using American-made aircraft to commit aggression. But the protestations seemed mostly pro forma; few countries had any real sympathy for the Iraqi despot, Saddam Hussein.

Three weeks later, Begin's Likud Party fared better in the national elections than anyone could have predicted at the start of the year. The Prime Minister formed a new Government, though he had to enlist several ultra-orthodox parties as partners along with the right-wing parties that normally allied with Likud.

The sudden 400 percent budget increase at the Orthodox-controlled Ministry of Religious Affairs was widely resented among the nation's secular majority. But one Cabinet appointment that got far less attention at the time — the naming of the militant, pugnacious Ariel Sharon as Minister of Defense — actually turned out to be the most significant decision the new government would make.

During Begin's first term, Sharon had been best known as the architect of the Likud Party's policy of accelerating the settlement of Jews in the occupied West Bank and Gaza Strip. As Minister of Agriculture and Chairman of the

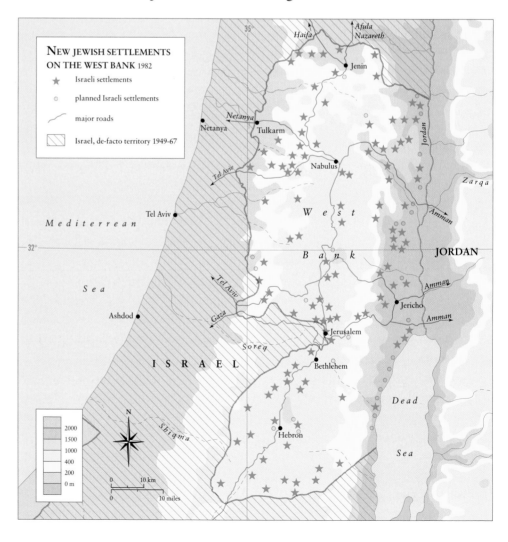

On the southern fringes of Jerusalem, new buildings at Armon Hanaziv in December, 1980, helped to ring the city with Jewish residents.

Settlement Committee, Sharon had directed an aggressive policy of promoting and encouraging new settlements. And by 1981 his policies had more than tripled the number of West Bank settlers, to about 18,000 Jews.

Most of these people were hard-line ideologues willing to live in small, bare, isolated settlements in the belief that they were guaranteeing continued Jewish control of the West Bank — part of the original Land of Israel, as they saw it. But the number of settlers was far smaller than the target of 300,000 that Sharon had set as his goal years before. So, starting in 1981 the focus of settlement policy began to change. The government began building "suburban" settlements, luxurious bedroom communities intended for average Israelis of all political persuasions who simply wanted a large, affordable place to live minutes away from their jobs in the cities.

Lured by the government's low-interest mortgages, opulent tax breaks and a host of other inducements, residents of Tel Aviv and Jerusalem moved to settlements including Ariel near Tel Aviv and Maale Adumim near Jerusalem, where large, well-appointed villas could be bought for the price of a cramped apartment in town. All of it cost the Government several billion dollars, adding to the nation's economic troubles.

Through all this, most of the nation's borders generally remained quiet. In April, 1982, Israel completed its withdrawal from the Sinai, overcoming loud and violent resistance at the end from the Jewish settlers there. After that, the Egyptian border remained peaceful, even after the Egyptian President, Anwar Sadat, was assassinated in September, 1981, by Egyptian fundamentalists who were resentful of the peace with Israel.

The borders with Syria and Jordan also had settled into cold but peaceful routines of mutual accommodation.

Every morning around 9:30 a Jordanian soldier in a powder blue uniform carrying a small bundle under his arm walked to the middle of the Allenby

ISRAELI FORCES STRIKE SOUTHERN LEBANON, TAKE P.L.O. OUTPOSTS

By THOMAS L. FRIEDMAN

BEIRUT, Lebanon June 6 — The Israeli Army invaded southern Lebanon by land, sea and air on Sunday in an attack aimed at destroying the main military bases of the Palestine Liberation Organization.

More than 250 Israeli tanks and armored personnel carriers, as well as thousands of infantrymen, rolled past the observation posts of the United Nations peacekeeping troops in southern Lebanon at 11 A.M. and fanned out across the frontier, according to a United Nations spokesman in Beirut.

By late Sunday evening the Israelis had taken several P.L.O. outposts in the craggy hills of southern Lebanon and were engaged in fierce firefights with the Palestinians for control of scores of other strongholds along the 33-mile front, stretching from the port city of Tyre to the foothills of Mount Hermon, the United Nations spokesman said.

In the first day of the invasion the Israelis besieged all their main targets — Tyre, Beaufort Castle, Nabatiye and Kawkaba — but the Palestinians stood their ground and did not flee north. The number of casualties was not known.

Israel said this morning that Beaufort Castle, a Crusader stronghold overlooking the border that the Palestinians have used as a communications and artillery base, was captured during the night by an Israeli infantry battalion. But the Palestinians denied that the castle had fallen.

It appeared that at least a few elements of Syria's force of about 25,000 men in Lebanon had become involved in confrontations with the Israelis.

The state-run Beirut radio reported Sunday night that Syrian artillery north of Hasbeya was exchanging fire with the Israelis on the eastern route of their advance. This could not be confirmed. In Damascus, a Syrian military spokesman said Israeli forces had come into contact with Syrian troops in three places, but it was not clear whether fighting had occurred.

The Israel radio broadcast a statement saying that the invasion was not aimed at the Syrians and that Israeli troops would not engage Syrian units as long as they stayed out of the fighting.

But the situation could become increasingly difficult if the Palestinians are forced to pull back into Syrian-controlled areas.

The New York Times June 7, 1982

Bridge, which spanned the Jordan River between Israel and Jordan. At the same time, an Israeli soldier in khakis, also carrying a bundle, approached from the other side.

Without exchanging a word, the two men traded bundles and returned to their respective countries — the Jordanian bringing home the day's Israeli newspapers and the Israeli bringing home the Jordanian papers. Back in Jerusalem and Tel Aviv, Israeli editors read the Jordanian papers so they could publish the schedule of Jordanian television programs, which were widely watched in Israel. In Amman, Jordanian editors did the same with the Israeli program listings. Jordan and Israel were officially at war, but both sides were more interested in knowing when "Dallas" or "Dynasty" would air on each other's television stations.

While the southern and eastern borders were generally quiet, Israel's northern border with Lebanon was an open sore. Years earlier, the Palestine Liberation Organization had set up its headquarters in Beirut, and southern Lebanon had become a Palestinian fief, ruled by well-armed P.L.O. fighters. From southern Lebanon, the P.L.O. launched hundreds of rocket and artillery attacks on northern Israel, and squads of P.L.O. guerrillas occasionally slipped over the border and carried out terrorist attacks against civilian settlements, often killing women and school children.

Israel struck back with ferocious air attacks on refugee camps and other presumed guerrilla encampments. But the Arab attacks continued, and Sharon began talking publicly about "cleaning up Lebanon," turning it into "an independent state that will live with us in peace."

His plan was to invade Lebanon to drive the P.L.O. out of the country. His second and equally important goal was to tip the political balance in Beirut in

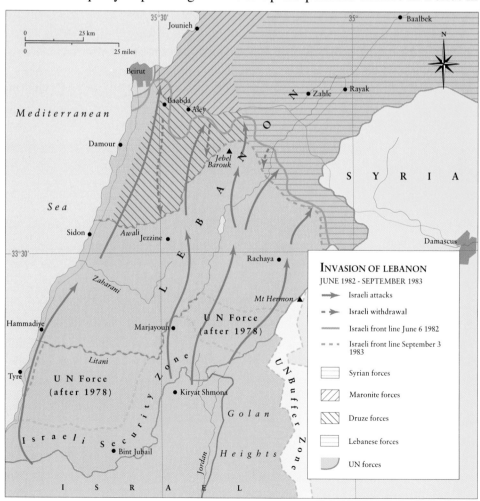

INVASION OF LEBANON
JUNE 1982 - SEPTEMBER 1983

→ Israeli attacks
⇢ Israeli withdrawal
— Israeli front line June 6 1982
--- Israeli front line September 3 1983
Syrian forces
Maronite forces
Druze forces
Lebanese forces
UN forces

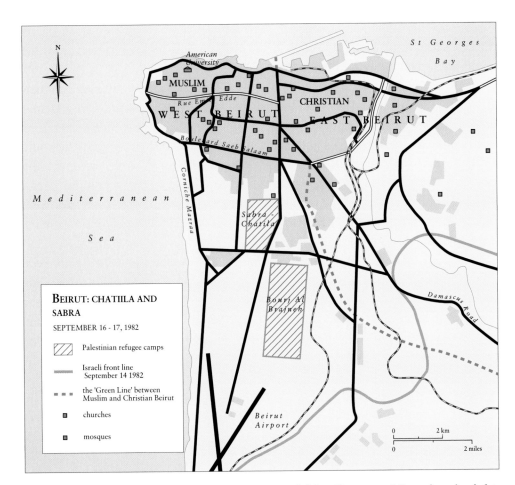

BEIRUT: CHATIILA AND
SABRA

SEPTEMBER 16 - 17, 1982

Palestinian refugee camps

Israeli front line
September 14 1982

the 'Green Line' between
Muslim and Christian Beirut

churches

mosques

favor of the Lebanese Christians, who seemed friendly toward Israel and might be enlisted against the P.L.O. They might even be able to expel the Syrians, who had 40,000 troops in Lebanon and had ended Christian domination of the country's political institutions.

In a secret meeting with Sharon in January, 1982, Bashir Gemayel, the head of the Phalange, the main Lebanese Christian militia, heartily agreed to the plan. And so on June 6, 1982, three Israeli divisions — 80,000 men — moved into southern Lebanon.

Sharon promised that the operation would last no more than two or three days, and said the goal was to establish a 25-mile "security zone" in southern Lebanon. But by the end of the third day the army had moved more than 25 miles north and was still going, with little Israeli loss of life.

Sharon's goal was to link up with the Phalangist forces in Beirut, and to cut the Beirut-Damascus highway in the east. The strategy ran the risk of a new war with Syria, and the Syrian troops did give battle in the east, halting the Israeli threat to the Bekaa Valley. But in the Beirut area, Israeli troops were able to link up with the Phalangists and cut off the Beirut-Damascus highway. After only a week's fighting, Israel found itself entrenched just outside Beirut, with a far larger war on its hands than anyone but Ariel Sharon had anticipated.

The offensive had driven thousands of P.L.O. guerrillas into the western, Muslim side of Beirut, where 15,000 of them were holed up among half a million other Muslim Arabs. Sharon was determined to drive the guerrillas out, but neither he nor anyone else in the Israeli Government was willing to risk heavy Israeli casualties by sending their troops into the city. Under their agreement with Israel, the Phalangists were responsible for this operation, but they developed cold feet.

Begin demanded that the P.L.O. withdraw from Beirut. When Arafat refused the Israeli forces massed just outside the city launched a furious artillery attack

An Israeli artillery attack on West Beirut in June, 1982.

that lasted two months. At times the artillery appeared to be aimed at known P.L.O. strongholds, while at other times the missiles and shells seemed to be fired indiscriminately into the city.

After weeks of American mediation, the P.L.O. agreed to withdraw, leaving Beirut by sea. One day in late August, guerrillas rolled toward the port in a deafening, nerve-racking crescendo as gunmen along the sidewalks, atop buildings, on dirt barricades and riding in cars, pointed their weapons skyward and blasted away in salute. There were also emotional scenes as guerrillas tearfully hugged wives and children, who had to remain behind in the devastation that Beirut had become. Much of west Beirut, particularly its Palestinian neighborhoods and refugee camps, had been reduced to rubble in the 75 days of Israeli invasion and siege.

The scene had the look of defeat for the P.L.O., though the guerrillas pointed out that they had fought the Israelis longer than any Arab army, and had held them off at the gates of their last redoubt.

Even so, they were scattered to seven Arab countries and an uncertain future. And as they left, the Syrians pulled some of their forces back across the border. Even Sharon's political goals seemed to be achieved when Gemayel, Israel's ally, was elected President.

Had Sharon pulled Israel's forces back then, the Israeli people probably would have accepted the war, even with all of the Government's deceptive statements and the hundreds of Israeli deaths.

But Sharon said he was unwilling to leave Lebanon until all P.L.O. guerrillas were out of Lebanon. Despite Palestinian disavowals, he claimed that at least 2,000 fighters were hiding in the refugee camps. Gemayel promised to clean out the camps, but less than a month later, before he could execute the operation, he was assassinated.

The Phalangists suspected P.L.O. involvement. Two days later, with the Israeli Army's tacit approval, Phalangist forces moved into the Sabra and Shatila Palestinian refugee camps in southern Beirut, promising to root out the remaining P.L.O. guerrillas. In fact, the Phalangists slaughtered every man,

Opponents of the war in Lebanon at a rally in Tel Aviv in September, 1982. It was the largest protest in Israeli history, with more than 400,000 participants

MASSACRE IN BEIRUT
The Four Days

WEDNESDAY, September 15: One hundred and one days after it invaded Lebanon in a campaign to drive the Palestine Liberation Organization out of its headquarters in Beirut, the Israeli Army began to enter the western, Muslim side of the capital.

It had not been Israel's original intention to take this final step. Having shelled the city so heavily that pressure on Yasir Arafat, the P.L.O. leader, to withdraw from the capital was overwhelming, the architect of the invasion, Defense Minister Ariel Sharon, was content to allow the Lebanese Army to perform the task of taking control of West Beirut and suppressing any armed Palestinians in the city or the Palestinian refugee camps on its southern fringes.

That all changed on Sept. 14, when Bashir Gemayel, the Lebanese President-elect, was killed by a bomb during a meeting with commanders of the Christian militia, known as the Phalange. Gemayel's Phalangist Party has been the dominant element in a coalition of Maronite Christian parties that has controlled East Beirut and a Christian enclave to the north, and Gemayel was the militia's commander before Lebanon's Parliament elected him to the presidency.

According to a statement by Sharon to the Israeli Parliament, moments after Gemayel's death became known, the Israeli Defense Minister contacted Prime Minister Menachem Begin and the two men decided that the Israeli Army should enter West Beirut.

Sharon argued that the Israeli presence was required, arguing that some P.L.O. guerrillas and Lebanese leftist Muslim militiamen remained armed and in the refugee camps, and that because control over West Beirut by the Lebanese Government was tenuous, there would be a potential for the P.L.O. to re-establish itself.

THURSDAY, September 16: By Thursday morning, the Israeli Army had the entire area around the Sabra and Shatila camps sealed off. No one could move in or out. A spokesman in East Beirut for the Israeli Army, formally known as the Israel Defense Forces, issued the following statement that day: "The I.D.F. is in control of all key points in Beirut. Refugee camps harboring terrorist concentrations remain encircled and closed. The I.D.F. calls on citizens to return to normal activity and on all terrorists and other armed persons to lay down their arms."

Around 6 A.M. Thursday, shellfire and gunshots could be heard in Sabra in the vicinity of Gaza Hospital, according to patients. Although the night had been calm, new groups of wounded people were streaming into the medical center.

The artillery fire, many of these patients later said, appeared to be coming from Israeli positions overlooking the camp to the west. Armed elements inside Sabra may also have been firing at targets outside the camp.

According to Sharon, after a meeting was held Thursday between the Phalangist liaison officers and the commander of Israeli units in the north, Maj. Gen. Amir Drori, "it was concluded that the armed force of Christian militiamen would enter Shatila from the south and west, would look out for and clear out the terrorists."

"And," Sharon added, "it was stressed that civilians — especially women, children and old people — should not be harmed."

By 3 P.M. Thursday afternoon, Phalangist commanders had assembled an estimated 1,500 men at the airport, in Israeli-controlled territory near Sabra and Shatila. The stage was set for a massacre.

According to a Lebanese Army soldier, the militia force going into the camps was composed primarily of Phalangist units consisting of men from Damur,

Saadiyat and Nameh. These are three Christian villages that were sacked by Palestinian forces in the early days of the Lebanese civil war.

The Lebanese soldier said that one Phalangist militiaman told him before going into the camps, "We have been waiting a long time for this day."

Sometime around 4 P.M. Thursday, according to residents of the Sabra and Shatila camps, armed men began moving in.

From the moment they entered, witnesses said, the militiamen made no apparent effort to distinguish between Palestinians and Lebanese, let alone between men, women and children.

What appeared to be entire families were found slain as they sat at the dinner table. Others were found dead in their nightclothes, apparently surprised by the militamen who burst in on them Thursday evening.

Some people were found with their throats slit. Others had been mutilated with some kind of heavy blade, perhaps axes.

According to Dr. Eivinu Witsoe, a Norwegian surgeon at Gaza Hospital and his colleague Dr. Per Maehlumshagen, beginning Thursday afternoon, a large number of casualties began flooding into the hospital: mostly men, women and children with gunshot wounds in the head, chest and stomach as well as a variety of shrapnel injuries.

From 8 P.M. Thursday until 5 A.M. Friday, the physicians said, they were busy treating patients.

The doctors said the first indication they had that a massacre might be taking place was when an 11-year-old boy, Milad Farouk, was brought into the hospital with three gunshot wounds. He told the doctors that Christian militiamen had burst into his house in Shatila and shot his mother, father and three siblings, one an infant. Then they shot him.

At the same time these wounded people were being treated Thursday evening, hundreds of people — the doctors estimate that there were anywhere from 1,000 to 2,000 of them — began flocking to the hospital and the nearby buildings to seek safety.

Pandemonium reigned. In the operating theater, the physicians said, Palestinian nurses were breaking down in tears in the middle of surgery out of fear for their lives. In the streets of Shatila, people were rushing about in terror. The dead and dying were being carried to the hospital by families, as no ambulance drivers would go out.

The scene was made all the more frightening, the doctors said, by the illumination flares that were being fired by Israeli troops over the camps and dropped by Israeli aircraft.

Sharon said the 81-millimeter flares were requested by the Phalangists to light their way. Residents in the camp say the sky was aglow most of the night.

Hirsch Goodman, the military correspondent of *The Jerusalem Post,* reported that he had been shown a cable sent at 11 P.M. Thursday from the head of the Phalangist units in Shatila to the Israeli command in East Beirut.

It said, Goodman wrote, "To this time we have killed 300 civilians and terrorists." The cable was immediately distributed in the command and sent to Tel Aviv, he reported.

FRIDAY, September 17: By Friday morning, most people in the camps were either in hiding or had fled. According to an Asian doctor at Akka Hospital who asked not to be identified, the fear there was such that almost all of the 500 people who had sought shelter there fled in panic, scattering in all directions. What happened to some of them is not known.

The Asian doctor said that in addition to himself, the only medical personnel left behind at Akka Hospital were five Palestinian staff members and six foreign nurses. He said there were also some patients in their rooms. None of them could walk.

At about 10:20 A.M., witnesses said, militiamen came to the hospital. Speaking Arabic in a southern Lebanese dialect, the witnesses said, they ordered everyone to come out with their hands up.

Three foreign nurses left the hospital under a white flag, according to the Asian doctor. He said they were accompanied by a Palestinian physician who worked at the hospital, Mohammed Ali Osman.

As they were leaving, a shot rang out, and the Palestinian doctor fell to the ground, dead.

At 2 P.M. Friday, a different group of militiamen came, wearing different uniforms, according to the Asian doctor. He said they started to molest one of the Lebanese nurses, whose name was Friyal. They stopped after she started screaming.

"Shortly after that we went down to the shelter," the doctor said, "and found that one of the Palestinian nurses down there had been raped repeatedly and then shot."

At approximately 3:45 P.M., witnesses say, yet another group of militiamen arrived at the Akka Hospital. The militiamen said they wanted to see the nurses. He told the men that the nurses had all fled.

At this point, according to the doctor, the militiamen asked to search the hospital. During the course of their work, they found a photograph of Yasir Arafat in the Asian doctor's room.

"You are a terrorist," one of the militiamen said to him.

At that point, the doctor said, he began to beg for his life. He was told to bring the nurses back to the hospital by 7 P.M., or else, the militiamen said, they would blow his head off.

Fortunately for the physician, by about 5 P.M. Friday, an International Red Cross convoy made it to the hospital and evacuated everyone left there. The doctor said that at about 5:30 P.M., as he was leaving the facility for safety, he saw at the southern end of Shatila what he estimated to be 80 to 90 bodies. They had been mixed together with sand and were being pushed by bulldozers.

This area can be seen very clearly with the naked eye from the Kuwaiti Embassy traffic circle — the site of an Israeli Army observation post, equipped with binoculars and a powerful telescope. All available evidence suggests that it is probable that Israeli soldiers were manning the post during the time of the massacre. The strongest evidence found by reporters who visited the observation station was in the form of Hebrew-language newspapers found on the floor. They were dated Thursday and Friday.

According to Sharon's statement before the Israeli Parliament, at about 11 A.M. Friday the commander of the Israeli division deployed around Beirut, Brig. Amos Yaron, met with Drori and "raised suspicions concerning the method of operation of the Phalangists."

According to Sharon, Drori then ordered the Phalangist liaison officer to halt the operation. It is clear from all accounts that by Friday afternoon things did quiet down somewhat in the camps, but there were still fires raging and shooting going on, according to people who were on the scene.

But at 4:30 P.M. Friday, after Drori was said by Sharon to have ordered an end to the operation, he and the Israeli Chief of Staff, Lieut. Gen. Rafael Eytan, met again with the Phalangists. At that time, Sharon said, it was "agreed that all of the Phalangists would leave the refugee camps on Saturday morning."

Israeli officers in East Beirut said what happened at the 4:30 Friday meeting was that the Phalangists told the Israelis that they needed more time to "clean up" the area.

Inside the camps, the militiamen already on the scene continued with their work. At some time between 4 P.M. and 5 P.M. Friday, a Reuters correspondent, Paul Eedle, spoke to an Israeli colonel just outside the Sabra camp and asked him about the operations taking place inside.

The colonel, who declined to be identified, told Eedle that his men were working on the basis of two principles: that the Israeli Army should not get involved, but that the area should be "purified."

SATURDAY, September 18: Men, women, girls and young boys were all rounded up by the militiamen. Some 500 to 600 people, possibly even more, were then herded together and marched at gunpoint down to the main street of Shatila, where they were forced to sit along the road. Beside them were a number of corpses that had already begun to decay.

With all of these refugees collected in Shatila, the final act was about to take place at the Gaza Hospital, where some 20 foreign doctors and nurses and two Palestinian medics were still caring for 37 patients.

At about 7 A.M., members of the medical staff recalled, six or seven militiamen came to the hospital and ordered everyone out.

Hiding with the group of foreign medical workers were two Palestinian male nurses who were trying to slip though the net of the militiamen.

"They were very frightened," Dr. Maehlumshagen recalled. "When we entered the Shatila camp, we discovered all of these people sitting along the main street. As we marched along, one of the militiamen pulled one of the Palestinian nurses out of the line and asked his identity."

"We asked them what they were going to do with him," the doctor said. "The militiaman said, 'You do your job and I will do mine.' They then took the man around a corner and we heard shots. That is all we know." Along the way, the other Palestinian nurse was pulled out of line as well, witnesses said. His fate is also unknown.

Several witnesses said that at one point, a man wearing a blue hospital uniform in the group of foreigners from Gaza Hospital was stopped by the militiamen and asked his nationality. When he replied "Syrian," the militiamen gunned him down in the middle of the street, in front of everyone.

According to Tineke Uluf, a Dutch nurse who was on the Gaza Hospital staff, the surviving doctors and nurses were taken to the Phalangist outpost at the traffic rotary, where a militiaman gave them a lecture, saying, "We are not fascists or racists, but respect the Geneva conventions."

Then they were allowed to cross the street to the Israeli lines, where they were given food and water and released. Two of them were subsequently allowed to return to the hospital to help care for the patients still there.

Meanwhile, back in Shatila, the militiamen were busy separating Lebanese and Palestinians they had taken prisoner, with men forced to sit along one part of the main street, the women along another. It was about 7:30 A.M.

Sometime later that morning the women and children were all released, and most of the men were marched off toward a nearby stadium. At some point on the way to the sports stadium, the militiamen turned their captives over to the Israelis, then left. The Israelis asked the men to sit under a stadium tier, tended to the wounded and gave everyone food and water.

Whatever the Israelis knew about the massacre by Saturday morning, and however disturbed they were by the events, some of the Palestinians say the Israeli soldiers threatened to turn them over to the Phalangists if they did not cooperate.

The New York Times February 23, 1975
By Thomas l. Friedman, an Op-Ed columnist, who won the Pulitzer Prize in 1983
and 1988 for his coverage of Lebanon and Israel.

woman and child they could find — more than 300 people in all.

As word of the massacre reached Israel, and the idea that Israel's leaders had allowed it to occur gained currency, the nation's dislike of the Lebanon war turned quickly to revulsion. On Sept. 24, in the largest public demonstration in the nation's history, more than 400,000 Israelis turned out to protest the war.

The criticism took a toll on Begin, who appeared to grow more and more depressed and unhealthy. In August, 1983, he announced that he would resign.

The Likud Party's choice for Prime Minister, Yitzhak Shamir, took over a nation riven with unhappiness and dissent. The new leader offered no clear plan for pulling Israel out of Lebanon. Worse, the nation's economic condition had fallen from bad to wretched. Inflation stood at an annual rate of 400 percent.

Government officials began suggesting that the nation was no longer able to secure foreign loans. The stock market virtually collapsed, and the nation's foreign currency reserves fell to critical levels.

Shamir, a lackluster leader at best, failed to stem the rising panic. And in that atmosphere, the Labor Party managed to rally the votes in the Knesset to bring down the Likud-led Government. The new election was scheduled for July 23, 1984.

The Labor Party won enough seats that its leader, Shimon Peres, was asked to form a government, but he was unable to secure enough acceptable partners to form a majority coalition. After weeks of effort, he agreed to an unusual coalition with Likud. Peres would be Prime Minister for two years while Shamir served as Foreign Minister. Then after two years, halfway through the term, the two men would trade places.

Peres instituted harsh wage and price controls and managed in relatively short order to cut the inflation rate to about 20 percent. He also pulled the troops out of most of Lebanon. Israel declared a "security zone" in southern Lebanon, a strip along Israel's northern border that was generally less than 20 miles deep. Israeli troops, working with an allied Christian militia, patrolled the area with the intent of preventing artillery attacks and commando raids into Israel.

Youths unfurling the outlawed Palestinian flag during a clash with Israeli soldiers in the West Bank city of Nablus.

But the trouble came from another direction.

In December, 1986, in Ramallah, a West Bank town north of Jerusalem, a 16-year-old Palestinian schoolboy walked up behind an Israeli soldier, pulled an ax out of his blue schoolbag, started shouting something about Palestine and began striking the soldier on the head.

The soldier was taken to a hospital with severe cuts. The youth was taken to prison. All the army spokesmen would say about the young Palestinian was that he was acting on his "own initiative" — that is, no one had ordered or paid him to do it.

That scene had been repeated several times over the previous year: young Palestinians using kitchen knives or sharpened screwdrivers attacking Israeli soldiers or civilians in broad daylight.

ISRAEL REVIEWS MILITARY TACTICS; SEES NO END TO PALESTINIAN DEFIANCE

By JOEL BRINKLEY

JERUSALEM, September 28 — After 408 days, 6,000 arrests, at least 361 deaths and many thousands of injuries, the Palestinian uprising still rumbles steadily along, barely deterred by Israel's ever-changing tactics for suppressing it. But now for the first time, Israeli Army officers as well as other leading officials are acknowledging with frustration and despair that nothing they can do will end it.

The army battled a record number of violent incidents in the West Bank and Gaza Strip in the month ending January 9.

The period saw 2,790 such clashes between Palestinians and soldiers, 60 percent more than in the month before. The number of Palestinians killed was 26, a number equal to that recorded in the uprising's first violent days. The resistance has not flagged despite the recent Israeli decisions to use steel and rubber bullets that harm instead of merely sting, to increase the use of plastic bullets that can injure or kill, and to widen the judicial and monetary penalties against demonstrators.

Last week the Israeli press quoted army officers as saying privately that they could see no end to the violence, no matter what the army did. The officers predicted with more than a little gloom that the army will be fighting the Palestinians this time next year, and perhaps the year after that, unless a political solution is found. Despite an improved environment for negotiation — the Palestine Liberation Organization has shown evidence of a conciliatory attitude — in Israel, movement toward peace still seems a long way off. And so the uprising rolls along.

"There's no question here of damaging the foundation," Defense Minister Yitzhak Rabin told a Parliament committee in discussing the uprising. "If we arrest 4,000 people, we won't be rid of the problem because if there really is a command that you'll arrest, another will arise, and a third. This is a clash with a wide public."

The Defense Minister also admitted that two of Israel's weapons against Palestinians — deportation of accused troublemakers and the demolition of their homes — were no longer proving useful as deterrents.

Late last week, Deputy Chief of Staff Ehud Barak said, "We can gradually, over a long period of time, reduce the level of violence. But we shouldn't think in terms of days, weeks, months."

The New York Times September 29, 1989

The young Palestinians were members of the post-1967 generation, who had spent all their lives under Israeli rule in the occupied West Bank and Gaza Strip. In discussions with Palestinian high school and college students, only a few said they would ever think of attacking an Israeli with an ax. Still, many seemed to share the attackers' rage. These students no longer seemed to believe violence was serving as a means toward a particular political objective; most said they had simply given up hope for any solutions. They were angry and just couldn't hold it in any longer. And as 1987 came to a close, they lashed out en masse.

No one planned it, and when the violence began no one foresaw what it was to become. The spark came in the Gaza Strip on December 9, when a car full of Palestinians collided with an Israeli truck, and four Arabs died. Rumors spread that the collision was deliberate, a reprisal for the stabbing death of an Israeli in a Gaza market the week before.

A short time later, several angry teenagers in Gaza's Jabaliya refugee camp surrounded an Israeli Army patrol car and began showering it with rocks and gasoline bombs. The officer in charge of the patrol opened fire, killing a 17-year-old and wounding two others.

The incidents, by themselves, were not that unusual. But the reaction certainly was. Rioting spread, first across the Gaza Strip and then the West Bank, and within a day or two it seemed as if every Palestinian youth had taken to the streets and begun hurling rocks at soldiers. Confronted with violent protesters, Israeli soldiers fired back, usually with rubber bullets but sometimes with live ammunition. By the end of a week, at least eight Palestinians were dead.

Every day the rioting grew worse; the death toll mounted until finally both sides began to realize this was not just another of the occasional flare-ups but a revolt with staying power. Every new death created a martyr who energized his friends and fellow villagers. These young men would throw more stones at

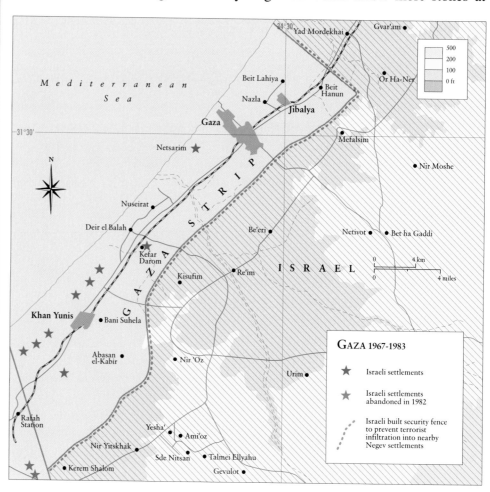

GAZA 1967-1983

★ Israeli settlements

⚝ Israeli settlements abandoned in 1982

Israeli built security fence to prevent terrorist infiltration into nearby Negev settlements

Palestinian couple waving to relatives in a prison camp near Gaza City.

A stone thrower being taken into custody in Nablus.

soldiers who would fire back, creating more martyrs.

"I will be killed fighting them, and my brother and my sister," one Palestinian youth said as he stood outside a martyr's home in the Bureij refugee camp in Gaza in the early weeks of the uprising. "We will struggle, as you see; we will struggle with stones and by killing ourselves."

Thousands of Israeli troops were deployed, and the new Israeli Defense Minister, Yitzhak Rabin, urged his soldiers to employ "force, might, beatings." Later he suggested they break bones. The army began rounding up Palestinians; by the first of January 1,000 were in custody. Most were sentenced to "administrative detention," six months in jail without formal charge or trial. The sentence could be renewed endlessly.

But the violence continued, and the rest of the Palestinian population of the territories joined the resistance to Israeli occupation. General strikes were declared. Palestinian businesses and schools closed. Arab workers refused to go to their jobs in Israel. The violence had become self-sustaining. By the spring of 1988, the Intifada, as the uprising was known in Arabic, had settled into a routine of daily strikes, protests and clashes that had led to the death of more than 150 Palestinians, along with deepening enmity on both sides.

In fact, the two sides had fought to a stalemate. Palestinian businesses were shuttered most of the time, and thousands of the community's leaders were dead or in Israeli prisons. On the days when West Bank villages weren't closed down because of general strikes called by the uprising's underground leadership, the Israeli military imposed curfews that kept everyone home.

In Israel, meanwhile, tourism had dropped to near zero, depriving the country of a critical source of income. The strikes severely hampered Israeli business

ETHIOPIAN JEWS AND ISRAELIS EXULT AS AIRLIFT IS COMPLETED

By JOEL BRINKLEY

LOD, Israel, May 25 — Israel fell into joyous celebration tonight as the Government announced the successful conclusion of an emergency airlift of 14,500 Ethiopian Jews, nearly the entire Jewish population, in just under 36 hours.

At the airport this morning, it was difficult as more joyful — the barefoot Ethiopians who cheered, ululated and bent down to kiss the tarmac as theto tell who wy stepped off the planes, or the Israelis who watched them aglow, marveling at this powerful image showing that their state still holds appeal, even with all its problems.

"We've stood up to our obligation and completed the operation bringing all the Jews," Prime Minister Yitzhak Shamir declared tonight. "It gives us a feeling of strength."

Israelis were no less wondrous at the operational accomplishment of ferrying so many people more than 1,500 miles in 40 flights over so short a time. The air force said 35 civilian and military airplanes, including one Ethiopian airliner, had been used in the operation.

At one point overnight, 28 aircraft were in the air at one time. All of the flights were crammed with passengers, often two or three people to a seat.

"We made history," said Aryeh Oz, who piloted one El Al 747 cargo plane. "It's the first time that any 747 or any air flying vehicle in the world ever carried 1,087 people. I don't think it will happen again."

"It was a very nice flight," said one of the smiling immigrants, 29-year-old Mukat Abag. "We didn't bring any of our clothes, we didn't bring any of our things, but we are very glad to be here."

A crew of doctors and paramedics was on each flight, expecting many of the immigrants to be sickly. A few were, and 140 people were taken from the airfield to hospitals. But the more common problem was pregnant women. Five babies were born aboard the planes.

The airlift proceeded through the night according to a complex schedule involving thousands of people in Israel and Ethiopia, the three dozen aircraft, and more than 400 buses at both ends.

The New York Times May 26, 1991

and industry.

And Israeli society grew ever more polarized. The uprising had driven about half of Israelis to believe even more fervently that Israel should just give up the West Bank and Gaza Strip and be rid of the Palestinian problem once and for all. The other half held that Israel should take even harsher measures to end the violence so Israel could keep the territories forever.

Caught in the middle were tens of thousands of Israeli soldiers, young draftees and middle-aged reservists who were sent to the West Bank or Gaza for several weeks at a time and asked to keep order. Hundreds were wounded in the first six months and several were killed. Few of them liked fighting the intifada. And when their service in the occupied territories was over, some were changed men.

"I don't see myself fighting against little children," Lieut. Uzyah Linder, 21, volunteered one summer afternoon. "I don't think it's my job. It's not what I was trained to do, and I don't feel proud. But I have no choice."

Lieutenant Linder said that the last time he was sent out on patrol, two weeks earlier, the army gave him a "cold weapon" — a wooden club. At times, he said, he found himself with little choice but to beat Palestinians not much more than half his age.

"When you identify a kid throwing rocks at you, or using a slingshot — and they're good at it — sometimes you have to apply force to catch them," he said. "I don't remember fighting 8- or 9-year-olds myself, but it's not uncommon."

One afternoon a few weeks later, Maj. Gen. Amram Mitzna, the senior military commander in the West Bank, visited the elite Golani infantry brigade camped near Nablus. General Mitzna stood before 100 Golani troops, who sat in semicircles on the ground, purple berets angled precisely on every head.

"Those of you who have served in the territories before, do you see any difference from the last time?" the general asked the paratroopers.

A young soldier, maybe 19, rose to his feet. "They're more united now," he said. "Every visit we are stoned and see Palestinian flags. One of them stood right in front of my rifle and didn't move. He wasn't afraid. They know our orders now. They know when we can shoot and when we can't. They're much more sophisticated now."

Another soldier stood up. "We prefer to be up in Lebanon," he said, "to be infantry as we are trained, not policemen here. The question is: Do we really need to take down every flag and wipe out all the graffiti? Do we really need to be here?"

For all the violence, the uprising was not the only issue occupying the attention of the nation. The Soviet Union, then in its death throes, began allowing Jews to emigrate, and many were choosing to move to Israel. They came by the tens of thousands, straining Israel's ability to receive them. But for a people criticized around the world for their handling of the Palestinian uprising, it was heartening for Israelis to see that somebody liked them.

By the summer of 1990, the uprising had been underway for two and one-half years and showed no signs of abating. At least 725 Palestinians had been killed, as well as 47 Jews.

In the midst of all this violence came signs that the situation was changing. The army reported that Yasir Arafat's faction of the P.L.O. had not carried out any terrorist attacks in months. A few months later, an internal intelligence report prepared for the Cabinet concluded that the only way to end the intifada was to open negotiations with the P.L.O. But Likud Party leaders angrily disputed both findings, and Shamir insisted he had no intention of talking to the P.L.O.

The emergency airlift known as Operation Solomon, brought 14,500 Ethiopian Jews to Israel in 1991. Identifacation numbers helped prevent the families from being separated.

A planeload of refugees arriving at Ben-Gurion Airport from Moscow in 1990. The collapse of the Soviet Union opened the floodgates of emigration for Russian Jewry.

Children in Tel Aviv awaiting the all-clear siren during a late night Iraqi Scud missile attack in January, 1991.

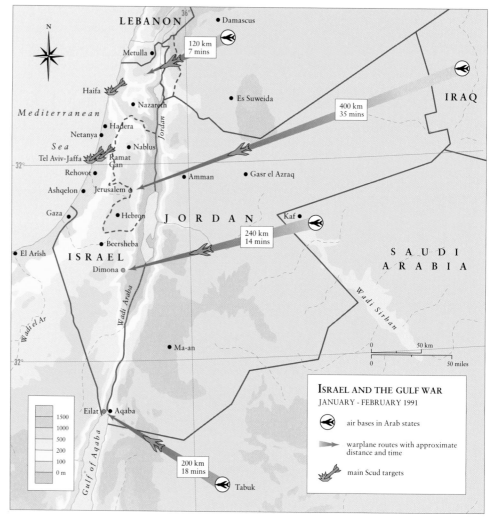

ISRAEL AND THE GULF WAR
JANUARY - FEBRUARY 1991

air bases in Arab states

warplane routes with approximate distance and time

main Scud targets

So the intifada raged on, so entrenched that only some outside force could change it. August, 1990, was the moment: Iraq invaded Kuwait, and the Palestinians were taken up by a new fervor: Almost alone in the world, they became passionate defenders of Saddam Hussein because of his outspoken support for their cause. Most of the rest of the Arab world joined the American-led coalition against Iraq.

In the occupied territories, the violence declined as Israelis and Palestinians watched the American and allied forces preparing to retake Kuwait. Each side prayed for opposite outcomes. Through the fall, Hussein hurled threat and vitriol at Israel, vowing to attack Israel if the United States attacked Iraq. And when the American-led air strikes against Iraq began in January, 1991, Hussein followed through, firing volleys of Scud missiles at the Jewish state.

The attacks were terrifying, but the damage was minor and deaths and injuries were few. Israel vowed to retaliate, but Washington urged restraint, saying Israeli attacks would cause problems for the delicate Arab-Western coalition assembled against Iraq. Israel reluctantly agreed, and as the Persian Gulf War ended Israel's political stock was at a record high, while the Palestinians' support for Saddam Hussein had cost them much of the sympathy and good will they had gathered. Crucially, Saudi Arabia, Iraq's leading Arab foe, cut off all contributions to the P.L.O., and Arafat's coffers soon were empty.

With this new political dynamic, the American Secretary of State, James A. Baker III, began an urgent round of negotiations, trying to arrange a regional peace conference between Israel and the Arab states. Shamir resisted, but the pressure from Washington was intense. And no matter how the negotiations turned out, Israelis could see that the status quo had already changed.

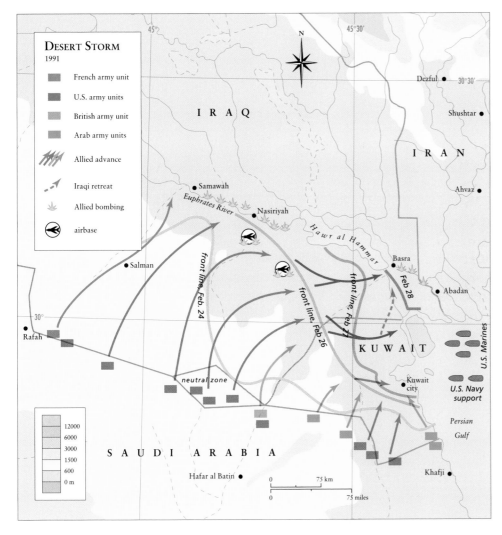

Chapter Seven: Breakthrough

Clyde Haberman

Palestinians hoisting their national flag on the walls of the Old City during a jubilant celebration of the Israeli-Palestinian peace accord in September, 1993.

By MID-1991, with the Persian Gulf war over and the Soviet Union gasping its last breath, the stage was set for Israel's first serious peace negotiations with the Arabs since its treaty with Egypt in 1979. First, the United States had to get deeply involved, because on their own the old enemies were not about sit down together. But in the fall of 1991 a peace conference finally got under way in Madrid, a turning point for Middle Eastern politics.

For President George Bush, the talks were an integral part of his agenda for a "new world order," and in those early days of the post-cold war era Washington usually got its way. Even a traditionally rejectionist Arab state like Syria felt, with its Soviet patron suddenly gone, that it could no longer resist the pressure. Where Syria led, its client government in Lebanon swiftly followed. As for Jordan, King Hussein had been meeting secretly with Israeli leaders for decades, so for him going public was no great leap.

That left the Palestinians, and on the Arab side no party went through a more wrenching change.

The political leadership, in the form of the Tunis-based P.L.O., was in tatters. Yasir Arafat's disastrous support of Saddam Hussein had pushed his organization to the brink of political oblivion, both in the Arab world and beyond. Palestinians in the occupied West Bank and Gaza Strip, people who knew Israel intimately, had grown weary of one failure after another in their struggle for independence. They wanted as much of a say in their own future as faraway P.L.O. bureaucrats, widely seen as incompetent and corrupt. It was clear that a new strategy was needed, for the intifada had run its course, producing by this point little more than ritualistic — and meaningless — street battles between Israeli soldiers and rock-throwing Arab youths.

Changes came in substance and style.

Not that the Palestinians abandoned their goal of an independent state, to be carved out of lands held by Israel since 1967, including East Jerusalem. But moderate forces holding sway in the territories — and, for that matter, in Tunis — had finally come to accept reality: Israel was here to stay, like it or not. It was useless to cling to the worn idea that anything short of immediate statehood amounted to a sellout. Palestinian autonomy in the West Bank and Gaza, within the framework of overall Israeli control, had become an acceptable first step.

The Palestinian image also underwent a transformation.

That is not to say that anti-Israel terrorism stopped. Indeed, before long Islamic extremists would give it a new terrifying face, in the form of suicide bombings that killed and maimed dozens of Israelis at a time. But the political face presented to the world after the Gulf War was no longer the scraggly beard and checkered kaffiyeh of Yasir Arafat. For peace talks with Israel, they selected delegates who went forth in suits, presenting themselves as the middle-class, Western-educated elite that in fact many were.

All this caught Prime Minister Yitzhak Shamir of Israel off guard. He and his Likud Party still took an absolutist hard line against territorial compromise, viewing virtually all Arabs as implacably hostile and Arafat as a terrorist outlaw. Lands captured in the 1967 war were Israel's forever, Shamir declared. To make that point abundantly clear, his government rapidly expanded Jewish settlements in the West Bank and Gaza, the Prime Minister defiantly vowing to build to "the horizon's edge."

There was also no love lost between Shamir and Bush.

The Israeli leader felt betrayed by the Americans. He had helped keep the anti-Saddam coalition together by sitting out the Gulf War and not striking back after Iraq fired Scud missiles at Israel's cities. But instead of agreeing that he owed Shamir a favor, Bush was pressing for a peace conference that the Israeli feared could put his country's survival at risk.

Then there was a matter of money. Some might call it blackmail.

With hundreds of thousands of immigrants pouring in from the former Soviet Union, stretching public finances thin, Israel wanted to borrow up to $10 billion for housing and other projects. Washington had promised it would cover any losses in the unlikely event of an Israeli default. But suddenly, the Bush Administration announced that these loan guarantees would not be forthcoming, after all.

ISRAEL AND ARABS, FACE TO FACE, IN QUEST FOR PEACE

By THOMAS L. FRIEDMAN

MADRID, October 30 — For the first time, Israel and all the Arab nations around it sat down face-to-face here today for peace talks aimed at settling their outstanding disputes and finding a way for Israelis and Palestinians to share the homeland they both claim as their own.

Representatives from Israel, Jordan, Syria, Lebanon and the Palestinians took their seats around a T-shaped meeting table in the Hall of Columns at Spain's Royal Palace. They had been invited there by the co-sponsors of the Middle East conference, President George Bush and President Mikhail S. Gorbachev of the Soviet Union, who gave the opening addresses.

The chief Arab and Israeli delegates to the conference were not scheduled to present their opening bargaining positions until Thursday, and today they spoke to one another only in body language and with their eyes. Sitting around the table, they exchanged furtive glances and blank stares as they listened to Mr. Bush and Mr. Gorbachev.

The awkwardness of these first encounters between adversaries who have never shared a formal conference table underscored both how far they have come and how far they must go before they approach anything resembling real peace. Nevertheless, after eight months of cajoling and arm-twisting by the United States, all were finally there.

"That old taboo that Arabs and Israelis cannot meet and cannot talk is now something that we want to relegate to history," Secretary of State James A. Baker 3d, the conference's architect, said afterward. "The road to peace will be very long and it will be very difficult. We have to crawl before we walk and we have to walk before we run, and today I think we all began to crawl."

President Bush used his opening speech to tell the Israelis that "territorial compromise is essential for peace," meaning that Israel will have to cede at least some of the territories it still holds as a result of the 1967 Mideast war — the West Bank, the Gaza Strip, the Golan Heights and East Jerusalem.

The New York Times October 31, 1991

Above: *The mood of the Madrid peace conference is captured on the faces of Dr. Haider Abdel-Shafi, the chief Palestinian delegate, and* **right,** *Israeli Prime Minister Yitzhak Shamir.*

A new Jewish settlement near the Arab town of Ramallah in the West Bank awaiting its occupants in July, 1992.

Under intense pressure, Shamir had no choice but to say yes to negotiations. But he extracted important concessions on the makeup of the Palestinian peace team. It had to be part of a joint delegation with Jordan, and no member could come from Jerusalem or be openly identified with the P.L.O., an organization then banned under Israeli law. The Palestinians were not happy with the restrictions, but they were hardly dealing from strength themselves.

On October 30, 1991, a peace conference opened in an 18th-century hall in Madrid, beneath glittering chandeliers and Renaissance tapestries. Shamir sat at a long table with representatives of Syria, Lebanon, Jordan and the Palestinians. The notion — always a fiction — that Tunis had no representation was quickly dispelled by Dr. Haider Abdel-Shafi, the chief Palestinian delegate, who invoked Arafat's name and mentioned "our acknowledged leadership": the P.L.O. Even though he had threatened to walk out if words like that were uttered, Shamir kept his seat.

Over all, the mood of the conference was bad and the oratory intransigent. As they had for decades, Arabs and Israelis accused each other of treachery and aggression. Though the peace talks would continue after Madrid, for the most part in Washington, they were not going anywhere. That stalemate suited Shamir fine. Later, an Israeli journalist would quote him as saying that he would have kept talking and talking for 10 years, all the while expanding settlements in the territories.

But if he was satisfied with the status quo, many of his fellow citizens were not. His uncompromising right-wing ideology had begun to frustrate them. Likud's rejection of any "land for peace" formula rang hollow. To a growing number of Israelis, it was clear that without territorial compromise there would be no peace.

On many fronts, the country was changing rapidly. The outside world had begun to look less hostile, even if the Prime Minister didn't think so. Dozens of countries, including Russia, lined up to establish diplomatic relations or to renew ties that were severed after 1967. Immigrants from former Soviet republics kept on coming. True, finding apartments and jobs for them was a headache. But Israelis were pleased to see that their country had become attractive to outsiders — and increasingly prosperous, too, with a per-capita income that reached the levels of southern Europe. Another sign of change was the introduction of cable television in the early 1990s, an important development for a country that had had no television at all until 1968 and then had made do with a single state-run network. For the first time, the world came into Israeli homes beyond the reach of military censors and a government that usually took a "father knows best" attitude toward its citizens.

Israelis were ready to live in "a normal country" and not stand forever on the parapet, rifles locked and loaded. But normality required less ideology and more pragmatism in relations with the Arabs. That essential step became possible in February, 1992, when Yitzhak Rabin defeated his archrival, Shimon Peres, to regain the leadership of the opposition Labor Party.

Peres was a proven loser at the polls, and Labor's rank and file had had enough. Rabin, at 70, was not entirely a blessing himself. His three years as Prime Minister in the 1970s were undistinguished and ended in his forced resignation in 1977 under a cloud of scandal. But Rabin was a respected former general, army chief in the Six-Day War. While ready for compromise with the Palestinians (to what extent was not made clear), he was no starry-eyed dove. Many voters were confident he would not give away the store, and that made him the choice of those who were tired of Likud and wanted peace, but a peace that did not undermine national security.

Labor's strategy for the June, 1992, general election was to emphasize the candidate over the party, an American style of campaigning then alien to Israel's collectivist politics. The tactic worked. Rabin won, taking office in July with an appeal to the country to stop thinking that "the whole world is against us." The new Prime Minister, until then the only native-born Israeli to hold that office, could not have set himself apart from the European-born Shamir more starkly. Shamir, whose family was wiped out in the Holocaust, viewed the world as anti-Semitic to its core. But Rabin declared, "We must overcome the sense of isolation that has held us in its thrall for almost half a century."

More substantive change soon came when the new government put a brake on rampant settlement-building in the territories. Not that the settlers' numbers stopped growing; birth rates were too high for that. Besides, even Rabin believed that West Bank communities near Jerusalem should be strengthened

A watchful mother in the West Bank settlement of Shiloh.

NOW IS THE MOMENT TO ACHIEVE PEACE, RABIN TELLS ARABS

By CLYDE HABERMAN

JERUSALEM, July 13 — Yitzhak Rabin took over as Israel's Prime Minister tonight, pledging to waste no time in the search for Middle East peace and appealing to Palestinians to take Israeli offers of limited self-rule seriously and not "lose this opportunity that may never return."

The need for bold, swift strides toward peace—including a proposed exchange of visits with Arab leaders—formed the core of Mr. Rabin's message to the new Parliament hours before it approved his Government, the first one in 15 years to be dominated by the Labor Party.

Mr. Rabin's inaugural speech, studded with biblical and poetic allusions, included no specifics on Palestinian self-rule and no concessions on the status of Jerusalem or the Golan Heights.

But it was more than an outline for peace. It was also a declaration that Israel had changed direction after 15 years of right-wing governance under the Likud Party, a clarion call to the country to stop thinking that "the whole world is against us."

"We must overcome the sense of isolation that has held us in its thrall for almost half a century," he said. "We must join the international movement toward peace, reconciliation and cooperation that is spreading over the entire globe these days, lest we be the last to remain, all alone, in the station."

With his remarks, Mr. Rabin offered himself as a pragmatic counterpoint to his Likud predecessor, Yitzhak Shamir, who left the office he had held for most of the last decade fiercely holding forth Israel as a special case among nations.

To underline his appeal for Middle East reconciliation, Mr. Rabin invited Palestinian leaders and heads of neighboring Arab countries to Jerusalem "for the purpose of talking peace" and said he was prepared to go immediately to Amman, Damascus and Beirut.

The New York Times July 14, 1992

and ultimately retained as part of Israel. But the days of approving brand-new settlements and of offering tax breaks and low-interest mortgages to encourage Israelis to move into them were over.

All that, however, did not end the mistrust between Israel and the Arabs. The so-called Madrid talks slogged on, but the negotiators were spinning their wheels. If anything, the climate was badly deteriorating as 1992 drew to a close.

One December morning, an Israeli border guard was kidnapped on his way to work by terrorists from the militant Islamic group Hamas. His body was found a few days later on a West Bank hillside. With his country in a rage and his image as a no-nonsense security man on the line, Rabin felt he had to act decisively. He ordered that more than 400 Hamas members and sympathizers be rounded up and taken to the border with Lebanon, where they were unceremoniously dumped. It was an audacious maneuver. Never before had mass deportations taken place on that scale.

As expected, Israel was roundly condemned, including by the United Nations. Palestinians were outraged, and their P.L.O.–backed delegates boycotted the peace talks. Some of this was political posturing; the P.L.O. didn't like Hamas any more than did Israel. But the deportations hit an ultra-sensitive nerve among Palestinians, who had always regarded forced evacuation from their homes and lands as the worst fate that could befall them. The international pressure on Rabin to relent was intense. Finally, he agreed to shorten the exile period for the Hamas deportees, who had set up camp in a desolate strip of southern Lebanon between Israeli and Lebanese army lines.

More than 400 Hamas members and sympathizers were deported to southern Lebanon in the winter of 1992. Bowing to international pressure, Israel allowed half of the deportees to return home nine months later.

By then, all parties were trapped in yet a new cycle of violence. March, 1993, was horrific. Fifteen Israelis were killed in a wave of Palestinian knifings. Finally, Rabin had had enough. He ordered that Palestinians be confined to the

West Bank and Gaza Strip, an action that prevented 120,000 laborers from reaching jobs in Israel.

Most Israelis were happy simply not to have all those Arabs around, even if it meant that construction work in their cities slowed to a crawl. But for Palestinians, being cooped up in their own territories was economically devastating. After a few days without work, many had trouble feeding their large families. Perhaps worse, this territorial closing, while not the first, was clearly not going to be a temporary expedient. It lasted for months, and it would be reimposed again and again, after every major act of Palestinian terrorism. The barricades would always be lifted eventually. But each time, a shrinking number of Palestinians was let back into Israel to work. Across Gaza and the West Bank, poverty widened, while faith in the peace process narrowed. It was an example of how the two sides looked at the world with different eyes. Where Israelis saw a necessary security measure, Palestinians saw collective punishment.

The gloom could not have been thicker. But unknown to all but a handful of people, a back-channel dialogue had begun between the Rabin Government and the P.L.O. Conducted largely in Norway, it led to what would become known as the Oslo accords.

The Oslo agreement, formally called the "declaration of principles," was beyond question the biggest step forward ever taken by these bitter enemies. At last, they recognized each other's legitimacy, and accepted that the only way out of their long struggle to the death was to share the postage-stamp-sized land that both called home.

Oslo rewrote history. It sealed the Arabs' recognition of Israel's rightful place in the Middle East, more even than the peace treaty with Egypt had. The P.L.O. had unequivocally acknowledged Israel's right to exist, effectively getting the coffin ready for its 1964 covenant, which called for armed struggle to "destroy

A homeless Palestinian family living in a Gaza cemetery in 1993. Closing the West Bank and the Gaza Strip in response to terrorist acts was economically devastating for the many Palestinians who had jobs in Israel.

RABIN, ARAFAT SEAL ACCORD AS CLINTON HAILS 'BRAVE GAMBLE'

By THOMAS L. FRIEDMAN

WASHINGTON, September 13 — In a triumph of hope over history, Yitzhak Rabin, the Prime Minister of Israel, and Yasir Arafat, the Chairman of the P.L.O., shook hands today on the White House lawn, sealing the first agreement between Jews and Palestinians to end their conflict and share the holy land along the River Jordan that they both call home.

At 11:43 A.M. on the sun-splashed South Lawn of the White House, Foreign Minister Shimon Peres of Israel and Mahmoud Abbas, the foreign policy aide for the Palestine Liberation Organization, signed a Declaration of Principles on Palestinian self-government in Israeli-occupied Gaza and the West Bank. Three thousand witnesses watched in amazement, including former Presidents Jimmy Carter and George Bush.

Mr. Rabin, whose face is etched with the memories of every Arab-Israeli war, captured in his remarks the exhaustion of all parties with the centuries-old conflict.

"We the soldiers who have returned from the battle stained with blood," he said, "we who have fought against you, the Palestinians, we say to you today in a loud and clear voice: "Enough of blood and tears! Enough!"

Mr. Arafat, relishing his moment of acceptance on the White House lawn, strove to give Mr. Rabin the appropriate response, declaring in Arabic: "Our two peoples are awaiting today this historic hope, and they want to give peace a real chance."

And President Bill Clinton, who gracefully shepherded Mr. Arafat and Mr. Rabin through their awkward moment of public reconciliation, hailed them both for their "brave gamble that the future can be better than the past."

The agreement, which will eventually allow Palestinians to run their own affairs as Israeli troops pull back within months from the Gaza Strip and Jericho in a first step, was reached during secret negotiations over the past few months between Israelis and Palestinians under the direction of Mr. Peres and Mr. Abbas, through the mediation of Norway.

The New York Times September 14, 1994

the Zionist and imperialist presence." And by recognizing the P.L.O., Israel had come to terms with a despised Arab leader, Arafat, whose name many Jews uttered in the same breath as Hitler's.

Oslo did not come about in a political vacuum, of course. Each side had its own compelling practical reasons for the secret talks, which began in early 1993 and went on for months.

The P.L.O. could no longer escape its disarray. Deprived of Saudi assistance in retaliation for its support of Iraq in the Gulf War, it saw its once-fat bank accounts were drying up, and Arafat's loyalists were losing ground to the Hamas Islamicists. He needed a deal with Israel to reaffirm his primacy.

The Rabin government was also ready, particularly the dovish wing led by Shimon Peres, now the Foreign Minister. At first, Rabin was skeptical, but he came around. Like Arafat, he had given up on the Madrid talks rules as a waste of time. He knew that history would judge him by what he did on the peace front, and Palestinians from the territories could not deliver the goods.

Norway may have seemed an unlikely catalyst. But Norwegian social scientists and Government officials had solid contacts among the Palestinians, in particular a group of academics who had done extensive research on social conditions in the territories. After the 1992 elections, some of them approached Yossi Beilin, the new Deputy Foreign Minister and a Peres disciple, and offered themselves as a bridge between Israel and the P.L.O.

The contacts began tentatively, through Israeli academics and through a senior P.L.O. figure, Ahmed Suleiman Khoury, better known as Abu Alaa. To Israelis, Abu Alaa was an acceptable partner. Unlike so many in the P.L.O., he had "no blood on his hands," meaning he not taken an active part in anti-Israel terrorism campaigns.

Gradually, as 1993 wore on, the contacts blossomed into full-blown government negotiations, some held on isolated Norwegian royal estates many miles from Oslo. Forced to live together for days at a stretch, the Palestinians and Israelis got to know and to respect one another, so much so that when tension rose they could defuse it with a joke. Terje Larsen, a key Norwegian intermediary, later described it this way: "It was an informal relationship: intense, complex, characterized by passionate and silent poetry."

Still, shared jokes and meals could not eliminate obstacles by themselves. Suspicions were not about to melt miraculously in front of a Norwegian fireplace. The talks dragged on through 14 sessions, from winter through spring and into summer, with ups and downs all the way and success never assured. But in late August, 1993, enough compromises had been made for a breakthrough.

The key element was that Israel would withdraw for the first time from Palestinian territories, starting with the Gaza Strip and tiny Jericho in the West Bank. In truth, most Israelis were sick of patroling Gaza anyway, of risking their soldier children's lives in squalid refugee camps seething with hate. But for Arafat, Gaza alone was not reward enough. He needed a West Bank foothold as well, to show Palestinians that they were truly on the road to their hoped-for state. The compromise: Jericho, which was relatively isolated and not a hotbed of anti-Israel fervor.

The deal called for Gaza and Jericho to be followed by further pullbacks by Israel's forces. Saved for last, but to be resolved no later than five years down the road, were the toughest issues of all: Jerusalem's political status, the fate of Israeli settlers, demands for the repatriation of Palestinian refugees who had gone abroad and, not least, the final status of the territories. Do they become an independent state or something else, perhaps part of a federation with Jordan?

Oslo's underlying philosophy was to put off explosive issues, like Jerusalem's future, that would lead immediately to a dead end. The idea was to do the possible first. Build trust, no small measure being Arafat's commitment to have the P.L.O. renounce sections of its charter that called for Israel's destruction. Only after mutual confidence had taken root could Israelis and Palestinians move to the next stage. Oslo's strength was its deliberate vagueness on many essential points. Unfortunately, as would become obvious later, the lack of specifics also was its weakness.

But in the dizzying summer of 1993, the "declaration of principles" took the world's breath away. Astonishingly, Israel and the Palestinians had allowed hope to triumph over their blood-soaked past. A year later, the three main political architects — Rabin, Arafat and Peres — would be rewarded with the Nobel Peace Prize.

The agreement was sealed at the White House on September 13, 1993. Though Israel and the P.L.O. had done this deal on their own, they still wanted, and needed, Washington's stamp of approval. Nothing better symbolized the new world they had bravely entered than a stunning moment when Rabin and Arafat, with President Clinton at their side, literally reached across history to clasp each other's hand.

It was an anguished act of symbolism for the Israeli leader, whose body English left no doubt that he still detested this longtime enemy. In an interview with a *New York Times* reporter only hours before, Rabin acknowledged that the prospect of that handshake made him retch. But he did it, with a ringing call for an end to the conflict, once and for all: "Enough of blood and tears! Enough!"

Indeed, during what would tragically turn out to be the last two years of his life, Rabin grew increasingly comfortable using the language of Israel's doves, declaring with deepening conviction that Jews were not meant to control occupy another people against its will.

There were still those details to be hammered out, though. What would security provisions be for Israeli settlers remaining in Gaza and near Jericho? Who would be in charge of the Allenby Bridge crossing from Jericho to Jordan? How

From left, Russian Foreign Minister Andrei Kozyrev, Israeli Prime Minister Yitzak Rabin, President Clinton, P.L.O. Chairman Yasir Arafat, and U.S. Secretary of State Warren Christopher, at the signing of Israeli-Palestinian peace agreement in September, 1993.

would a Gaza-to-Jericho "corridor" through Israel actually work? Coming up with solutions would take months, usually at a cost to the trust that the two sides strove so hard to build.

But on May 4, 1994, in Cairo, they came to terms. True to form, Arafat staged some last-minute theatrics during the signing ceremony in an attempt to squeeze one more concession from the Israelis. It didn't work, though, and at last the agreement was signed. A week later, hundreds of P.L.O. soldiers, now called police officers, rode into Gaza and Jericho from staging areas in Egypt and Jordan. They thrust automatic rifles skyward in triumph. Huge crowds cheered

Residents of Jericho celebrating the arrival of the Palestinian police force and autonomy from Israel in May, 1994.

King Hussein and Yitzak Rabin after signing the Israeli-Jordanian peace treaty in October, 1994, ending 46 years of war.

as Israeli flags came down at army compounds and police stations for the first time in 27 years, replaced by the green, red, black and white colors of Palestinian nationalism.

And those celebrations were but a prelude to an extraordinary event that would have been dismissed as a fantasy of world politics less than a year earlier.

On July 1, in a whirl of dust and excitement, Yasir Arafat roared into the Gaza Strip from the Sinai Peninsula, his first return to the land of his birth in three decades. With tears in his eyes, he knelt and kissed the ground, then went on to address thousands before getting down to business as chairman of the new Palestinian Authority. His speech was remarkable not for its content (indeed, it was humdrum and the crowd began to drift away well before he finished his remarks) but for the remarkable fact that he got to deliver it in the first place.

In those days, the Middle East's capacity for hopeful surprises seemed limitless. Almost obscured by the Israeli-Palestinian drama was the way Oslo opened the door for Israel to complete a treaty with Jordan. King Hussein was far too cautious to strike a deal on his own unless Arafat went first. But Oslo freed him to bring his own secret talks out into the open, to the glee of most Israelis, who genuinely liked him. In October, 1994, with Clinton once again on hand, the King and Rabin signed a peace treaty — Israel's second with an Arab country — on a patch of desert along their border that was newly cleared of land mines.

Those were heady times for Israel. Morocco and Tunisia established economic relations. Qatar discussed a possible natural-gas deal. Private capital flowed in from overseas. Israeli officials visited Oman. Even Syria resumed peace negotiations, and while those talks would prove to be more shadow than substance, they contributed to a sense that anything was possible in this new Middle East.

The problem was that powerful specters of the old Middle East remained, hate-filled and well-armed. In 1994, rejectionists among both Israelis and Palestinians launched a wave of unparalleled terrorism that claimed scores upon scores of lives, shaking the peace process to its core. In almost no time, optimism turned to despair.

Improbable though it was for most Israelis, the first shocking blow was delivered not by an Arab but a Jew. It came in Hebron, a West Bank city that is sacred to Muslims and Jews alike but that is also steeped in hatred, a place where the Israeli-Palestinian conflict has had some of its darkest moments.

Jews and Muslims revere Hebron as the resting place of biblical patriarchs and matriarchs, most of all Abraham, the father of both religions. Hebron has extra meaning for Jews because it was King David's capital for seven years, until he moved to Jerusalem. At the heart of the struggle over Hebron is the Cave of the Patriarchs, where Abraham is believed to be buried and above which sits an imposing stone shrine known for centuries by Muslims as the Ibrahimi

JEWISH SETTLER FIRES INTO HEBRON MOSQUE; RABIN DENOUNCES 'MURDER'

By CLYDE HABERMAN

JERUSALEM, February 25 — On the bloodiest day in the occupied territories since Israel captured them in 1967, a Jewish settler killed 29 and wounded an estimated 125 others today, spraying them with automatic rifle fire as they knelt together in prayer at a shrine venerated by both Muslims and Jews.

The gunman, Dr. Baruch Goldstein, a 37-year-old resident of Kiryat Arba, opened fire on the Muslim worshipers at dawn in a mosque at the Cave of the Patriarchs in the tinderbox West Bank city of Hebron. The terrorist attack came as the victims were gathered to offer prayers as part of Ramadan, the Muslim holy month of fasting.

The Brooklyn-born settler, a follower of the anti-Arab Rabbi Meir Kahane, was apparently beaten to death by the worshipers after they overcame their initial terror.

It remained unclear tonight whether the settler was motivated by revenge for recent attacks against Jews in the territories, or whether the massacre was an act of calculated political terrorism aimed at provoking confrontations that would cause the peace accord to unravel. The Israeli-Palestinian agreement calls for a gradual transition to Palestinian self-rule in the occupied West Bank and Gaza Strip.

The massacre sent shock waves through the Middle East and beyond, raising fears for the Israeli-Palestinian peace accord and prompting President Clinton to summon both sides to Washington for nonstop negotiations aimed at keeping the peace effort alive.

The chairman of the P.L.O., Yasir Arafat, described the killings as a "true blow to the peace process."

A spokesman for Prime Minister Yitzhak Rabin said that the Prime Minister denounced the massacre as "a loathsome, criminal act of murder" and telephoned Mr. Arafat and told him that he was "ashamed as an Israeli."

The New York Times February 26, 1994

A victim of the Hebron massacre is rushed to the hospital.

AT LEAST 20 KILLED IN TERRORIST BOMBING OF BUS IN TEL AVIV

By CLYDE HABERMAN

TEL AVIV, October 19 — A powerful bomb tore apart a crowded bus in the heart of Tel Aviv city today, killing at least 20 people and wounding 48 others in one of the deadliest terrorist attacks in Israeli history.

Believed by Israeli officials to have been carried by a Palestinian Islamic extremist on a suicide mission, the bomb packed such force that it sent people flying through the air, ripped bodies to pieces and reduced the bus to a charred, barely recognizable shell. Initial reports said that 22 people were killed in the blast, but medical officials later scaled the death toll back to 20, The Associated Press reported.

"We saw a horrible picture," said a man who was standing on Dizengoff Street, Tel Aviv's equivalent to New York's Broadway, when the explosion occurred during the morning rush hour. "The bus seemed to be lifted into the air. The roof flew. The place looked like a battlefield."

Responsibility for the attack was taken by Islamic militants from the Hamas organization, and Prime Minister Yitzhak Rabin vowed angrily tonight to crack down on the group and "wage a battle to the bitter end." Mr. Rabin did not spell out what actions he had in mind, saying he would raise them with his Cabinet ministers at an emergency meeting on Thursday, but he suggested that some proposals would bring objections from civil-rights advocates.

"I think that ways need to be found for Hamas suicide attackers to know that not only they may be killed by their actions but that their homes and the homes of their families may be damaged," he said in a television interview held a few hours after he had cut short a visit to Britain and returned to Israel.

He also raised the possibility of arrests for long periods without formal charges, a procedure known as administrative detention.

"We, the executive arm, must be allowed by the legislative arm to use the tools that will enable us to combat terrorism of such a radical nature," the Prime Minister said, "They are not in our hands today."

The New York Times October 20, 1994

Above:*Victims of a Palestinian suicide bomber are removed from the wreckage of a bus in Tel Aviv.*

Mosque.

In 1929, egged on by the mufti of Jerusalem, Arabs in Hebron rampaged against the small Jewish community there, massacring 67 people, razing synagogues and burning Torah scrolls. That was what people usually meant when they talked about "the Hebron massacre," until February 25, 1994, when Arabs got their own martyrs to intolerance.

Early that morning, a fanatical West Bank settler who was originally from Brooklyn, Dr. Baruch Goldstein, walked into the Ibrahimi Mosque — fully armed, dressed in his army uniform and unchallenged by Israeli soldiers on guard duty. As Palestinians knelt in prayer, Goldstein opened fire. Within moments, he got off enough shots to kill 29 people and wound dozens of others before he himself was killed.

Later, Israelis dismissed this settler as a madman. Some argued that it would be unfair to compare his isolated act to the anti-Jewish marauding by large numbers of Arabs in 1929. Nonetheless, most Israelis felt deep shame over this new massacre, including Rabin, who stood before Parliament and declared settlers bent on murder to be outcasts, "a shame on Zionism and an embarrassment to Judaism."

One could say, however, that Goldstein ended up killing not only Arabs but also many Jews.

Freed by the Hebron massacre from even the semblance of restraint, Hamas and another militant group, Islamic Jihad, declared war on Israeli civilians. In April, suicide bombers killed 13 people in the northern towns of Afula and Hadera. In October, Palestinian gunmen opened fire on a popular pedestrian street in the heart of Jerusalem, an area called Nahalat Shiva. That same month, the country was enraged when a young Israeli soldier who also had American citizenship, Nachshon Wachsman, was kidnapped by Hamas loyalists masquerading as Orthodox Jews. As the kidnapping saga unfolded over several days, a mesmerized and horrified world watched anxiously. It ended badly, with Wachsman killed in a botched Israeli rescue mission — on the very day it was announced that Rabin, Peres and Arafat had won the Nobel prize.

Bad quickly went to worse. A suicide bomber killed 22 people on a Tel Aviv bus, also in October. Another 19 Israelis, almost all young soldiers, were blown

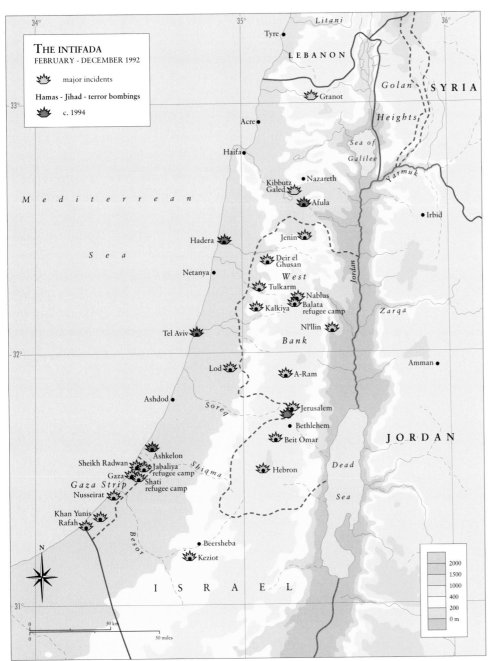

The Intifada
FEBRUARY - DECEMBER 1992

major incidents

Hamas - Jihad - terror bombings

c. 1994

The winners of the 1994 Nobel Peace Prize: Arafat, Peres and Rabin in Oslo.

apart in January, 1995, at a rural bus stop, this time by two suicide bombers. The carnage went on and on. Hamas seemed to have an inexhaustible supply of young recruits willing to kill themselves along with Jews for a promised place in paradise. Rabin vowed that the violence would not to stop the peace talks. But each explosion made that pledge harder to fulfill.

Again and again, Israel sealed off the West Bank and Gaza to keep Palestinians out of sight. But as before, that only deepened the poverty and frustration on Palestinian streets. In Gaza, the growing anger turned against Arafat, who was now being denounced by militants as Israel's stooge. Doubts that he would govern democratically were confirmed as he arrested political opponents and harrassed journalists. One devastating Friday in November, 1994, his security forces lost its discipline and opened fire on Palestinian street protestors, killing 10 and wounding many more.

The new year limped along without progress, and on both sides disillusioned people asked what had become of their peace dividend. Palestinians were worse off economically, and Israelis felt unsafe in their own cities. By mid-1995, Rabin acknowledged to a *New York Times* reporter that "everyone has got his doubts." But he insisted he would stay on course.

Chapter Eight: Hopes and Fears

Serge Schmemann

Israeli children light memorial candles to mark the first anniversary of the Rabin assassination.

THE CLEAR, WARM EVENING of Saturday, Nov. 4, 1995, began as an unexpected triumph for the supporters of the Oslo agreements. After a summer of hard negotiations, two suicide bombings and regular anti-Oslo demonstrations and protests, the Labor Party decided the time had come for its supporters to step forward.

The turnout was brilliant. Tens of thousands of Israelis gathered on the main square of Tel Aviv, Israel's "secular capital," to sing and cheer and revel in their solidarity. But nothing so symbolized the moment as the public embrace of Yitzhak Rabin and Shimon Peres, the Prime Minister and Foreign Minister who had overcome a bitter, lifelong political rivalry to join in forging the peace.

They were as different as east and west — the one a prototypical Israeli warrior, rough-mannered, hard-drinking, brutally candid, happiest poring over military plans with fellow generals; the other a Polish gentleman who looked naked without a necktie, who had never served in the army, who was happiest in a book of poetry or bantering with French Socialists. They had both been there from the beginning — Rabin was a hero of the 1948 war, Peres a lieutenant and disciple of Ben-Gurion — and they had both made extraordinary contributions to the establishment of the State of Israel — Rabin as warrior and leader, Peres as architect of its nuclear program and its military industry.

But in their parallel tracks they had always been rivals, sometimes enemies. When Rabin became Prime Minister in 1992, he named Peres his Foreign Minister, but with the humiliating condition that the central elements of Israeli foreign policy, dealings with the Arabs and with the Americans, remain with the Prime Minister. Peres accepted. A man who never succeeded in translating his

vision and integrity into popularity or electoral victory, he had made a career of achieving successes from whatever perch he had. From a seemingly toothless Foreign Ministry, he secretly fashioned the Oslo deal, and sold it to a skeptical Rabin. The parallel tracks finally merged, Rabin's credibility and native charisma with Peres's vision and diplomatic doggedness, to break the cycle of hostility with the Palestinians.

Now, standing before thousands of their euphoric followers, the two old antagonists clenched hands and joined in singing — growling was probably closer to the fact — the sentimental "Song of Peace." Characteristically, Rabin required a crib sheet and Peres knew it by heart.

After it ended, as Rabin was walking to his car, a 23-year-old religious nationalist named Yigal Amir, who had managed to mingle unchallenged with the waiting drivers and police, walked up behind Rabin and fired three bullets into him. "It hurts, but it's O.K.," the old warrior declared on his way to the hospital. By the time he reached it, he was dead.

The assassination was a traumatic revelation of the depth of the division among Jews over fundamental questions of identity, religion, peace — over the very destiny of Israel. However great their internal differences, the Israelis had always felt united against the common danger from without to their existence as a people. But the Oslo agreement had changed that.

Roughly half the nation had never fully accepted the notion of "land for peace." They wanted security, like every Israeli, an end to terror bombings, to the stone-throwing "intifada" of the Palestinians, to the international censure that came with repressing another people. But their Israel was not another small country on the Mediterranean; it was the Land of Israel, the arid patch of rugged highlands, desert and coastal plains that God had granted His chosen people, and from which they had been separated for 2,000 years of wretched suffering and dogged faith. They had forged their state after an unspeakable genocide; they had defended it against extraordinary odds. And when the soldiers stood weeping in June, 1967, at the Western Wall they had finally reclaimed, they had vowed never to relinquish this land. Israelis who perceived themselves as neo-Zionists moved onto the hilltops of what they called Judea and Samaria, the bib-

RABIN SLAIN AFTER LARGE PEACE RALLY BY ISRAELI ZEALOT

By SERGE SCHMEMANN

JERUSALEM, November 4 — Prime Minister Yitzhak Rabin, who led Israel to victory in 1967 and began the march toward peace a generation later, was shot dead by a lone assassin this evening as he was leaving a vast rally in Tel Aviv.

Mr. Rabin, 73, was struck down by one or two bullets as he was entering his car. Police immediately seized a 27-year-old Israeli law student, Yigal Amir, who had been active in support of Israeli settlers but who told the police tonight that he acted alone.

The police said Mr. Amir had also told them that he had tried twice before to attack the Prime Minister.

It was the first assassination of a prime minister in the 47-year history of the state of Israel, and it was certain to have extensive repercussions on Israeli politics and the future of the Arab-Israeli peace.

Mr. Rabin was to lead his labor party in elections scheduled for November next year, and without him the prospects for a labor victory, and of a continuation of his policies, were thrown into question.

In the immediate aftermath, Foreign Minister Shimon Peres, Mr. Rabin's partner in the peace negotiations, automatically became acting Prime Minister. It was widely expected that he would be formally confirmed as Mr. Rabin's successor.

Mr. Rabin, who rose to national prominence as commander of the victorious Israeli army in the 1967 Six-Day War, became the second Middle Eastern leader, after President Anwar el-Sadat of Egypt, to be killed by extremists from his own side for seeking an Arab-Israeli peace. Mr. Sadat, the first Arab to make peace with Israel, was assassinated in 1981.

Mr. Rabin and his Labor Government have come under fierce attack from right-wing groups over the peace with the Palestinians, especially since the agreement transferring authority in the West Bank to the Palestinian Liberation Organization was reached in September. Mr. Rabin has been heckled at many of his appearances in recent weeks and his security has been tight.

The New York Times November 5, 1995

Above: *Enraged and grief-stricken Israelis wait outside the hospital where Rabin was taken after the shooting.*

SETTLEMENTS OF CONTENTION
1989 -1991

immigration of Russian Jews:

over 25,000

17,001 - 25,000

7,001 - 17,000

7,000 or under

West Bank settlements, all under 1000:

lical names for the occupied West Bank; new Jewish neighborhoods sprouted in a ring around Jerusalem.

Out of that religious-nationalist vision emerged zealots for whom the Oslo deal came as a devastating blow. Suddenly the face of the enemy shifted from outside to within, to the Jew who would surrender the divinely ordained patrimony of his people for an illusory peace, for the sybaritic lifestyle of Tel Aviv and the approval of a fickle world. For these zealots, whether ultra-Orthodox rabbis or militant settlers, the reality that the West Bank was settled by 1.5 million Palestinians, that Israel would never find security until it made peace with the Palestinians, was no match for the grand vision of the Land of Israel.

The assassin was not an isolated madman. The investigation revealed that Yigal Amir's ideas were widely shared among Jewish youths raised on an intoxicating brew of guns and religious nationalism and fired by rabbis who found sanction for their zeal in the Torah and the Jewish law. Under the spell of these rabbis, Amir and the company he kept at Bar Ilan University, which combined Orthodox discipline and contemporary curriculum, had reached the conclusion that Rabin, as the man who signed the Oslo accords, could be deemed under Jewish law a "pursuer" — a person who poses so great a threat that it is legitimate and right to kill him.

The assassination was not entirely a thunderbolt from the blue. The skies had been darkening for some time.

Over the summer preceding the assassination, two more Hamas suicide bombers had struck, blowing up buses in Tel Aviv and Jerusalem, as the military wing of the militant Islamic movement waged a rearguard action to undermine a peace it viewed as surrender to the "Zionist occupation." Many of the

Israelis who had accepted the Oslo accords did so in the tentative expectation that in exchange for ceding lands to their nemesis Yasir Arafat and his Palestine Liberation Organization, Israel would finally get security. But each exploding bus, each Hamas communiqué lauding a new "martyr" and vowing more attacks, eroded that slim faith and strengthened the voice of the zealots. At one particularly strident rally on Jerusalem's Zion Square, at which the leader of the opposition Likud Party, Benjamin Netanyahu, and other speakers took turns denouncing the Oslo accords, a few extremists distributed leaflets in which Rabin was depicted as a Nazi.

On the Palestinian side, too, disillusion had been spreading. Again and again, claiming their need for security as the reason, the Israelis would seal off Gaza and the West Bank, blocking tens of thousands of Palestinians from jobs in Israel. To the Palestinians, this was evidence that Israel was not interested in a fair peace, but only in its own security, whatever the cost to the Palestinians. The United Nations estimated that each day of closure cost Gaza $2 million, eating up whatever aid was flowing in and leaving many Gazans in even worse condition than they had experienced under Israeli occupation. The economic misery contributed to growing disenchantment with Arafat and the administrators he brought with him, many of whom proved to be corrupt and authoritarian political figures.

In the immediate aftermath of the assassination, however, the Oslo process seemed irreversible. The moving eulogies at Rabin's graveside by King Hussein and President Bill Clinton elevated the warrior-turned-peacemaker to a martyr for the cause of peace. A horrified public surged massively to the political left, while the right sank into a surly defensiveness. Many a conservative quietly jerked anti-Oslo stickers off his car. Netanyahu, who had been slightly ahead of Rabin in the polls before the assassination, sank behind under allegations — mostly exaggerated or unfair — that he had not done enough to counter the "incitement" of the right-wing extremists. Rabin's widow Leah demonstratively refused to shake Netanyahu's hand at the funeral.

King Hussein at Rabin's funeral: "He had courage, he had vision and he had a commitment to peace. As long as I live, I'll be proud to have known him, to have worked with him, as a brother and as a friend and as a man."

129

As 1996 dawned, a Hamas bomb-maker named Yahya Ayyash, whom the Israelis knew as "the engineer" and held responsible for fashioning the terrible weapon of suicide bombings, took a call on a cellular phone at his home in Gaza City and was instantly killed by explosives concealed in the device. Though Israel never acknowledged responsibility, the killing had all the hallmarks of an Israeli hit, and the Shin Bet secret service did not conceal its satisfaction, especially after having been publicly disgraced for the security lapse of the Rabin assassination.

The timing of the hit was to prove disastrous. The peace was enjoying unprecedented popularity on both sides. Israeli troops had withdrawn on schedule from one Palestinian town after another in the West Bank — Jenin, Tulkarem, Kalkilya, Nablus, Ramallah, and, finally, on Christmas Eve, Bethlehem. Each withdrawal was marked by euphoric Palestinian celebrations presided over by Arafat. The newly freed territories plunged into an election campaign, Arafat appeared to be making headway in political talks with Hamas, there had been no terror attacks for several months.

The killing of Ayyash punctured the mood: to Palestinians, it was not just retaliation, but evidence that Israel still perceived itself as an occupying power. Tens of thousands of Palestinians turned out for Ayyash's funeral in Gaza, Arafat's lieutenants prominent among them. Anyone who was there knew it was only a matter of time before Hamas would strike back.

Palestinians at the funeral of Yahya Ayyash, "The Engineer," in January, 1996.

Yet for a while, the political process continued apace. The Palestinian elections on January 20 were rated a success, as huge numbers of voters turned out despite a Hamas boycott. Arafat was overwhelmingly elected Chairman of the new Palestinian National Authority, and voters also chose a new, 88-seat Palestinian Legislative Council in which many independent candidates scored well against Arafat's candidates.

At this point, Peres made a fateful choice. Buoyed by continuing high ratings in the polls, satisfied by the progress on the Palestinian agreement, convinced that president Hafez al-Assad of Syria was not prepared for a quick agreement, Peres decided to move national elections up from October to May, 1996, hoping thus to garner a solid, five-year mandate for the final status talks and for negotiations with Syria.

The first two suicide bombs went off in the early morning of Sunday, February 25, one at a bus stop in Ashkelon, the other aboard a bus in Jerusalem. The following Sunday, another bomb went off on a bus in Jerusalem, and on the next day, March 4, a suicide bomber detonated his charge outside a popular shopping plaza in Tel Aviv. More than 60 Israelis were dead; the public was in utter rage and despair.

In the tragic logic of the Middle East, the momentum toward peace generated by one act of violence, the assassination, was abruptly reversed by new violence. Peres suspended the withdrawal from Hebron, the last of the West Bank

Grieving for young friends who died in a suicide bombing at a Tel Aviv shopping mall in March, 1996.

NETANYAHU NARROW VICTOR; RELIGIOUS PARTIES SCORE HEAVILY

By SERGE SCHMEMANN

JERUSALEM, May, 31 — Confirmed as the winner in Israel's leadership race by the narrowest of margins, Benjamin Netanyahu turned today to the task of reassuring anxious Arab neighbors and shifting candidates for a new cabinet.

After counting absentee ballots through much of the day, the Israeli Election Commission finally declared Mr. Netanyahu the winner over Prime Minister Shimon Peres by 29,457 votes, 1,501,023 to 1,471,566.

Mr. Netanyahu made no public statement, and his victory address is not expected until Sunday evening. But his bustling camp reported that he had received a call from President Clinton, who invited him to Washington, and that Mr. Netanyahu had telephoned the leaders of Jordan and Egypt.

His associates also said the Prime Minister–elect's candidates for the key ministries of Foreign Affairs and Defense would be men from the moderate end of the spectrum in the conservative Likud.

Given the closeness of the vote, the last-minute endorsement of several ultra-Orthodox rabbis probably gave Mr. Netanyahu the critical boost over the top. Apparently in a gesture to his new partners, Mr. Netanyahu, television cameras in tow and a black yarmulke on his head, made a stop today to pray at the Western Wall.

The tightness of the election was underscored by the fact that 145,000 voters had cast blank ballots for Prime Minister, indicating disenchantment with both candidates. About 12,000 of those were cast by Arabs, many presumably to register their anger over the Israeli military operation in Lebanon last month.

The Election Commission also confirmed a new Parliament in which small parties will hold almost half the seats and religious parties will have an unprecedented representation, with more than a fifth of the votes.

The official count cleared Mr. Netanyahu, who at 46 will be Israel's youngest Prime Minister, to start shaping a coalition in Parliament and forming a Cabinet. Only when his Government is accepted by Parliament will he be formally sworn in, the eighth person to serve as Prime Minister since the founding of the state in 1948.

The New York Times June 1, 1996

cities under Israeli control, and ordered draconian measures against the Palestinians, sealing off all West Bank cities and villages and threatening even tougher measures unless Arafat immediately cracked down on Islamic militants. The Clinton Administration moved quickly to prevent fatal damage to the Oslo process, convening a summit meeting against terrorism in Egypt and pushing Arafat to undertake credible and deep action against terror.

The Israeli-Arab struggle is a many-headed dragon, and before long another head was spewing flames, this time in southern Lebanon. The guerrilla war there was always a smoldering sore. Since withdrawing from the rest of Lebanon after the invasion of 1982, the Israeli Army and the South Lebanon Army, a Lebanese militia trained and maintained by Israel, had maintained a buffer zone inside the Lebanese border ranging in depth from a few miles in the west to 16 miles in the east. This zone was the stage for a low-level, hit-and-run war between the Israelis and the guerrillas of Hezbollah. In April, an escalation of the struggle led to charges by each side that the other was violating an informal agreement against firing on civilians. Israelis, still raging over the suicide bombings, cried out for action. Peres, his standing slipping since the terror attacks, acquiesced, and on April 11, the Israeli Army launched an attack by land and air.

Initially, Israeli military chiefs bragged of pinpoint hits with "smart bombs," even in downtown Beirut. The Israeli strategy was to stampede residents of southern Lebanon northward and to selectively strike at the Lebanese infrastructure, creating a steadily growing problem for the Lebanese Government and its Syrian patrons until they were forced to rein in Hezbollah. A similar strategy had worked in Lebanon once before, resulting in a reduction of hostilities in 1993.

But then on April 18, an Israeli artillery barrage struck a United Nations camp where hundreds of civilians were taking refuge, killing more than 70. In an echo of the 1982 furor over the Sabra and Shatila refugee camp massacres, Israel went abruptly from military offensive to diplomatic defensive, condemned around the world as an arrogant aggressor. Peres, too, was on the defensive. With the renewed sense of insecurity and frustration, the final weeks of the Israeli campaign found Netanyahu drawing closer and closer to Peres.

Then 46, Benjamin Netanyahu was a new phenomenon in Israel's clanny politics. "Bibi," as he was universally known, went to high school in Pennsylvania and studied architecture and business at M.I.T. He had mastered television and image-shaping, and had returned to conquer the Likud in the political equivalent of a hostile takeover, working the party machines and the new primaries while the veterans and the hereditary party "princes" — men like Ariel Sharon, Dan Meridor and Zeev "Benny" Begin — wrangled among themselves.

But for all his American inflections, in Netanyahu's veins there ran the blood of a stern Zionist. In Israel, he and his two brothers had all been members of one of the toughest Israeli commando units, the Zayeret Matkal.

The turning point in Netanyahu's life was the death of his older brother, Yonatan, while commanding the legendary mission to rescue Jewish hostages at the Entebbe Airport in Uganda. Yoni and Bibi were exceptionally close, and the death galvanized Netanyahu to organize a conference on terrorism. It proved an enormous success, and before long, Netanyahu was recruited by the Israeli Ambassador to Washington, Moshe Arens, as his deputy. There, and at a subsequent positions as the Israeli Ambassador to the United Nations and as spokesman at the Foreign Ministry, Netanyahu demonstrated and polished his communication skills and prepared to capture the Likud. After its loss in the

1992 elections, the party woke up to find itself under a young, brash, telegenic newcomer.

But the takeover had a price: resented by the Likud elite, Netanyahu put his trust in a small coterie of advisers loyal personally to him, and on his own television skills. A telling early example of his response to crisis came when the thrice-married Netanyahu received anonymous warnings of a compromising video cassette. His reaction was to rush to the television station and pre-emptively acknowledge an extramarital affair, and to accuse a Likud rival, David Levy, of leaking the damaging rumors. The video turned out to be a hoax.

Netanyahu's campaign against Peres was slick and effective. The ballot was the first in which Israelis elected the Prime Minister directly, and the personalized approach fit perfectly with Netanyahu's skills and youth. Aided by an American image-molder, he focused on Israeli anxieties over the peace, hammering away at Peres as a dreaming liberal who had "subcontracted our security to Arafat." One especially devastating Likud spot showed Arafat leading Peres by the hand, followed by the sound of breaking glass. By contrast, Peres tried to ride his dwindling lead, waging a mild campaign that focused on images of prosperity and showed the 72-year-old politician surrounded by admiring youths. In the end, on May 29, ultra-Orthodox rabbis and new immigrants from Russia pushed Netanyahu over the top by a few hundred votes.

The birth of the new government was chaotic. The new electoral system had been intended to bring more order to Israeli politics by putting the Prime Minister above the party fray. The effect was the exact opposite: After casting one ballot for Peres or Netanyahu, voters felt free to cast their second for the party that represented their special interest, leaving Netanyahu with a welter of

An Orthodox Jew entering the disputed underground tunnel which runs from the Western Wall to the Arab quarter of the Old City.

small parties from which to form his government. His final coalition consisted of his Likud, three religious parties, three splinter parties and a Russian émigré party — all of them less loyal to the Prime Minister than to their own constituents and interests.

Before long, it became evident that adept as Netanyahu was in coming to power, he had little idea how to wield it. His grand plans to reign like an American president crumpled as Knesset members blocked his plans for independent councils of national security or economic advisers, and his attempt to create an Israeli Camelot with his wife and small sons was soon dashed by the intense scrutiny of the tabloids. Above all, he and his small clutch of advisers came under siege from the issue that ultimately determines the shape of all Israeli politics — relations with the Arabs. Netanyahu had come to office preaching a dual message. He pledged to abide by the Oslo accords, and at the same time made no secret of his disdain for them. He declared that everything was open to negotiation, and at the same time declared that he would never cede Jerusalem or the Golan Heights, nor permit a Palestinian state, nor freeze settlement construction in the West Bank. The result was stagnation of the process and frustration on all sides. As the crises multiplied and the criticism in the press became ever shriller, Netanyahu's sound-bites became increasingly bitter attacks on what he perceived as hostile elites — the military, the intelligence services, the media, the opposition. "They" were all under the control of the left, they were out to thwart him.

On the Arab and Palestinian front, relations began to deteriorate almost immediately after Netanyahu was sworn in. In July, Egypt summoned an Arab summit meeting to issue a critical assessment of the new Israeli Government, and in August, Syria created an alarm by moving commando units to the foot of Mount Hermon on Israel's northern border. Relations with the Palestinians eroded as week after week, Netanyahu put off meeting Arafat. The humiliation of the purported "peace partner" was compounded by actions like the demolition of Palestinian buildings in Jerusalem's Old City. When Netanyahu and Arafat did finally meet in September, the tensions were palpable.

The explosion came in late September, when the right-wing mayor of Jerusalem, Ehud Olmert, went into the Old City in the middle of the night with a band of soldiers and opened a back entrance to a tunnel running by the Western Wall of Solomon's Temple Mount. The entrance was an old dispute. To the Palestinians, the mount was the Haram al-Sharif, the Noble Sanctuary, the third holiest site of Islam, and any digging under it was a violation of the status quo. Perhaps in another context the Muslims might have accepted the entrance, but in an atmosphere of pent-up frustrations and humiliations, an eruption because of the tunnel was certain.

Rioting by Palestinians in Bethlehem, in response to the tunnel opening in September, 1996.

JERUSALEM 1967 - 1997

Jewish areas

Arab areas

Jerusalem city limits

Arafat, Netanyahu and King Hussein (obscured) at a White House meeting in October, 1996.

The protest took a nasty and unexpected turn. After Israeli soldiers pelted demonstrators in Ramallah with rubber bullets for a few hours, a Palestinian policeman opened fire with real bullets at the Israelis. Suddenly, the Israelis' worst fears about the peace were reality: throughout the West Bank and Gaza, Israeli and Palestinian police were shooting it out. More than 60 Palestinians and 15 Israelis were killed, and the entire process was in danger of disintegrating in violence.

Once again the United States stepped in, summoning Netanyahu and Arafat to an emergency meeting with President Clinton and King Hussein in Washington. The result was an agreement to immediately restart the negotiating process and

Israeli soldiers providing security as construction began at the site of a new Jewish neighborhood in Arab East Jerusalem.

THE NEW PALESTINIAN STATE
1997

- areas of Israeli control
- areas of joint control
- areas of Palestinian control

quickly conclude an Israeli withdrawal from Hebron.

The new negotiations opened promptly, with Secretary of State Warren Christopher arriving to give each side a personal nudge. Just as quickly, they changed from a search for a pragmatic solution to a bitter test of wills, with battles over every comma. When an agreement was finally reached on January 15, 1997, it was only after exhaustive efforts and threats from Dennis Ross, the American mediator. The Hebron agreement raised a fleeting hope that the peace process was "back on track," and Netanyahu flew off to the United States in February to have his back publicly patted by President Clinton. But the satisfaction was short-lived. The Prime Minister's right-wing constituents, simmering over what they viewed as their leader's cave-in to the Americans, confronted him immediately on his return with a new challenge: build a new Jewish neighborhood in Arab-populated East Jerusalem, or fall. On February 26, Netanyahu gave the go-ahead to the new project, called Har Homa.

The next blow fell a week later. Under the Hebron agreement reached in January, Netanyahu had obliged himself to make three more withdrawals from the West Bank by mid-1998, with the first by March 6. But instead of the sizable transfer the Palestinians anticipated, the Cabinet voted to cede only 2.8 percent of lands that had been under full Israeli control. Arafat, already seething over Har Homa, refused to accept the land and froze all further negotiations. Unexpectedly, the sharpest criticism came not from the United Nations or hostile Arab states, but from King Hussein, the Arab leader considered most sympathetic to Netanyahu and to Israel in general. The king voiced a profound anguish over Netanyahu's actions in a letter that was leaked to the press.

"My distress is genuine and deep over the accumulating tragic actions which you have initiated at the head of the Government of Israel, making peace — the worthiest objective of my life — appear more and more like a distant elusive mirage," wrote King Hussein. "I could remain aloof if the very lives of all Arabs

NETANYAHU AND ARAFAT AGREE ON HEBRON PULLOUT

By SERGE SCHMEMANN

JERUSALEM, January 15 — Meeting in the middle of the night at a military base between Israel and the Gaza strip, Prime Minister Benjamin Netanyahu and the Palestinian leader, Yasir Arafat, today finally sealed the long-delayed deal on a partial Israeli withdrawal from Hebron.

After three and a half months of all-night negotiating sessions, mutual recriminations and regular declarations that agreement was either imminent or impossible, the end was announced in a brief statement at 2:45 A.M. by Dennis Ross, the American mediator who cajoled and pressured the negotiations through most of the ordeal.

With Mr. Netanyahu on his right and Mr. Arafat on his left, Mr. Ross declared, "I'm very pleased to announce on behalf of the two leaders that they have reached agreement on a protocol on Hebron redeployment and on a 'note of agreement' on non-Hebron issues." Mr. Ross said the agreement detailing Israel's withdrawal from 80 percent of Hebron was "indeed a fair and balanced approach to dealing with concerns each side had."

He added that the accompanying note, which is formally a statement by the United States, "really lays out a road map for the future." "Taken together," he said, "these two documents represent a very important building block in terms of developing relations between the two sides and in terms of laying out a pathway of greater hope and the possibilty of peace in the Middle East as a whole." Mr. Ross said the two leaders had placed calls to President Clinton, President Hosni Mubarak of Egypt and King Hussein of Jordan, all of whom had played various roles in the difficult talks.

Shortly after the agreement was announced, President Clinton said, "It brings us another step closer to a lasting peace in the Middle East." ... "Once again, the forces of peace have prevailed over a history of divisions."

Mr. Clinton praised Mr. Netanyahu and Mr. Arafat, and he pointedly mentioned King Hussein, declaring that he deserved "special recognition and gratitude for his work for peace." But the President tempered his elation with acknowledgement of the problems that remain in working out final details of the accord and in reaching a lasting peace in the region. "In short, this is not a time to relax," he said.

The New York Times January 15, 1997

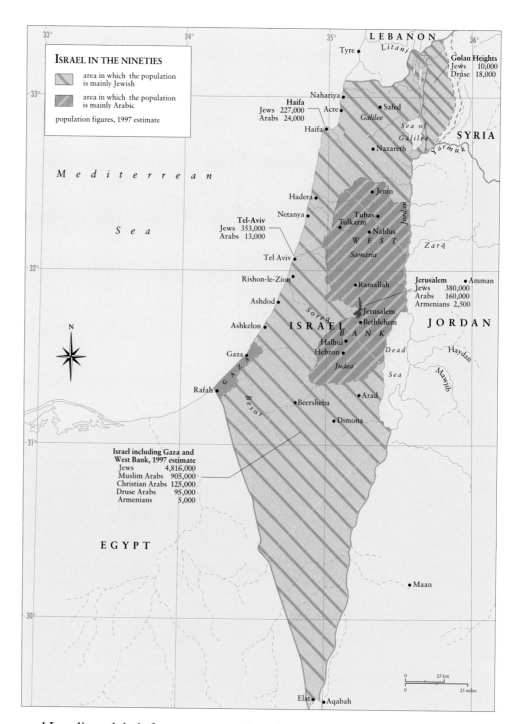

and Israelis and their future were not fast sliding towards an abyss of bloodshed and disaster, brought about by fear and despair."

The West Bank erupted. Day after day, Palestinian youths pelted Israeli soldiers with rocks in Bethlehem, Hebron and Ramallah, and the Israelis responded with volleys of tear gas and rubber bullets. On March 22, a suicide bomb ripped through a crowded cafe in Tel Aviv, killing three women in the first such attack in more than a year. Netanyahu accused Arafat of personally giving the "green light" to the resumption of terror.

For once, even the Americans seemed out of ideas. A year after Netanyahu's election, the bright light that was Oslo seemed to be flickering and fading.

There were those who argued that the process was irreversible, that eventually Israelis and Palestinians would recognize that however great their mutual distrust and animosity, they had no choice but to coexist in the same parched, ancient corner of the earth. But as Israel prepared for its 50th anniversary, it was still a nation profoundly divided over competing visions of its destiny and purpose, and still groping for a fair and lasting peace with its neighbors.

Crossing point in the Old City: A Jewish worshipper on his way to the Western Wall passing an Arab on his way to prayers.

Nation Builders
Leaders Who Shaped Israel
By Correspondents of The New York Times

Yigal Allon

YIGAL ALLON, one of Israel's most prominent military and political figures and a hero of the first Arab-Israeli war, died after a heart attack. He was 61 years old.

Mr. Allon gained prominence as the leader of Palmach, the commando strike force that operated before the establishment of Israel. After entering Parliament in 1955 he held a series of Cabinet posts, including those of Deputy Prime Minister and Foreign Minister in the last Labor Government, which was headed by Yitzhak Rabin.

He was best known for a peace plan bearing his name that he put forward after Israel captured Arab territory in the Six–Day 1967 war. The plan proposed restoring most of the West Bank territory to Jordan while retaining Israeli para-military settlements along the Jordan River, which forms the border with Jordan. A corridor through this line of settlements was to link the two parts of the Kingdom of Jordan.

The plan was rejected by King Hussein of Jordan, dismissed by the United States Government and never formally adopted by an Israeli government. However, it still represents the thinking of the mainstream Labor Party.

Prime Minister Menachem Begin, commenting on Mr. Allon's death, said: "Allon was a national hero. He was one of the outstanding officers during the War of Independence and served his people with fidelity and devotion in the highest-ranking positions."

Mr. Allon was buried in Kibbutz Ginosar, a collective settlement overlooking the sea of Galilee that he helped found in 1937 and where he made his home until his death. When he held high office he returned to the kibbutz for weekends and holidays and took his turn as a member working in the dining room, the fields or an electronics factory.

World statesmen were entertained at the kibbutz by Mr. Allon, the last being Gen. Kamal Hassan Ali, Egyptian Defense Minister, who was there the previous afternoon. Upon hearing the news of Mr. Allon's death General Ali expressed shock and sorrow and phoned Mrs. Allon from Tel Aviv to offer condolences.

Two hours after the general left the kibbutz, Mr. Allon complained of chest pains. The kibbutz doctor took him by ambulance to a hospital in Afula, 50 miles north of Jerusalem. He died not far from from his birthplace, Kfar Tabor, which was founded by his father, Reuven Paicovitch.

His parents sent him to an agricultural school to learn farming, and he also learned soldiering in a cell of Haganah, the secret Jewish organization. He was one of the first members of Palmach, Haganah's elite striking force. During WWII, he smuggled Jewish survivors of the Holocaust ashore in Palestine in defiance of British law. Later in the war he fought alongside British soldiers against the Vichy French.

When Israel proclaimed independence and Haganah surfaced as the sovereign state's new army, Mr. Allon commanded a Palmach force that fought major battles against the Arabs. He pursued the Egyptians from the Negev into Sinai to the outskirts of El Arish but was ordered back by Prime Minister David Ben-Gurion under pressure from the United States. Among Mr. Allon's prisoners was a young officer named Gamal Abdel Nasser, who later became President of Egypt.

Leaving the army after the war, Mr. Allon, who was a socialist, tried politics as a member of Parliament for a few years but resigned his seat in midterm to take up a research fellowship at Oxford. A writer on military subjects, he discontinued his studies in 1961 when Mr. Ben-Gurion recalled him to join the Government as Minister of Labor. He remained in the Cabinet until Labor was voted out of power in 1977.

His political base in the kibbutz movement was strong enough to protect his Cabinet seat but not to get him the offices he most coveted. He was offered the defense portfolio on the eve of the Six–Day War but it went to Moshe Dayan under pressure of public opinion and the threat of a Cabinet crisis. As deputy to Prime Minister Levi Eshkol he expected to succeed on Mr. Eshkol's death, but the party brought Golda Meir out of retirement.

In his last campaign for a party leadership he lost a preliminary round to the party chairman, Shimon Peres, but announced he would be a candidate at the party's national convention.

The New York Times
February 29, 1982

Abba Eban

ABBA EBAN, whom the world has for decades considered the voice of Israel, was looked upon subsequently by many of his own compatriots as a fringe radical.

"I don't think I have moved at all politically," Mr. Eban said in an interview at the King David Hotel, one of his favorite haunts. "But the center of gravity here has moved — to the right. By standing still and saying the same things I said 40 years ago, I suddenly find myself on the fringe."

"When I go abroad I still can speak for Israel in

terms of its achievement," Mr. Eban added, with a hint of regret. "But, frankly, when I look back at the speech I gave at Israel's birth to get us into the United Nations, I would not dare make that same speech now. The rhetoric was too utopian. Now I would be much more reserved. I would definitely not use the phrase that we will be 'a light unto the nations.'"

A picture published on the front page of every Israeli newspaper two weeks ago seemed to capture Mr. Eban's current situation perfectly. The picture showed him sitting at a meeting of the central committee of the Labor Party, which had been convened by Foreign Minister Shimon Peres and Defense Minister Yitzhak Rabin for the sole purpose of verbally flagellating Mr. Eban for having dared to issue a report that was critical of the Labor leadership for its role in the Jonathan Jay Pollard spy scandal.

In the photograph, Mr. Eban, 72 years old, was looking up toward a Labor leader, who was showering him with insults. On Mr. Eban's face was an expression of such intense bewilderment and anguish that the picture was almost painful to view.

Although public-opinion polls showed an overwhelming majority of Israelis sided with Mr. Eban in his criticism of Mr. Rabin's and Mr. Peres's handling of the Pollard affair, this did not change the status of the elder statesman, who is more of an outsider in Israeli politics now than ever before.

True, he was always an outsider socially, and he never had half the party following in Israel that he had in New York City; he was a little too eloquent, a little too clever, and a little too much of a Cambridge upper-class gentleman to ever really fit in with the native-born Israelis.

Born in South Africa in 1915, he was educated at Cambridge and taught Oriental languages there before being assigned to Allied headquarters in Jerusalem to help train Jewish volunteers in World War II.

"When Eban first appeared, with his remarkable tongue, everyone loved him as a kind of boy wonder," said Shabtai Teveth, the biographer of Israel's founding father, David Ben-Gurion. "Then, in 1968, when Ben-Gurion decided to prepare the next generation for rule, Eban, Peres and Moshe Dayan were singled out for political succession.

"Eban was promoted not so much as a vote-getter, but as a kind of ornament. But when the old guard died, and Dayan, Peres and Rabin took over, Eban was shoved aside. The others felt he saw Israeli problems through foreign eyes." Finally, Mr. Teveth said, when Sephardic Jews from Moslem countries became the majority in

Israel, Mr. Eban was made still more marginal.

"Eban was foreign to this new ethnic majority, both socially and politically," Mr. Teveth said. "If in the old Israel he was admired for his talents, in the new Israel his talents were not recognized, and he was resented by many for his dovish views. Ironically, though, he is the true heir to the vision of Ben-Gurion, not Peres and Rabin."

Heir or not, today Mr. Eban speaks in his eloquent voice only for himself and the small group of Israeli intellectuals who share his views. Although he is still a Labor Member of Parliament, and is chairman of the Foreign Affairs and Defense Committee, Mr. Eban said the political ground has been moving from under his feet since 1967.

"Although the Six–Day War was a tremendous military salvation and political gain, and enabled us to get the peace with Egypt, we went a little bit crazy intellectually as a result of it," he said in his cultivated Oxbridge accent.

"We interpreted the war as not just a victory, but as a kind of providential messianic event that changed history permanently and gave Israel the power to dictate the future."

Many Israelis, Mr. Eban said, lost sight of the reality that the Arabs remained intact, none of their capitals had been occupied, and their power of refusal was largely untouched.

Nonetheless, this post-1967 euphoria continued, he said, and, with the seven-year tenure of Menachem Begin, produced a new kind of Zionism.

"The central themes of Zionism originally were liberalism, tolerance and an ethical emphasis, coupled with an understanding that we had to reach some kind of an agreement with the Arabs," Mr. Eban said. "This has given way in recent years to a new Zionism that used to be on the fringes but is now creeping to the center of respectability.

"It says say that we will not give any territory back; if the Arabs don't like it here they can get the hell out, and if they stay we will not give them all of their human rights, and being Jewish is more important than being democratic."

The Israeli elder statesman is convinced that his country is heading for a disaster by holding on to the West Bank and Gaza Strip, with their 1.3 million Palestinian inhabitants.

The occupation, he said, is "deforming and defacing our society "

"It is wasting our resources, and it is not necessary for our security," he said.

"We have to remember that all of the original creations that gave Israel its fascination were created in the little Israel, before the state was established that is, the kibbutz movement, the Hebrew language, the early institutions of learning,

the emphasis on science and the pioneering spirit."

Paradoxically, Mr. Eban says he finds he has difficulty convincing many American officials and American Jews of these views, partly because they continue to be wedded to a mythical image of an infallible Israel that he himself helped to generate in his youth.

By THOMAS L. FRIEDMAN
The New York Times
June 14,1987

[Mr. Eban lives in the Israeli coast town of Herzliya north of Tel Aviv, but he has spent long periods abroad in recent years, particularly in New York City. He has lectured across the globe, taught at Columbia and Princeton and now is a professor at George Washington University, where he lectures on international relations after the Cold War, a subject he has also written about in a book titled *The New Diplomacy*. Currently Mr. Eban is working on a film for PBS on the Arab-Israeli peace process, a follow-up to a well-known PBS series he hosted on the history of the Jewish people.]

Menachem Begin

MENACHEM BEGIN, the Israeli Prime Minister who made peace with Egypt, lived much of his life in the opposition. A Jewish underground leader before Israel gained independence in

1948, he openly fought the established Zionist leadership of the struggle against British rule. Then for nearly three decades, he headed Israel's major opposition party.

Ultimately and to many Israelis, surprisingly, his minority bloc ousted the Labor Party, which had governed continuously in the three decades since statehood, and Mr. Begin, as party leader, became Prime Minister. He was to govern an ever more divided and troubled nation.

Mr. Begin, who led Israel from May 1977 until he resigned as Prime Minister in 1983, stretched the national mood from great pride to deep dismay. He guided the nation to a peace treaty with Egypt, the first such pact with an Arab country. But he also presided over a bitterly divisive war against Palestinian guerrillas in Lebanon.

If the treaty with Egypt, which brought Mr. Begin a shared 1978 Nobel Peace Prize with President Anwar el-Sadat, represented a high point in his political leadership, the war in Lebanon in 1982 and the stalemate that followed, with its steady toll of dead and wounded, were its low point.

Started with the announced aim of evicting Palestinian guerrillas from operating too close to Israel's border with Lebanon, it brought Israeli troops to the outskirts of Beirut. It enmeshed Israel in the lethal sectarian politics of Lebanon, and led to a costly and indecisive occupation.

The invasion in June, 1982, was seen by Israelis at first as a justified response to years of border harassment. But when the Israelis advanced to the outskirts of Beirut and bombed and shelled the Lebanese capital for 10 weeks, criticism and anguish arose.

Dissent reached a peak in the fall of 1982, when Lebanese Christian militia units entered Palestinian refugee districts at Sabra and Shatila that were supposedly under Israeli guard and killed hundreds of people.

The massacre led to an independent investigation ordered by the Israeli Government, which concluded that Israeli troops watched the killing from a distance and did nothing to stop it. Mr. Begin survived in office, but was shaken politically.

His medical problems — he had suffered three heart attacks — became an increasing burden. And in November, 1982, his wife of 43 years, Aliza, died while he was on a trip to the United States. Thereafter, Mr. Begin became increasingly listless, participating little in debate in Parliament, taking less and less interest in politics and limiting his public appearances. On August 28, 1983, he announced that he planned to quit and on September 15 he formally resigned as Prime Minister. He lived the remainder of his life as something of a recluse.

When he became Prime Minister, Mr. Begin represented both political and stylistic change. He brought a new demeanor to the Prime Minister's office with his remote manner, a sharp contrast to the earthy and informal style of his Labor Party predecessors. Unlike the bulk of Israeli politicians, he was seldom seen other than in his suit and tie.

And he moved the country in a distinctly different ideological direction. Hours after his election victory, he visited an Israeli settlement in the occupied West Bank, which had been captured in the 1967 war, declaring it part of "liberated Israel." Labor Governments had avoided such declarations, but to Mr. Begin the West Bank was Judea and Samaria, Jewish land dating back to biblical times.

His government did not formally annex the West Bank, as it did the Golan Heights, a Syrian promontory captured in 1967. But under Mr. Begin, the occupied territory of the West Bank began to be heavily settled by Israelis.

He was also to return some Arab land taken in battle, a strip of Syrian territory won in 1973 and a town on the Golan Heights taken in 1967. But the most significant territorial withdrawal, and for Mr. Begin the most personally wrenching, was in the Sinai Peninsula, which Israel returned to Egypt in three stages from 1979 through 1982. Jewish settlements in Sinai were abandoned despite intense protest by their residents.

The Sinai withdrawal was the last stage of a process that began with Sadat's landmark visit to Jerusalem in November, 1977, six months after Begin took office.

The Egyptian president, frustrated by the intransigence of Arab neighbors in dealing with Israel, had hinted that he was prepared to go it alone in seeking peace and had said he would even travel to Jerusalem, in pursuit of that goal. Begin responded with an invitation.

On a warm November evening, the wheels of the presidential aircraft, Egypt 01, touched down at Ben-Gurion International Airport. Begin stepped forward and said: "I am waiting for you, President, and all the ministers are waiting for you."

Sixteen months of arduous negotiations followed, including the marathon talks at Camp David, Maryland, with President Jimmy Carter. The process culminated in the Israeli-Egyptian peace treaty signed in Washington on March 26, 1979.

The treaty gave Begin one of the great satisfactions of his career. He explained his feelings in a forceful and eloquent speech in Parliament.

"Why is this peace treaty so important?" he asked. "This is the first peace treaty Israel ever signed, the first peace treaty after five wars in which we have lost 12,000 of our people. Our aim, our yearning and our dream is to smash this helix of hatred. We must sign this treaty because it is a human act of the highest degree."

At the White House signing, Begin said it was "the third greatest day of my life" — after the establishment of the State of Israel in 1948 and the unification of Jerusalem in the 1967 war.

But Mr. Begin's wariness toward the Arabs remained undiminished. In June, 1981, he ordered the bombing of an Iraqi nuclear reactor near Baghdad. This was followed in July by two weeks of bombing in Lebanon.

In December, he pushed through Parliament a measure to annex the Golan Heights. This drew sharp criticism from Washington and other capitals, but Begin held his ground. When the Reagan Administration suspended a strategic cooperation pact with Israel and imposed financial sanctions because of the Golan annexation, Begin said Israel was being treated like a "vassal state."

His relations with Egypt also changed. After Sadat was shot to death by Muslim extremists in October, 1981, his successor, President Hosni Mubarak, seemed determined to calm the hostility toward Egypt in the rest of the Arab world because of its peace treaty with Israel. Relations between Egypt and Israel cooled, especially after the invasion of Lebanon the following year.

Mr. Begin was more accustomed to an adversarial relationship. His was a life that until 1977 had been spent almost entirely in opposition — to the mainstream of Jews in his native Poland, to both the German and Russian invaders of his homeland in World War II, to the established leaders of the Jewish military struggle against British rule in Palestine and to the decades of Labor Party government in Israel.

He believed fiercely, and contentiously, that the Jews had a right to a national homeland and that it should range over the land of their biblical forebears. This was Zion and he was a dedicated Zionist, if a follower of the Zionist Revisionist organization founded by Vladimir Jabotinsky.

Mr. Begin was marked forever by the Holocaust, which had wiped out all vestiges of his former life in Poland. The pursuit of those goals was a thread that ran through his life. He was to spend much of his time explaining and trying to justify what some considered extreme actions and statements.

The best-known of those occurred in 1946, when Irgun Zvai Leumi, the underground terrorist faction he headed during the final years of the British mandate in Palestine, blew up a wing of the King David Hotel in Jerusalem, the headquarters of the British administrators of Palestine. The attack killed 90 people, among them Jewish and Arab employees as well as British officials.

By 1946 the British authorities were conducting an intensive hunt for Mr. Begin, placing a price of $8,000 on his head. Later, it was raised to $50,000.

The Irgun, often working with weapons and explosives purchased from the Arabs, set about breaking the grip of colonial rule. Begin, in his book *The Revolt*, explained the group's actions this way: "The arrest of British officers in order to secure the annulment of a death sentence, the arrest of more officers which did not prevent the murder of our captive comrades, the whipping of officers in retaliation for the whipping of our young soldiers, hangings in retaliation for hangings."

In April, 1948, the Irgun attacked an Arab village, Deir Yassin, in which more than 200 men, women and children were killed.

Mr. Begin also struggled fiercely against David Ben-Gurion, the mainstream Zionist leader and head of the regular Jewish force in the fight for nationhood. Two months after the Deir Yassin assault, the freighter *Altalena,* loaded with arms and ammunition and 900 men recruited by the Irgun, came under fire from regular Jewish forces. Ben-Gurion feared that the new Government of Israel might be overthrown or that civil war might break out after the fight against the Arabs was over.

In the first elections for Parliament, in January 1949, Mapai, the Labor Party, emerged with 44 seats; the left-wing Mapam won 15, the religious bloc 16, and Begin's Herut Party 14.

Leading the opposition, he was suspended from Parliament for organizing demonstrations and was forever demanding apologies in Parliament and being asked to apologize in turn. He would demand preventive war, for example, only to hear an opponent say that "anyone who does so is a criminal against the Jewish nation." A policy dispute would become personal.

He cooperated with the Labor Party only once. From 1967 to 1970, Mr. Begin served in a war coalition, then withdrew when Israel began to consider an American proposal that would have linked withdrawal from the occupied territories with peace.

In 1973, Mr. Begin broke an embargo on domestic criticism of the Government's action in failing to accurately gauge Arab intentions leading to the war. The Arab attack on Yom Kippur, he said, only underscored the need to retain occupied territories.

He resisted every pullback agreement, and in 1975 derided Secretary of State Henry A. Kissinger for telling us to trade territory for legitimacy. "We don't need legitimacy," Mr. Begin stated emphatically "We exist. Therefore we are legitimate."

Early in 1977, with the Labor Government riddled by dissension and tainted, in the view of some, by corruption, Mr. Begin finally achieved the political recognition that had so long eluded him. Though weary from a heart attack two months before the election, he emerged with an upset victory and was asked to form a government.

Several things brought about his victory: The Labor Party had become increasingly identified with worsening inflation, frequent strikes and a stagnant economy. Its scandals led to the creation of the Democratic Movement for Change, which drew a valuable 15 seats of 120 from Labor in the election, and then briefly joined the new Likud coalition.

In addition, a "second Israel" of Jews from North Africa and the Middle East, the poor of the cities and new towns, had grown to become the nation's majority, and these people were attracted to Mr. Begin. Despite his European origin, they felt that he, too, had been outside the establishment, and he promised greater militancy toward the Arabs.

He began as Prime Minister with familiar militancy. He visited a West Bank settlement, Elon Moreh, the day after the 1977 election and declared: "We stand on the land of liberated Israel. There will be many Elon Morehs. There will be many, many settlements in the coming weeks."

The first settlements, similar to those under Labor Governments, were isolated defense posts, with armed farmers tilling fields. Later settlements were built nearer Arab towns, and then within them, such as in Hebron. By 1982, about 30,000 Israelis lived on more than 100 such settlements. New highways encouraged commuting from prefabricated towns to jobs in Tel Aviv.

Israel, under Mr. Begin, changed the unit of currency from the pound, a vestige of British rule, to the shekel, a coin used by the ancient Hebrews. And Parliament, under his leadership, formally declared all of Jerusalem, a city divided into Jewish and Arab sectors before the 1967 war, to be the nation's undivided and eternal capital — an act that was not recognized by most other countries.

Mr. Begin retained power in 1981 after his right-wing Likud bloc emerged with a one-seat lead over the Labor alignment of Shimon Peres. His margin of success came from the religious parties, which enabled him to form a fragile governing coalition.

Mr. Begin, a brilliant speaker and writer, was also an enigma: often soft-spoken, mild-mannered and personable. Yet this slight but firmly built man, who dressed in gray and never lost the hand-kissing tradition of his early years in Poland, was described as having the flinty looks of a movie terrorist.

There was no doubt about his dramatic flair. Once during a speech in the immigrant quarter of Jerusalem, he began to describe the "guarantees" for Israel that were being offered by American diplomats seeking to encourage Arab negotiations. His voice rose and his manner grew intense. He pointed higher and higher, as if searching for something, until he had everyone looking skyward.

"Guarantees, guarantees — maybe there you will find guarantees," he said, adding, as he pointed to the ground, "Not here!"

Menachem Wolfovitch Begin was born on Aug. 30, 1913, in Brest, when it was still part of the czarist Russian Empire. The area was returned to Poland in 1921, occupied by the Soviet Union in 1939 soon after Hitler's attack on Poland, overrun by the Nazis after Hitler turned on Stalin and attacked the Soviet Union in 1941, and ceded to Moscow in 1945.

Zionism was central to Mr. Begin's childhood. His father, Dov Zeev Begin, had been educated in Berlin and traveled widely. Dov Begin's travels brought him into contact with Jewish nationalists, the Zionist "heretics," as they were called by the traditionally minded.

At 15 he joined Betar, the Zionist Revisionists' youth movement, and was trained in the use of weapons. Ten years later, with a law degree from Warsaw University, he headed Betar, which by then had 70,000 members in 600 Polish communities.

"My friends and I labored to educate a generation to be prepared not only to toil for the rebuilding of a Jewish state but also to fight for it, suffer for it and, if needs be, die for it," he said, paraphrasing Jabotinsky.

Mr. Begin fled from Warsaw ahead of the advancing Germans in 1939 and was in Polish-controlled Vilna in 1940 when the Russians occupied the city, now Vilnius, Lithuania. He obtained a visa to go to Palestine but gave it to a friend he thought would have more trouble.

The Russians soon arrested him, accusing him of being a Zionist and a British agent, and sent him to Siberia. His wife, whom he had married a year earlier, went on to Palestine, convinced that she could do nothing to help her husband. Later, she became quietly influential in his political life while remaining out of the limelight. Besides their son, Benjamin, who became a leader of the Likud Party, they had two other children — Hasia and Leah.

Though sentenced to eight years in a labor

camp, he was released by the Soviet Union in 1941 in an agreement with the Polish government-in-exile that freed 1.5 million Poles. Mr. Begin found his sister, the family's only other survivor, then joined the Free Polish Army. That took him to Iran and to Palestine.

Having learned English by listening to the BBC, he served in the British Army in Palestine as a conscripted interpreter until the end of 1943. Then he took over the leadership of the Irgun underground in the battle for a Zionist homeland.

"From my early youth," Mr. Begin said later, "I had been taught by my father, who went to his death at Nazi hands voicing his faith in God and singing 'Ehatikvah,' that we Jews were to return to the land of Israel — not go, travel or come, but to return."

By JAMES FERON
The New York Times
March 10, 1992

David Ben-Gurion

DAVID BEN-GURION, symbol of the tough state of Israel, achieved a lifelong dream.

Born in Russia in 1886, he died on December 1, 1973 in the young state of Israel. Short, round, with a nimbus of white hair flaring angrily from a massive head, "BG," as he was known to many,

attained world leadership by firmly concentrating on the achievement of a dream, the birth and triumphant survival of a Jewish homeland amid a sea of hostile Arabs. Mr. Ben-Gurion was chairman of the Jewish Agency, the executive body of the World Zionist Organization, through the critical years of rising Arab nationalism, of Nazism, of World War II and of the postwar diplomatic struggle between Britain and the Jews of Palestine.

When Britain finally gave up the Palestine mandate, it was for Mr. Ben-Gurion who proclaimed the Jewish state, his moment of supreme test. For on that same day, May 14, 1948, the Arab armies began their invasion of the fledgling state.

Jerusalem was besieged by TransJordan's Arab Legion. In the Judean hills and in Galilee, Jewish settlements were under attack by Syrian and Iraqi forces, while Egyptians invaded from the south. The 62-year-old leader put on battle dress and assumed the direction of military operations.

He was de facto Premier and Minister of Defense. Many of his decisions were questionable. He ordered a costly and ineffective attack to drive the Arab Legion from Jerusalem. But he had surrounded himself with young and competent officers such as Yigal Yadin, Yigal Allon and Moshe Dayan.

The Arabs, who lacked unity of command, were soon routed. To Mr. Ben-Gurion fell most of the credit for having won the first Jewish campaign since that of Judas Maccabeus 2,000 years before. He became an almost mystical figure to many Zionists: the wise patriarch who embodied all the traditional virtues and who would ultimately lead Israel to triumph over the ring of Arab enemies.

He embittered millions of others. He alarmed the United Nations and ensured the continued hatred of the Arab states by adopting a policy of swift and ruthless retaliation for Arab raids on Israel. Although an armistice was arranged by the United Nations, technically Jordan, Lebanon, Syria and Egypt remained at war with Israel, and border incidents were frequent after the war of 1948-49.

Mr. Ben-Gurion also alienated many American Jews by insisting that all true Zionists must live in Israel. Disturbed by the influx of Oriental Jews, which he feared would transform Israel into "just another Levantine state," Mr. Ben-Gurion dreamed of a vast migration of Jews from the Soviet Union and the United States.

In the early years only 5,000 American Jews were "ingathered," a scant migration that drew scornful reproaches from Mr. Ben-Gurion. The feud between Mr. Ben-Gurion and a large segment of American Jewry dated from August,

1957, when he said at a Zionist ideological conference in Jerusalem that a sound Jewish life was not possible outside Israel. "There seems to be a general agreement," he said, "that a Jew can live in America, speak and read English and bring up his children in America and still call himself a Zionist. If that is Zionism I want no part of it."

In subsequent speeches Mr. Ben-Gurion reiterated his belief that Jewish life in the outside world had a dim future. His dogmatism alienated potential friends of Israel among both Jews and gentiles. Non-Zionist Jews resented his insistence that Judaism was not a mere religion but a nationalistic ethos.

Almost every Zionist faction in the United States joined the mounting protest. On Israel's role, though, Mr. Ben-Gurion insisted that essentially Judaism was a nationality and Israel was the only sovereign spokesman for the world's Jews. In June, 1962, he again infuriated American Jewish leaders at a Jerusalem conference by equating Judaism with nationality.

Stanley H. Lowell, chairman of the New York City Commission on Intergroup Relations, retorted: "You aren't the only answer to Jewish living, Jewish creativity and Jewish survival. This generation and the next generations to come shall and will remain part and parcel of the great American experience of democracy."

In later years, though, with the 1967 and 1973 wars and increased United States aid, the old man's idea of Zionism came to be the accepted one. The anti-Zionist organizations became virtually extinct; by 1970, American immigration to Israel was reaching 10,000 a year. At home, Mr. Ben-Gurion managed to rule elements of the population, even members of his own Mapai party, by methods that often seemed autocratic.

He never enjoyed sharing authority, and he chafed under Israel's system of proportional representation, which assures religious parties of representation in the government. These parties were often in bitter disagreement with Mr. Ben-Gurion, who opposed their dream of a theocracy. His Mapai party, although dominant, was never able to win a clear majority in the Knesset, or Parliament; this was a cause of the formation of 11 coalition governments in Israel, including the provisional government that was set up in April, 1948.

In March, 1949, Mr. Ben-Gurion became Premier in the first regularly constituted Government of Israel. Such political marriages into coalitions were usually brief and stormy. The Socialist Mapai had little in common with the small left wing labor parties and religious groups that were persuaded to join coalitions in exchange for concessions in legislation or for a ministerial post or two.

Mr. Ben-Gurion would become so frustrated that he would resign and retire to his four-room cottage in Sde Boker, a kibbutz that was his favorite retreat, in the stony Negev Desert. The mere threat of resignation was enough to force the concessions Mr. Ben-Gurion demanded.

The only Israeli with enough stature to offer alternative leadership was Moshe Sharett, another Mapai stalwart. But Mr. Sharett was considered too cautious, too temporizing. Israelis thought they needed daring leadership to meet the growing threat brought on by Egypt's acquisition of Communist-bloc arms, by the nationalization of the Suez Canal and by the military alliance between Egypt and Syria. Mr. Ben-Gurion resigned several times, but his retirements to Sde Boker were fleeting except for one interval: In December, 1953, he turned over his office and leadership to Mr. Sharett, explaining that he felt "tired, tired, tired."

For 14 months he stayed in Sde Boker compiling "Rebirth and Destiny of Israel," a collection of his addresses and essays and working at agriculture in the kibbutz while his wife helped in the communal kitchen. In retirement he cast his long shadow over the country; soon, in February, 1955, he was called to Jerusalem to resume the post of Minister of Defense, which he had held throughout his Premiership.

He also assumed leadership of the Mapai and again became Premier in November, 1955. Under Mr. Ben-Gurion, Israel adopted a policy that led to war. There had been a flurry of frontier incidents. Israel complained that the United Nations truce supervision teams were futile instruments for checking Arab commando raids.

Mr. Ben-Gurion mounted large-scale retaliatory operations aimed at destroying what he called guerrilla bases across the frontier. To United Nations observers, the border incidents about which the Israelis complained often appeared hardly serious enough to warrant the thunderous retaliation visited upon the Arabs by the Israelis.

In balance at least five or six Arabs died for every Israeli killed. In December, 1955, after Syrians had fired on Israeli fishing craft in the Sea of Galilee, Mr. Ben-Gurion ordered his army into Syrian territory. A network of Syrian coastal positions was blown up, and 50 Syrian solders were killed. The raid was ill-timed politically.

On that same day the temperate Mr. Sharett, then Foreign Minister, was waiting in Washington for an answer to his request for Western arms to offset Communist arms that were reaching Egypt. News of the raid shocked and vexed the State Department. Mr. Sharett returned empty-handed, furious with Mr. Ben-

Gurion, whom he accused of having undermined his mission. Mr. Ben-Gurion not only refused to modify his retaliation policy but also told Mr. Sharett that diplomacy was to be subordinated to security.

In June, 1956, he ousted Mr. Sharett and chose as his new Foreign Minister Mrs. Golda Meir, a former Milwaukee teacher, whom he could trust to follow his line. Tensions rose during the summer of 1956, and in September a major retaliatory action led by General Dayan, then chief of the Israeli armed forces, resulted in the deaths of 37 Jordanians.

Termed fascist actions, Mr. Ben-Gurion defended them as "self-defense," and he told his Parliament that the greatest menace to Israel was an impending attack by "the Egyptian Fascist dictator," President Gamal Abdel Nasser. He proclaimed: "We will never start a war. We do not believe that wars provide comprehensive solutions to historic problems."

Weeks after he had spoken those words Mr. Ben-Gurion, in complicity with France and Britain, launched a "preventive war" to knock out President Nasser's army. Israeli forces overran the Gaza Strip, the tiny corner of the old British Palestine mandate administered by Egypt, and plunged deep into Sinai. Mr. Ben-Gurion's objective was the fall of President Nasser and the signing of a peace treaty with Egypt.

By prearrangement, Britain and France moved to seize the Suez Canal. Port Said fell to the British and French forces. The invasion by the three nations was on the verge of success. Then the roof fell in. President Dwight D. Eisenhower was furious at Britain and France for having committed open aggression while the West was reaping moral capital over the Hungarian revolt.

So the United States supported United Nations demands that the invading forces vacate Egypt promptly and unconditionally. Faced also by threats of Soviet intervention, Britain and France withdrew their forces in 27 days.

But Israel balked. Mr. Ben-Gurion wanted to keep the Gaza Strip. He also wanted assurances that the Gulf of Aqaba, the northern arm of the Red Sea, would be open to Israeli shipping. The gulf had been denied to Israeli ships for six years by Egyptian guns commanding the narrow passage at Sharm el Sheik.

Mr. Eisenhower insisted that no nation invading another in the face of United Nations disapproval should set conditions on its withdrawal. Aggression, he said, must not be rewarded. Mr. Ben-Gurion defied the world for weeks, flouting successive General Assembly orders to get out of Egypt.

His Parliament had approved a defiant resolution committing Israel never to yield either the gulf or Gaza. But when President Eisenhower cut short a vacation to warn of "pressure" if Israel failed to cooperate, the tough little Premier knew the game was up. Tired and drawn from pneumonia contracted after a PT boat ride in the Gulf of Aqaba, Mr. Ben-Gurion went before his Cabinet to propose more flexibility in Israel's position. He had learned the art of compromise.

Mr. Ben-Gurion was born in Plonsk, Poland, on October 16, 1886. His name was David Green, and his father was Avigdor Green, an unlicensed lawyer who wore a silk top hat and a frock coat rather than the fur hat and caftan traditionally worn by the men of his community.

David was to adopt the pen name "Ben-Gurion" as a journalist in Jerusalem. He thought it had a resonant Old Testament ring — it was the name of one of the last defenders of Jerusalem against the Roman legions. The Hebrew word "Ben" means "Son of" and "Gurion" means "Lion Cub." Mr. Ben-Gurion's mother, Sheindal, died during the birth of her 11th child.

David, her sixth, was 10 years old at the time. The tone of the family was vigorously intellectual. There were discussions of Socialism and the newly re-emerged Zionism advocated by the Viennese journalist Theodor Herzl at the historic Jewish conference at Basel, Switzerland, in 1897.

Mr. Ben-Gurion's formal education did not go much beyond the Plonsk Jewish schools, but he acquired an excellently stocked mind through wide reading, particularly in history. Possessed of tremendous concentration, he became in his lifetime a keen student of Greek and Eastern philosophies. He achieved a brilliant reputation as a linguist through his mastery of English, Russian, Greek, Yiddish, Turkish, French and German. He read but did not speak Arabic. He also studied Spanish. In Plonsk he was active in the Poale Zion movement, which combined Zionism and Socialism. Plonsk was in Russian Poland, and the revolutionary movement against the Czars was followed by pogroms there.

Many Polish and Russian Jews emigrated. In 1906, kindled by Mr. Herzl's aim for a Jewish commonwealth, David Green was one of a group of young Plonsk Jews who went to Palestine. On his first night in Palestine he wrote in a letter to his father "I did not sleep. I was amid the rich smell of corn. I heard the braying of donkeys and the rustle of leaves in the orchards. Above were massed clusters of stars against the deep blue firmament. My heart overflowed with happiness."

Mr. Ben-Gurion was repelled by the political apathy of the Jewish settlers — there were about 60,000 Jews in Palestine when he arrived. He joined the small Workers party, Poale Zion, which was to emerge as Mapei, and soon became one of its leading organizers and propagandists. Today Mapai is moderately Socialist, probably no more leftist than the British Labor Party, and has little in common with doctrinaire Marxism.

Mr. Ben-Gurion worked for a time as a farm laborer for wages just sufficient to provide him with a room and one meal a day. He displayed a natural ability to negotiate in labor disputes, and he soon had considerable prestige among his fellow workers. Articles signed "Ben-Gurion" began to appear in the Poale Zion party newspaper, and Mr. Ben-Gurion was elected to the three-man administrative presidium of the party at the 1907 Jaffa conference.

At that conference he succeeded in having this platform plan adopted: "The Party will strive for an independent state for the Jewish people in this country." In that year, to prevent difficulties for his father in Plonsk, Mr. Ben-Gurion returned to Russia to do his military service. He served for one week, deserted and made his way back to Palestine.

The success of Enver Pasha's "Young Turk" movement in Turkey in 1908 led Mr. Ben-Gurion and many of his associates to believe that reasonable coexistence could be established between the new and supposedly liberal Turkish Government and the Jewish community in Palestine, which was in the Ottoman Empire.

Mr. Ben-Gurion and several other Zionist leaders went to Constantinople to study Turkish law and administration, hoping to enter the Turkish Government as representatives of Jewish Palestine. Russia had left the war and the United States had entered it. Mr. Ben-Gurion believed that the best interests of the Palestine Jews lay with Turkey.

But by 1917 there were indications that the Turks might not be on the winning side. Mr. Ben-Gurion helped organize two Jewish battalions in the United States and Canada to serve with the British in the Middle East. He served as a corporal in one of the battalions, with the Royal Fusiliers in Egypt, but saw no action.

The Balfour Declaration of 1917 established the principle of a Jewish homeland in Palestine, and in 1922 the British were entrusted by the League of Nations with a mandate for Palestine. Chaim Weizmann, the intellectual who was to become the first President of Israel, headed the workers' Zionist movement mostly from London.

Mr. Ben-Gurion preached Jewish working-class solidarity on the scene in Palestine. To a group of Zionist delegates he once said "Let me inform you gentlemen that Zionism has no content if you do not constantly bear in mind the building of the Jewish state. And such a state is only possible on the basis of a maximum number of workers, and if you cannot understand that, woe to your Zionism."

The Jewish Legion had been formed too late to contribute much to the defeat of Turkey, but its existence provided Mr. Ben-Gurion with a fine channel for propaganda. He proselytized for the Poale Zion party among the 3,000 legionnaires. It was largely because of his initiative that Histadrut, the General Federation of Labor, was formed in 1920, with Mr. Ben-Gurion as Secretary General. The powerful body, now quartered in a modern Tel Aviv skyscraper that enemies of Mr. Ben-Gurion called the Kremlin, expanded into banking, health plans, contracting, agriculture, marketing, education, insurance, transportation, employment agencies, collectives and cooperatives of every kind.

Over the next five years Mr. Ben-Gurion campaigned for the union of Palestine's labor parties, and in 1930 the Mapai was formed. In 1935 he became chairman of the Jewish Agency, the executive body of Zionism. Mr. Ben-Gurion had many opponents in the general Zionist movement. Vladimir Jabotinsky was one leader of a nationalist movement opposed to what many Zionists believed to be Mr. Ben-Gurion's strong Socialist views.

In 1936, Palestinian Arabs staged a bloody revolt against increasing Jewish influence, and the next year Mr. Ben-Gurion favored a partition of Palestine as recommended by a Royal Commission under Earl Peel. The Arabs rejected the proposal, and the British dropped the plan. London's policy became clearly pro-Arab, and in 1939 the British Government issued a White Paper that limited Jewish immigration to Palestine and land purchases there and was aimed at insuring a permanent minority status for the Jews there.

After Britain declared war on Germany the Jews in Palestine pledged support against the common enemy but continued their resistance to British policy, which they considered a threat to their existence. Mr. Ben-Gurion put it this way: "We shall fight in the war against Hitler as if there was no White Paper, but we shall fight the White Paper as if there were no war."

During the war years he was preoccupied with these aims and internal matters in Palestine. And the mass extermination of German Jews intensified his desire to establish a Jewish homeland. In 1945 he visited displaced persons camps in Germany and told a conference of survivors: "We shall not rest until the last one of you who so desires shall join us in the land of Israel to build the Jewish state together with us."

Mr. Ben-Gurion believed that if the Jews in

Palestine could not defend themselves they would be driven out by the Arabs. From 1907, when he was with "Hashomer," the armed guard movement, while he was a labor leader in Sejera, a small isolated village in Galilee, he acted in the belief that the Palestinian Jews would have to protect themselves. When the United Nations, on November 29, 1947, resolved to partition Palestine into Jewish and Arab states, Mr. Ben-Gurion assumed the security portfolio of the Jewish Agency Executive.

He planned and supervised the transformation of the Haganah from an illegal underground military arm of the Jewish Agency into the Israel Defense Forces. He sent men to Europe to buy arms, including World War II surplus equipment, and to recruit Jewish war veterans to operate the planes, tanks and artillery with which the Haganah had had no experience. They came from the United States, Canada, South Africa, South America and most European countries.

Mr. Ben-Gurion obtained funds from Jews in the United States and bought machinery to establish an arms industry. From time to time Mr. Ben-Gurion cooperated with the British against terrorists, yet armed clashes were narrowly averted. During the mandate the Irgun Zvai Leumi, an extreme nationalist group, had conducted terrorist activities against the British Government.

Unlike the Haganah, it had spurned the authority of the official Jewish leadership. During a United Nations truce, the Irgun ran the landing ship *Altalena* ashore at Tel Aviv with weapons and volunteers. Mr. Ben-Gurion ordered Haganah troops to fire at the ship, which blew up.

Men were killed and wounded on both sides. The *Altalena* affair was one of the most controversial events in Mr. Ben-Gurion's career as Premier. Many Israelis never forgave his order, which deprived Israel of badly needed weapons and nearly touched off a civil war.

Others said it had been one of the most courageous and statesmanlike actions of his career. They believed that by handling the situation firmly in that crucial period Mr. Ben-Gurion had established once and for all that there was no authority in the state but the Government of Israel and in fact averted a civil war. After the truce, renewed sharp fighting with the Arabs secured the Negev and central Galilee for Israel.

Armistice agreements with Egypt, Lebanon, Syria and Jordan in 1949 ended the hot war for the time being. Although large-scale immigration had nearly doubled the population, it was still necessary to maintain military preparedness. The Israelis by 1951 found it necessary to take drastic steps to bolster the economy. Mr. Ben-Gurion came to the United States on a fund-raising drive.

He was received with enthusiasm and initiated the sale of $500 million in Israeli Bonds. This time Israel abandoned her foreign policy of "non-identification" and openly aligned herself with the United States in the cold war. Previously, Israel, in her independence struggle, had bought arms from Soviet-bloc countries and had enjoyed good relations with the Soviet Union, one of the first nations to recognize the State of Israel.

At home Mr. Ben-Gurion wrestled with succeeding Cabinet crises until the day in 1953 when he decided that he had had enough for a while. In an article written for *The New York Times* from his retreat at Sde Boker on his retirement, he said: "No single person alone can determine the fate of a nation. No man is indispensable. In war there may be a commander or statesman on whom much or even all depends. Not so in time of peace. The fate of a country depends upon its own character, its ability, its capacity, its faith in itself, its sense of responsibility, both individual and collective. A statesman who sees himself as the determining factor in the fate of his country is harmful and dangerous."

But for 15 years Mr. Ben-Gurion made most of the decisions for Israel, and the most fateful were to come after he had returned to Jerusalem in 1955 and had begun leading the nation on a more adventurous path. Although his country was in reality a ward of the United States, absolutely dependent on financial aid from Washington and from American Jewish groups, Mr. Ben-Gurion refused to permit any outside meddling in her affairs.

He showed his freedom from American controls early by ignoring strong Washington pressure to put Israel's capital in Tel Aviv, rather than in Jerusalem, which the United Nations had proposed as an international city. The United States has refused to move its embassy from Tel Aviv to Jerusalem.

In domestic politics, Mr. Ben-Gurion also defied strong forces, notably the ultra-Orthodox religious groups. Once during an interminable Knesset debate over whether swine — forbidden to Jews as food — should be bred in Israel, Mr. Ben-Gurion remarked that if the Lord had objected to pigs He wouldn't have led them to Noah's Ark. Another time he shocked rabbis in the Knesset by announcing that after a study of Exodus he had concluded that only 600 Jews — not 600,000 as the Bible maintained — could have left Egypt and crossed the Sinai Desert.

Mr. Ben-Gurion was a profound student of the Bible. His speeches were enriched with references to the heroes and Prophets of the Old Testament. He had had little formal education, but his intellectual curiosity led him, at 56, to learn Greek so he could read the Septuagint, the Greek version of the Old Testament.

At 68 his interest turned to the Dialogues of Buddha, and he began learning Sanskrit to understand them fully. He already knew enough yoga to stand on his head, and photos of Mr. Ben-Gurion in bathing trunks, inverted on the Mediterranean sands, invoked wry comment. Friends insisted, however, that Hazaken — the Old Man — as he was affectionately called, was sharper-witted upside down than most of his opponents right side up.

The most serious domestic challenge to Mr. Ben-Gurion's rule came as a result of the celebrated "Lavon affair." A former protégé of Mr. Ben-Gurion, Pinhas Lavon, had risen in the Histradrut until his political influence was so considerable that he was regarded as a possible heir to the national leadership. Mr. Ben-Gurion fell out with Mr. Lavon and sought to destroy his power.

A cloak-and-dagger fiasco, involving the collapse of an Israeli spy network in Egypt, gave Mr. Ben-Gurion the chance in 1955 to force Mr. Lavon's resignation as Defense Minister. The scandal smouldered for six years. Few Israelis knew what the affair was about. The press was allowed to print only the state censor's approved phrase, "a security disaster in 1954."

The Egyptian Government charged in 1954 that it had uncovered an Israeli spy ring that planned to blow up British and American consular offices to sabotage relations between Cairo and the Western powers. But in December, 1960, the Lavon affair burst into the news again. Mr. Lavon was able to prove at a meeting of the Israeli Cabinet that forged papers had been part of the evidence that forced him from office.

Mr. Ben-Gurion stormed from the room, but even this did not prevent his Cabinet from clearing Mr. Lavon of responsibility for the 1954 fiasco. Mr. Ben-Gurion followed his usual tactic of bringing down the Government by resigning. But this time other members of his six-party coalition were so disturbed that they refused to join him in a new government.

Hoping to silence his critics, Mr. Ben-Gurion called for new elections. The results, he conceded, were "a national disaster," for Mapai slipped from 47 seats to 42 in the 120-seat Knesset. After lengthy dickering, however, he formed a new Cabinet and meanwhile the Mapai Central Committee had destroyed Mr. Lavon's base of power by ousting him as Secretary General of the Histradrut.

Mr. Ben-Gurion suffered the bitter fate that overtakes a statesman who has been around too long. He became a bore to his people, and they rejected him. He resigned as Premier in June, 1963, because of "personal needs." He said later that he wanted to write a history of the Jews' return to their homeland.

But in semiretirement he erupted sporadically, like a cooling volcano. He became increasingly critical of Levi Eshkol, the new Premier, and the estrangement between the two grew wider when Mr. Ben-Gurion proclaimed that Mr. Eshkol was "unfit to lead the nation." He demanded a reopening of the Lavon affair.

But the country was bored by the 10-year-old scandal, and Premier Eshkol refused an inquiry into the almost-forgotten fiasco. Mr. Ben-Gurion's efforts to return to politics ended in humiliation. The Mapai Central Committee refused to put him on the party's list for the 1965 election.

So he formed Rafi, a splinter party, taking with him a handful of younger politicians, including General Dayan, the former Chief of Staff. The new party ran a poor fourth with less that 9 per cent of the vote, and won 10 seats in Parliament. Mr. Ben-Gurion's wife died in 1968 and the old warrior spent much of his time thereafter in solitary contemplation.

In 1968, after his small Rafi party decided to join the newly formed Israel Labor party, a number of Rafi members led by Mr. Ben-Gurion broke away. They formed the Independent National List and won four Knesset seats in 1969. He remained in the Knesset until 1970, when he delivered a hand-written resignation note to the speaker, Reuven Barkatt, and, dry-eyed, left the chamber for good.

Afterward, he told a visitor to Tel Aviv that he had found farm work more satisfying than politics. And he had this to say about Soviet intentions in the Middle East: "They want to get the two oceans, the Atlantic and the Pacific. So first of all they must have the Mediterranean, and it is not easy to get that without the Arabs. They want the Arabs, I do not think they are interested in destroying Israel, because if they do, the Arabs will not need them."

On the territories that Israel occupied in the 1967 Arab-Israeli war, Mr. Ben-Gurion took a relatively dovish position: "I consider peace more important than territory," he said. "The area we had before the Six–Day War would be enough to take in all the Jews."

He continued: "For peace, I would be for giving back all the captured areas, with the exception of Jerusalem and the Golan Heights." As to his old theme on the need for further immigration, he said Israel still needed "another five or six million" Jews. But he observed wryly, "I don't believe that all Jews will settle in Israel — unless the Messiah comes."

On the sometimes controversial question of what constitutes being a Jew, Mr. Ben-Gurion later told a visitor to Sde Boker, "The essence of being a Jew, in my opinion, is the idea of the Prophets — not the Torah, but the Prophets. They have two ideas: You must love one single God and you must lead a moral life. That is all that matters."

"Later on," he continued, "when we Jews lost our independence and we had to live in ghettos and were hated, then our leaders provided other things and rules about things to wear and say. They needed these things to keep Jews together as a nation."

He said that now that Jews again had a homeland and independence, the rituals and practices had faded in significance against the Prophets' more general messages.

In his last years Mr. Ben-Gurion aged considerably. His nimbus of white hair seemed to grow wispier, and his thoughts sometimes rambled. He spent much of his time in his cluttered study at Sde Boker, living among his books and in the past. There was a large portrait of his wife, a map of Israel, a vase of desert roses among the awards and mementos.

On his desk, there was always a Bible and a bottle of apple juice. He was well, he participated in kibbutz activities — dedicating a new garden, leading a Bible-study group, pressing Tel Aviv for a teachers' training institute for the settlement. His time was devoted to study, reflection, writing, and a teeming correspondence with Jews all over the world. He produced three big books in his last years, including the 862-page *Israel: A Personal History,* published in 1971.

On rare occasions, he made public appearances. In early 1971, he toured the fortifications along the Suez Canal with Gen. Haim Bar-Lev, then the Chief of Staff, engaging in the banter he loved. The old man was shown a bunker. "What kind of Hebrew word is 'bunker'?" he asked. An escort explained: "We use 'bunker' because we have not yet got around to Hebraizing defense terminology. On offense, we have no foreign words." Ben-Gurion talked with a soldier. "You're younger than I," he said, "perhaps you can tell me when there will be peace." The soldier replied: "Who knows? It depends on the Arabs."

"And on us!" the patriarch put in. In 1971, on his 85th birthday, he publicly rejected an appeal from Mrs. Meir that he give up his splinter party and rejoin Mapai. Mrs. Meir nonetheless went to the celebration in Sde Boker, and they talked for a bit — after five years of silence.

His last appearance was in May in Tel Aviv for Israel's 25th anniversary. He sat bent over a grandstand watching the pomp, wearing a farmer's hat. He had become a symbol of the past, a much-loved grandfather hovering at the edge of the thoughts and aspirations of the embattled nation.

He said little about the October war, though he was quoted as having referred sarcastically to the arguments among Israeli generals following the Egyptian and Syrian surprise attacks: "They think they're generals now."

In his last years, Mr. Ben-Gurion argued that the Israeli Government was not genuinely democratic. Old opponents replied that it was Mr. Ben-Gurion himself who had introduced authoritarian ways into Israel during his years as Premier.

Even these opponents conceded that he and his wife had never stood much on ceremony.

When Mrs. Ben-Gurion was asked once whether her husband should be addressed as "Prime Minister" or "Mr. Ben-Gurion," she reportedly said, "Call him Ben-Gurion. Anyone can be a prime minister, but not everyone can be a Ben-Gurion."

By HOMER BIGART
The New York Times
December 2, 1973

Ben-Gurion briefed by Moshe Dayan as they fly over the Sinai Peninsula in 1956.

Itzhak Ben-Zvi

ITZHAK BEN-ZVI, president of Israel from 1952 to 1963, died in his residence in Jerusalem. He was 78 years old.

The President's health failed after his return from an African tour in August. He entered the hospital on April 1 and returned home three weeks later.

Mr. Ben-Zvi, Israel's second President, was reported to have had cancer and his condition deteriorated steadily. He lapsed into a coma before his death at 7:05 A.M.

Speaker of the Knesset (Parliament), serves as acting president until the Knesset elects a successor within 30 days.

Itzhak Ben-Zvi was a lifelong leader of the generation of militant young Zionists who settled in Palestine before World War I and shaped the movement that created Israel after World War II.

He was a faithful partner of Ben-Gurion in the moderately socialist Labor Zionist group that became the Mapai party, the dominant political force in Israel. Mr. Ben-Zvi was two years older, a head taller and more easy-going than Mr. Ben-Gurion, Israel's Premier.

When Israel's first President, Dr. Chaim Weizmann, died in 1952, Mr. Ben-Zvi was the Mapai nominee to succeed him. On the third ballot in the Knesset, the left-wing Mapam political party swung behind him to break a deadlock with a candidate of the Orthodox religious and political parties.

In 1957 no one stood against him for a second five-year term; 76 members of the Knesset voted for him and the remaining 18 who were present abstained. In the next election there was no candidate against him, but the vote was 62 to 42 because many members objected on principle to a third term for any President.

The duties of an Israeli President are mainly symbolic. Mr. Ben-Zvi performed them with dignity but without any change in his plain egalitarian style. Through his interest in Jewish immigrants whose heritage differed from that of the dominant East European group, he sought to unify the younger generation. This attitude of goodwill to all was perhaps his chief asset at President.

When the President's salary was raised, over his protest, to $6,000 a year, he announced that he would donate half of it to research, which, next to Zionism, was his lifelong preoccupation.

His humble quarters in Jerusalem were open to visitors from all walks of life, particularly during the festivals of Passover and the Tabernacles, and on the first day of each month. He continued to worship in the small synagogue he had attended as a private citizen, and to take part in its weekly Talmud class. On Friday afternoons he worked at his old desk in the Ben-Zvi Institute for Research on Oriental Jewish Communities.

Mr. Ben-Zvi was the last recourse of Adolf Eichmann after the death sentence against the former Nazi in 1962 for complicity in the wartime murder of millions of Jews. The president rejected the appeal for clemency and Eichmann was hanged several hours later.

Czarist pogroms drove Mr. Ben-Zvi to Palestine in 1907. He had visited the Middle East three years earlier, but returned to his parents in Poltava, in the Ukraine, where he was born November 24, 1884. His name was Isaac Shimshelevitz. In Israel, he adopted the Hebrew form, which means Isaac, son of Zvi.

He attended the traditional Hebrew school as a child, went to the Government high school in his city and later studied natural science at the University of Kiev. He taught Hebrew and Russian at the university to earn enough money to visit Palestine.

With a record of having helped to found the Zionist labor movement in Russia, the young Ben-Zvi went back to Jerusalem as a teacher. He was a founder of the first Hebrew high school there in 1909 and a year later became editor with Mr. Ben-Gurion of the journal Haachdut.

Mr. Ben-Zvi and Mr. Ben-Gurion were often referred to as "the twins." They were sent to

Constantinople to study Turkish law. They collaborated in the literary field and then, with Josef Springzak, brought together a group of guardsmen known as Hashomer. This defense unit became the Haganah after World War I.

When Jemal Pasha, Governor of Syria, exiled Messrs. Ben-Zvi and Ben-Gurion from Palestine in 1916, "the twins" came to the United States. After organizing the Hechalutz (pioneer) movement here, they returned home to form the Jewish Legion, a unit that fought beside the British in driving the Turks and Germans from Palestine.

A Zionist delegate of the British Labor party since 1908, Mr. Ben-Zvi became a Government official in Palestine in 1920. He resigned a year later in protest against a British order temporarily suspending immigration to Palestine.

He had already helped to organize the Histadrut in 1920 as the Federation of Jewish Labor in Palestine. In 1929 he took part in the Zurich conference that led to the establishment of the Jewish Agency for Palestine.

Mr. Ben-Zvi returned to government service in 1927 on the Municipal Council of Jerusalem. Four years later he became chairman of the Vaad Leumi, the Jewish National Council, which represented 90 percent of the Jewish community for the 30 years of the British mandate in Palestine.

He represented the Jews of Palestine at the coronation of King George VI of Britain in 1937. Seven years later he was elected president of Vaad Leumi and, in 1948, he was one of the 37 signers of Israel's Declaration of Independence. He presented a copy of this document to the United States the same year at a ceremony in this country on the Freedom Train, which carried the American Declaration of Independence to cities thoughout the United States.

Upon the establishment of Israel as a nation in 1948, he was elected to the Knesset.

Mr. Ben-Zvi, throughout his political career, continued his work on Middle East lore and archeological research. He collaborated with Mr. Ben-Gurion on "Eretz Israel in Past and Present" in 1918.

His "The Book of the Samaritans" was published in 1935, and five volumes of research and articles on Moslem culture appeared in 1937. He became chief of the Institute for the Research of Jewish Communities in the Middle East at the Hebrew University that same year. In 1958 he published his history of the Jews, *The Exiled and the Redeemed*.

Mr. Ben-Zvi succeeded Dr. Weizmann as honorary president of the Hebrew University. He also received an honorary degree from the Jewish Theological Seminary of America. Britain granted him the order of the British Empire.

His widow, the former Rachel Yanait, was an agricultural engineer. The couple lived for many years in a tar-papered wooden shack in the Rahavia district of Jerusalem. Their official residence when he became President of Israel was a three-room prefabricated bungalow of the type erected for immigrant families in villages.

A son, who is a farmer, and a daughter also survive. A younger son was killed resisting the Arab military forces in 1947. The little shack in which the family used to live was moved to Beit Keshet, the collective settlement where the younger son had lived.

The New York Times
April 23, 1963

Moshe Dayan

MOSHE DAYAN, the Israeli soldier-statesman, died of a heart ailment in Tel Aviv's Sheba Medical Center. He was 66 years old.

Mr. Dayan was rushed to the medical center around midnight, complaining of chest pains and shortness of breath.

A former Chief of Staff, Defense Minister and Foreign Minister, he was an architect of Israel's campaigns in the 1967 and 1973 wars as well as the Camp David accords that led to the peace treaty with Egypt.

He resigned as Foreign Minister in October 1979, citing differences with Prime Minister Menachem Begin over policy towards the Palestinian Arabs in the occupied West Bank and Gaza Strip.

Mr. Dayan headed his own political party, called Telem, in the last elections, but it won only two seats. Despite the absence of a power base, he continued to make his voice heard on the major issues facing Israel, especially relations with the Arabs.

His health had been poor in recent years. In June, 1979, he had a malignant tumor removed from his colon and part of his intestine, then underwent chemotherapy and radiation treatment, according to friends. His appearance deteriorated markedly; he grew drawn and frail. Some who saw him recently noticed that the vision in his one good eye seemed to be failing.

The Israeli radio and television reported that his condition in the hospital deteriorated with respiratory problems and loss of blood pressure. His death was attributed by a government official to a heart attack.

Moshe Dayan was known as a general who made war, a diplomat who made peace and a political figure who stirred repeated controversy in his homeland.

Although single-minded in his passionate Israeli nationalism, he was a complicated man in other ways. His complexity was mirrored in his disparate features: the long youthful face, the forceful mouth, the distinctive high cheekbones and the famous, tough-looking eyepatch.

Those striking features, the delight of cartoonists and cameramen, became known around the world during Mr. Dayan's long and varied career in the service of Israel.

Mr. Dayan was vulnerable physically, almost frail, a short man, continually beset by ailments. He admitted to being hard of hearing. Old wounds caused him pain. Sometimes he wore a back brace.

"I need a completely new body," he wearily told an interviewer in 1978. "I need parts replacing, the whole thing. My eye, my back."

His military career started in 1939, when he joined a Jewish militia force. Later, as chief of staff, he emerged a hero in the 1956 war with Egypt. As a military planner, he was instrumental in the strategy that enabled Israel to capture vast areas in the 1967 war.

But, as defense minister, he was severely criticized for Israel's setbacks in the first days of the Arab attack in October 1973.

Then, as foreign minister, he played a key role in negotiations that led to the signing of the Israeli-Egyptian peace treaty.

Mr. Dayan's devotion to Israel was reflected in his private life. He built up a vast collection of Holy Land antiquities that nourished his near-mystic sense of Israel's past. His writings, notably his autobiography and a book about archeology, *Living With the Bible,* were in part hymns to his country.

Like other world leaders, Mr. Dayan was sometimes criticized and sometimes out of favor. But he was a remarkably resilient man who seemed blessed by good fortune. Prime Minister Golda Meir called him "altogether too lucky." An Israeli writer, Amos Elon, noted that he was "always landing on his feet."

Though Mr. Dayan was by and large a hero to the Israeli people, he was generally a loner. Mr. Elon called him "this gloomy, lonely, gifted man — too cunning, too admired, too hated, too ambiguous, too glamorous, too extravagant, too famous."

He crowned the achievements of his long public career, in the eyes of some, by helping to overcome lingering barriers to the peace agreement with Egypt.

Deeply involved in the treaty negotiations since the beginning in October, 1978, Mr. Dayan met with Prime Minister Begin in Jerusalem on the evening of March 12, 1979, when agreement seemed unlikely, and he urged that a last attempt be made to work out a compromise with the Egyptian position.

It was a crucial moment. President Carter was in Jerusalem, preparing to leave for home the next morning without having resolved the obstacles to peace.

Mr. Dayan then met with Secretary of State Cyrus R. Vance and suggested some approaches that made the Secretary feel further peacemaking efforts must be justified. Mr. Dayan was also on hand the next morning, with Prime Minister Begin and President Carter, when additional discussions were held about a compromise involving the question of Israeli access to oil from Sinai fields and other issues.

Within 24 hours, Israel and Egypt had agreed to the treaty terms.

Earlier, in 1977, Mr. Dayan obtained the Foreign Minister's post through another exercise in flexibility and enterprise. He quit the Labor Party shortly after it was humiliated in a general election by Likud, Mr. Begin's political bloc, and accepted the Prime Minister's offer of the post.

From the viewpoints of Mr. Begin and Mr. Dayan, the move made sense. The two were in substantial agreement on foreign policy and dealt with each other in the past. And Mr. Dayan's international standing was expected to be helpful to the prime minister.

Mr. Dayan's switch brought a flood of denunciation from the Labor Party, where grandstand appeals to unity and fierce internal rivalries were customary. But Mr. Dayan calmly kept his own counsel, making few comments, and the hullabaloo died down.

As foreign minister, he played a key role in the negotiations and maneuvering that preceded the signing of the Israeli-Egyptian peace treaty in March, 1979.

Yet in October, 1979, Mr. Dayan quit his Cabinet post, complaining about what he said was the Begin government's failure to carry out the Camp David provisions for autonomy for the residents of the West Bank and Gaza Strip.

Undaunted, he formed his own party, Telem, for the Israeli parliamentary elections last June, but won only two seats in the 120-member parliament. He blamed himself for the disappointing showing.

In newspaper interviews during the campaign, he criticized the government and called for the unilateral withdrawal of Israel's military governments from the Gaza Strip and West Bank, leaving the Palestinians in those areas to administer their own affairs.

After the elections, Mr. Begin talked to Mr. Dayan before forming a new government. But Mr. Dayan reportedly asked, as a condition of joining it, that he be put in charge of the negotiations with the United States and Egypt on granting self-administration to the Palestinians of the Gaza Strip and West Bank. Mr. Begin turned him down.

Through the years he held repeated secret meetings with King Hussein of Jordan, most recently during his time as Mr. Begin's foreign minister. Recalling that last meeting in a subsequent book, Mr. Dayan said he came away feeling certain that no deal could be struck with the King.

Mr. Dayan's passionate concern for Israel and its future continued until the end of his life. In *Breakthrough: a Personal Account of the Egypt-Israel Peace Negotiations,* a book published in 1981, he said his country would allow no "foreign sovereignty" on the West Bank. He also said that Israeli military forces and settlements must remain and that no Palestinian nation should be allowed.

In his last published writing, an article that appeared in the Israeli newspaper Yedioth Ahronoth, he expressed some uncertainty about future Israeli-Egyptian relations in light of the death of the Egyptian president, Anwar el-Sadat.

He said be believed that "the new government of Egypt will carry through" the letter of the peace agreement, but added, "As for its spirit, that is another question completely."

Mr. Dayan's military career was even more turbulent than his political life. He weathered a storm over the 1973 war, when Israel suffered reverses in the first days of fighting, after misjudging signs that an Arab assault was imminent. For a time he was relegated to a minor role as an ordinary member of parliament.

The basis for Mr. Dayan's prominence in Israeli political life was the glory he earned in the earlier Arab-Israeli wars. After serving as commander of the Jerusalem front during the 1948 conflict, he pursued military studies at the Camberley Staff College in Britain and headed Israel's General Staff from 1953 to 1958.

In the 1956 war, troops under his command swept through Egyptian positions to occupy the Sinai Peninsula and the Gaza Strip within six days. But the Israelis subsequently withdrew from the land they had seized — three times the size of Israel — on orders from the Government, which was under pressure from the United Nations and the United States.

General Dayan chose to be with his troops as they took down their blue-and-white Israeli flags before handing over the land to United Nations troops.

"A commander's place is with his men during a bitter withdrawal," he observed at the time "Even more than in time of conquest."

Mr. Dayan's 1967 military triumph was sweeter. Two days before that war broke out, he was called back by the Israeli Government — he was minister of agriculture — to serve as defense minister. He declared that Israel welcomed diplomatic support in its confrontation with the Arabs but did not wish "anyone else to fight for us."

Two days later, his forces staged surprise predawn attacks. Israeli war-planes knocked out opposing Arab air forces before their planes could get off the ground.

Israeli tanks and armor churned through the Sinai Desert, once again seized the Gaza Strip, and moved west-ward to the Suez Canal before a ceasefire was arranged.

That victory, coming after much Arab bluster, was ascribed to brilliant staff work and to courage by Israelis, notably tank officers in the field. It also embodied Mr. Dayan's longstanding concern with his nation's security.

In *Living With the Bible,* he wrote, "The future borders of Israel have been my closest concern since the establishment of the state."

Despite the criticism of Israel's early performance in the 1973 conflict, Mr. Dayan later argued that the war's final outcome had a crucial bearing on the decision by President Sadat to seek peace with the Israelis.

In giving his explanation of Mr. Sadat's action,

Mr. Dayan wrote: "Egypt was defeated, and it ended with Israel's forces being closer to Cairo than in the previous wars. Sadat learned something from this. He nullified his alliance with Russia, sought closer relations with the United States and announced that he favored peace."

Mr. Dayan remained outspoken where military affairs were concerned. In June of 1981, speaking in telephone interviews, he said that Israel had developed the capacity to make nuclear weapons and could produce bombs on short notice if the Arabs did so.

"We don't have any atomic bomb now, but we have the capacity, we can do that in a short time," he said in what was believed to be the first confirmation by an Israeli who had been in a position of authority of what was widely assumed about Israel's nuclear potential.

"If the Arabs are willing to introduce nuclear weapons into the Middle East," he went on, "then Israel should not be too late in having nuclear weapons, too."

Mr. Dayan's other great interest was with the Holy Land's past. When he was in his home in a suburb of Tel Aviv he liked to relax in its large yard, which was filled with antiquities he had unearthed.

Over years of diligent archeological activity, Mr. Dayan put together one of the world's most valuable and extensive private collections of ancient Middle East relics. It included sarcophagi, burial urns and ancient plaques that he had removed from burial sites.

In an appraisal of *Living With the Bible* in *The Times Book Review,* Amos Elon charged that the collection had been "assembled partly through illicit excavations."

"No public prosecutor has ever dared to file charges," Mr. Elon noted, although Mr. Dayan's private excavations often came in for bitter denunciations in Israeli newspapers.

Mr. Dayan pursued his passion for the past even when it involved physical danger. An ancient burial cave collapsed on him as he was excavating near Tel Aviv in 1969, and he might have died had it not been for the lucky chance that a boy had seen him enter the cave.

Over the years, Mr. Dayan was so successful as an antiquities sleuth that a noted Israeli archeologist, Prof. Benjamin Mazar of Hebrew University, remarked that Mr. Dayan, with his one eye, could see more than 10 professional archeologists.

Trying to explain his passion, Mr. Dayan wrote: "My parents, who came from another country, sought to make the Israel of their imagination, drawn from the Bible, their physical homeland. In somewhat the reverse way, I sought to give my real and tangible homeland the added dimension of historical depth."

Moshe Dayan was born on May 20, 1915, the first child in Degania A, the first kibbutz established in what is now Israel.

A farming and dairy center, the kibbutz is on the southern shore of the Sea of Galilee. It was founded by Zionists in 1909, destroyed by Arab troops in 1948 and rebuilt by citizens of the new Israeli state.

Mr. Dayan's parents, as he wrote in his autobiography, were settlers from Europe who had come "to the land of Israel, experiencing with their whole being, heart and body, the revolutionary transition from the Russian disapora to the unknown."

His father, Shmuel Dayan, was raised in the Ukraine, the son of a poor itinerant peddler. Shmuel Dayan's grandfather and great-grandfather had been rabbinical judges, known in Hebrew as "dayanim." Shmuel Dayan's peddler father took the singular form of the word, "dayan," as his family name.

In 1908, Shmuel Dayan, an ardent Zionist, settled in what was then Turkish-ruled Palestine and became a farm worker and later a watchman at a vineyard before joining Degania A.

Moshe Dayan's mother, Dvorah, was the daughter of a lumber merchant in the Ukraine. Also a dedicated Zionist, she went to the Holy Land in 1913 and met and married her husband on the kibbutz.

Mr. Dayan attended the agricultural secondary school in the village of Nahalal and was trained in the Haganah, a Jewish militia force. He was jailed in 1939, when the Haganah was declared illegal by the British authorities, who then controlled Palestine under a League of Nations mandate. He was released to fight with the British Army in World War II.

He lost his left eye during Allied action in Syria when a French bullet struck binoculars that he was holding to his eyes.

In 1935, Mr. Dayan married Ruth Schwartz, who was later active in Arab-Israeli cultural relations. They were divorced in 1972. He married Rachel Corem a year later. Technically, he was married three times. In the 1930s, he married a young German-Jewish woman to legalize her immigration to Palestine, but quickly divorced her.

Mr. Dayan is survived by his wife; two sons, Assaf, an actor, and Ehud, a farmer, and a daughter, Yael, a writer, all from his first marriage; and five grandchildren.

A Sample of Comments by Dayan
On Battle

"When I go into battle, I am 100 percent sure I

will win and come out safely. I believe, with my luck and skill, that I'll manage between the bullets and they will not get hold of me. You have to feel that way or you'll never come out of it."

"During battle, when I see shells exploding around me, I am able to be calm. Most people, when they hear a shot, their body jerks. Mine doesn't. I'm not proud of that. When I hear bullets whistle, I know it's not birds singing, but I have no physical reaction."

On Death

"I've lost one eye, had a finger clipped, busted my back, paralyzed a vocal cord and had cancer of the colon. So I'm no Olympic athlete. So what? I hope you'll believe me. I find it very hard to convince other people. I don't mind dying and never have. Not that I want to die—I just don't give a damn."

On His Relations with Arabs

"When we argue, they know I'll keep my word. I say, 'Unless you cease sheltering terrorists who sneak into our villages and kill innocent farmers and children, I will destroy your villages' — and they know I mean it. So we have a normal relationship where we trust one another."

On Politics

"So this is the way I'm involved in politics: not to pull strings and to organize groups, but to learn and understand our homeland — its reality, its future. I am one of the very few in this country, who know this country, not only every inch, but seven feet deep. The history of the country is not only what is on the surface. I know the history, not only the Bible, but the archeology and the history and the story of the Jewish people."

On Himself

"I'm not a kibbutznik, I don't like being cooped up with others. Emotional partnership, sociability and absolute egalitarianism are not in keeping with my nature."

On Certitude

"There are not 'ifs' or 'buts'. You can show no doubt — only black and white. Except at night, when you are alone, you can look at it and wonder if maybe you were wrong. But you never show it."

On Terrorism

"We cannot prevent every water pipe from being blown up nor every tree from being uprooted. We cannot prevent the murder of workmen in a citrus grove or of families fast asleep in their beds. But we can set a high price for our blood. A price too high for the Arab world, the Arab armies and the Arab governments to pay."

Independence Day Address, 1954

"The army does not commemorate the fallen in just one single memorial hour, once a year. The entire life of the army, its strength, its spirit, are interwoven with them."

Addressing Troops at Start of 1967 War

"They outnumber us but we shall overcome them. We are a small people but a brave one. We are peace-loving but prepared to fight for our lives and country. The population at our rear will bear their suffering stoically. But the supreme effort will be required of you, the soldiers, the fighting men in the air, on land and on the sea, of those manning the border settlements and spearheading the armored columns. Soldiers of the Israel Defense Army, our hope and our security rest with you today."

On Archeology

"What I really like is to remove the lid of the land. In the first three or four yards, you discover the way it was four or five thousand years ago. Even at that time, it was not Jewish everywhere. Always there were Canaanites here with others. Nor do I need to find a Jewish dwelling. It's enough that I open the door of a house that existed a few thousand years ago — whether it be Canaanite or Jewish or Philistine."

By ERIC PACE
The New York Times
October 17, 1981

Moshe Dayan at his home in 1975.

Levi Eshkol

ONE OF THE American agencies that has long dealt with Israeli financing developed a telegraphic designation some years ago for Levi Eshkol. It was "farmer."

That was when the Russian-born Israeli was finance minister, a post he held under David Ben-Gurion for 11 years. As premier of Israel, the designation remained apt in many ways.

At 71 years of age, Mr. Eshkol retained the appearance of a man of the soil. His manner was earthy, his approach direct. In fact, farming was to have been his career, but malaria interrupted it and he was recruited for public service.

As premier and minister of defense — a dual responsibility that Mr. Ben-Gurion also shouldered — Mr. Eshkol sent Israeli armor into Jordan on a retaliatory raid, and he spoke to his Cabinet of efforts to seal his country's borders with Jordan and Syria.

The decision to strike firmly, and at Jordan, after months of border terrorism brought criticism from many quarters, abroad and at home, but the premier was not singled out.

This was partly because of his natural reticence, an unwillingness to put himself forward personally as spokesman for Israel's policies. The tendency is for the Government, rather than the Premier, to take the credit when it is due and to absorb the blame when that is forthcoming.

Mr. Ben-Gurion tended to be identified with Israel, its hopes and fears. Mr. Eshkol, a man who relied much more on consensus, remained more obscure.

He was not without critics. A joke going the rounds before a border crisis dealt with a group of army officers who were planning, in typical Middle East fashion, to take over the government. They failed, however, because they were unable to find the government.

Mr. Eshkol, an expert at conciliation, served for many years as Mr. Ben-Gurion's trouble shooter. He used his talents to achieve compromises thought by his admirers to have been impossible, and by his critics to be unnecessary.

"They call me a moderator," he once told a colleague. "Yes, I moderate until I get what I want."

It was Mr. Eshkol's fate to follow the more dramatic Ben-Gurion, a challenge not unlike the one Harry Truman faced after the death of Franklin D. Roosevelt.

The premier was born October 25, 1895, in the railway junction town of Oratovo, near Kiev. The family name was Shkolnik, but Mr. Eshkol Hebraized it after Israel became independent. One meaning of both Shkolnik and Eshkol is scholar, or educated person.

His mother came from a rich family; his father was a Hassid, a religious man. Young Levi had nine brothers and one sister, but tutors were brought in to help the children and relatives and friends came around to talk of Zion and Palestine.

In 1914, when he was 19, he made the move to Palestine — to a Tel Aviv of two dozen low buildings, a "hearty village built on the sands." Soon he was working as a laborer, then as a farmer and finally, in the 1920s timeframe, in the organizations that were to become the political backbone of Israel.

When the Nazis seized power in Germany in the 1930s, Mr. Eshkol was working with the Jewish Agency for Palestine, as it was then known, to aid new immigrants. Between 1950 and 1952 he served as treasurer of the Jewish Agency and Minister of Agriculture, and then he took on a decade's work as finance minister. When Mr. Ben-Gurion retired, he picked Mr. Eshkol to lead the country.

In 1965 Mr. Eshkol won a sturdy election victory on his own, turning aside a challenge by Mr. Ben-Gurion, who had become disenchanted with his successor.

Mr. Eshkol's election success had been followed by a year of economic troubles and increasing border tension. Government efforts to moderate what it called "an overheated economy" led to some of the worst unemployment in Israel's history and a severe strain on the coalition government.

Critics said that the heart of the problem was an unwillingness by the premier to make unpopular moves. He has been criticized for operating the premier's office as he did the finance minister's office — on a year-to-year basis

The premier led a quiet personal life with his wife, Miriam, a former Knesset (Parliament) librarian who came to Israel from Rumania in 1932 at the age of 5. The Premier had four daughters by two previous marriages.

The Eshkol humor was illustrated when the premier spoke of his daughters to a member of the office staff who was celebrating the first of a first child, a girl.

"There's an old Hebrew saying that a first-born girl is a sign of subsequent sons," Mr. Eshkol said. "I know, I have four signs."

The New York Times
November 21, 1966

Chaim Herzog

THROUGHOUT one morning, at 40-minute intervals, the new ambassadors of five countries presented their credentials to President Chaim Herzog, who was leading such ceremonies for the last time.

They were purely routine political rituals, and Mr. Herzog had seen more than his share. Nevertheless, they underlined how much Israel's international position had changed since he began the first of his two five-year terms in 1983.

"We have a ceremony every Rosh ha-Shanah, the New Year," he said. "All the diplomatic corps comes to greet you. At that time, one side of our big hall was enough to accommodate the whole diplomatic corps in one line. The diplomatic corps that came last time occupied the length of two walls in a double line."

In 1983, Israel was a pariah for many countries, especially in the third world and the Soviet dominated bloc, where fallout continued from a 1975 United Nations resolution that had equated Zionism with racism. Mr. Herzog, Israel's delegate to the United Nations when that fateful vote was taken, had stood before the General Assembly and defiantly torn the text of the resolution in two.

Since then, a few big "isms" have come crashing down, but not Zionism. Some 40 countries that used to shun Israel rushed in the last few years to establish or renew diplomatic relations. And in 1992, the General Assembly repealed its 1975 vote, giving Mr. Herzog the last laugh.

"Of the three countries that presented the Zionism as racism resolution, one has relations with us although no embassy — that is Benin," he said in an interview in his book-lined office in Jerusalem. "Two still don't have relations — one which has relations with nobody, namely Somalia, and one which is in great trouble, namely Cuba. They were the three sponsors of that resolution, these bastions of democracy and freedom."

A courtly man with a trim mustache and wisps of a brogue from northern Ireland, where he was born 75 years ago, Mr. Herzog is tailor-made for the Israeli presidency, a position designed more for grace than power, a symbol of unity for a country whose many diverse elements find precious few points of agreement.

Chaim Weizmann, Israel's first president, once groused that "the only thing I can stick my nose into is my handkerchief." But that was selling the office short, said Mr. Herzog, who insisted that despite his reserved style he has left his mark on the four prime ministers with whom he has worked.

Many Israelis waited to see whether the presidential residence in Jerusalem took on new colors on May 13, 1993, when it got a new tenant, Chaim Weizmann's nephew, former Defense Minister Ezer Weizman.

Mr. Weizman, elected in March by the Israeli Parliament, the Knesset, was anything but understated, and his relationship with Prime Minister Yitzhak Rabin was anything but warm. Few Israelis would have bet the farm on total circumspection from him.

There was no such concern with Mr. Herzog, a career army man for much of what he said unblinkingly had been "a very interesting life," including a stint as chief of military intelligence. But discretion does not mean silence, and he has sought to stretch the presidency by speaking out on issues that government leaders could not or would not tackle.

Over the years, he advocated greater rights for Israel's Arab and Druse populations, and strove to isolate Rabbi Meir Kahane and his aggressively anti-Arab Kach Party. Mr. Herzog also lobbied hard for sweeping change in Israel's electoral system, which has produced a maze of parties, frequent parliamentary deadlock, blatant political extortion and public discourse that often gave off more heat than light.

"Frequently, when you have an altercation of some sort, the inevitable statement calling on people to calm down is: This is not the Knesset," he said with a disapproving shake of the head. "I regret very much that I didn't succeed to get the whole electoral system changed far more radically."

One presidential power is the right to pardon convicted criminals, and Mr. Herzog set off bitter disputes in the mid-1980s when he used it to pardon agents of the Shin Bet security service and its director, who was accused of having ordered the summary execution of two Palestinian bus hijackers.

"I condemned what had happened," Mr. Herzog said in his defense. But Israel was in a war against terrorism, he added. "To take all these people and put them on trial, and have each one bringing all sorts of evidence to prove that he wasn't the worst and so on, could have torn the Shin Bet to pieces just when we didn't need that."

There were also outcries after he commuted the sentences of members of a so-called Jewish underground that had tried to kill local Palestinian officials. He said later that lightening the sentences for some and forcing them to condemn what they had done helped bring about a ruinous split in the organization.

There was another conspicuous shift during Mr. Herzog's long tenure: Israel, mired more than a decade ago in an unpopular war in Lebanon, is now talking peace with its Arab neighbors and the Palestinians. Yes, he says, it is a slow and fragile process that makes many Westerners impatient. Then again, he adds, the West does not really understand this region.

"Things in the Middle East develop according to the rules of the Middle East market," he said. "You don't put down the price immediately. You don't pay what you're asked for. You bargain. You walk away. You break off. You look annoyed. It takes a long time before you finally do a deal."

By CLYDE HABERMAN
The New York Times
May 4, 1993

[Mr. Herzog, who worked on his memoirs and resumed practicing law after his presidency, died of heart failure in Tel Aviv on April 17, 1997.]

Vladimir Jabotinsky

VLADIMIR JABOTINSKY, author, lecturer and world leader of the New Zionist Organization, died in the youth camp of the Zionist group at Hunter, New York, of a heart attack, according to news sources. He was 59 years old.

Mr. Jabotinsky, who had been living at 10 West 74th Street since his arrival in this country from London on March 13, 1940, headed the Jewish Legion in Palestine during World War I. Before his death, he had been working on a plan to raise a similar army to fight against Italy and Germany and also had been conducting a drive for mass emigration of Jews to Palestine from Eastern and Central Europe.

He left a widow, Anna, who was in London, and a son, Erl, who was in prison in Palestine because of his nationalistic activities on behalf of the Jewish population of that country

Mr. Jabotinsky stirred intense loyalty among his followers and bitterness among his opponents in the Zionist movement. His leadership was more pronounced in Eastern Europe and in Palestine — from which he was banned — than in the United States, but on his last visit here last March more than 5,000 persons overcrowded a hall to hear him speak. They constituted the largest group ever gathered in New York under so-called Revisionist auspices.

Mr. Jabotinsky had the multiple appeal of poet, soldier, orator and personal fire and magnetism. His sincerity could hardly be questioned, even by those leaders of other Zionist parties to whom he was anathema. At times he and his followers were denounced as traitors to Jewry, as Jewish Fascists, as trouble breeders, as foes of labor, even as gunmen. But imbued as he was with the ideal of a self-defending Jewish State in Palestine, and with a nature preferring forthrightness to compromise, it was natural that he should be constantly in the center of controversy.

Mr. Jabotinsky himself was once sentenced to 15 years in prison for organizing an anti-Arab defense force, but served only three months. After his exile by the British his son, Erl, continued active and with the development of the extra quota immigration project, openly backed by his father's organization, furthered it to the extent of being jailed himself.

He was born in Odessa, Russia, in 1880 and became something of a literary and linguistic prodigy. He went to high school in his home city, but later studied in Switzerland and Italy. Mr. Jabotinsky did much translating, including the works of Dante and Poe. He translated the "Divine Comedy" into Russian while taking a law degree in Rome.

Five years after his first Zionist poem appeared in a St. Petersburg monthly, Mr. Jabotinsky became politically active in the movement. He was a delegate to the Sixth Zionist Congress at Basel in 1903, and his influence rose steadily. But the aspect of his career which brought him international attention and led ultimately to his differences with the other leaders was his organizing and leading of the Jewish Legion which fought on the British side in the Near East during World War I. He earned an honorary lieutenancy.

Returning to England in 1920 after his release from jail, he became an executive of the World Zionist Organisation, but in 1921 resigned because of differences with Dr. Chaim Weizmann, whose policy was, to the founder of the Jewish legion, one of surrender. Thus the Revisionist movement grew up around him, insisting on more than a Jewish cultural center or unofficial homeland in Palestine. It had only four delegates at the 1925 world meeting, the figure rising to fifty-eight in 1931. That year the organization had one of its most turbulent sessions, the Revisionists bolting on July 13. Mr. Jabotinsky, facing a breach in his own ranks, took a voluntary six months leave from the leadership.

He had visited America in 1926, arriving with no fanfare, totally ignored by the Zionist Organization of America and by all but a handful of sympathizers. His next visit, in 1935, saw the Revisionists better organized here and able to muster almost 4,000 persons for his first public speech. With the outbreak of another war and the concentration of interest on the refugee problem, his followers in this country increased. The world Revisionist movement became known as the New Zionist Organization, and it was aided here in its refugee work by a new group called the American Friends of a Jewish Palestine. The leadership of the Z. O. A. remained strictly aloof, but the Jabotinsky cause, espoused by a well-known liberal rabbi, Dr. Louis I. Newman, took a firmer grip here. It remained, at the same time, a distinct minority.

Mr. Jabotinsky was a small man with a firm chin and a lock of gray hair prone to cut down across his brow. His English was excellent, and he was equally fluent in Russian, French, German, Italian, Hebrew and other tongues — nine in all. His oratory was neither as superbly paced nor as resonant as that of Dr. Stephen S. Wise, nor as direct and keyed to understatement as that of Dr. Weizmann — but it had an uneven brilliance all its own. Mr. Jabotinsky clenched his small fist often in the course of a speech, without shaking it. That was the key to the intensity of feeling which characterized him.

The New York Times
August 5, 1940

Ephraim Katchalski

IMMEDIATELY after the balloting by the 120-member parliament, it was announced that Dr. Katchalski, one of Israel's most distinguished scientists, would change his surname to Katzir in accordance with a government policy requiring Hebrew names for state officials.

Dr. Katchalski, who assumed the largely ceremonial presidential post, succeeded Zalman Shazar, who retired at the expiration of his five-year term on May 25, 1971. He was the fourth President of Israel and the youngest in the office also held by the late Dr. Chaim Weizmann, Israel's first president, and the late Itzhak Ben-Zvi.

In his nonpolitical office the president accepts the credentials of foreign ambassadors, signs treaties and laws, then summons a member of parliament to form a government after elections.

Although the office is nonpolitical, the selection followed bitter infighting among members of the dominant Labor party, whose nomination is tantamount to election.

Some of that struggle was reflected in the balloting, in which Dr. Katchalski won by a vote of 66 to 41 over his sole opponent, Ephraim Uhrbach, candidate of the National Religious party. Nine ballots in the secret proceedings were left blank — an apparent protest against the maneuvering that attended the nomination of Dr. Katchalski March 22, 1971.

Until a few days before the nomination it had been expected that the Labor candidate would be Yitzhak Navon, Deputy Speaker of Parliament and a member of a faction of the party led by Defense Minister Moshe Dayan.

Another faction, led by Premier Golda Meir, secured Dr. Katchalski's agreement to run, and he came away with a narrow margin — 58 votes — in the 650-member Central Committee of the party.

The President was born May 16, 1916, in Kiev, a son of Yehuda and Golda Katchalski, who emigrated to Palestine in 1922.

He won a master's degree at Hebrew University in Jerusalem in 1937 and a doctorate in 1941. From 1941 to 1948 he held posts at the university and as a research fellow at the Brooklyn Polytechnic Institute and at Columbia University.

During the War of Independence in 1948, Dr. Katchalski headed the science corps of Haganah, the Jewish underground. When his name was placed in nomination before the Labor party, Foreign Minister Abba Eban said that it was still too early to reveal developments by the scientist that had been vital to victory.

In 1949, Dr. Katchalsi became head of the Department of Biophysics at the Weizmann Institute of Science in Rehovoth; two years later he was named department head, a post he held until February, 1970. He intended to continue research while serving as president.

An internationally recognized authority on proteins, he was the first scientist to synthesize a complex protein molecule used in scientific research in immunology.

For many years he served as chief scientific adviser to the Israeli Defense Ministry. His older brother, Dr. Aharon Katzir, who headed the Polymer Research Department at the Weizmann Institute, was killed May 30, 1970, in the terrorist massacre at the Tel Aviv international airport.

Dr. Katchalski and his wife, the former Nina Gotlieb, have two children. He lectures frequently at universities abroad, holds memberships in numerous scientific organizations and has won several awards for his work.

The New York Times
April, 1971.

[Today, at 81, Dr. Katzir (Katchalski) is still active in the world of science doing various research work. He lives in Rehovoth.]

Abraham Isaac Kook

REGARDED AS THE PROPHET of religious Zionism, Rabbi Abraham Isaac Kook, the first Ashkenazic Chief Rabbi in British-ruled Palestine, saw the modern return of the Jews to their homeland as the beginning of their divine redemption.

A religious mystic and Talmudic scholar who advocated the integration of secular studies with religious learning, Rabbi Kook stood between the traditionally closed world of the anti-Zionist Orthodox establishment in Palestine and the militant secularism of the young Zionist pioneers.

He was criticized by the Orthodox rabbis for his support of Zionism, seen by them as a heretical movement hastening what should be a Messianic redemption. He in turn criticized the new Jewish nationalists for their abandonment of religion and what he considered their neglect of spiritual needs in favor of material achievements. "The dimension of holiness must regain its scope in our national and Zionist movement," he wrote, "for only therein is the source of abiding life."

Rabbi Kook argued that Judaism should be a synthesis of Orthodoxy, nationalism and liberalism, an early formulation of what was later to become the credo of religious Zionism in the early years of the State of Israel.

Born in Griva, Latvia, in 1865, Rabbi Kook went beyond the traditional Talmud studies of the Jewish ghetto of Eastern Europe to explore the Bible, Hebrew language, general philosophy and Jewish mysticism. After serving as the rabbi of two Lithuanian towns, he came to Palestine in 1904 and became the chief rabbi of Jaffa. In 1919 he was appointed Chief Rabbi of Jerusalem, and in 1921 Chief Rabbi of Palestine, serving until his death in 1935.

Rabbi Kook's prolific writings on mysticism and religious philosophy served as guides to generations of religious Zionists. His son, Rabbi Zvi Yehuda Kook, succeeded him as head of the Merkaz Harav yeshiva which he had founded in Jerusalem in 1924, leading his disciples toward an increasing identification with a more potent brand of religous nationalism.

On the eve of the 1967 Arab-Israeli war, Rabbi Zvi Yehuda, in a speech to his students, appealed for a return of the Jews to the Biblical cities of Hebron, Nablus and Jericho in the West Bank. When they fell to Israeli forces in the fighting, Rabbi Zvi Yehuda's students saw it as a step toward messianic redemption.

Their fervor produced the religious nationalist movement, Gush Emunim, whose leaders founded the first Jewish settlements in the West Bank and spearheaded what became known as the "Greater Land of Israel" movement, dedicated to keeping the lands captured in 1967. In their interpretation, Rabbi Kook's messianic vision of Zionism lost its liberal dimension and became a rallying cry for a total commitment to the land, to what Rabbi Kook called the "sacred connection" between the Jewish nation and the Land of Israel.

By JOEL GREENBERG
The New York Times

Golda Meir

GOLDA MEIR, a one-time teacher in Milwaukee who became Prime Minister of Israel, died at the age of 80.

Mrs. Meir had been in Hadassah Hospital since August for treatment of an undisclosed back ailment. Earlier a hospital spokesman said she had also been suffering from liver infection and jaundice.

Hadassah Hospital said later that Mrs. Meir had had leukemia for 12 years, including the years 1969-1974, when she was Prime Minister. The hospital spokesman said that the illness was kept under control until recently, when viral hepatitis developed.

Mrs. Meir was semiconscious in the last days. At the moment of death her two children, a sister and other members of her family, as well as former political aides, were at her bedside.

Death came at 4:30 P.M. The news was broadcast to the nation an hour and a half later, after strict observance of the Sabbath had begun.

There was little public reaction in the largely deserted streets of Jerusalem and other cities. Israelis who heard the news expressed deep grief and said the country had suffered a grave loss.

President Yitzhak Navon conveyed his sympathy and that of the nation to the family. "Your sorrow is that of all Israel," he said.

Shimon Peres, chairman of the Labor Party, in which Mrs. Meir had long been a leading figure, described her in a statement as "one of the great women in Jewish and world history" and as a "stalwart lioness." He recalled tributes paid to her by President Anwar el-Sadat of Egypt during his visit to Israel in November, 1977, and added that "the Labor movement is in deep mourning."

Prime Minister Menachem Begin was informed in Oslo, where he arrived earlier in the day for the presentation on Sunday of the Nobel Peace Prize, awarded jointly to him and President Sadat. During the flight to the Norwegian capital in an Israeli military plane, the Prime Minister requested news of Mrs. Meir's condition by radiotelephone and was informed that she was in her last hours.

Mr. Begin said he would stay in Oslo to receive the peace prize. Officials said they expected him to be back in Jerusalem for the funeral, probably on the following Monday.

The Israeli Cabinet was to meet in special session the next day, after the Sabbath, to express the nation's mourning and to approve arrangements for a state funeral. The meeting was summoned by Deputy Prime Minister Yigal Yadin, who said Mrs. Meir's death was a "tragedy for the entire Jewish people."

According to an official, the body was taken to the modern building of Parliament, on Jerusalem's western outskirts. At 10 A.M. the next Sunday there were to be prayers for the dead and eulogies by national figures. Later the body would lie in state until 6 P.M.

No decision appeared to have been made immediately as to the burial site. An Israeli who knew Mrs. Meir speculated she might have left instructions to be buried in the cemetery of a kibbutz in the Negev that her daughter, Sara had helped found.

For five years Golda Meir was Prime Minister of Israel. Her often-stated ambition was to see Israel accepted by its Arab neighbors and living in peace. With firmness and determination, she sought but failed to achieve these aims. "We say 'peace' and the echo comes back from the other side, 'war,'" she once lamented. "We don't want wars even when we win."

It was her fate to lead the Israeli Government when the forces of Egypt and Syria attacked in October, 1973, in a costly war that Israel almost lost before it could mobilize and fight to an inconclusive end, in which both sides would claim tenuous victories.

"We do not rejoice in victories," she said. "We rejoice when a new kind of cotton is grown and when strawberries bloom in Israel."

Mrs. Meir left office in 1974. When President Anwar el-Sadat of Egypt made the dramatic announcement of his decision to visit Jerusalem in November, 1977, Mrs. Meir — who was in New York for the opening of the Broadway show "Golda," an account of her life starring Anne Bancroft — hailed it as a brilliant move but advised a wait-and-see attitude pending more concrete results.

When President Sadat arrived in Israel, he seemed more at ease with her than with any of the other prominent Israelis he saw, and she gave him a gift for a newly born grandchild. He later confided to interviewers that he would have preferred to negotiate with her because he regarded her as a "tough old lady" who had the will to persevere on the road to peace.

Her toughness was legendary while she ran the Israeli Cabinet. After she left the Labor Party, which she had led, became more fractious than ever and, beset by charges of corruption, went down to a stunning defeat in the spring of 1977 at the hands of a right-wing coalition led by Menachem Begin, who became Prime Minister. After that, the Labor Party experienced a bewildering slide into something close to irrelevance in the political arena.

Mrs. Meir had a gift for making complex issues appear simple and expressing her views in plain but emotional terms: "Our generation reclaimed the land, our children fought the war, and our grandchildren should enjoy the peace." Even when she spoke to an audience of thousands, it could sound as though she was speaking in her living room.

At a small gathering in New York, Mrs. Meir heard an overdramatized version of an appeal she had made to President John F. Kennedy for arms. "If I had spoken to Kennedy so beautifully," she commented, "I would have gotten more arms." Once when an aide suggested a statement to make to waiting reporters, she rejoined, "You can't improve on saying nothing." Her mother used to advise: "When you say no, you never regret it."

Golda Mabovitch was born on May, 3 1898, in Kiev, in the Russian Empire. Her first memory was of her father nailing boards over the front door during rumors that a pogrom was imminent. "If there is any explanation necessary for the direction which my life has taken," she said years later, "perhaps it is the desire and the determination to save Jewish children from a similar scene and from a similar experience."

"I have a pogrom complex — I have, I plead guilty," she went on. Alluding to the six million Jews killed by the Nazis, she added: "There are many Jews who don't have complexes any more. But we who lived through it have a complex of gas chambers."

In Russia life was not far from death. "I was always a little too cold outside and a little too empty inside," she recalled. Her food was sometimes given to her younger sister, Zipke; their older sister, Sheyna, often fainted from hunger.

In 1906 the family emigrated to the United States, where Golda's father had spent three years in Milwaukee saving to prepare the way. When he could find employment he worked as a carpenter, and his wife set herself up in a small grocery, the bane of Golda's existence. Beginning at age 8, Golda had to run the store each morning while her mother was at the market buying supplies. The child arrived late for school every day, having cried all the way from home.

At age 11 she organized her first public meeting and gave her first public speech, to raise money for school textbooks. Not many years later her mother pressed her to give up the idea of high school, spend her days working in the grocery and marry a much older man, a Mr. Goodstein. At age 14 Golda ran away to live with Sheyna in Denver, where she met her future husband, a gentle, erudite sign painter named Morris Myerson, another emigrant from Russia.

After an argument with Sheyna, Golda, now 16, moved out and was given shelter by two of Sheyna's friends. She got a job measuring skirt linings, and in later years found herself involuntarily glancing at hems.

Her father wrote to her that if she valued her mother's life she would come home, so she did, aged 18, to plunge into a confusion of enthusiasms: socialism, teaching, public speaking, Zionism. When there were attacks on Jews in the Ukraine and in Poland, she helped organize a protest march in Milwaukee. Her home became a center for visitors from Palestine. "I knew that I was not going to be a parlor Zionist," she wrote.

She pressed her reluctant husband-to-be to go to Palestine, and when he agreed, in 1917, they were married. They left in 1921, on a trip that included a mutiny and near starvation. She had learned much about freedom in America, she loved her first adopted country, but she never knew a moment of homesickness for it.

Much later, in jest, she echoed her Israeli compatriots' complaint against Moses: "He dragged us 40 years through the desert to bring us to the one place in the Middle East where there was no oil." The only heavy industry in Palestine was the manufacture of chocolate, she recalled. "Why does it taste so sandy?" she asked, and was told that sand was the only natural resource.

The new immigrants — she, her husband, her sister Sheyna, with whom she had been reconciled, and Sheyna's children — had no one to help them. Many others found the struggle too much and left, and Mrs. Meir was to say later: "I have always felt sorry for those people, because to my mind, the loss has always been theirs."

Golda and Morris Myerson applied to join Kibbutz Merhavia, whose name means "God's wide spaces," and were rejected because a majority of the members suspected that she would not be willing to do physical labor. Furious at this attitude, she persisted and was finally accepted. Afterward, she said jokingly that she was accepted only because of her phonograph and records.

On the kibbutz she worked herself to exhaustion picking almonds, planting trees, caring for chickens. "The kibbutz made me an expert in growing chickens," she said. "Before I was afraid to be in a room with even one chicken."

When her husband could bear communal life no longer, she agreed to leave the kibbutz. They moved briefly to Tel Aviv, then to Jerusalem, where Golda Myerson gave birth to a son, Menachem, and a daughter, Sarah, endowing them with the inalienable right to share the family's poverty. Mrs. Myerson spent hours each day doing the laundry for Menachem's nursery school to pay for his tuition. "Was this what it was all about?" she asked herself. "Poverty, drudgery and worry?"

In 1928 she became secretary of the women's labor council of Histadrut, which meant supervising the vocational training of immigrant girls. Her marriage was breaking up, and accepting the job, which required frequent travel, was tantamount to recognizing the breakup. She and the children moved to a tiny apartment in Tel Aviv, and for years she slept there on the living-room couch. Her husband died in 1951; characteristically, she was away at the time.

She made frequent fund-raising trips, and a woman reproached her for not talking sentimentally enough to make women in the audiences cry; tears were useful in raising money. "Tears don't have to be elicited from anyone in the Zionist movement," she replied. "God knows there is always enough to cry about."

In 1934 she joined the executive committee of Histadrut, then a kind of shadow government for the eventual independent state of Israel. In 1938, while attending a conference in Evian-les-Bains on refugees as a "Jewish observer from Palestine," she raged inwardly at the complacent manner in which official representatives expressed sympathy for the plight of Germany's Jews, then explained that their countries could not offer refuge.

In the Balfour Declaration of 1917 the British Government promised "the establishment in Palestine of a national home for the Jewish people." The Jewish population in fact nearly quintupled during the British mandate, mostly through immigration, up to May 1939 just before World War II broke out. At that time the British, fearing an Arab shift toward the Axis powers, issued a white paper severely restricting Jewish immigration. David Ben-Gurion, who was to play a vital role in securing Israeli independence fixed the lines of Jewish opposition:

"To the white paper and fight the white paper as if there were no Hitler."

Mrs. Myerson became a member of the War Economic Advisory Council set up by the British authorities in Palestine. When the war ended and the British kept Jewish survivors of concentration camps in European detention centers, she went to work for the clandestine entry into Palestine of Jewish immigrants, and joined a hunger strike in sympathy with them. "There is no Zionism except the rescue of Jews," she said.

Years after Israel won independence, Mrs. Meir — she had since Hebraized her name, as did others — said that she did not know if Ernest Bevin, the British Foreign Secretary, who bitterly opposed Jewish immigration to Palestine, was insane or just anti-Semitic or both. "Those responsible for British policy cannot forgive us for being a nation without their approval," she said, "They cannot understand that the problem of the Jews of Europe was not created for the sole purpose of embarrassing the British Government."

When Zionist leaders in Palestine were arrested in 1946, she was one of the few left free. "Golda, they didn't take you yet?" Mr. Ben-Gurion's wife, Paula, kept asking in phone calls repeated often enough to make their recipient almost wish she had been taken.

Mrs. Meir began running things. She took over Zionist negotiations with the British and meanwhile kept in close touch with leaders of the armed Jewish resistance who opposed the British and fought Arab guerrillas.

Finally a United Nations Special Committee on Palestine visited the country, recommended partition and the establishment of a Jewish state, and the world organization voted approval, with the United States and the Soviet Union voting with the majority. Upon Arab refusal to accept the decision, Palestine's Jews realized that war lay ahead and that they needed arms and money. Though warned that she should not expect much help, Golda — few now bothered to use her second name — left for America and collected $50 million.

On her return she undertook delicate political negotiations with King Abdullah of TransJordan, grandfather of King Hussein of Jordan. Disguising herself as an Arab woman, she traveled to Amman, Abdullah's capital, to urge him to keep his promise to her not to join other Arab leaders in an attack on the Jews. He asked her not to hurry the proclamation of a state. "We have been waiting for 2,000 years," she replied. "Is that hurrying?"

On May 14, 1948, she was one of 25 signers of Israel's independence declaration. "After I signed, I cried," she said. "When I studied American history as a school-girl and I read about those who signed the Declaration of Independence, I couldn't imagine these were real people doing something real. And there I was sitting down and signing a declaration of independence."

By May 15 Israel was under attack from the armed forces of Egypt, Syria, Lebanon, Transjordan and Iraq. Bearing what was in effect Israel's first passport, Mrs. Meir was sent to the United States again to raise more money. At home, the new state confounded the expectations of its Arab enemies by holding off their attacks and establishing its authority.

Later that year Israel named Mrs. Meir as its first Minister to the Soviet Union, an assignment for which she felt unqualified: her Russian was practically forgotten and she knew little about diplomacy. She did know a lot about communal living, however, and when she took up her post she ran the embassy as a kibbutz, with everyone, including the envoy, taking turns at the chores.

When she turned up at Moscow's Central Synagogue thousands of Russian Jews, defying the Government's hostility, flocked to welcome her and express their solidarity with Israel. "If you had sent a broomstick to Moscow," she said later, "and said it represented the State of Israel, it would have received the same welcome."

Mrs. Meir left Moscow and entered the Israeli Parliament in 1949, serving until 1974. From 1949 to 1956, years of severe economic difficulty, she was Minister of Labor. The meat ration was 3.5 ounces a day — "just so that we didn't forget that there is meat in the world," said Mrs. Meir.

When the Cabinet was trying to deal with a series of assaults on women, a minister suggested barring women from the streets after dark. The Minister of Labor protested: "Men are attacking women, not the other way around. If there is going to be a curfew, let the men be locked up, not the women."

People often asked Mrs. Meir if she felt handicapped at being a woman minister. "I don't know," she would reply. "I've never tried to be a man."

She campaigned vigorously for money to house the tens of thousands of immigrants who were living in tent cities and overwhelming the young state's facilities. Levi Eshkol, then Finance Minister, had his priorities, and they were not hers.

"You can't milk a house," he said. "But you can milk a cow. If you want money you can have it — but only for cows." She threatened to resign, but stayed on and got money, though not as much as she wanted, to provide homes for those willing to join the adventure of a Jewish state.

"The period since we won our independence has been the first for many, many centuries, during which the words 'Jewish Refugee' are no longer heard," she said later. "There is no such thing any more because the Jewish state is prepared to take every Jew, whether he is a skilled worker or not, whether he is old or not, whether he is sick or not. It doesn't make a particle of difference."

In 1956 she became Foreign Minister, succeeding Moshe Sharett, and served under Prime Minister Ben-Gurion. A man of strong ideas and powerful will — it was he who prevailed on Golda Myerson to change her name — he is said to have called her the only man in his Cabinet.

She, Moshe Dayan and Shimon Peres flew in secret to France in 1956 to lay plans for collaborating in the attack on Egypt, which had nationalized the Suez Canal and closed the Strait of Tiran, the link between the Gulf of Aqaba and the Red Sea. When war came Israel took less than 100 hours to capture the Gaza Strip and all of Sinai; France and Britain, however, after landing at the northern end of the Suez Canal Zone and driving southward under the pretext of separating the Egyptian and Israeli armies, were forced by United States and Soviet pressure to withdraw.

Israel, also pressed by the two super-powers, later pulled out of Sinai, and the United Nations sent a peacekeeping force to open the Strait of Tiran. This force remained until 1967, when it was withdrawn at the request of President Nasser of Egypt in a prelude to a new war that lasted only 6 days.

During subsequent negotiations at the United Nations, the Iraqi Foreign Minister at one point exclaimed from the rostrum of the General Assembly: "Mrs. Meir, go back to Milwaukee — that's where you belong!"

She was an architect of Israel's policy of extending technical assistance to developing African nations, a policy that improved relations until the Arab oil embargo swept the Africans into line against Israel. Asked by Billy Graham, the evangelist, for the secret of Israeli success in Africa before the embargo, she replied: "We go there to teach, not to preach."

When Mr. Ben-Gurion gave up office and then split with Levi Eshkol, Israel's third Prime Minister, Mrs. Meir sided with Mr. Eshkol, becoming his strongest supporter. Though it was fashionable to say that hers was the stiffest backbone in the Cabinet, she said: "I have never believed in inflexibility except when Israel is concerned."

"If we are criticized because we do not bow," she said, "because we cannot compromise on the question 'To be or not to be,' it is because we have decided that, come what may, we are and we will be."

As Foreign Minister she worked an 18-hour day. After two years her chief of Cabinet suggested she take a vacation. "Why?" she said. "Do you think I'm tired?" "No," he said, "but I am." She replied: "So you take a vacation!"

But in 1965, after much illness and the exhaustion of years of unremitting labor, she resigned from the Cabinet. "I won't go into a political nunnery," she assured Mr. Eshkol, refusing an offer to be Deputy Prime Minister on the basis that it was better to be a full-time grandmother than a part-time minister. She moved out of the Foreign Minister's large residence and went back to cleaning, cooking, ironing and shopping. Bus drivers often would make unscheduled stops to let her off near her home or detour to take her right to the door.

Her party soon pressed her to be its secretary general, and she agreed.

In 1967, when Israel lived in the shadow of renewed war, Prime Minister Eshkol delivered a radio address to the nation, for which he was criticized because he sounded far from inspiring and stumbled over his words. Mrs. Meir defended him: "A leader who doesn't hesitate before he sends his nation into battle is not fit to be a leader." To young volunteers who rushed to Israel during the Six-Day War and were preparing to return home, Mrs. Meir said: "You were ready to die with us. Why don't you live with us?"

Israel had won a brilliant and overwhelming victory. As the cease-fire took effect, Mrs. Meir commented, "The only alternative to war is peace and the only road to peace is negotiations."

"There is nothing Israel wants so much as peace," she added. "With all the bleakness of the desert, the desert of hate around us is even more bleak.

"We have been obliged to become good soldiers, but not with joy," she said. "We are good farmers with joy. It's a wonderful thing to go down to a kibbutz deep in the Negev and remember what it was — sand and sky, maybe a well of brackish water — and to see it now green and lovely. To be good soldiers is our extreme necessity, but there is no joy in it."

At the same time she warned: "There cannot be quiet on one side of the border and shelling on the other. We will either have peace on both sides or trouble on both sides."

"I understand the Arabs wanting to wipe us out," she noted, "but do they really expect us to cooperate?"

Though insisting that the Arabs would eventually have to negotiate and recognize Israel's right to live, she reinforced a reputation for stubbornness, and later complained that "intransigent" had become her middle name. "Hitler took care of six million Jews," she said. "If we lose a war, that's the end forever — and we disappear from the earth. If one fails to understand this, then one fails to understand obstinacy. We intend to remain alive. Our neighbors want to see us dead. This is not a question that leaves much room for compromise." She called Israel's secret weapon "no alternative."

In Israel there was growing debate about how to reach an understanding — and peace — with the Arabs. Mrs. Meir noted that Israel had doves and hawks, but she had found no one who wanted to turn himself into a clay pigeon. When foreign powers pressed Israel to return to its pre-1967 boundaries, she retorted that the war had started along those lines.

Critics argued that she failed to understand the Palestinians or even to recognize them as a national entity, and that she was anything but sympathetic to their just desires for recognition and land. "Do the Arabs need another land?" she asked. "They already have fourteen. We have only one."

To the complaint that she was intransigent and refused to seize opportunities for negotiation, she insisted that the Arabs refused to speak to Israel.

Speaking to an audience in New York just after the 1967 war, Mrs. Meir said: "Is there anybody who can honestly bid the Israelis to go home before a real peace? Is there anyone who wants us to begin training our 10-year-olds for the next war? You say no. I am sure that every fair-minded person in the world will say no, but — forgive my impertinence — most important of all the Israelis say no."

She was a popular, effective speaker. From a news conference at the National Press Club in Washington:

Q. Your grandson, Gideon Meir, age 7, says that you are the best gefilte-fish maker in Israel. What is your recipe?

A. My grandson. I'm afraid he's not very objective about me. I'm not very objective about him, either.

On Mr. Eshkol's death in February, 1969, the Labor Party selected her as its candidate for Prime Minister. That was not exactly the retirement she had in mind — "Being 70 is not a sin," she said, "It's not a joy, either' — but she accepted and won Parliament's vote of confidence.

Pressing for a meeting with the Arabs, she proclaimed her readiness to go to any length except national suicide to secure peace. "If Nasser chooses New York for negotiations, it's all right," she said. "If he wants to go to New Jersey, that's fine too. If he says Geneva, we agree. I'm even prepared to go to Cairo — how about that! — to sit down at the table."

"Arab officials will have to overcome the shock of meeting us not on the battlefield but at the negotiating table," she added.

"Suppose we want to return territory we have taken," she noted. "To whom? We can't send it to Nasser by parcel post."

Upon the death of President Nasser in September, 1970, Israeli officials saw a new opportunity for peace under Mr. Sadat, his successor. In 1972 President Nicolae Ceausescu of Rumania told Mrs. Meir that President Sadat was agreeable to a meeting, and when she urged that it be arranged, Mr. Ceausescu said he would be in touch; but she related later that she never heard from him again.

In January, 1973, she did hear from the Vatican, which had never recognized Israel, that Pope Paul VI was ready to receive her. "Before we went to the audience," she recalled, "I said to our people: 'Listen, what's going on here? Me, the daughter of Moshe Mabovitch the carpenter, going to meet the Pope of the Catholics?' So one of our people said to me, 'Just a moment, Golda, carpentry is a very respectable profession around here.'"

The Pope had hardly opened the conversation before the daughter of Moshe Mabovitch spoke her mind. "I didn't like the opening at all," she recalled. "His Holiness had said he found it hard to understand the Jewish people, who should be merciful, behaved so fiercely in its own country. I can't stand it when we are talked to like that, so I said to the Pope: 'Your Holiness, do you know what my earliest memory is? A pogrom in Kiev. When we were merciful and when we had no homeland and when we were weak, we were led to the gas chambers.'"

She had decided to look the Pope in the eye, and not lower her eyes under any circumstances. "There were moments of tension," she said. "I felt that I was saying what I was saying to the man of the cross, who heads the church whose symbol is the cross, under which Jews were killed for generations."

Mrs. Meir knew many bitter moments and difficult meetings, few more galling than her encounter with Chancellor Bruno Kreisky of Austria, whose background was Jewish but who had acceded to an Arab request that an Austrian transit camp for Soviet Jewish immigrants to Israel be closed. She could not persuade him to change his mind, and she never forgave him.

The greatest critic of her years as prime minister came with the war in October, 1973. Although she felt that Egypt and Syria might be planning an attack, she accepted the reassurances of her military leaders and held off mobilizing the reserves. "I shall live with that terrible knowledge for the rest of my life," she wrote in her autobiography.

In the first days of the war, with Israeli forces overwhelmed by superior numbers and firepower, Mrs. Meir lived endless hours of apprehension and exhaustion. "I couldn't even cry when I was alone," she wrote later. Finally, when Egypt and Syria faced defeat, the Russians, as they had in 1967, demanded a cease-fire, to which the United Nations agreed.

During subsequent negotiations between the United States and Israel, Mrs. Meir came to have ambivalent feelings about the role of Henry A. Kissinger, the Secretary of State. To force Israeli compliance with American wishes, the United States threatened economic retaliation and the negotiations were broken off.

By this time Mrs. Meir had handed over the Government to Yitzhak Rabin, having told the party leadership "It is beyond my strength to continue carrying this burden." When she left office, on June 4, 1974, she was 76 years old, but she was still not prepared to go into that political nunnery, so she went on speaking her mind.

During a talk at Princeton a student asked her, in a reference to Yasir Arafat, the Palestinian guerrilla leader: "What if Arafat offered to recognize Israel?" The prospect seemed so ludicrous that Mrs. Meir, bowdlerizing, replied: "There's a saying in Yiddish, 'If my grandmother had had wheels, she would would have been a carriage.'" When another student asked for details of the Soviet Union's presence in the Middle East in men and in missile bases, she replied: "It was too much before and it's too much now."

At the end of her life she was still feeling guilty about the years during which she had neglected her children and about her failure to devote herself to the kibbutz rather than to public life. "There is a type of woman who cannot remain at home," she once wrote. "In spite of the place her children and family fill in her life, her nature demands something more; she cannot divorce herself from the larger social life. She cannot let her children narrow her horizon. For such a woman there is no rest."

The New York Times
By Israel Shenker
December 9, 1978.

Yitzhak Navon

A POPULAR AND FOLKSY Labor Party politician who did not want to be "kept on a pedestal" was elected the country's fifth President. The chief of state, Yitzhak Navon was the first Israeli-born leader and the first from Israel's Sephardic majority to hold the largely ceremonial political post.

"You elected me, so don't come to me later with complaints," he joked as a parliamentary delegation formally told him that he had been chosen to succeed President Ephraim Katzir on May 29.

Mr. Navon, whose name is pronounced na-VOHN, said in an interview that he was worried by such well-wishers as a pistachio nut vendor in Jerusalem who told him "I'm glad you'll be president but I suppose I'll lose a customer."

Mr. Navon resigned his seat in parliament on being elected to the five year Presidential term by a larger margin than any given his four predecessors — 86 votes, with 23 abstentions and 11 members absent. He was unopposed.

Prime Minister Menachem Begin's candidate, Yitzhak Chavet, a nuclear physicist, withdrew when it became clear that the vast majority in parliament preferred Mr. Navon.

All of the President-elect's predecessors were born in czarist Russia and all belong to the Ashkenazic community of Jews from Eastern and Central Europe.

Mr. Navon's election was calculated to hearten the Mediterranean Jews, or Sephardim. Although a majority in Israel, the Sephardim have tended to consider themselves underrepresented in top positions of authority.

Mr. Navon said he planned to dedicate himself to reducing economic, social and emotional frictions among the various Jewish communities in Israel, who come from 102 countries and speak 81 languages.

The new president could have embarrassed the Begin government if he spoke his mind on international affairs, since he had been a strong critic of its foreign policy and advocated greater flexibility in peace negotiations with the Arabs. However he could not impair the government's ability to execute its policies since virtually everything he did must have been authorized by a Cabinet minister.

The main function is to consult party leaders after national elections or in case a government falls, and then call upon a member of parliament to try to form a new government likely to win a vote of confidence.

A scion of a highly respected Sephardic family that has lived in what is now Israel for 10 generations, Mr. Navon fits comfortably in the upperechelon of the Israeli political structure, which is dominated by the Ashkanazim. But his deep Sephardic roots show in the way he pronounces Hebrew, his speeches, which is replete with classical expressions and cultural interests. He has written books and stories on the folklore of Sephardic communities, one of which was turned into a hit musical. Titled *The Sephardic Orchard*, it told of life in a section of Jerusalem.

While he projects his own Sephardic personality, Mr. Navon resents what he calls "professional Sephardic Types who demand positions or public offices solely on the grounds they belong to an underrepresented society."

As a Labor Party member of parliament, he had sought the party's nomination for the speakership of parliament, the presidency of Israel in 1973 and the chairmanship of the World Zionist organization, but each time when his goal seemed within reach he was blocked by the old guard leadership, apparently because he once bolted the regular party organization and joined his political mentor, the late David Ben-Gurion, in political opposition.

However, the party leaders fully exploited his popularity, and talents in the national elections last year, when he was Labor's star performer in television broadcasts.

Mr. Navon, who was born in 1921, has been at the center of Israeli political life since 1952 when he met Mr. Ben-Gurion. The Prime Minister had asked for a teacher of Spanish because he wanted to read *Don Quixote* in the original. Foreign Minister Moshe Sharett sent Mr. Navon, then his political secretary to Mr. Ben-Gurion who liked him and kept him as his own political secretary.

He stayed with Mr. Ben-Gurion 11 years until the Prime Minister resigned in 1963. Mr. Navon had been so wedded to his job that he did not take a wife until Mr. Ben-Gurion retired. Then, at the age of 42, he married Ofira Erez, psychologist and one-time beauty contest winner. They have two children — a 5-year old daughter and a 4-year old son.

When Mr. Ben-Gurion broke with Labor and organized the Rafi Party to contest the 1965 elections, Mr. Navon followed his mentor. He was elected to his first term in parliament on the Rafi ticket but later returned to the Labor fold. Although never included in a Labor cabinet, he was appointed chairman of the important Foreign Affairs and Security Committee. He also served five years as chairman of the World Zionist Council, a sort of parliamentary body that guides the World Zionist Organization between Zionist congresses.

The New York Times

[After retiring from political life in 1990, Mr. Navon has been active in religious societies, and has written several plays and literary works.]

Benjamin Netanyahu

A **CONVERSATION** with Israelis about Benjamin Netanyahu inevitably comes around to how "American" he is.

Some say it with admiration, some with disdain, but they talk of his American accent, his American education, his Kennedy-style clan and the American name he once tried — Ben Nitay.

Above all they talk about his mastery of "American-style" politics, by which people here mean his mastery of pungent sound bites and packaged issues. That Mr. Netanyahu's image was massaged by an American, Arthur Finkelstein, came as a surprise to no one.

But behind Mr. Netanyahu's "Made in U.S.A." facade is a very Israeli core, a native "sabra" reared on militant Zionism, honed in an elite commando unit and chary of ever giving an inch to his enemies, whether politicians or Arabs.

His heroes are his father, the historian Benzion Netanyahu, an ardent follower of a right-wing school of Zionism that held as early as 1925 that the Jewish claim to the entire Land of Israel was unquestionable and non-negotiable, and his brother, Yonatan Netanyahu, whose death leading the commando raid to free Jewish hostages at Entebbe in 1976 turned him into an Israeli military legend.

The question frequently posed, now that the 46-year-old "Bibi" (as he is universally known) has been chosen by Israelis to lead them through the end of the century, is whether his comforting talk of continuing his predecessor's pursuit of peace, albeit with more concern for security, is only an "American" sales pitch or a genuine shift in his inherited outlook.

The final judgment will come with time. But already now, when stripped of the smooth euphemisms and evasions, there is a consistency to his statements, a combination of his father's brand of unyielding Zionism and his brother's sacrifice, whose heroism proclaimed that the response to terrorism must to be direct, immediate and vicious.

While Mr. Netanyahu has accepted Palestinian self-government in areas already granted them, he has never even suggested a readiness to cede Israeli sovereignty over any part of Jerusalem, or the West Bank, or the Golan Heights, nor to curtail Israel's right to take whatever measures it deems necessary to safeguard its security, even if this means entering areas under Palestinian control.

Though he avoided saying in his campaign whether he would invest more money into Jewish settlements in the West Bank, he has made clear that the Labor Party's ban on their expansion will be lifted.

Mr. Netanyahu also indicated what he meant by negotiating with Arabs during a campaign debate with Prime Minister Shimon Peres. The Arabs, he said, were "realistic" — "when they see a weak government like Peres's, they demand everything, they get everything, and they demand more." When they came up against a tough government, he might have continued, that same realism would curb their demands.

Mr. Netanyahu's campaign was a combination of American packaging and native ruthlessness. It was a style that proved especially suitable to the first election in which voters were asked to choose not only parties, but also a personality.

Focusing sharply on popular fears and emotions, reducing issues of war and peace to sharp slogans, Mr. Netanyahu relentlessly chipped away at Peres's early lead.

"The way of Peres brought neither peace to Israel nor real security. It brings us fear," Mr. Netanyahu declared. "It is not one of my dreams to tour the palaces of Europe with Arafat, as Peres has been doing."

The "Americanization" of Mr. Netanyahu began in 1963 when he was 14, and his father took a teaching job in Pennsylvania. Young Bibi finished high school and, after five years of military service, enrolled at M.I.T., where he took a master's degree in business administration. It was also in the United States that he made the first two of his three marriages.

His years in the United States, which encompassed the Vietnam War and the election of Ronald Reagan, had a distinct impact on Netanyahu. But he ardently denied during the campaign that he ever contemplated staying in America. "Not for a single moment," he declared in the debate. "I come from a Jewish, Zionist family, with roots here for 100 years."

Mr. Netanyahu emulated his scholarly father by writing two books on international terrorism, and he served with distinction in the same unit as his brother Yonatan, the Sayeret Matcal, in which their younger brother, Iddo, also served.

His entry into politics traces to the death of his brother. Returning to Israel, aged 27, he organized a series of memorial seminars on terrorism that attracted considerable attention. Among those impressed by Mr. Netanyahu's performance was Moshe Arens, then Ambassador to the United States, who plucked Mr. Netanyahu from a job as a furniture salesman and made him his deputy.

He was soon delegate to the United Nations, a position in which he became a fixture on American television talk shows and popular with conservative American Jews.

Back in Israel as Deputy Foreign Minister, Mr. Netanyahu gained further renown as the Israeli spokesman during the Persian Gulf war. Quick, succinct and good-looking, he was the voice of Israel day after day on every international network. After Likud lost in the 1993 national election, Mr. Netanyahu scrambled past the established figures of the Israeli right to seize the party chairmanship, in the process making numerous enemies in his own party.

After the assassination of Prime Minister Yitzhak Rabin, the perception that he condoned or even incited the radical right led to a steep plunge in his standing in the polls. His fortunes changed with four suicide bombings, which turned many Israelis against the governments policies.

Thereafter the race was neck-to-neck to the very end.

On most days of the campaign, Mr. Netanyahu was accompanied by his third wife, Sara, and sometimes by the older of their two young sons. He also has a daughter from his first marriage, Noa, 18, who lives in New York and will return to Israel next year for military service.

Mr. Netanyahu's paternal grandfather, also an ardent Zionist, settled in Palestine in 1920, changing his name from Mileikowsky to Netanyahu, which means "given by God." Mr. Netanyahu's father divided his life between American and Israel. Mr. Netanyahu was born in Israel on October 21, 1949. That makes him not only the youngest Israeli Prime Minister, but also the first to be born after the state was founded in 1948.

By SERGE SCHMEMANN
The New York Times
June 1, 1996.

Shimon Peres

BY RIGHTS, Shimon Peres should rank as one of the greatest figures in Israeli history. He was at David Ben-Gurion's right hand at the founding of the Jewish state, he built up its awesome defenses, he held every major government post, and he started the peace effort with the Palestinians.

But in the end, Mr. Peres will be remembered as the man who could not win.

Three times before, he led Labor in national elections, and three times he lost. This election was his fourth and, at 72, almost certainly his last, and this time his chances to redeem his failures and to crown his life's work seemed most solid.

With Yitzhak Rabin, his predecessor, Mr. Peres had opened a dialogue with the Palestinians that won plaudits in the West and a shared Nobel Peace Prize. Given four more years, he was certain that a comprehensive Middle East peace — the elusive dream so many other statesmen had pursued without success — was his to make.

Yet once again fate seemed determined not only to deny him the prize, but to humiliate him in the process.

Mr. Peres may have erred when he tried to capitalize on the wave of sympathy that followed Rabin's assassination and advanced the elections from October to May, 1996. No sooner had he done so than the Islamic militants of Hamas sent suicide bombers into Israel to avenge the assassination of their star bomb-maker, Yahya Ayyash, and the ensuing carnage reduced Labor's lead to a narrow margin.

Even then, trusting even that shrunken lead, Mr. Peres waged a low-key, statesmanlike campaign while Benjamin Netanyahu, his young, hawkish challenger, hammered away at Israeli fears and insecurity. In retrospect, it seemed that if Peres had not rushed to move up the polls, he might have used the extra months to consolidate his own standing and image.

After the assassination of Mr. Rabin, Mr. Peres tried to assume some of the mantle of tough guy, donning a leather jacket to inspect troops, slapping brutal restrictions on the Palestinians after the suicide bombings, sending warplanes on an aggressive raid into Lebanon. But the polls showed that none of those efforts earned him any points with Israeli Jews, and only lowered his standing with Arabs.

Some thought he might have done better to stay with his vision of peace. In the past, his popularity was highest when he acted on principle — when he pulled Israel out of a disastrous invasion of Lebanon in 1984, when he ordered severe economic measures to conquer hyperinflation in 1988, when he engineered the peace with Yasir Arafat in 1993.

Though not given to public displays of anger or emotion, the reputation of a loser was one to which Mr. Peres was obviously sensitive. On the eve of the election, when polls were showing him losing his edge, an interviewer ventured, "Maybe you're not a winning candidate."

"What do you want me to tell you — that I am nice, that I am a genius?" Mr. Peres snapped back.

But while Mr. Peres preferred to attribute his failures to the machinations of his rivals and the vagaries of politics, there was also the fact that he never succeeded in translating respect and even admiration into popularity or trust.

He was perceived as an intellectual, a visionary, an idealist, a statesman. But there was also a stigma that followed him throughout his 50-year political life of being elusive, deceitful, a spinner of intrigues. Perhaps it came of a political career in which he shifted from hawk to dove and joined with Likud in two "national unity" governments. Or it came of being a polished European intellectual in a land whose heroes were blunt, native-born soldiers. But he never succeeded in fully shaking it.

Mr. Peres's failures as leader and campaigner will long be dissected. But in the end, his major failure was probably his inability to overcome the apprehensions among half his countrymen about the longterm advantages of his peace effort. For a nation that equates peace with security, the vision of a new Middle East fades before the bloody reality of suicide bombings — especially with Mr. Netanyahu there to drive the message home.

But nobody will accuse Mr. Peres of wavering in his faith in his ability to achieve a comprehensive peace, if only he was given the chance. Asked last February whether he was the right man to lead Israel to this peace, he said: "I'm not sure I'm the right man. But I'm sure I have the right idea."

In the end, half of his countrymen concluded that he was not the right man. But if history shows that he did have the right idea, then his four electoral defeats might still be vindicated.

By SERGE SCHMEMANN
The New York Times
May 31, 1996.

Yitzhak Rabin

PRIME MINISTER Yitzhak Rabin of Israel, who was shot dead at age 73, was a soldier turned statesman who led his country into uncharted territory to make peace with the Palestinians and put an end to the wars, bloodshed and terrorism that had plagued his country since its founding.

It was General Rabin, the commander in chief of Israel's armed forces in 1967, who had led the lightning strike that captured broad swaths of Arab territories. Twenty-six years later, on September 13, 1993, it was Prime Minister Rabin who reluctantly extended his hand to Yasir Arafat, leader of the Palestine Liberation Organization, to put a symbolic seal of approval on an accord that would lead to the return of much of that territory and to Palestinian self-rule on the Israeli-occupied West Bank and the Gaza Strip.

In an extraordinary ceremony on the South Lawn of the White House, one that few had ever expected to see, Mr. Rabin came face-to-face with Arafat — the man who had been reviled for decades by Israelis as the mastermind behind one attack after another on their people, the man with whom the following year he and his foreign minister, Shimon Peres, would share the Nobel Peace Prize.

"The time for peace has come," Mr. Rabin declared. "We, the soldiers who have returned from battles stained with blood, we who have seen our relatives and friends killed before our eyes — we who have come from a land where parents bury their children, we who have fought against you, the Palestinians — we say today in a loud and clear voice: Enough of blood and tears. Enough."

Speaking as much to his own people as to the astonished world that was watching, Mr. Rabin explained in mournful tones how painful and how necessary it was for Israel to take this step. "It's not so easy — either for myself as a soldier in Israel's war nor for the people of Israel — It is certainly not easy for the families of the victims of the war's violence, terror, whose pain will never heal, for the many thousands who defended our lives and their own and have even sacrificed their lives for our own. For them this ceremony has come too late."

But he said Israel was not seeking revenge. It was seeking peace.

The tragedy was that some of Mr. Rabin's own people were seeking revenge. As Mr. Rabin came closer to achieving his goal of peace, a wide schism opened within the Israeli populace. Much of the bitterness of those opposed to making peace with Israel's historic enemies was directed at Mr. Rabin, and he became the soldier who paid the ultimate price to make peace.

He had been unrelenting in his drive to institutionalize that peace. Only a month ago, Mr. Rabin took part in another White House ceremony to mark the beginning of another withdrawal from the West Bank. This time the handshakes with Arafat were less reluctant and the peace process was well established.

Mr. Rabin was the only one of Israel's eight prime ministers to have been born in the land of Israel, a Sabra who had not experienced the long history of attacks on European Jewry and the horror of the Holocaust. With his election, Israel turned over its leadership from the fathers to the sons and he appealed for a new vision. On taking office in 1992 for his second term as prime minister, Mr. Rabin said it was time for Israel to jettison its siege mentality.

"No longer is it true that the whole world is against us," he said. He accepted his election as a mandate to make peace. One of his first steps was to put a freeze on all new construction in the occupied territories.

For their part, the Palestinians were ready to deal. With the end of the cold war and the collapse of the Soviet Union, the P.L.O. was deprived of diplomatic, financial and military support. At the same time, the P.L.O. was reeling from the loss of contributions from wealthy Arab states angered by Arafat's support of Iraq during the 1991 Persian Gulf war.

To achieve agreement with the Palestinians, Mr. Rabin followed the lead of Foreign Minister Peres, a Labor Party colleague and longtime political rival. They had fought for decades over the leadership of the party and the country, but they joined forces in the search for peace. To the opposition that branded Mr. Rabin a traitor, the prime minister replied that peace must be made with enemies, not with friends.

Mr. Rabin had been at the center of the major events in his nation's history for five decades. In 1948, he fought in the siege of Jerusalem during Israel's war of independence. In 1967, as chief of staff of the Israeli Army for the three years before the June war, he brought to fighting strength the formidable force that rolled over three Arab armies in six days. Later, as Ambassador to the United States he helped assure Israel a steady supply of sophisticated weapons. In his first term as Prime Minister he negotiated the crucial and lasting disengagement of Israeli and Egyptian forces in the Sinai, which paved the way for the Camp David accords. And as defense minister, in 1986, he presided over the withdrawal of Israeli forces from Lebanon although he continued to respond with force to terrorist attacks.

As a boy growing up in Palestine, Mr. Rabin wanted to be an agronomist, and attended the Khadouri Agricultural School in Galilee where he won the High Commissioner's Gold Medal as the best student in Palestine. But like many patriotic young people of his time he gave up his childhood ambition and joined the Palmach, the elite strike force of the Haganah underground Jewish army, saw action in World War II and developed into a brilliant military tactician.

He also developed into a politician. Israelis trusted him for his single-minded devotion to the good of the country and he was repeatedly asked to accept high government positions. But he was the antithesis of the convivial party man. Taciturn, introspective, controlled, intensely private, he had almost no close advisers and reached decisions independently, often announcing them in an authoritarian manner that alienated the party leadership. He spoke in a deep monotone that made his public personality seem colorless, and even in private he was almost devoid of humor.

Mr. Rabin was born in Jerusalem on March 1, 1922. His father, Nehemiah, who came from a poor family in Ukraine, had escaped from Czarist Russia and gone to Palestine by way of Chicago and St. Louis. In Palestine, he became a trade union organizer in the labor movement of David Ben-Gurion. His mother, Rosa Cohen, born to a well-to-do family in Gomel, Russia, was active in politics and became the dominant influence on the young Mr. Rabin. Theirs was a home where young Yitzhak was taught that public service was a duty and where, he remembered, "It was a disgrace to speak about money."

He was 7 years old when Arabs began attacking Jewish settlements. Later, during the 1936 Arab riots and general strike, he was at the Khadouri school where he was trained in the use of arms by Yigal Allon, who was later to become his commander and his mentor. Five years later, during World War II, Moshe Dayan, then a young commander in the Haganah, invited Mr. Rabin to join the Palmach. As part of the British invasion of Greater Syria, which was in the hands of the Axis powers, Mr. Rabin was sent across the border. The youngest in his unit, it was his job to climb up telephone poles to cut the wires so the collaborationist Vichy French forces could not call up reinforcements.

In June 1945, just after the end of the war in Europe, Mr. Rabin commanded a daring raid to liberate about 200 illegal Jewish immigrants held by the British in a camp at Athlit, on the Mediterranean just south of Haifa. The exploit was said to be the prototype for a similar raid in the novel *Exodus,* and Mr. Rabin the prototype for Ari Ben Canaan, the hero, played in the movie version by Paul Newman. But the shy Mr. Rabin always insisted that he was not the fictional Ari Ben Canaan.

Mr. Rabin was arrested by the British and imprisoned for six months in a camp in Gaza. Soon after he was released the British turned the problem of Palestine over to the United Nations, which, in 1947, voted for partition into a Jewish and an Arab state.

The Arabs attacked, and as hostilities intensified between the Jews and the Arabs, Mr. Allon, then the commander of the Palmach, appointed Mr. Rabin his deputy. During the 1948 Israeli war of independence, Mr. Rabin commanded the Har-El Brigade, a makeshift unit that failed to take Jerusalem for Israel but kept open the vital supply lines between Jerusalem and the sea. Later, with the rank of colonel, he served on the southern front against Egyptian forces.

When Mr. Rabin disclosed in his 1979 memoir his role in forcing 50,000 Arab civilians to leave their homes at gunpoint during the war of independence, there was a furor in Israel, where officials had long denied that Arab civilians were pushed out of their lands.

In the middle of the war, on August 23, 1948, Mr. Rabin married Leah Schlossberg, who had joined the Palmach and served in his battalion. They had two children, a son, Yuval, and a daughter, Dalia, and three grandchildren. They all survive him.

Mr. Rabin's first venture into diplomacy came when he was sent to the island of Rhodes as part of the delegation to the Israeli-Egyptian armistice talks in 1949.

In 1953, having finally committed himself to a career in the army, Mr. Rabin went to England to study at the British Staff College at Camberley. Back home he went on to hold a series of high posts in the Israeli Army, mainly involving manpower training, and was named chief of staff in 1964.

He became Israel's top expert on military matters. Even as he rose through the ranks, he became known as the man who who knew more than the generals. Eventually, he became a general himself.

The army that fought the Six–Day War in 1967 was essentially Mr. Rabin's army. Shabtai Teveth, professor of history at Tel Aviv University, said, "It was the army he trained, planned, built and armed in his three years as Chief of Staff." But, he added, "There his glory ends."

His "glory" ended when, on the eve of the fighting, Mr. Rabin suffered a nervous collapse.

In his memoir, he wrote of going to see Mr. Ben-Gurion, then in retirement. He went in search of encouragement but instead got a dressing-down. Mr. Ben-Gurion, he wrote, scolded him for mobilizing the reserves after President Gamal Abdel Nasser of Egypt closed the Straits of Tiran. "You have led the state into a grave situation," Mr. Ben-Gurion told him. "We must not go to war. We are isolated. You bear the responsibility."

Mr. Ben-Gurion's words reverberated in his ears as he worked himself into a state of physical and mental exhaustion. He recovered in time to carry out his duties during the war, but some observers thought he was not functioning normally and was only being "propped up" so that the troops and the people would not lose confidence in their leader.

Whatever the source of Mr. Rabin's difficulties, the results achieved by his army were astonishingly clear. At the end of the war Hebrew University conferred on him an honorary doctorate. In a modest, occasionally poetic speech, he said he accepted the honor not for himself but as the representative of an army of civilians who had never been trained for conquest, of battle-hardened paratroopers who had leaned on the stones of the Wailing Wall and wept at the capture of the Old City of Jerusalem. He spoke about his army, but perhaps even more about himself.

"Our Sabra youth, and most certainly our soldiers," he said, "do not tend to be sentimental and they shrink from any public show of feeling. But the strain of battle, the anxiety which preceded it, and the sense of salvation and of direct confrontation with Jewish history itself cracked the shell of hardness and shyness and released wellsprings of emotion and stirrings of the spirit."

In 1968, Mr. Rabin was appointed ambassador to the United States, where he became known as an effective advocate for Israel and a master at procuring sophisticated American weapons. In his five years as ambassador he developed a close relationship with Henry A. Kissinger, President Richard M. Nixon's national security adviser and later his secretary of state. Kissinger called on him for intelligence about troop movements in the Middle East and even consulted him on Vietnam.

Shortly after he returned to Israel in 1973, Mr. Rabin entered national politics for the first time. Then, on Yom Kippur, while the country was in the middle of an election campaign, Syria and Egypt launched a surprise attack. The country's leaders — Prime Minister Golda Meir and her Minister of Defense, Dayan — were held responsible for the country's lack of preparedness in that October war.

The Labor Party managed to win enough votes to form a new Government, and Mr. Rabin won a seat in Parliament in his first attempt at election and was given the post of minister of labor. But within a month of forming her Cabinet, Meir resigned and the party turned to Mr. Rabin, who had been out of power at the time of the war and was therefore untainted by the heavy casualties.

In 1974, Mr. Rabin became Israel's fifth prime minister and, at 52, its youngest. "The time has come," he said, "for the sons of the founders of the state to take over their role."

Mr. Rabin became the first Israeli Prime Minister to make an official visit to West Germany. He also said he met secretly with King Hussein of Jordan six times in an unsuccessful effort to open peace negotiations with him. His government weathered the Arab oil embargo and the skyrocketing prices of oil, and negotiated a second Sinai disengagement with the Egyptians.

During his term as Prime Minister, Mr. Rabin faced down terrorists who hijacked an Air France plane en route from Tel Aviv to Paris. At first, he was seen as weak because he waited several days before dispatching an assault group to Entebbe, Uganda, where the plane and almost 100 Israeli citizens were being held hostage. When he finally approved a military operation and, when the daring raid succeeded, he was hailed as a hero.

But in 1977, his image was damaged when an Israeli newspaper disclosed that he and his wife had violated currency laws by maintaining bank accounts in the United States after he had returned home. At first he lied about how much money was in the accounts and, finally, he was forced to step down, opening the way for the victory of Menachem Begin and the Likud Party.

Mr. Rabin bounced back from the scandal not because he was a skilled politician, but because he was not a politician at all. He returned to government as minister of defense in a Labor-Likud national unity coalition that presided over the Israeli pullout from Lebanon. His was the policy of the "iron fist," promising swift retaliation for guerrilla raids against Israelis withdrawing from southern Lebanon.

Sitting in his office at the defense ministry one evening in 1987, he looked back at his life with satisfaction tinged with disappointment. His disappointment, he said, was in what he saw as a loss of national spirit, the failure of the creators of the state to pass on their sense of commitment.

Of his most satisfying moment he had no doubt — the liberation and unification of Jerusalem in 1967.

But there was more, a legacy delivered that day in 1993 when he led the country to come to terms with the Palestinians, "to live together on the same soil in the same land."

He acknowledged the risk. But in going to Washington to endorse the agreement, he said, "We have come to try to put an end to the hostilities so that our children, our children's children, will no longer experience the painful cost of war."

By MARILYN BERGER
The New York Times
November 5, 1995.

Yitzhak Shamir

YITZHAK SHAMIR is a man with a reputation for saying no.

He opposed the Camp David accords; he opposed the peace treaty with Egypt, and he opposed the Cabinet's decision to withdraw the Israeli Army from Lebanon.

But as he prepared to reclaim the office of prime minister for his Likud bloc — a job he held previously from October 1983 to September 1984 — Mr. Shamir dropped several hints that his hard-line reputation, though well deserved, should not necessarily be considered a guide for future action.

A favorite story of his is one that an Israeli delegation brought back from Bucharest after a meeting with Romania's President, Nicolae Ceausescu. A member of the delegation asked Ceausescu whether he thought Mr. Shamir would continue with peace efforts, to which the Romanian leader replied, according to Mr. Shamir, "Without doubt he will continue — and you will see, he will surprise you."

No one expected that Mr. Shamir would suddenly moderate his views. But as a man who may have faced his last hurrah in political life, he seemed eager to leave at least some mark on that elusive diplomatic phenomenon known as the "Middle East peace process" — although just what kind of mark that might be remained to be seen.

He refused to relinquish any part of the Israeli-occupied West Bank, Golan Heights or Gaza Strip. But he seemed to be aiming toward some kind of permanent, "de facto" arrangement with the Arabs.

"Of course I will try to improve our contacts with all our neighbors," Mr. Shamir said during an interview in his office. "I don't say that I will accept their positions. That's impossible. But we will try to discuss and find common ground. You don't have to be desperate. Never be desperate. That is my slogan."

"I am not afraid of taking risks," he added. "We have to take risks for peace. I admit, there is a Palestinian problem. They are not happy to live under our rule. We have to find a solution without giving up our rights in the territories. A very large majority of Israelis is against giving up our rights. And the Arab side is not yet ready for compromises. It's a fact. Therefore, we have to find a stable solution — not a permanent solution — a stable solution, a modus vivendi. I have some ideas. I don't want to speak about them now, but I have some ideas."

Mr. Shamir is no stranger to risks. He has lived close to the edge most of his adult life. Although he can be amiable and avuncular in his dealings with the public, this exterior masks a steely character underneath that is capable of the most brutally tough decisions. When Mr. Shamir decided to begin writing his memoirs, no one doubted that if he were to write them in a frank and open manner they would make for some fascinating reading.

Mr. Shamir's family name was Jazernicki when he was born on October 15, 1915, in a Hasidic village in eastern Poland. He broke off his law studies at the University of Warsaw and emigrated to Palestine in 1935. His father, a leader of the Jews in his home village, remained behind with the rest of his family and they were all wiped out by the Nazis.

Mr. Shamir joined the Irgun Zvai Leumi, one of the underground Jewish terrorist organizations directed against the British occupation of Palestine. When the Irgun split in 1940, Mr. Shamir sided with the most violent faction, headed by Abraham Stern, which later became known as the Stern Gang.

After Stern was killed by the British in 1942, Mr. Shamir became one of the three leaders. During his tenure, the Stern Gang was held responsible for many deeds, including the 1944 assassination of Britain's minister of state for the Middle East, Lord Moyne, and the 1948 assassination of Count Folke Bernadotte of Sweden, then a United Nations representative in the Middle East.

After the State of Israel was established, Mr.

Shamir remained underground — but legally — by joining the Mossad secret service in 1955, where he rose during 10 years to be chief of its European operations.

In 1965, Mr. Shamir cast away his trenchcoat and retired from espionage. After a stint in private business — he managed a small rubber factory near Tel Aviv — he entered politics in 1970. At the age of 55, he joined Menachem Begin's right-wing Herut Party, the core of the present day Likud bloc. Gradually, he worked his way up through the party ranks.

After Mr. Begin was elected Prime Minister in 1977, he had Mr. Shamir appointed Speaker of parliament. Three years later, Begin promoted him to foreign minister, and when Begin suddenly decided to quit politics in October 1983, Mr. Shamir was elected by the party to succeed him as prime minister, a job he held until the stalemated elections of July, 1984, produced the national unity government.

For the time being, Mr. Shamir concentrated on perpetuating the national unity coalition, which, he contended, is not only what the public wants but was best for Israel.

"Many of the recent achievements on the economic front and in the international arena have to be put on the credit of the national unity government," Mr. Shamir said. "One party alone never could have achieved them. When Peres is going to talk to Mubarak or to Hussein or to others, if he has my backing, he can afford to do it. And it makes the prospects for peace better. Peres knows it very well. He can always say to his negotiating partners, 'You must know, I have Shamir there back home and I have to get his agreement.'"

"It is not always pleasant — not for Peres and not for me," Mr. Shamir said. "And I don't know what will happen in the next 25 months, but I really feel that it is worthwhile."

By THOMAS L. FRIEDMAN
The New York Times
October 21, 1986

[Yitzhak Shamir stepped down from Likud leadership in March, 1993. As Likud's elder statesman, he travels to the U.S. and Europe to visit Jewish communities. He is not a member of parliament, but remains active in politics, and is a sharp critic of prime minister Netanyahu as being too soft and indecisive in dealing with the Palestinians. Mr. Shamir lives in Tel Aviv.]

Moshe Sharett

MOSHE SHARETT, premier of Israel from 1953 to 1955, died of cancer in Jerusalem at the age of 70. His death was announced in a joint statement by the government, the World Zionist Organization and the Knesset (parliament).

Mr. Sharett was chairman of the World Zionist Executive and served uninterruptedly in the Knesset since Israel was established in 1948.

"The Jewish people have been bereaved of a leader of the state, a pilot of the movement and a teacher of the nation," the joint announcement said.

Mr. Sharett, seriously ill for a long time, was readmitted to Hadassah Hospital after his condition suddenly worsened. He fell into a coma the next day.

In his will, opened in the presence of his family at his deathbed, Mr. Sharett requested that they refrain from announcing his death by posting mourning notices in the street. He also requested no eulogies during the funeral and internment.

Mr. Sharett's body laid in state in the courtyard of the Jewish Agency building in Jerusalem throughout the next day. A funeral service was held in Jerusalem.

Also, in accordance with his will, Mr. Sharett was buried in Tel Aviv's Old Cemetery next to the graves of his brothers-in-law and close friends Eliahu Golomb, founder and leader of the Haganah, the Jewish underground during the British occupation of Palestine, and Dov Hos, a Zionist leader.

For 15 years before the birth of Israel, Mr. Sharett made history mainly as the official responsible for Israel's foreign relations. He was in effect foreign minister of the shadow cabinet of the embryo Jewish State, as head of the Political Department of the Zionist Executive, and presented his people's case in the chancelleries and embassies of the world and before international bodies.

Those were years of frustration and heartache with rare moments of encouragement.

But when the United Nations voted in 1947 to partition Palestine into Jewish and Arab states, Mr. Sharett's personal prestige was at its peak.

On returning from New York to Tel Aviv in 1948 to sign the Declaration of Independence, cheering crowds followed him from the Tel Aviv Museum to the home of his aged mother in Rothschild Boulevard, where he walked after the historic ceremony.

On that day, when the Israeli Government became official, Mr. Sharett slipped naturally into the office of Foreign Minister, which he held until 1956. But he continued to experience frustrations.

At home, he was under cross-fire from leftists criticizing his pro-Western orientation and by irredentists opposing his moderation with the Arabs.

However, that period was also full of compensation and moments of elation, as when Mr. Sharett led his government's delegation to Lake Success, to accept United Nations membership in 1949.

After a stormy debate, fierce with Arab opposition, Israel was voted in, 377 to 12, and Mr. Sharett rose to pledge the country's "loyalty to the fundamental principles" of the charter.

"We enter this Assembly in a spirit of humility, anxious for guidance and enlightenment," he said.

The next day at an emotional ceremony outside United Nations headquarters, he led the singing of "Hatikvah," the Jewish anthem, as the blue and white Israeli flag, bearing the Star of David, took its place among the flags of the world.

"This star of David, which has been used by our oppressors, which we have carried with us in our trials and tribulations, which accompanied our pioneers when they broke new ground in the wilderness, this flag, which has been a rallying point for the forces of Jewish people struggling to achieve the liberation in our ancestral home, is now marking our full emancipation," he declared.

The happy period ended abruptly. David Ben-Gurion reassumed the helm in 1955 after Mr. Sharett had served as Premier for two years. Mr. Ben-Gurion lost patience with his temperate and cautious foreign minister. He served notice that one or the other must go, and Mr. Sharett accordingly resigned.

The statesmanlike and dignified manner in which he stepped down earned Mr. Sharett renewed admiration and esteem. He received warm ovations whenever he appeared publicly.

He retained his seat in parliament and continued to be active in the Mapai party, but assiduously declined august state appointments. He became head of Am Oved, the General Labor Federation's publishing house.

In 1956, he assumed the chairmanship of the World Zionist Executive and finally found a satisfying outlet for his abilities. He applied himself to his new post with zeal, attempting to breathe new life into the movement that had been flagging since its goal of creating a Jewish state had been reached.

A polished linguist of great personal charm and urbane courtesy, Mr. Sharett became even better known around the world as he traveled extensively, trying to persuade Zionists that they still had a vital function, recruiting young blood for the movement and promoting Hebrew education in the Diaspora.

Mr. Sharett was born October 15, 1894 in Kherson, in the Ukraine, and was brought to Turkish-ruled Palestine at the age of 12. His father, Yaakov Tchertok, was a member of Bilu, a Russian-Jewish organisation dedicated to agricultural colonization of Palestine.

The family changed its name to Shertok in Palestine and after the establishment of Israel, to Sharett, Hebrew for "serve."

In line with Bilu ideals, the family's first home in Palestine was a farm in a remote Arab village in the hills of Ephraim. The venture was an economic disaster and in 1909 the family moved to Ahuzat Bait, a suburb of Jaffa that was to develop into the city of Tel Aviv.

During the two years the young immigrant spent on the farm, he mastered Arabic and studied his neighbors' customs and morals, gaining knowledge that was to influence his career.

Mr. Sharett was in the first graduating class of the Herzlia Gymnasium in Tel Aviv. While there, he joined a semi-clandestine idealistic clique that pledged its members to choose occupations that would benefit the Jewish community in Palestine.

Most of the members became farmers. Mr. Sharett was chosen to go to Istanbul to study law and equip himself to defend Palestine Jews against abuses by corrupt Ottoman officials.

His law studies were interrupted by World War

I and Mr. Sharett had to decide between going underground, risking detention as a Czarist subject or becoming an Ottoman citizen and joining the army. He chose the latter and was commissioned an officer.

For his extraordinary linguistic abilities he was assigned as interpreter for a high ranking German officer commanding a Turkish unit. In that post, he traveled widely and became familiar with the region.

After the war and Britain's Balfour Declaration, which pledged the establishment of a Jewish national home, Mr. Sharett went to London and enrolled in the School of Economics and Political Science. He paid his way by working as a translator and giving Hebrew lessons. He was also active in Zionist affairs then.

In 1925, when the General Federation of Labor started its daily, Davar, Mr. Sharett was called back to Tel Aviv to join the editorial staff. Davar initiated an English-language supplement in 1929, and Mr. Sharett became editor.

His work attracted the attention of Chaim Arlosoroff, head of the Political Department of the Zionist Executive, who invited him to join his staff. Mr. Sharett became Mr. Arlosoroff's right-hand man, particularly in relations with Arabs.

During that period, Mr. Sharett developed a warm relationship with Emir Abdullah of Trans-Jordan, later the King. A Persian rug presented to him by the Arab ruler was one of his most-treasured possessions.

Mr. Arlosoroff was murdered on the Tel Aviv seashore in 1933 and later that year the Zionist Congress elected Mr. Sharett to succeed him. Thus, at 37, he entered the front rank of Zionist leadership.

In addition to the history he helped mold, Mr. Sharett left his imprint on the Hebrew language. He coined scores of new words and used the prestige of his official positions to spur their widespread use. He was also instrumental in getting other people's creations adopted.

He was fluent in Hebrew, English, Russian, French, German, Turkish and Arabic and Yiddish. He translated poetry from several languages into Hebrew and also wrote two books.

He was survived by his widow, Zippora, whom he married when they were students in London; two sons, Yaakov and Chaim; a daughter, Mrs. Yael Medini; a sister, Mrs. Eliabu Colomb; a brother, Yehuda Sharett, a composer; and eight grandchildren.

The New York Times
July 8, 1965

Ariel Sharon

ARIEL SHARON was a soldier from childhood who grew up to be one of Israel's most vocal and uncompromising hawks, on the battlefield and in politics.

An outspoken Cabinet member in a generation of Israeli administrations, Mr. Sharon's imprint is most apparent in the West Bank and Gaza, where he aggressively pursued the construction of Jewish settlements. And it was Mr. Sharon, as defense minister under Prime Minister Menachem Begin, who orchestrated the 1982 invasion of Lebanon, which cost hundreds of Israeli lives and brought down Israel's first conservative government.

The invasion was the end of a military career that began six years before the birth of Israel, when at the age of 14, Ariel Sharon joined the Haganah, the underground Jewish militia, on the cooperative farm where he was born in Kfar Malal, outside Tel Aviv. In the army, he fought in every major military campaign in Israeli history, leading infantry units and a paratroop division and working in intelligence.

He retired as a general in 1973, but a few months later was called back to active duty to lead an armored division in the Yom Kippur War. He retired again, but his association with the armed forces truly ended only when he was forced to resign as defense minister in the aftermath of the invasion of Lebanon.

On June 6, 1982, Mr. Sharon ordered the army

into Lebanon, with the stated purpose of forcing Palestinian guerrillas out of firing range of northern Israel, which had for years endured sporadic rocket and artillery barrages.

Mr. Sharon promised to stop his army after it had advanced 25 miles into Lebanon. Instead, his fighters moved on to Beirut, another 25 miles to the north. The real objectives of the invasion were revealed when Israel demanded that the Palestine Liberation Organization, which was headquartered in Beirut, withdraw from Lebanon. When Yasir Arafat, the P.L.O. leader, rejected the demand, the Israelis began shelling the city.

After a two-month bombardment that devastated the capital and left more than 17,000 dead, most of the victims Palestinian or Lebanese civilians, Arafat finally acquiesced.

With the P.L.O. leadership decamped to Tunis, its guerrillas dispersed. But the cost was great.

Stripped of his portfolio, Mr. Sharon remained active in government and quickly recovered, as he had from his war injuries, to re-enter the political fray, with his ambitions, including his dream of becoming prime minister, unscathed.

Officially, General Sharon entered politics after the 1973 war, and he did so in characteristic fashion, by forming his own party, which was tiny and attracted little support during its brief life. But he won a seat in parliament in 1973 and joined the Herut wing of the Likud bloc. Saying he was bored, he quit parliament a year later, reportedly miffed that he had not been appointed a government minister. But he bounced back in less than a year, accepting an appointment as security adviser to Prime Minister Yitzhak Rabin.

In 1977, he was again elected to parliament and was chosen by prime minister Menachem Begin as minister of agriculture, a job he approached with vigor, stretching its boundaries beyond the traditional duties to exercise his influence over the administration of Jewish settlements in the occupied territories. He fully expected to become Mr. Begin's defense minister when the job came open in 1980, but Mr. Begin kept the portfolio for himself for political reasons, eventually surrendering it to General Sharon in 1981. He became one of Mr. Begin's greatest admirers and most trusted advisers, and in the time they served together, references to the Begin-Sharon Government were not uncommon.

Despite his loss of the defense post, he went on to become minister of industry and trade in 1984 under the national unity government and minister of housing in 1990, under Prime Minister Yitzhak Shamir. Housing was broadly defined, conferring on General Sharon the opportunity to further fortify Jewish settlements in the West Bank and giving him the responsibility of finding homes for the Soviet Jewish emigrés who were streaming into Israel. Again, in the Shamir administration, Sharon was said to be a "shadow prime minister." Indeed, each portfolio he was handed by — or, as was the case in 1996, wrested from — succeeding administrations expanded so that his power was felt throughout the government.

In July, 1996, when a Likud coalition was elected by the slimmest of margins, General Sharon was considered to be chief among the conservative powerbrokers who delivered the votes the new prime minister, Benjamin Netanyahu, needed, but he was shunned by Mr. Netanyahu before the elections and left out when it was time to divide the spoils. In time, he was named minister of national infrastructure, a new Cabinet post assembled from responsibilities carved out of other ministries, much to the dismay of his fellow Cabinet members, but the appointment came about only after the foreign minister, David Levy, threatened to resign unless a spot was found for General Sharon.

The job gave him broad jurisdiction over nearly every resource he needed to continue his crusade for Jewish settlements: Roads, housing in rural areas and settlements, negotiation of water rights and some fuel and transportation responsibilities. He was empowered almost immediately when Mr. Netanyahu lifted the previous Labor government's ban on expanding settlements. In addition to the settlements, he made it a priority over the years to build networks of new roads that bypass Arab areas and link clusters of Jewish settlements.

Mr. Sharon's aggressive settlement-building, even after the establishment of Palestinian self-rule, was seen as an obstacle to peace efforts and thus earned him the wrath of several administrations in Washington.

Mr. Sharon was not intimidated by political pressure, however, and said so outright on more than one occasion around the Middle East.

In September of 1982, when Bashir Gemayel, Lebanon's new President and an ally of Israel, was assassinated just days after he was elected, Israeli troops swarmed into west Beirut. They stood by and did not intervene when Christian Phalangists raided the Palestinian refugee camps of Sabra and Shatila. Several hundred Palestinian civilians were killed in the raid, and a government commission investigating the massacre found the defense minister among those indirectly responsible for the deaths and recommended his resignation. General Sharon saw himself as a scapegoat and considered this action to be the deepest form of betrayal, one Jew turning in another, the one thing his father had implored him never to do.

He was not fazed by outside pressure, either, and said on more than one occasion that he did not recognize the Oslo accords Israel signed with Palestinian leaders. The old general has said many times that he believes Arabs and Jews can coexist peacefully, but in his vision of coexistence, Israel is always in charge.

By HELEN VERONGOS
The New York Times

Zalmon Shazar

ZALMAN SHAZAR, the nation of Israel's third President, died in Jerusalem, a day before his 85th birthday.

His death was announced officially by President Ephraim Katzir, Parliament and the Government after sunset marked the end of the Jewish sabbath. He died at the Hadassah University Hospital, which he entered suffering from renal malfunctioning.

The body of the president laid in state in Jerusalem and burial took place on Mount Herzl in the capital.

Mr. Shazar served two full terms as president, from 1963 until 1973. The tenures culminated seven decades of service to the cause of Jewish national revival.

He is remembered largely for his fiery orations, delivered in an arm-waving thunderous style once popular in Eastern Europe.

When Israel was established in 1948, Premier David Ben-Gurion proposed sending Mr. Shazar to Moscow as ambassador. The Kremlin declined to accept him. It was said the Russians feared the impact the firebrand might have on Soviet Jews.

Mr. Shazar was born in Czarist Russia on October 6, 1889. His name was originally Schneor Zalman Rubashov; like most leading officials of the Jewish state, he changed his name to a Hebrew sounding one when he assumed high office. The name "Shazar" is made up of the initials of his previous name.

Mr. Shazar's Zionist activities over the years were mainly in Hebrew literature and culture. They began in Russia when he became a translator in a Zionist publishing house.

He first went to Israel in 1911 when the country was under Turkish rule and was called Palestine, but he returned to Russia for his army service. He settled in Tel Aviv in 1924 after the British conquest of Palestine.

With the founding of Davar, the daily newspaper of the General Federation of Jewish Labor, or Histadrut, he joined the staff, and in 1944 became editor-in-chief.

At the same time Mr. Shazar was active as a leader of the Labor party in the Zionist movement and the Vaad Leumi, the elected body representing Palestinian Jews. He traveled to Europe and America on national missions. He was among the founders of Hehalut, a European movement that trained young Jews for pioneering life in Palestine.

Mr. Shazar participated in a hunger strike protesting British restrictions on Jewish immigration to Palestine and was the author of various manifestos about the Nazi holocaust. In 1948 he helped draft the Israeli proclamation of independence.

In 1949 Mr. Shazar became Israel's first minister of education. In a quivering voice, he announced in Parliament that education would be free and compulsory. However, he was considered a poor administrator, and Premier Ben-Gurion replaced him.

He was then elected to the executive of the World Zionist Organization and headed the department for Jewish education outside Israel. He remained in the post until 1963, when Parliament elected him to succeed the late Yitzhak Ben Zvi as president of Israel, a mainly ceremonial office.

As president, Mr. Shazar continued to focus on literary and cultural affairs. He set up a personal fund to help writers and publishers and organized groups in the official residence for the study of the Bible and events in contemporary Judaism.

He also pursued his own literary activities. During his presidency, he expanded a Hebrew book of essays about personalities he had met in his public career and published a volume of Yiddish poems.

Mr. Shazar acquired a thorough education in traditional Jewish studies at home in Russia and his secular higher education in the Academy for Hebraic Studies in what was then St. Petersburg and the universities of Freiburg, Strasbourg and Berlin. He majored in history and philosophy.

He thus felt equally at home in the world of the Talmud and in the world of European culture.

Mr. Shazar's family belonged to the Lubavitcher Hasidic sect. His given names were those of the founder of the movement, Schneor Zalman. Although a Socialist, Mr. Shazar retained the traditional attachment to the Hasidic movement.

He regularly attended the annual festivities in Kfar Habbad, a Lubavitcher village near Tel Aviv, on the anniversary of the release of Schneor Zalman from a Czaris prison.

As president, Mr. Shazar shunned protocol and on visits to the United States insisted on going to Brooklyn to pay respects to Rabbi Menachem M. Schneerson, the head of the sect. Mr. Shazar maintained that it would be unseemly for the rabbi to call on the President.

His widow, the former Rachel Katznelson, was an author, journalist and labor and political leader in her own right.

By MOSHE BRILLIANT
The New York Times
October 6, 1974

Ezer Weizman

EZER WEIZMAN, a blunt-talking swashbuckler who evolved from a hawkish general into a leading voice for peace with the Arabs, was elected by parliament to be Israel's seventh president.

A befuddled and embarrassed legislature had to vote twice because the first time, for reasons unclear, it wound up with 124 ballots being cast — four more than its membership.

But in the end everything came out as expected: The 68-year-old Mr. Weizman, a former defense minister and air force commander who had quit politics, completed his comeback by defeating Dov Shilansky, a former Speaker of Parliament. The vote was 66 to 53, with one blank ballot.

The new president's five-year term began on May 13, when he succeeded Chaim Herzog, who held the basically ceremonial but potentially influential position for a decade. It is the president, for example, who chooses a politician to form a government when the politicians cannot decide among themselves.

For Weizman, victory was the culmination of a personal odyssey. His uncle, Chaim Weizmann, was a founder of Israel and its first president. ("My father decided that one 'n' was good enough for us," Weizman has said, explaining the difference in spelling.) The Israeli presidency can be an important forum and Mr. Weizman, who was a driving force behind the 1978 Camp David peace accords between Israel and Egypt, hinted he would use the office as a bully pulpit.

In the past, generating sharp disputes as he went along, he called for more rapid strides toward peace with Israel's Arab neighbors and direct negotiations with the Palestine Liberation Organization. He was said to have talked with the P.L.O. himself in 1989, when such contacts were illegal, and although he never confirmed or denied it, he was forced out of a left-right unity government that then prevailed.

While the parliamentary vote reflected party politics, some commentators viewed it as a sign that the Israeli mainstream is now prepared to consider compromises for peace.

Two questions about the new president were on many Israeli minds.

One was whether he would be able to control his often tart, occasionally crude language in a position regarded here as a unifying force. The other was how he would get along with Prime Minister Yitzhak Rabin, who was the Israeli armed forces chief of staff during the 1967 Middle East war, when Weizman was Rabin's deputy.

A decade later, Mr. Weizman disclosed that Mr. Rabin had collapsed and disappeared for a day nearly two weeks before the start of the 1967 war, which ended with Israel's stunning six-day victory. Years later, relations between the two men remain glacial.

Born in Tel Aviv on June 15, 1924, in what was then British-ruled Palestine, Mr. Weizman served with the Royal Air Force in World War II, then helped build the Israeli Air Force, the cutting edge of this country's military.

A hawk then on issues of land and peace, he engineered the Likud Party campaign that brought Menachem Begin to power in 1977. A year later, he played a pivotal role at Camp David, forming a close friendship with President Anwar el-Sadat of Egypt.

At first gradually, then rapidly, Mr. Weizman became disenchanted with Mr. Begin, finally leaving Likud in the mid-1980s for the Labor Party and drifting toward ever more dovish views.

Although he said nothing about how he might translate his views into action, Weizman clearly had that question on his mind. "I think I know what I'm forbidden to do," he said to laughs from backers. "But it's still not clear what I'm permitted to do."

By CLYDE HABERMAN
The New York Times
March 25, 1993

Chaim Weizmann

CHAIM WEIZMANN, a founder of Israel died in his home in Rehovoth, near Tel Aviv, after a long illness. He would have been 78 years old on November 27, 1952.

Respiratory inflammation was declared to be a principal cause of his death.

Dr. Weizmann, a world famed chemist, was an early Zionist and the natural choice to be Israel's first president when the new nation came into being May 14, 1948.

Chaim Weizmann's life was sufficiently full of adventure, romance, accomplishment and fulfillment to have been lived by a dozen men. He was a world-famous scientist, a statesman, leader of a forceful political movement, an intellectual and, above all, a great humanitarian.

In the three-quarters of a century through which he lived, he experienced every emotion: reward, for priceless scientific achievement; despair, for when the great prize seemed lost; and triumph, when the prize — his lifelong dream of a Jewish home in Palestine — was achieved.

Few great men have had more humble beginnings. He was born on November 27, 1874, in the village of Motele, near Pinsk, Russia. He lived to become the first president of the modern state of Israel and to see pour into its borders the hundreds of thousands of homeless, abandoned European Jews.

Many strong men and women, people of great courage, skill and ability, have contributed to the growth of Israel. His life epitomized the task of all of them in transforming Palestinian deserts into sections of rolling forests, lush olive and orange groves, irrigation and water-powered projects and centers of science and industry in the undeveloped Middle East.

Theodor Herzl was the founder of the modern Zionist movement; Dr. Weizmann gave it practical direction. He acted as a moderator among the bitterly quarreling Zionist factions.

Perhaps his principal contribution to the movement came as a result of his work as a scientist in the first World War. His reward was the Balfour Declaration. It became the key to ultimate Zionist victory.

As head of the British Admiralty Laboratories from 1917 to 1919, Dr. Weizmann developed a process for the manufacture of synthetic acetone at a time when the British needed it desperately. He isolated certain organisms found in cereals and horse chestnuts and within a month had created synthetic acetone for British explosives.

He was also credited with having suggested to David Lloyd George the strategy of the campaign against Turkey which resulted ultimately in Allenby's victorious march on Jerusalem. For all these services the British prime minister asked him what he wanted in return.

Dr. Weizmann refused any monetary reward or a title, and said "There is only one thing I want — a national home for my people."

The Balfour Declaration, issued in November 1917, followed. It was Britain's promise to facilitate the Jews in making a homeland in Palestine and was hailed as the Magna Carta of the Zionist movement.

It was supported by a joint resolution of the Congress of the United States and led Jews everywhere to believe the redemption of Palestine was assured. The declaration was a central factor in Jewish aspirations even in the darkest days when war, then changes in British policy, including support of the Arab position, seemed to doom the whole idea of a Jewish homeland.

Dr. Weizmann was the third child of Reb Oizer and Rachel Czermerinsky Weizmann. His father was a timber merchant, of modest means, who managed with his wife the remarkable task of sending nine of their fifteen children to universities. He went first to cheder (Jewish religious school) until he was 11 and then the Gymnasium in Pinsk, where he made a brilliant record in science and mathematics.

Years later when he was reputedly asked by Lord Balfour, the British Foreign Secretary, if there were many Zionists like him, Dr. Weizmann, whose celebrated remarks were legendary, replied, "The roads of Pinsk are paved with them."

He left Russia in 1894 and spent the next four years in Germany at the Technische Hochschule of Darmstadt and Berlin-Charlottenburg. When a favorite professor joined the staff of the University of Freiburg in Switzerland, Dr. Weizmann went there to study. He received a doctorate in science in 1900.

Within a year, he took a position as lecturer in organic chemistry at the University of Geneva, where he taught and continued his research until 1904. He became affiliated, meanwhile, with the Zionist movement.

It was in Geneva that he met Vera Chatzman, a medical student, whom he married in 1906. They had two sons Benjamin and Michael, who was killed in 1944 while flying on patrol with the British Royal Air Force.

Dr. Weizmann left Geneva to accept a post at the University of Manchester in England and in 1910 he became a naturalized British subject. He received a D.Sc. from the British university in 1909 and an LL.D. in 1919.

The only major Zionist conference which Dr. Weizmann failed to attend was the first, in 1897, after Herzl published *Der Judenstaat*.

At the age of 27, Dr. Weizmann had dared to criticize Herzl as "too visionary," and in 1900, at the Fourth Zionist Convention, he emerged as the leader of the Democratic Zionist faction.

This group opposed both the political Zionists, who wanted political guarantees for the establishment of a Jewish home in Palestine, and the practical Zionists who wanted to settle Jewish colonies in the Holy Land without regard to political guarantees. Dr. Weizmann helped reconcile their differences.

His first speech to the biennial Zionist Congress in 1903 proposed the establishment of a Hebrew University. The proposal was accepted at the Eleventh World Zionist Congress in 1913. Five years later he had the honor of laying the cornerstone of the Hebrew University on Mount Scopus in Palestine.

On his first visit to Palestine in 1907 he was instrumental in founding the Palestine Land Development Company. This was typical of his ability to convert ideas into practical realities.

For 15 years, while teaching chemistry at the University of Manchester, he headed the "Manchester Group" of British Zionists. In 1906 he met Mr. Balfour, who was on an electoral campaign and convinced him that Palestine rather than Uganda, British East Africa, which had been offered by the British, was the proper homeland for the Jews.

After his distinguished services on behalf of the British in the first World War, the main task he assigned himself was to remind the British of their promise to aid in the establishment of the Jewish national home.

His efforts led to his appointment as chairman of the first Zionist Commission, established in March, 1918, and recognized by the British as an official advisory body on all Jewish questions. He appeared before the Paris Peace Conference in support of his cause. Dr. Weizmann visited the Arab Prince Feisal in his camp near Amman around this time and convinced him that the proposed Jewish national home held no existing threat to the Arabs and that Jewish-Arab cooperation was desirable. He won Arab support to help carry out the Balfour Declaration, and reached an agreement with Feisal for large-scale Jewish immigration into Palestine and the protection of Arab rights.

The Zionist delegation was given a hearing before the Supreme Council of the Peace Conference on February 27, 1919 at which Robert Lansing, the United States secretary of state, asked if the term "a Jewish national home" meant an autonomous government.

Dr. Weizmann replied that they did not ask for the immediate creation of a Jewish administration but he quite clearly expressed his hope that he would some day see a Jewish majority in Palestine and the ultimate creation of a Jewish state.

The Zionists found shortly afterward that their principal difficulties were only beginning. The League of Nations had to be organized and a mandate system worked out. It was not until August, 1924, that the status of Palestine as a mandated territory was legalized.

From 1920 to 1931, and in 1935, Dr. Weizmann, as president of the World Zionist Organization, found it necessary to compromise with the British and the Arabs and to appease his various Zionist opponents. Civil war in Palestine between the Jews and Arabs added to his difficulties. The Arabs insisted that Palestine had been exclusively theirs for 13 centuries; the Jews maintained the right of prior occupation and historical connections related to their conquest of Palestine in 1200 B.C. Blood flowed freely in frequent clashes.

In the second World War, the British rejected his proposal to train a Jewish Army. They did train a Jewish battalion but that did not come into existence until 1944.

No Jewish mission was invited to the United Nations Conference in 1945 and it was not until 1948, when the Anglo-American Commission of Inquiry on Palestine was created, that Dr.

Weizmann again had an opportunity to make an official plea for a Jewish home and unrestricted immigration.

In October, 1947, he headed a delegation from the Jewish Agency which presented its case before the United Nations Special Committee on Palestine. He accepted at that time the principle of partition of Palestine into Jewish and Arab states provided that the Jews were free to form a "free national unit." On November 30, 1947, the U.N. General Assembly approved partition, and Jews danced in the streets of Tel Aviv.

Partition was threatened temporarily when the American delegation to the U.N. switched its position and pressed for a trusteeship. This proposal was turned down, and on May 19, 1948, simultaneously with the withdrawal of the British from Palestine, the Provisional Government of the new State of Israel was created.

On May 16, the 37 council members of the provisional government elected him president. The honor was accepted on the next day by Dr. Weizmann at his suite here at the Waldorf-Astoria Hotel, crowning his life's work.

"I dedicate myself to the service of the land and people in whose cause I have been privileged to labor these many years," he pledged in his message of acceptance.

Dr. Weizmann's first official act of state was to visit President Truman on May 25 at the White House, where he appealed for funds to build the new country and an end of the arms embargo which kept the Jews from getting munitions from the United States. An export-import loan of $100,000,000 was authorized several months later, but no action was subsequently taken on the arms embargo.

He was the honorary chairman of the board of directors of Hebrew University and director of the Daniel Sieff Research Laboratory. His home was in Rehovot near the $4,000,000 Weizmann Institute of Science, which was created for him as a tribute from American Jews.

Dr. Weizmann paid his first visit to the United States as President of Israel in April, 1949. At a dinner on behalf of the Weizmann Institute, where he was the guest of honor, he blueprinted the foreign policy of his nation as friendship with all nations whose policy was, similiarly, friendship to Israel regardless of "whether or not they diverge among themselves."

It was in May, soon after his return to Israel, that Dr. Weizmann realized another significant goal in his life when he United Nations admitted Israel as a member nation. This came after he had talked with President Truman during his visit here to participate in celebrations commemorating the first anniversary of the founding of the new State of Israel on May 4.

It was also in 1949, in June, that Dr. Weizmann finally surrendered his British citizenship to become a citizen of Israel. And it was two months later that he participated in ceremonies when the body of Theodore Herzl was brought "home" to Israel from Vienna to be buried on Mount Herzl.

At the time of his 75th birthday on November 27, 1949, he stood by while the nation which granted him the title of being its "father" gave him an eighteen-gun salute. He foretold its future by saying on a visit to Geneva that "just as some people live by the sword, we will live by science."

On his 75th birthday he was content, as on many other days, to gaze with failing eyes from his home in Rehovoth, across the orange groves, to the white buildings of the Weizmann Institute. Construction of the institute started in 1944 and each year large sums of money were contributed here toward additional buildings.

Although in poor health, Dr. Weizmann continued actively as president of Israel and president of the Executive Council of the Weizmann Institute.

In July, 1950, he urged support of United Nations measures to end the war in Korea. Later the same year he was confronted with the fall of his Cabinet and the formation of a new one. Early in 1951 he was again confronted with the collapse of the coalition Cabinet under Prime Minister David Ben-Gurion, but despite continued illness he carried on the duties of his office.

He presided over the first meeting of Israel's new thirteen-man coalition Cabinet on Nov. 3, 1951 and continued to work at his home in Rehovoth, until removed to a hospital four weeks later.

Dr. Weizmann was re-elected president in November, but a move to name him life president was dropped after several political parties failed to go along with the proposal.

His illness drastically curtailed his activities in his second term as president, but he was able to serve as host to Mrs. Franklin D. Roosevelt on her tour of Israel in February, 1952. From his sickbed, he issued a message on the fourth anniversary of the republic the next April 28.

Addressed to "all citizens of Israel and to all members of the House of Israel," it said: "On this solemn day I would say this to all my brethren, the future of Israel rests on three foundations — brotherly love, constructive effort and peace near and far."

His chief work in chemistry was in three fields of research: the synthesis of polycyclic sub-stances, the production of acetone and butyl alcohol and their derivatives and the development of protein foodstuffs for use as meat substitutes.

Throughout the years of turmoil and violence he had remained a moderate and in 1931, when he relinquished his post as head of the world Zionists, he refused to give ground on this issue. He expressed his philosophy in a three-hour "farewell address." His words then might just as well have summed up his views in 1949. He said:

"With a strong national home in Palestine built up peacefully and harmoniously, we may expect, in cooperation with the Arabs, also to open up for Jewish endeavor the vast areas which for their development, need intelligence, initiative, organization and finance.

"The constant formulation of excessive demands endangers the safety of the mandate. We have been searching for other ways and means. In this quest I have not always been successful, but in laying down my office, formally and definitely, today, I feel that I have brought the movement a little nearer to its goal. That goal we shall reach."

The New York Times
November 9, 1952

Yigal Yadin

YIGAL YADIN, military hero of Israel's War of Independence and archeologist of Masada and the Dead Sea Scrolls, died of a heart attack in Hadera, Israel. He was 67.

Born March 21, 1917, in Jerusalem, to a famed archeologist, Eliezer Sukenik, Mr. Yadin intertwined a life of archeology, military affairs and politics.

In 1947, shortly after obtaining his M.A. degree in archeology from Hebrew University, he became chief of operations for the Haganah, the clandestine forerunner of the Israeli Army. At the time he Hebraicized his name to Yadin, which means "he will judge."

A general before he was 30, Mr. Yadin outsmarted an Egyptian force in the Negev campaign of December, 1948. He surprised the Egyptians by sending his troops down a long-lost desert road built 2,000 years ago by the Romans.

In 1949, Mr. Yadin served as negotiator with the Egyptians in armistice talks on the Greek island of Rhodes. That year, he visited Lausanne, Switzerland, where he studied the Swiss Army's reserve system.

On his return to Israel, he molded the military along Swiss lines with a large number of reservists and a relatively small standing force.

"Every Israeli citizen is a full-time soldier who is on leave 11 months of the year," he reputedly said.

In 1952, after a falling out with Prime Minister David Ben-Gurion, Mr. Yadin retired from the army, where he had been chief of staff.

Mr. Sukenik died the next year, and Mr. Yadin moved to fulfill his father's dream, the return of all of the Dead Sea Scrolls to Israel.

On November 29, 1947, the eve of Israel's War of Independence, Mr. Sukenik had made a dangerous trip to Bethlehem where, for 50 pounds, he bought three of the seven scrolls, which were written almost 2,000 years ago. But war enveloped Palestine and the trail of the other fragile scrolls was lost.

In 1954, on a visit to the United States, Mr. Yadin purchased the four other scrolls for $250,000.

He continued his archeological activities in the Holy Land, working as he once put it, "with Bible in one hand and trowel in the other."

Digging at Hazor, Mr. Yadin said he unearthed the remains of Solomon's city gates and confirmed much of the exploits of Joshua in the Bible.

In 1960, under army protection against Jordanian guns facing the western shore of the Dead Sea, he led an exploration of Dead Sea caves. The search was rewarded with the discovery of 15 letters written by Simon Bar Kochba, a Jewish guerrilla who led the last revolt of the Israelites against the Roman Empire in 132 to 135 A.D.

From 1963 to 1965, Mr. Yadin led 5,000 volunteers from all over the world to excavate Masada. The evidence unearthed at this natural rock fortress proved, Mr. Yadin said, the historical accounts that, in 73 A.D., 976 Jewish defenders committed suicide rather than surrender to Roman legions.

Mr. Yadin continued to decipher scrolls that gave insights into life during biblical times. One described the beauty of Sarah, wife of Abraham. Another described an argument between the parents of Noah over his paternity.

He wrote numerous books on his archeological work, and for almost three decades taught archeology at Hebrew University.

In the mid-1970s, Mr. Yadin was drawn back into political life.

He served on a government commission investigating Israel's lack of military preparedness in the 1973 war.

Against a background of scandals in the Labor government, Mr. Yadin entered political life by forming in 1977 a new political party, the Democratic Movement for Change.

For a third party in Israel, the party did well, winning 15 seats in parliament. Mr. Yadin joined in a ruling coalition with the right-wing Likud bloc. The Likud leader, Menachem Begin, became prime minister and Mr. Yadin became deputy prime minister.

In government, Mr. Yadin repeatedly sought to block what he considered to be the indiscriminate building of Jewish settlements on the occupied

West Bank. Mr. Yadin's moderate stand had little effect on the policies of the Likud bloc and the Democratic Movement disbanded in 1981.

Seen as a dove in foreign affairs, Mr. Yadin participated actively in peace negotiations with Egypt in 1977. During breaks in the talks, Mr. Yadin was often seen chatting about pipes and tobacco blends with a fellow pipesmoker, President Anwar el-Sadat.

The New York Times
June 29, 1984

Ovadia Yosef

PERHAPS the most powerful cleric in Israeli politics, Rabbi Ovadia Yosef, a religious scholar and former Chief Rabbi, reigns supreme as the revered spiritual leader of Shas, the strictly Orthodox party of Sephardic Jews of Middle Eastern and North African origin.

Commanding the unwavering obedience of Shas's political leadership, Rabbi Yosef has repeatedly held the fate of Israeli governments in his hands. Both major Israeli parties, Likud and Labor, have needed an alliance with Shas to give them the required parliamentary majority to form governing coalitions, and their leaders have routinely courted Rabbi Yosef's support.

Born in Baghdad in 1920, he came to Jerusalem with his family when he was four and was ordained in 1940. He served as judge on Sephardic religious courts in Jerusalem and Cairo, and in 1947 was elected deputy chief rabbi of Egypt. He returned to Israel in 1950, served on rabbinical courts and was appointed Chief Rabbi of Tel Aviv in 1968. He became the Sephardic Chief Rabbi of Israel in 1973, serving a ten-year term.

But only after ending his years of service in the Orthodox religious establishment did Rabbi Yosef gain his towering political stature. In 1984 he launched Shas as a national party with his protégé, Aryeh Deri, presenting it as the authentic voice of the traditional Sephardic community in Israel.

Advocating a return to the traditional values of religion and offering low-cost education and social services in economically depressed communities of Sephardic Jews, Shas quickly built up a grass-roots following across Israel, gaining 10 seats in parliament in the 1996 national elections.

Rabbi Yosef has presided over the party's network of synagogues, schools and youth clubs, hammering home the religious message of Shas, an acronym for Sephardic Torah Guardians, and its call for ethnic pride. The party boasts that it is "restoring the old glory" of Sephardic Jewry after years of discrimination by an Israeli establishment dominated by Ashkenazic Jews of European origin.

Wearing the turban and embroidered black robe he wore as chief rabbi, Rabbi Yosef appears at mass Shas rallies, lionized by speakers as "the glory of the generation." A scholar known for his phenomenal command of Jewish texts, he gives religious lessons followed by thousands who come to hear him and listen to his talks on radio and televised broadcasts.

Unlike religious nationalist leaders, Rabbi Yosef has been a voice for moderation regarding Israel's relations with the Arabs. In a ruling in 1989 he came out in favor of a territorial compromise in order to bring peace. "If we can give back the territories and thereby avoid war and bloodshed, we are obliged to do so, under the Rule of Saving Life," he said, referring to the land captured by Israel in the 1967 Arab-Israeli war.

He traveled to Cairo in 1989 to meet President Hosni Mubarak of Egypt, and has also received Nasser Youssef, the chief of the Palestinian Authority's security forces.

By JOEL GREENBERG
The New York Times

Israel Almanac

Presidents of Israel
Date of Office

Chaim Weizmann	February 17, 1949	—	November 9, 1952
Itzhak Ben-Zvi	December 12, 1952	—	April 23, 1963
Zalman Shazar	May 21, 1963	—	May 24, 1973
Ephraim Katzir	May 24, 1973	—	May 28, 1978
Yitzhak Navon	May 29, 1978	—	May 5, 1983
Chaim Herzog	May 5, 1983	—	May 12, 1993
Ezer Weizman	May 13, 1993	—	

Prime Ministers of Israel
Date of Office and Party Membership

David Ben-Gurion	1948	—	1954	(Mapai)
Moshe Sharett	1954	—	1955	(Mapai)
David Ben-Gurion	1955	—	1963	(Mapai)
Levi Eshkol	1963	—	1969	(Mapai)
Golda Meir	1969	—	1974	(Labor)
Yitzhak Rabin	1974	—	1977	(Labor)
Menachem Begin	1977	—	1983	(Likud)
Yitzhak Shamir	1983	—	1984	(Likud)
Shimon Peres	1984	—	1986	(Labor)
Yitzhak Shamir	1986	—	1992	(Likud)
Yitzhak Rabin	1992	—	1995	(Labor)
Shimon Peres	1995	—	1996	(Labor)
Benjamin Netanyahu	1996	—		(Likud)

Foreign Ministers of Israel
Date of Office

Moshe Sharett	May 15, 1948	—	June 18, 1956
Golda Meir	June 18, 1956	—	January 12, 1966
Abba Eban	January 13, 1996	—	June 2, 1974
Yigal Allon	June 3, 1974	—	June 19, 1977
Moshe Dayan	June 20, 1977	—	October 23, 1979
Yitzhak Shamir	March 10, 1980	—	October 20, 1986
Shimon Peres	October 20, 1986	—	December 23, 1988
Moshe Arens	December 23, 1988	—	June 12, 1990
David Levy	June 13, 1990	—	July 13, 1992
Shimon Peres	July 14, 1992	—	November 22, 1995
Ehud Barak	November 22, 1995	—	June 18, 1996
David Levy	June 18, 1996	—	

Defense Ministers of Israel
Date of Office

David Ben-Gurion	May 14, 1948	—	January 25, 1954
	February 21, 1955	—	June 23, 1963
Pinhas Lavon	January 26, 1954	—	February 20, 1955
Levi Eshkol	June 24, 1963	—	June 2, 1967
Moshe Dayan	June 2, 1967	—	June 2, 1974
Shimon Peres	June 2, 1974	—	June 20, 1977
	November 4, 1955	—	June 18, 1996
Chaim Weizmann	June 21, 1977	—	May 28, 1980
Menachem Begin	May 28, 1980	—	August 5, 1981
	February 14, 1983	—	February 23, 1983
Ariel Sharon	August 5, 1981	—	February 14, 1983
Moshe Arens	February 23, 1983	—	September 13, 1984
	June 11, 1990	—	July 13, 1992
Yitzhak Shamir	March 15, 1990	—	June 10, 1990
Yitzhak Rabin	September 14, 1984	—	March 15, 1990
	July 13, 1992	—	November 4, 1995
Yitzhak Mordechai	June 18, 1996	—	

ISRAEL: National Statistics

Data include West Bank and Gaza Strip

Capital city: Jerusalem

Area: 21,060 sq km (Land area 20,620 sq km)

Population: 5,946,000 (1997 estimate)

Population density: 282 people per sq km

Population change: 4.4% per year increase

Urban population: 92% of population

Birth rate: 21 per 1,000 people

Death rate: 7 per 1,000 people

Health care, population per doctor: 350 people

Life expectancy: Males 75, Females 78 years

Infant mortality: 10 per 1,000 live births

Fertility rate: 3 children per female

Age groups: 0-14 yrs 31%, 1-59 yrs 57%, 60+ yrs 12%

Ethnic groups: Jewish 81%, Arab 19%

Languages: Hebrew, Arabic (English widely used)

Religions: Jewish 82%, Muslim 14%, Christian 2%

Land use: Arable 17%, grass 7%, forest 6%

Employment: Agriculture 4%, industry 22%, services 74%

Annual income: $13,760 per person

Origin of income: Agriculture 7%, industry 24%, services 69%

Energy: Production, 0.01 tons, consumption, 3.27 tons

Trade: $7,110 per person

Currency: Shekel = 100 agorat

Roads: 14,000 kilometres

Railroads: 600 kilometres

Adult literacy: 95%

Educational expenditure: 6.0% of GNP

Military expenditure: 11.1% of GNP

Aid received: $352 per person

The Regional Military Balance 1997

Israel

Army Personnel	134,000
(Reserves)	365,000
Tanks	4,300
Artillery	1,550
Air Force Personnel	32,000
Combat Aircraft	449
Navy Personnel	9,000
Major Warships	5
Smaller Craft	50

Strategic Forces

It is widely reported that Israel possesses a nuclear capability with perhaps 100 warheads.

Means of delivery may include Jericho I, range c. 500 km and Jericho II, tested between 1987 and 1989 with an estimated range of 1,500 km.

Egypt

Army Personnel	310,000
(Reserves)	150,000
Tanks	3,650
Artillery	4,000
Air Force Personnel	30,000
Combat Aircraft	449
Navy Personnel	20,000
Major Warships	15
Smaller Craft	43

Iraq

Army Personnel	350,000
(Reserve)	600,000
Tanks	c. 2,700
Artillery	2,400
Air Force Personnel	30,000
Combat Aircraft	310
Navy Personnel	2,500
Major Warships	1
Smaller Craft	14

Lebanon

Army Personnel	47,500
Tanks	330
Artillery	200
Air Force Personnel	800
Combat Aircraft	3
Navy Personnel	600
Major Warships	0
Smaller Craft	14

Saudi Arabia

Army Personnel	70,000
National Guard	57,000
Tanks	1,050
Artillery	448
Air Force Personnel	18,000
Combat Aircraft	218
Navy Personnel	13,500
Major Warships	8
Smaller Craft	29

Jordan

Army Personnel	90,000
(Reserves)	30,000
Tanks	1,050
Artillery	730
Air Force Personnel	8,000
Combat Aircraft	95
Navy Personnel	650
Major Warships	0
Smaller Craft	5

Syria

Army Personnel	315,000
(Reserves)	500,000
Tanks	4,600
Artillery	2,080
Air Force Personnel	40,000
Combat Aircraft	579
Navy Personnel	6,000
Major Warships	5
Smaller Craft	27

Sources for national and military data: Philip's Geographical Digest; 1997 Statesmen Yearbook; Israeli Embassy, London; International Institute for Strategic Studies

Note: artillery includes self-propelled and towed guns.

Historic Headlines from
The New York Times

The New York Times

LATE CITY EDITION
Weather: Sunny and milder today; fair and mild tonight, tomorrow. Temp. range: today 58-77; Tuesday 57-74. Temp.-Hum. Index yesterday 67. Full U.S. report on Page 90.

VOL. CXXI ... No. 41,864   © 1972 The New York Times Company   NEW YORK, WEDNESDAY, SEPTEMBER 6, 1972   15 CENTS

9 ISRAELIS ON OLYMPIC TEAM KILLED WITH 4 ARAB CAPTORS AS POLICE FIGHT BAND THAT DISRUPTED MUNICH GAMES

MRS. MEIR SPEAKS

A Hushed Parliament Hears Her Assail 'Lunatic Acts'

By TERENCE SMITH
Special to The New York Times

JERUSALEM, Sept. 5 — Her voice heavy and trembling with emotion, Premier Golda Meir today denounced "these lunatic acts of terrorism, abduction and blackmail, which tear asunder the web of international life."

Speaking to a hushed and somber parliament before the fate of the Israeli hostages held captive in Munich was known, she said, "It is inconceivable that the Olympic events should continue as long as our citizens are under the threat of being murdered in the Olympic Village."

She called on all the nations participating in the Olympics to do "whatever is necessary" to rescue the nine Israelis taken hostage by Arab guerrillas in an early-morning attack in which two other Israelis were killed.

[Official sources in Jerusalem said early Wednesday that the Cabinet would meet later in the morning and that there would be no statement on the deaths of the hostages until then.]

Cabinet Still Firm

Although she was not explicit, Mrs. Meir left the impression that Israel would continue to refuse the guerrillas' demands for the release of 200 Palestinian commandos held in this country. Cabinet sources said the Government remained committed to its hard-line policy of neither dealing with nor making concessions to the guerrillas.

Most Israelis seemed stunned by the news of the bizarre attack on the Israeli athletes, which was first reported here on a radio broadcast at 9 A.M. (3 A.M. Tuesday, New York time). Although Israeli citizens traveling abroad have been attacked by Palestinian guerrillas before, the Olympics seemed to many an unlikely setting.

"The games were going so well," one Jerusalem news dealer said, "and now this."

In parliament, where the members had gathered in an extraordinary session to confirm the Justice Minister, the attack was the sole topic of conversation.

Cabinet Ministers and members of parliament sat in the building's modern, sun-washed dining room waiting for additional news from Munich. Each hour on the hour, the large room grew silent and the ministers gathered four deep around a radio as the Israeli radio summarized the develop-

A copter making a test run before picking up Arabs involved in the attack on Israelis. At rear is the Olympic Tower. Sign in German says, "Olympic Village, Gate 6."

752 Air-Conditioned Cars Ordered for City Subways

By EDWARD RANZAL

Mayor Lindsay announced yesterday that 752 new air-conditioned subway cars had been ordered for $210.5-million. He said the contract was the largest ever signed in the country for the purchase of passenger railroad cars.

The first group of cars, which will be manufactured by the Pullman - Standard Company, are to be delivered by 1973.

The cars will provide a quieter ride than present equipment, according to Dr. William J. Ronan, chairman of the Metropolitan Transportation Authority.

The new equipment, which will be used on the IND and BMT lines, will enable the authority to phase out more than 1,200 pre-World War II cars, which are smaller than the new ones. A study is being made, Dr. Ronan said, to produce an air-conditioned unit that can be used in cars in the smaller tunnels of the IRT system.

20% of Fleet by '75

Each car will cost more than $273,000. The city will provide one-third of the total funds—the money has been provided in the city's 1972-73 capital budget—and the Federal Urban Mass Transportation Administration will supply the rest.

By 1975 more than 20 per cent of the city's fleet of nearly 7,000 subway cars will consist of new air-conditioned cars.

The first order under the contract will be for 454 cars at

Berrigan and a Nun Get Prison Terms In Letter Smuggling

By JOHN KIFNER
Special to The New York Times

HARRISBURG, Pa., Sept. 5— The Rev. Philip F. Berrigan—cleared of charges that he led a plot to kidnap President Nixon's adviser on national security affairs, Henry A. Kissinger —was sentenced in Federal District Court here today to four concurrent two-year terms for smuggling letters out of the Lewisburg Penitentiary.

Sister Elizabeth McAlister, also cleared of the plot charges, was sentenced to one year in jail and three years' probation for smuggling letters.

Moments after the sentences were announced, Government attorneys moved to dismiss the first three substantive counts of their indictment, confirming that the Justice Department would not seek a retrial of the controversial "Harrisburg Seven" case.

The Government charged Father Berrigan, Sister Elizabeth, two other Roman Catholic priests, a former priest, a former nun and a Pakistani scholar with conspiracy to kidnap Mr.

West German policemen talking with a spokesman, right, for Arabs who invaded Israeli quarters at Olympic Village

A West German Army ambulance passing through the heavily guarded gate at the military airfield in Fürstenfeldbruck, near Munich, after the commandos and the hostages landed in three helicopters.

A 23-HOUR DRAMA

2 Others Are Slain in Their Quarters in Guerrilla Raid

By DAVID BINDER
Special to The New York Times

MUNICH, West Germany, Wednesday, Sept. 6—Eleven members of Israel's Olympic team and four Arab terrorists were killed yesterday in a 23-hour drama that began with an invasion of the Olympic Village by the Arabs. It ended in a shootout at a military airport some 15 miles away as the Arabs were preparing to fly to Cairo with their Israeli hostages.

The first two Israelis were killed early yesterday morning when Arab commandos, armed with automatic rifles, broke into the quarters of the Israeli team and seized nine others as hostages. The hostages were killed in the airport shootout between the Arabs and German policemen and soldiers.

The bloodshed brought the suspension of the Olympic Games and there was doubt if they would be resumed. Willi Daume, president of the West German Organizing Committee, announced early today that he would ask the International Olympic Committee to meet tomorrow to decide whether they should continue.

Policeman Killed

In addition to the slain Israelis and Arabs, a German policeman was killed and a helicopter pilot was critically wounded. Three Arabs were wounded.

There were some reports that two of the hostages said to have been killed might still be alive. "It is a dim hope," said Dr. Bruno Merk, the Interior Minister of Bavaria, "but I am skeptical on this point."

The bloodbath at the airport that ended at 1 A.M. today, came after long hours of negotiation between German and Arabs at the Olympic quarters in the Olympic Village where the Arabs demanded the release of 200 Arab commandos imprisoned in Israel.

Finally the West German armed forces supplied three helicopters to transport the Arabs a their Israeli hostages to the airport at Fürstenfeld-bruck. From there all were to be flown to Cairo.

A Boeing-707 provided by the Lufthansa German Airlines was waiting.

Two of the terrorists, carrying their automatic rifles, walked about 170 yards from the helicopters to the plane. And then they started back to pick up the other Arabs and the hostages.

Positions Cited

As the Arabs were returning, German sharpshooters reportedly opened fire from the darkness beyond the pools of light

PARLEY REJECTS HIJACKING TREATY

U.S. - Canadian Project for Penalizing Nations Aiding Air Pirates Rebuffed

By ROBERT LINDSEY
Special to The New York Times

Nixon Tightens Security In U.S. Against 'Outlaws'

By TAD SZULC
Special to The New York Times

WASHINGTON, Sept. 5 — Secretary of State William P. President Nixon said today that Rogers issued this statement on "extra security measures" would behalf of the Administration: be taken in the United States "There are no words which to protect American citizens as can fully express our reaction well as visiting Israelis from to today's tragedy at the Olympic possible attacks by Palestinian pic Games. I know I speak for

GAMES SUSPENDED; RITES IN ARENA SET

Halt Is the First Since 1896, When the Classic Resumed
—Egypt Team in Forfeit

By NEIL AMDUR
Special to The New York Times

PULLOUT SECTION ON SIGNING OF MIDEAST PEACE TREATY, PAGES A11 TO A18

"All the News That's Fit to Print"

The New York Times

LATE CITY EDITION

Weather: Mostly sunny, cool today; clear, cold tonight. Sunny tomorrow. Temperature range: today 32-48; yesterday 36-49. Details on page C12.

VOL.CXXVIII . . . No.44,169 | NEW YORK, TUESDAY, MARCH 27, 1979 | 25 cents beyond 50-mile zone from New York City. Higher in air delivery cities. | 20 CENTS

EGYPT AND ISRAEL SIGN FORMAL TREATY, ENDING A STATE OF WAR AFTER 30 YEARS; SADAT AND BEGIN PRAISE CARTER'S ROLE

United Press International

Leaders join hands after signing pact. President Anwar el-Sadat signed first, followed by Prime Minister Menachem Begin. President Carter was witness.

OPEC PARLEY WEIGHS NEW OIL PRICE RISES AND CUTS IN OUTPUT

Saudis Say They Will Try to Resist Big Increases — Carter Puts Off Decisions on Energy

By PAUL LEWIS
Special to The New York Times

GENEVA, March 26 — Pressure for another large increase in world oil prices built up today at the opening of a meeting of oil ministers of the 13 member nations of the Organization of Petroleum Exporting Countries.

The advocates of a sharp new oil price rise, of anywhere from 20 to 35 percent from current levels on April 1, also urged other oil producers to reduce output. The aim would be to keep world markets tight as Iran resumes exports to insure that the new price levels stick.

But Saudi Arabia, the world's largest oil exporter, resisted pressure for price jumps, pointing out that they could do severe damage to the economies of both the developing and the industrialized world. "There is worry particularly about the effects of price changes on developing countries," OPEC's secretary general, René Ortise, said.

Effort to Reduce Increases

Sheik Ahmed Zaki Yamani, Saudi Arabia's oil minister, interviewed after tonight's session, said the ministers faced a "deadlock," with the Saudis feeling that the increases demanded by Iran and Libya were "too steep." Observers here interpreted his stance as an effort to cut probable increases to more moderate levels.

The ministers have not yet voted themselves the power to take any pricing action at the current two-day session but are expected to do so tomorrow. A simple majority vote would grant the meeting such authority.

On the question of possible punitive cutbacks in supplies, reflecting displeasure with some consuming nations' positions on the Palestinian question, Iraqi representatives said such moves were possible, particularly against Egypt. But they carefully noted that no such moves were planned by OPEC, although the "oil weapon" could re-emerge if conditions returned to the situation of 1973.

Carter Decisions Deferred

In Washington, meanwhile, Administration officials said that President Carter's decisions on various energy proposals, expected Thursday, would be deferred, apparently because key White House officials had not been able to devote enough time to the controversial plans. [Page D12.]

When Sheik Yamani entered the OPEC

Continued on Page D12, Column 3

Mood of Peace Seems Somber And Uncertain

By BERNARD WEINRAUB
Special to The New York Times

WASHINGTON, March 26 — Shortly after 6 A.M. today, President Anwar el-Sadat arose in the residence of the Egyptian Ambassador and began wandering around the five-bedroom house.

He scanned the morning newspapers, pedaled a stationary exercise bicycle, nibbled a slice of unbuttered toast, sipped a glass of orange juice and, by 7 A.M. turned on the television to watch the morning news.

Less than one mile away, in a guarded ninth-floor suite at the Washington Hilton Hotel, Prime Minister Menachem Begin of Israel peered out the windows at the traffic moving along Connecticut Avenue.

He turned away and, carrying a cup of tea, walked to a writing desk and began working on the emotional speech that he would deliver in mid-afternoon at the White House ceremony ending 30 years of war between Israel and Egypt.

It was the start of a day marked by paradox — a triumphal day of peace that seemed curiously somber, a day of celebration blurred by protests in the heart of Washington, a bright day shadowed by uncertainty.

"There is, you know, a sense of trepi-

Continued on Page A9, Column 1

Photographs for The New York Times by TERESA ZABALA

Treaty Impact Still Unknown

'Hopes and Dreams' but 'No Illusions' for Carter

By HEDRICK SMITH
Special to The New York Times

WASHINGTON, March 26 — The elusive, unprecedented peace treaty that Egypt and Israel signed today has enormous symbolic importance and the potential for fundamentally transforming the map and history of an entire region, but the agreement faces an uncertain future.

News Analysis

Israel has now won what it has sought since 1948 — formal recognition and acceptance from the most powerful Arab state and the ultimate prospect of exchanging ambassadors and entering into a full range of normal relations.

For all the violent denunciations that this historic breakthrough aroused in the Arab world, the best diplomatic estimate here is that the treaty has markedly reduced the risk of a major war in the Middle East for a considerable time by removing Egyptian strength from the active Arab arsenal.

And it has demonstrated American capacity to influence events in the Middle East despite the setbacks Washington has suffered since the overthrow of the

Continued on Page A10, Column 5

CEREMONY IS FESTIVE

Accord on Sinai Oil Opens Way to the First Peace in Mideast Dispute

By BERNARD GWERTZMAN
Special to The New York Times

WASHINGTON, March 26 — After confronting each other for nearly 31 years as hostile neighbors, Egypt and Israel signed a formal treaty at the White House today to establish peace and "normal and friendly relations."

On this chilly early spring day, about 1,500 invited guests and millions more watching television saw President Anwar el-Sadat of Egypt and Prime Minister

Transcripts of statements at signing are on page A11. Texts of treaty and Camp David accords are on pages A12, A13 and A14.

Menachem Begin of Israel put their signatures on the Arabic, Hebrew and English versions of the first peace treaty between Israel and an Arab country

President Carter, who was credited by both leaders for having made the agreement possible, signed, as a witness, for the United States. In a somber speech he said, "Peace has come."

'The First Step of Peace'

"We have won, at last, the first step of peace — a first step on a long and difficult road," he added.

Later, at a state dinner, Mr. Begin suggested that Mr. Carter be given the Nobel Peace Peace, and Mr. Sadat agreed.

At the signing ceremony, all three leaders offered prayers that the treaty would bring true peace to the Middle East and end the enmity that has erupted into war four times since Israel declared its independence on May 14, 1948.

By coincidence, they all referred to the words of the Prophet Isaiah.

"Let us work together until the day comes when they beat their swords into plowshares and their spears into pruning hooks," Mr. Sadat said in his paraphrase of the biblical text.

'No More War,' Begin Says

Mr. Begin, who gave the longest and most emotional of the addresses, exclaimed: "No more war, no more bloodshed, no more bereavement, peace unto you, shalom, saalam, forever."

"Shalom" and "salaam" are the Hebrew and Arabic words for "peace."

The Israeli leader, noted for oratorical skill, provided a dash of humor when in the course of his speech he seconded Mr. Sadat's remark that Mr. Carter was "the unknown soldier of the peacemaking effort." Mr. Begin said, pausing, "I agree, but as usual with an amendment" — that Mr. Carter was not completely unknown and that his peace effort would "be

Continued on Page A10, Column 1

Judge Bars Hydrogen Bomb Article After Magazine Rejects Mediation

By DOUGLAS E. KNEELAND
Special to The New York Times

MILWAUKEE, March 26 — A Federal District Court judge here, acting only after his suggestion for an attempt at out-of-court settlement was turned down, granted the Government's motion for a preliminary injunction today to keep The Progressive magazine from publishing an article about the hydrogen bomb.

In so doing, Judge Robert W. Warren became the first Federal judge ever to issue an injunction imposing prior restraint on the press in a national security case.

The magazine's attorneys said they would file an appeal shortly with the United States Court of Appeals for the Seventh Circuit in Chicago.

Court's 'Awesome Responsibility'

Before announcing his decision this afternoon, Judge Warren, a former Wisconsin Attorney General, acknowledged that he considered it an "awesome responsibility."

"Stripped to its essence, then," he said, "the question before the court is a basic confrontation between the First Amendment right to freedom of the press and national security."

The judge said "a mistake in ruling against The Progressive will seriously infringe cherished First Amendment rights." However, he added, "a mistake

Continued on Page B12, Column 3

INSIDE

Michigan State Wins

Michigan State became the National Collegiate basketball champion by defeating Indiana State, 75-64, at Salt Lake City. Page C13.

H.R.A. Administrator Quits

Blanche Bernstein, the Human Resources Administrator, resigned rather than accept Mayor Koch's offer to stay in the job without power. Page B1.

Palestinians, Reacting to the Pact, Go on Strike and Denounce Egypt

Special to The New York Times

BEIRUT, Lebanon, March 26 — Vowing revenge, staging strikes and protest marches and calling for punitive measures against Egypt, Palestinians and other Arabs reacted angrily today against the signing of the Egyptian-Israeli peace treaty in Washington.

Yasir Arafat, chairman of the Palestine Liberation Organization, vowed to chase Americans out of the Middle East and to "chop off the hands" of President Carter, President Anwar el-Sadat of Egypt and Prime Minister Menachem Begin of Israel. He spoke to a group of guerrilla recruits at the Sabra Palestinian camp here as effigies of the three signers were burned.

The inhabitants of Lebanon's 15 Palestinian camps protested the signing today by refusing to work, as did many Lebanese Moslems. Similar protests were staged in the occupied West Bank of the Jordan River and the Gaza Strip, and in the Arab Old City of Jerusalem a grenade exploded tonight, wounding five tourists.

Iran Government Condemns Pact

In Teheran, the Iranian Government condemned the treaty, and 30 Arab students took over the Egyptian Embassy there. Protesters also stormed the Egyptian Embassy in Kuwait, where 250,000 Palestinians live, forming the largest foreign community in that small country. In Damascus, Syria, demonstrators occupied the offices of the Egyptian airline, Egyptair.

Meanwhile, foreign and finance ministers of Arab League countries gathered today in Baghdad, Iraq, for a meeting tomorrow on possible economic and political measures against Egypt. The countries had vowed last November to hold such a meeting if the Egyptian-Israeli peace treaty was signed, but Saudi Arabia, Egypt's principal foreign backer, has been trying to exercise a moderating influence.

King Hussein of Jordan flew to Damascus and Baghdad during the day in what was believed to be an effort to coordinate the positions of hard-liners and moderates at tomorrow's Arab meeting.

Gromyko Comments on Treaty

In Damascus, Foreign Minister Andrei A. Gromyko of the Soviet Union ended a three-day visit to Syria today by joining with President Hafez al-Assad in denouncing the peace treaty, saying it appeared bound to increase tension in the Middle East. A joint Soviet-Syrian communiqué said the treaty was aimed at perpetuating the Israeli occupation of Arab lands, the annexation of Arab East

Continued on Page A10, Column 5

TUESDAY, MARCH 27, 1979

The New York Times

L+   A11

'إنهاء حالة الحرب'

'לשים קץ למצב המלחמה'

'To bring to an end the state of war'

From the Preamble to the Egyptian-Israeli Treaty.

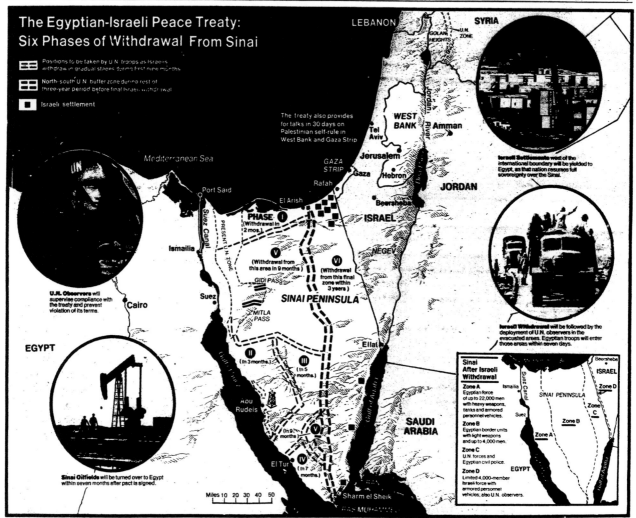

The Egyptian-Israeli Peace Treaty:
Six Phases of Withdrawal From Sinai

Photographs by Al Ahram, Israel Press Photo Agency, Associated Press and The New York Times

---

"…we three…will vigorously wage peace."

Following is a transcript of President Carter's remarks at the treaty signing yesterday at the White House, as recorded by The New York Times:

During the past 30 years, Isreal and Egypt have waged war. But for the past 16 months, these same two great nations have waged peace.

Today we celebrate a victory, not of a bloody military campaign, but of an inspiring peace campaign. Two leader who loom large in the history of nations, President Anwar Sadat and Prime Minister Menachem Begin, have conducted this campaign with all the courage, tenacity, brilliance and inspiration of any generals who have ever led men and machines onto the field of battle.

At the end of this campaign, the soil of the two lands is not drenched with young blood. The countrysides of both lands are free from the litter and the carnage of a wasteful war.

Mothers in Egypt and Israel are not weeping today for their children fallen in senseless battle. The dedication and determination of these two world statesmen have borne fruit. Peace has come to Israel and to Egypt.

I honor these two leaders and their Government officials who have hammered out this peace treaty which we have just signed. But most of all, I honor the people of these two lands whose yearning for peace kept alive the negotiations which today culminate in this glorious event.

First Step of Peace

We have won, at last, the first step of peace. A first step on a long and difficult road. We must not minimize the obstacles which still lie ahead. Differences still separate the signatories to this treaty from one another. And also from some of their neighbors who fear what they have just done.

To overcome these differences, to dispel these fears, we must rededicate ourselves to the goal of a broader peace with justice for all who have lived in a state of conflict in the Middle East.

We have no illusions. We have hopes,

Continued on Page A13

"Let there be no more despair or loss of faith."

Following is a transcript of President Anwar el-Sadat's remarks at the treaty signing yesterday at the White House, as recorded by The New York Times:

President Carter, dear friends. This is certainly one of the happiest moments in my life. It is a historic turning point of great significance for all peaceloving nations. Those among us who are endowed with vision cannot fail to comprehend the dimension of our sacred mission. The Egyptian people with their heritage and unique awareness of history have realized from the very beginning the meaning and value of this endeavor. In all the steps I took I was not performing a personal mission. I was merely expressing the will of a nation. I am proud of my people and of belonging to them.

Today a new dawn is emerging out of the darkness of the past. A new chapter is being opened in the history of coexistence among nations, one that's worthy of our spiritual values and civilization. Never before have men encountered such a complex dispute which is highly charged with emotions. Never before did men need that much courage and imagination to confront a single challenge. Never before had any cause generated that much interest in all four corners of the globe.

Men and women of good will have labored day and night to bring about this happy moment. Egyptians and Israelis alike pursued their sacred goal undeterred by difficulties and complications. Hundreds of dedicated individuals on both sides have given generously of their thought and effort to translate the cherished dream into a living reality. But the man who performed the miracle was President Carter. Without any exaggeration, what he did constitutes one of the greatest achievements of our time. He devoted his skill, hard work and above all his firm belief in the ultimate triumph of good against evil to insure the success of our mission. To me he has been the best companion and partner along the road to peace.

With his deep sense of justice and genuine commitment to human rights

Continued on Page A13

"Let us turn our hearts to our heroes and pay tribute.…"

Following is a transcript of Prime Minister Menachem Begin's remarks at the treaty signing yesterday at the White House, as recorded by The New York Times:

Mr. President of the United States of America, Mr. President of the Arab Republic of Egypt, Mr. Vice President, Mr. Speaker of the House of Representatives, Mr. Speaker of the Knesset, members of the Cabinets of the United States, of Egypt and Israel, member of the Congress and the Knesset, your excellencies, chairman of the Board of Governors of the Jewish Agency, chairman of the executive of the Zionist organization, Mrs. Gruber, the mother of the sons, distinguished guests, ladies and gentlemen:

I have come from the land of Israel, the land of Zion and Jerusalem and here I am in humility and with pride as a son of the Jewish people, as one of the generation of the Holocaust and the redemption. The a...cient Jewish people gave the world a vision of eternal peace, of universal disarmament, of abolishing the teaching and the learning of war. Two prophets, Yeshayahu Ben Amoz and Micah Hamorashti, having foreseen the spiritual unity of man under God, with these words coming forth from Jerusalem gave the nations of the world the following vision expressed in identical terms: And they shall beat their swords into plowshares, and their spears into pruning hooks. Nation shall not lift up sword against nation. Neither shall they learn war anymore. Despite the tragedies and disappointments of the past, we must never forsake that vision, that human dream, that unshakeable faith.

Peace is the beauty of life. It is sunshine. It is the smile of a child, the love of a mother, the joy of a father, the togetherness of a family. It is the advancement of man, the victory of a just cause, the triumph of truth. Peace is all of these and more and more. These are words I uttered in Oslo on Dec. 10, 1978, while receiving the second half of the Nobel Peace Prize. The first half went

Continued on Page A13

"All the News That's Fit to Print"

The New York Times

Late Edition

Weather: Chance of morning showers today, sunny and cool this afternoon; clear tonight. Mostly sunny tomorrow. Temperatures: today 63-67, tonight 45-49; yesterday 60-78. Details, page C31.

VOL.CXXXV. No. 46,559 NEW YORK, FRIDAY, OCTOBER 11, 1985 — 50 cents beyond 75 miles from New York City, except on Long Island — 30 CENTS

U.S. INTERCEPTS JET CARRYING HIJACKERS; FIGHTERS DIVERT IT TO NATO BASE IN ITALY; GUNMEN FACE TRIAL IN SLAYING OF HOSTAGE

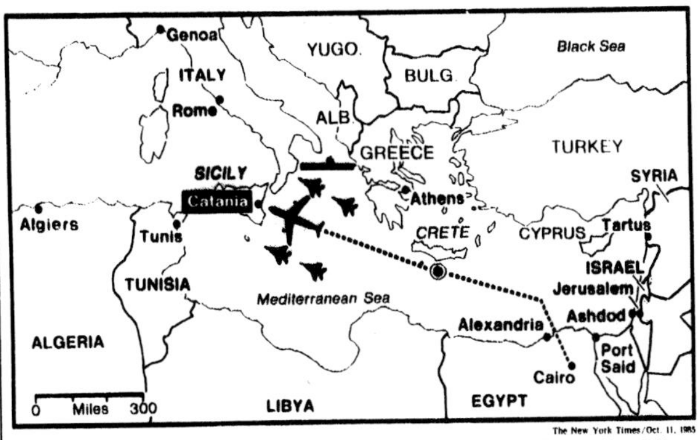

The New York Times/Oct. 11, 1985

Planes from the carrier Saratoga near Albania intercepted jet south of Crete and escorted it to Sicily.

OFFICIALS SAY C.I.A. DID NOT TELL F.B.I. OF SPY CASE MOVES

Court Papers Assert Suspect Told Colleagues He Might Give Secrets to Soviet

The following article is based on reporting by Stephen Engelberg and Joel Brinkley and was written by Mr. Brinkley.

Special to The New York Times

WASHINGTON, Oct. 10 — The Central Intelligence Agency failed to notify the Federal Bureau of Investigation after it learned more than a year ago that Edward L. Howard was considering becoming a Soviet spy, Government officials said today.

According to court records, Mr. Howard told two agency employees in September 1984 that he was thinking of disclosing classified information to the Soviet Union.

Law Calls For Reporting

The bureau has sole responsibility for domestic espionage investigations and, under Federal law, the intelligence agency and all other Government agencies are supposed to report suspected espionage to the F.B.I. It is illegal for the C.I.A. or any other Federal agency to carry out surveillance or other actions within the United States to stop potential spies.

Mr. Howard, 33 years old, a former intelligence agency officer who is now a fugitive, has been charged with espionage, accused of giving Soviet officials details of American intelligence operations in Moscow. Federal officials have called the disclosures serious and damaging.

Soviet Defector Was the Key

Federal officials said the C.I.A. told the F.B.I. nothing about Mr. Howard until after the bureau began an investigation this fall based on information from a Soviet defector, Vitaly Yurchenko, who had been a senior official of the K.G.B., the Soviet intelligence agency.

The bureau began surveillance of Mr. Howard last month, but he slipped out of his home at night and is believed to have fled the country.

Senator Patrick J. Leahy, the Vermont Democrat who is vice chairman of the Select Committee on Intelligence, said today: "If the C.I.A. did not give the F.B.I. adequate information

Continued on Page B8, Column 4

BUOYANT CAPITAL HAILS THE ACTION

Moynihan Sums Up the Mood: 'Thank God We Won One'

By BERNARD WEINRAUB

Special to The New York Times

WASHINGTON, Oct. 10 — Reagan Administration officials and legislators reacted exuberantly tonight to the news that American warplanes had seized the four hijackers who apparently killed an elderly American aboard an Italian cruise ship.

"Thank God we've won one," said Senator Daniel Patrick Moynihan, Democrat of New York.

The comment summed up the mood in this startled capital after years of witnessing the Carter and Reagan administrations struggling in vain to cope with Middle East terrorism and attacks against the United States.

Iran Crisis Recalled

Officials pointed out that it was nearly six years ago that Iranian revolutionaries seized the United States Embassy in Teheran and virtually made a hostage of the Carter Administration. Mr. Carter found himself unable to fulfill his threats against terrorists and, in the case of a military raid to rescue the Americans held hostage in Iran, failed in a humiliating manner.

Mr. Reagan took office after criticiz-

Continued on Page A11, Column 4

Port in Israel Described as Target Of Terrorists Who Seized Vessel

By THOMAS L. FRIEDMAN

Special to The New York Times

JERUSALEM, Oct. 10 — The four Palestinians aboard the Achille Lauro intended to stay aboard as passengers until the cruise liner reached Ashdod, Israel, and then planned either to shoot up the harbor or take Israelis hostage, according to Israeli, Palestinian and other Arab informants. The Israelis were to be held to bargain for the release of 50 Palestinians held in Israeli jails.

The leader of the faction that ordered the operation, Mohammed Abbas, also known as Abul Abbas, is a close associate of Yasir Arafat, the chairman of the Palestine Liberation Organization, and was reportedly sent by Mr. Arafat to deal with the hijackers after their original plan to infiltrate Israel at Ashdod had gone awry.

Crew Discovered Arms Cache

According to the informants, the four members of the group aborted their plans and seized the ship when their weapons were discovered by the crew after the Achille Lauro had left Alexandria on Monday. The informants say the original plan and the hijacking were part of a bungled attempt to exact revenge for Israel's raid last week on the P.L.O. headquarters near Tunis.

When relations between the P.L.O. and Italy seemed jeopardized by the seizure of the ship and an American passenger was killed by the apparently panicked hijackers, Mr. Arafat and Abul Abbas ordered the hijackers to return to Port Said and surrender.

This picture was pieced together from information provided by Israeli Foreign Ministry and military officials, Arab analysts in Beirut and a statement issued today in Nicosia, Cyprus, by a spokesman of Abul Abbas's faction in the Palestine Liberation Front, one of the guerrilla groups in the Palestine Liberation Organization.

A copy of the statement was delivered to Reuters in Nicosia and virtually all its main points have been confirmed by Israeli or Arab sources.

The statement, which apologized to the cruise passengers for the hijacking, was believed to be the first time that a Palestinian guerrilla group has expressed regret for an attack. It was apparently occasioned by widespread condemnation of the incident in Italy and in the Arab world.

Retaliation Was Aim

According to Arab and Palestinian sources in Beirut and Nicosia, the gunmen had planned the assault on Ashdod in retaliation for the Israeli attack on the P.L.O. headquarters in Tunisia, in which about 60 people were killed. The message to Israel was to have been: "If you can reach out 1,500 miles and strike at us, we can reach out 1,500 miles and strike back at you."

Israeli merchant marine and Government sources say Israel has been on the lookout for seaborne attempts at infiltration. The sources noted that Israeli naval vessels had been observed and photographed by unidentified men when they docked at Western European ports. Now that overland routes into Israel — from Lebanon, Jordan

Continued on Page A14, Column 1

PRAISE FOR PILOTS

Weinberger Will Not Say if Navy Planes Would Have Used Force

By BILL KELLER

Special to The New York Times

WASHINGTON, Friday, Oct. 11 — Secretary of Defense Caspar W. Weinberger praised Navy fighter pilots early this morning for "high military skill" in intercepting an Egyptian plane carrying four hijackers of an Italian cruise ship.

Mr. Weinberger, briefing reporters on the operation, refused to say whether the four F-14's from the aircraft carrier U.S.S. Saratoga had been prepared to use force if necessary to divert the Egyptian aircraft.

Mr. Weinberger also disclosed, in an apparent reference to American military special operations units reportedly deployed to the region, that before the hijackers of the Italian ship, the Achille Lauro, surrendered, the United States was "prepared to take action against the ship." He added, "We were prepared to do that, I think, effectively and successfully."

Details of Interception

Mr. Weinberger provided the first details of the interception.

He said the Saratoga was steaming west in the Eastern Mediterranean on a routine exercise near Albania when she received orders at about 9 P.M. local time Thursday to prepare for an interception.

At about 11 P.M., four swept-wing F-14 fighter planes took off, shortly before the Egyptian aircraft did so. Pentagon officials said two E-2C surveillance planes, smaller versions of the Awacs eavesdropping aircraft, had left the Saratoga earlier to track the Egyptian airliner. In addition, two KA-6 tankers accompanied the fighter planes in case they needed refueling.

'Very Good Intelligence'

Mr. Weinberger would not provide details of how the officers aboard the Saratoga knew the Egyptian plane was leaving the Cairo airport, or how they were certain they had the right plane. "I would say that we had very good intelligence," he said.

The fighters circled in the darkness near the island of Crete south of Greece and intercepted the Egyptian plane, a commercial Boeing 737 chartered by the Egyptian Government, at about 12:30 A.M., Mr. Weinberger said, and made radio contact.

"They were waiting in international

Continued on Page A10, Column 1

FLOWN FROM CAIRO

4 in Custody in Sicily — Washington Says It Wants Extradition

By BERNARD GWERTZMAN

Special to The New York Times

WASHINGTON, Friday, Oct. 11 — An Egyptian plane carrying the hijackers of an Italian cruise ship was intercepted by American Navy jets as it flew toward Tunisia Thursday night and was forced to land in Italy, the White House announced. A spokesman said the four terrorists had been taken into custody by Italian authorities.

In a late evening news conference, Larry Speakes, the White House spokesman, said President Reagan had ordered the dramatic military action after learning that Egypt had turned down repeated American pleas to prosecute the four gunmen and was flying them to freedom. The hijackers are believed to have killed an elderly American tourist aboard the cruise ship.

No Shots Fired

The United States intends to seek "the prompt extradition" of the hijackers from Italy, Mr. Speakes said. Later, Defense Secretary Caspar W. Weinberger said the United States hoped the Italians would waive their right to try the hijackers and would allow them to be prosecuted in the United States.

Mr. Speakes said that the Egyptian plane, a commercial 737 airliner with armed Egyptian security men aboard, was intercepted by the F-14's from the aircraft carrier Saratoga north of

News session excerpts, page A12.

Egypt in international waters. The F-14's "diverted" the plane to a joint Italian-NATO base at Sigonella in Sicily. Mr. Weinberger said four F-14's were involved.

The incident occurred without the American planes having to fire a shot, Mr. Speakes said.

Troops Surround Plane

He said the Egyptian aircraft had been headed for Tunisia but that the Tunisian Government had refused to grant it landing rights. For that, he said, the United States was grateful. Mr. Weinberger said the Egyptian plane had also been refused permission to land by authorities in Athens.

After the Egyptian plane landed, it was surrounded by American and Italian troops, Mr. Speakes said. Mr. Wein-

Continued on Page A10, Column 4

Orson Welles Is Dead at 70; Innovator of Film and Stage

Orson Welles, the Hollywood "boy wonder" who created the film classic "Citizen Kane," scared tens of thousands of Americans with a realistic radio report of a Martian invasion of New Jersey and changed the face of film and theater with his daring new ideas, died yesterday in Los Angeles, apparently of a heart attack. He was 70 years old and lived in Las Vegas, Nev.

An assistant coroner in Los Angeles, Donald Messerle, said Welles's death "appears to be natural in origin." He had been under treatment for diabetes as well as a heart ailment, his physician reported. Welles's body was found by his chauffeur.

An Unorthodox Style

Despite the feeling of many that his career — which evoked almost constant controversy over its 50 years — was one of largely unfulfilled promise, Welles eventually won the respect of his colleagues. He received the Lifetime Achievement Award of the American Film Institute in 1975, and last year the Directors Guild of America gave him its highest honor, the D. W. Griffith Award.

His unorthodox casting and staging for the theater gave new meaning to the classics and to contemporary works. As the "Wonder Boy" of Broadway in the 1930's, he set the stage on its ear with a "Julius Caesar" set in Fascist Italy, an all-black "Macbeth" and his presentation of Marc Blitzstein's "Cradle Will Rock." His Mercury Theater of the Air set new standards for radio drama, and in one performance panicked thousands across the nation.

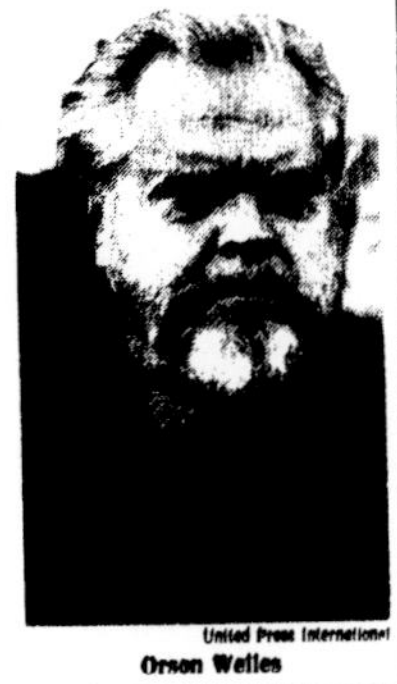

United Press International

Orson Welles

In film, his innovations in deep-focus technology and his use of theater esthetics — long takes without close-ups, making the viewer's eye search the screen as if it were a stage — created a new vocabulary for the cinema.

By age 24, he was already being described by the press as a has-been — a cliché that would dog him all his life. But at that very moment Welles was creating "Citizen Kane," generally considered one of the best motion pictures ever made. This scenario was re-

Continued on Page B6, Column 1

A B C D E F

INSIDE

40 Salvador Soldiers Killed

A leftist rebel unit killed at least 40 Salvadoran soldiers and wounded 68 in a raid on the main army training base near La Unión. Page A3.

Yul Brynner Is Dead

The actor and director, the quintessential Siamese monarch in "The King and I," died in New York at the age of 65. Page B7.

Dodgers Go 2 Games Up

The Dodgers beat the Cardinals, 8-2, in Los Angeles and lead by 2-0, in the National League playoff, which shifts to St. Louis tomorrow. Page A29.

Hostage's Death: 'A Shot to Forehead'

By E. J. DIONNE Jr.

Special to The New York Times

PORT SAID, Egypt, Oct. 10 — Passengers from the hijacked Italian cruise liner were quoted today as describing how the terrorists had dragged an elderly American tourist in his wheelchair to the ship's side and shot him in cold blood.

The most vivid account, based on interviews with some of the more than 400 people held hostage aboard the Achille Lauro, came from the Italian Ambassador to Egypt, Giovanni Migliudo. The Ambassador told reporters that he had put together his account of the killing after six hours of interviews.

He said the killing of the tourist, Leon Klinghoffer, had taken place on Tuesday when the ship was near Tartus, Syria.

Answer 'Slow in Coming'

"The hijackers had asked to be put in contact with the Italian and U.S. Ambassadors in Damascus to demand the liberation of 50 Palestinians held in Israel," the Italian news agency, ANSA, quoted the Ambassador as saying. "But the answer was slow in coming and to exercise further pressure, the hijackers decided to kill a first hostage."

Mr. Migliudo said that all the American and British passengers on the ship were forced to lie on the deck.

"The hijackers pushed him in his chair and dragged him to the side of the boat where — in cold blood — they fired a shot to the forehead. Then the body was dumped into the sea, together with the wheelchair," the Ambassador said.

The Ambassador's story was one of many that emerged today as the ship, the Achille Lauro, lay under a searing sun in the Suez Canal harbor here.

The Austrian Ambassador to Egypt,

Continued on Page ...

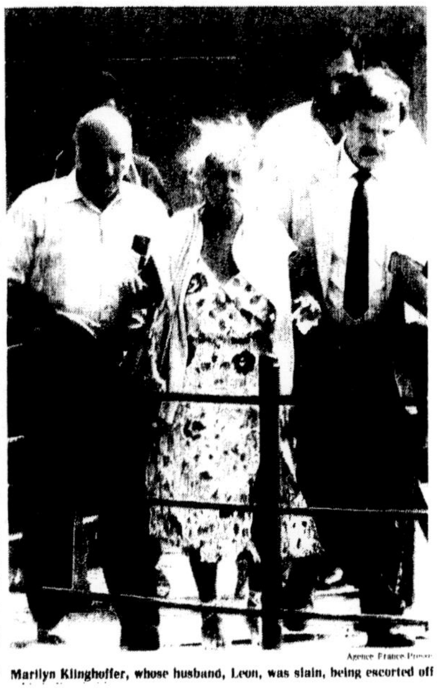

Agence France-Presse

Marilyn Klinghoffer, whose husband, Leon, was slain, being escorted off

"All the News That's Fit to Print"

The New York Times

Late Edition

Weather: Mostly sunny and cold today, westerly winds; clear and cold tonight. Partly sunny and milder tomorrow. Temperatures: today 30-35, tonight 20-25; yesterday 20-41. Details on page 46.

VOL.CXXXV . . No. 46,637 — Copyright © 1985 The New York Times — NEW YORK, SATURDAY, DECEMBER 28, 1985 — 60 cents beyond 75 miles from New York City, except on Long Island — 30 CENTS

AIRPORT TERRORISTS KILL 13 AND WOUND 113 AT ISRAELI COUNTERS IN ROME AND VIENNA

REAGAN TO TRADE TELEVISION TALKS WITH GORBACHEV

New Year's Day Greetings Are to Be Broadcast at Same Time in Both Nations

By GERALD M. BOYD

Special to The New York Times

LOS ANGELES, Dec. 27 — President Reagan and Mikhail S. Gorbachev have agreed to exchange videotaped New Year's Day greetings that are intended for broadcast in the United States and the Soviet Union, the White House announced today.

The announcement said the exchanges would give Mr. Reagan his first chance to talk to the Soviet people directly on television and would give the Soviet leader the same chance to speak to the American people.

The announcement came as Mr. Gorbachev, in Moscow, offered a cautiously upbeat assessment of relations between the Soviet Union and the United States, saying points of "potential convergence" had emerged in arms control talks. [Page 3.]

'Barbaric Methods' Assailed

Shortly before the announcement, Mr. Reagan, who flew here today to begin a weeklong vacation, issued his latest statement condemning the Soviet intervention in Afghanistan.

The statement, noting the sixth anniversary of the intervention, accused the Russians and their surrogates of resorting "to barbaric methods of waging war" to try to crush a liberation effort in Afghanistan. Mr. Reagan said the United States stood "squarely on the side of the people of Afghanistan."

The videotape exchange will achieve a longtime Administration goal of having Mr. Reagan talk on Soviet television.

Three to Five Minutes Long

Late today, the news divisions of the American networks indicated that they all planned to broadcast both addresses.

The speeches, both of which are to be broadcast on Wednesday, are to be three to five minutes long and will contain New Year's greetings, the officials said. One White House aide said Mr.

Continued on Page 3, Column 5

Further Growth In the Economy Forecast for '86

But Inflation and Jobless Rate Worry Analysts

By ROBERT D. HERSHEY Jr.

Special to The New York Times

WASHINGTON, Dec. 27 — The United States economy seems headed for a fourth consecutive year of expansion in 1986, but its course will be marred by gradually rising inflation and stubbornly high unemployment, according to a consensus of business and academic forecasters.

The possibility of a recession, which at various times in the last year has seemed just over the horizon, has receded and is no longer regarded as an apparent threat.

One important reason is the roaring bull market in stocks and bonds. By making investors richer, it has raised both confidence and the outlook for consumer spending, which accounts for two-thirds of the economy.

'Rather Sluggish Fashion'

"The prospects for the economy in 1986 are quite good," said A. Gilbert Heebner chief economist for the Philadelphia National Bank, in a prediction that typifies current professional thinking. "It's going to seem like more of the same, with the economy growing but in a rather sluggish fashion."

The Reagan Administration, for its part, is believed to have tentatively adopted a 4 percent growth forecast for next year, somewhat higher than that of most private analysts.

To be sure, few economists or politicians are satisfied with the current rate of American growth, less than 2.5 percent for 1985 after 6.6 percent in 1984. This year's rate has been barely enough to keep unemployment from rising and it has left industry with large amounts of idle productive capacity.

Moreover, agriculture and parts of the oil, real estate and banking industries are in disarray despite an expansion that this month reached its third anniversary. Weak farm and crude oil prices, as well as a glut of unrented office space in some cities, could cause more problems for banks in 1986.

Yet most economists predict solid growth for 1986. They cite several factors for this tempered optimism. Both

Continued on Page 31, Column 4

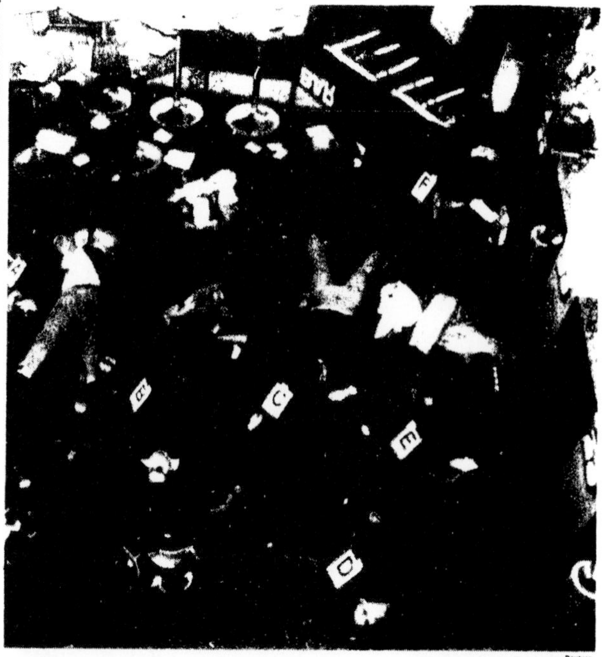

Reuters

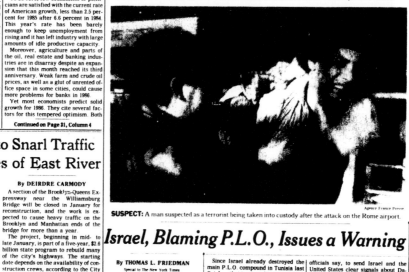

VICTIMS: Bodies bearing tags affixed by police on the floor at Leonardo da Vinci Airport near Rome.

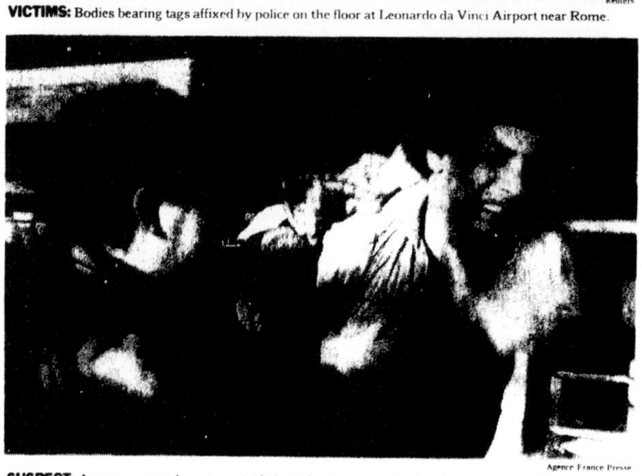

Agence France Presse

SUSPECT: A man suspected as a terrorist being taken into custody after the attack on the Rome airport.

4 ATTACKERS KILLED

Gunmen Fire Into Crowds and Throw Grenades Near Lines at El Al

By JOHN TAGLIABUE

Special to The New York Times

ROME, Dec. 27 — Terrorists hurled grenades and fired submachine guns at crowds of holiday travelers at airports in Rome and Vienna today in attacks on check-in counters of El Al Israel Airlines.

Authorities quoted by news services said the gunmen had killed at least 13 people, including 4 Americans, and wounded 113 in the two attacks. Four terrorists were killed, and three others were wounded and captured.

While El Al appeared to be a target in both attacks, the authorities said the terrorists in Rome had also thrown grenades and fired indiscriminately with Soviet-made assault rifles into crowds of New York-bound passengers checking in at Pan American World Airways and Trans World Airlines.

Terrorists Not Identified

The assailants, who were not immediately identified, left the two airline terminals strewn with bloodied and torn bodies, luggage, overturned furniture and broken glass.

Israeli Government officials asserted that the Palestine Liberation Organization might be responsible, but P.L.O. officials here and in Tunis denied any role in the apparently coordinated attacks.

Witnesses at the airport in Vienna said panic broke out as the explosions and firing began, with passengers and airport staff throwing themselves to the ground and crawling desperately for cover. [Page 4.]

Gunmen Jumped and Shrieked

Similar accounts were given in Rome, where survivors described chaos amid thundering explosions and raking bursts of gunfire unleashed by young masked men in blue jeans who jumped up and down and shrieked as their victims fell. Bystanders screamed and dived for cover.

"It was an inferno — they started throwing hand grenades and firing with submachines guns," said one witness who was wounded in Rome, Dora Silvestri. "We all threw ourselves to the ground. Blood spread over the floor. I

Washington said the attackers were "beyond the pale of civilization." Page 5. These comments were echoed worldwide. Page 6.

fell on the body of a girl, and a grenade splinter hit me in the face."

As the weary and shaken travelers caught in the airport attacks returned to New York, some of them told of their minutes of terror in a series of interviews. [Page 6.]

The authorities said seven terrorists were apparently involved — four in the attack in Rome, which began shortly after at 9 A.M. (3 A.M. New York time), and three in the attack in Vienna, which started a few minutes later.

At Leonardo da Vinci Airport at Rome, three terrorists were slain and one was seized after being wounded in a gun battle with the police and plainclothes Israeli security men in the terminal. Security had been increased there after recent hijackings and official warnings that airports might be attacked during the Christmas holidays.

A total of 13 people were killed in the Rome attack, including the three terrorists, and 70 wounded.

[A wounded American man died later at a Rome hospital, The Associated Press reported from Rome.]

At Schwechat Airport in Vienna, 3 were killed, including a gunman, and 47 wounded, one of them critically.

Two of the terrorists in Vienna were seized after a wild car chase and a run-

Continued on Page 4, Column 3

Israel, Blaming P.L.O., Issues a Warning

By THOMAS L. FRIEDMAN

Special to The New York Times

JERUSALEM, Dec. 27 — Although the Palestine Liberation Organization denied involvement in the attacks in Rome and Vienna, Israeli officials blamed the guerrilla group today and made it clear that Israel would respond at the appropriate time and place.

"Israel is shocked and outraged by these two new acts of senseless terror against innocent civilians," a Foreign Ministry statement said.

"The terrorist attacks come against a background of declarations by the head of the P.L.O., and those Arab states that support this organization, that these terrorists will cease terrorist operations outside of Israel. Israel will continue its struggle against terrorism in every place and at any time it sees fit."

Syrian Missiles in Lebanon

Meanwhile, Israeli analysts said Israel's ability to retaliate for the attacks had been limited by Syria's decision to move mobile surface-to-air missiles into Lebanon.

In the past, Israel has often retaliated for terrorist attacks abroad by bombing Palestinian guerrilla bases in Lebanon, regarding these as convenient "return addresses."

To do so now, however, Israeli jets would have to penetrate the new curtain of surface-to-air missiles Syria has drawn over the Bekaa region in Lebanon, which could lead to an all-out war with Syria, the analysts said.

Since Israel already destroyed the main P.L.O. compound in Tunisia last October, that too is no longer an option for retaliation. The analysts said new P.L.O. offices in Baghdad would not be easy to reach and were widely dispersed. This would seem to leave as the only option for retaliation a more surgical strike against specific individuals, the analysts said.

A Political Statement

To appreciate the full Israeli quandary, officials said, it must be understood that the Syrian decision to deploy the SAM-6 and SAM-8 mobile batteries a few miles inside Lebanon, for the second time in a month, was as much a political statement as a strategic military maneuver.

It was apparently designed, Israeli officials say, to send Israel and the United States clear signals about Damascus's intentions to change some of the rules in the Middle East.

To begin with, said Itamar Rabinovich, an authority on Syria at Tel Aviv University, the Syrians are apparently trying to establish a new relationship with Israel in Lebanon after the Israeli withdrawal.

While Israel wants to hold onto all of its old perquisites in Lebanon, particularly its freedom to fly reconnaissance missions over the Syrian-controlled Bekaa, the Syrians want to reverse once and for all this free Israeli access to their neighboring client state.

"By sending the missiles back, the

Continued on Page 5, Column 1

Road Repairs to Snarl Traffic On Both Sides of East River

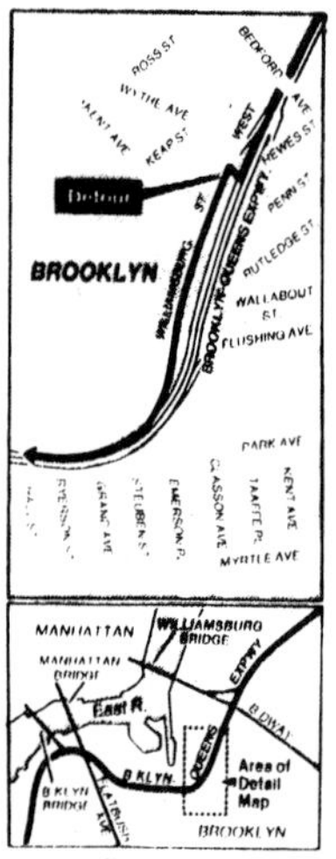

The New York Times / Dec. 28, 1985

Williamsburg Bridge will carry more Manhattan-bound traffic.

By DEIRDRE CARMODY

A section of the Brooklyn-Queens Expressway near the Williamsburg Bridge will be closed in January for reconstruction, and the work is expected to cause heavy traffic on the Brooklyn and Manhattan ends of the bridge for more than a year.

The project, beginning in mid- to late January, is part of a five-year, $2.6 billion state program to rebuild many of the city's highways. The starting date depends on the availability of construction crews, according to the City Bureau of Traffic Operations.

70,000 Vehicles a Day

Westbound traffic on the expressway, which the Traffic Bureau says is used by about 70,000 vehicles a day, will be rerouted at the Wythe Avenue exit in Brooklyn onto Williamsburg Street West for two and a half blocks. Cars will be able to get back on the expressway at the Flushing Avenue entrance.

Williamsburg Street West has been widened by a lane and a shoulder has been added. The Flushing Avenue entrance has also been widened by a lane.

"It is not an easy detour, not one we look forward to," said Traffic Commissioner Samuel I. Schwartz.

The detour is not expected to be able to carry all the traffic, but according to Abel Silver, a spokesman for the City Transportation Department, some of the vehicles that normally take the Brooklyn and Manhattan Bridges into

Continued on Page 26, Column 1

INSIDE

A
B
C
D
E
F

3 on Miami Force Arrested

Three members of the Miami police force were charged with murder in the drownings of three men thought to have been dealing in drugs. Page 8.

West Side Rail Proposal

New York State and New York City are studying the possibility of a light rail line — perhaps a monorail — on Manhattan's West Side. Page 25.

For Families of 2 Americans, Sudden Sorrow

By SARA RIMER

Natasha Simpson, the 11-year-old daughter of a foreign correspondent in Rome, was on her way to New York with her family for a three-week vacation with friends and relatives. John Buonocore 3d, a 20-year-old student, was on his way home to Wilmington, Del., after a semester in Rome, just in time for his father's 50th birthday.

Both died at Leonardo da Vinci Airport in Rome yesterday. They were among the 14 people killed there when terrorists hurled hand grenades and opened fire with submachine guns into crowds of holiday travelers. The Associated Press said two other Americans, Frederick Gage, of Madison, Wis., and Don Maland, of New Port Richey, Fla., were also killed.

Natasha Simpson was killed apparently as her father, Victor L. Simpson, a New Yorker who is the news editor for The Associated Press in Rome, tried to shield her from the bullets. Mr. Simpson, 43, was wounded in the right wrist and hand.

'Put His Arm Around Her'

"I think he put his arm around her to try and push her down and that's how he injured his finger," said his wife, Daniela Petroff Simpson, who was reached by telephone at her parents' home in Rome.

Mrs. Simpson, 40, had been outside the terminal walking the family terrier while her husband and two children — Natasha and 9-year-old Michael — checked in for their flight to Kennedy International Airport. Then she heard the exploding grenades.

"Suddenly there was a shattering noise as if something were collapsing," Mrs. Simpson, who is also a journalist, told The Associated Press in Rome. "And then there were machine-gun bursts. Two distinct machine-gun bursts. And then silence. I rushed into screams and cries and saw my husband dripping blood from his hand and my son on the floor shot in the stomach."

Mr. Simpson and his son were hospi-

Continued on Page 6, Column 3

Index

References in this index in bold face are
for maps or pictures

A

G

Galilee, shelled by Syrians from Golan Heights, 76
Gath, 19
Gaza, 19, 129
Gaza Strip, 83, **108**, 114, 120
    Israeli military rule in, 82
    Jewish settlers in, 98
    outline for autonomy, 94
    rioting spreads, 108
Gemayel, Bashir, head of Lebanese killed by bomb, 103
    Phalange, Christian militia, 101
Genisis, book of, 15
Germany, Federal Republic of, 62
    pays compensation for Jewish property seized under Nazis, 63
Golan Heights, 67, 70, 134
    annexed by Israel, 1981, 90
    captured 1967, 76, **77**
    disengagement agreement, 1974, **91**
    raids from, 60
Golani infantry brigade, 110
Golden Age, 19
Goldstein, Dr. Baruch, attacks Ibrahimi Mosque, 124
Goliath, slain by David, 20
Gulf War, 1991

H

Hadera, 124
Haifa, 72
Hamas, Aviv, 128
    Ayyash, Yahya, "the engineer" bomb maker, 130
    deportees camp in southern Lebanon, 118
    militant Islamic group, 118, 124, 125
    suicide bombers in Jerusalem and Tel Aviv sympathizers, deported, 118, 120
Hamid, Abdul, Ottoman Sultan, 33
Haganah (defense) formed, 36
Hanukkah, (Festival, Feast of Lights), 23

Har Homa, new Jewish suburb, East Jerusalem, 137
Hebrew, "the tongue of Canaan", 19
    chosen as Jews national language, 36
Hebron, 74, 123
    massacre, 123
    revered resting place of patriachs, 123
Herod, King of Judea, 23
Hersh, Seymour M., reporter, 81
Herut, party (revisionists), 53
Herzl, Theodor, lawyer and journalist, 32, 74
    convenes Zionist Congress, 29, **33**, 49
Herzog, Chaim, 72, 79
Hezbollah, 132
Holocaust, 42, **42**, **43**, 46, 53, 55, 63, 92
Homo sapiens sapiens, 15
Hussein, King of Jordan, 71, 73, 114,137
    Signs Peace Treaty, 1994, **122**, 123, 136
Hussein, Sadam, President of Iraq, 98, 113

I

Immigrant camps, **56**
Immigration, see also Aliyah, 36, 37, 40
    Ethiopian Jews, airlift of, **111**
    from the Magreb, 58
    from East European regimes after 1957, 62
    from Soviet Union, 110, 115
    Russian Jews arrive by air, **111**
    source of, **57**
Independence, Declaration of, 48,
Intifada, Palestinian uprising, **107**, 109, 110, 113, 114, **125**, 127
Invasion of Lebanon, **100**
Isaiah, 19
Islam, new faith established, 27
Islamic Jihad, militant group, 124
Israel,
    boycott by Arab States, 57
    counter attack to Arab invasion, **52**
    culture, 19
    Israel in the 90s, **138**

kingdom splits after death of Solomon, 21
kingdom united under Saul, 20
"lost tribes of", 21
new state, 1948, recognised by International community, 50
Northern kingdom falls to Assyrians, 722 BC, 21
public demonstration against war in Lebanon, **102**, 107
recognition of new State by USA, 48
settlements, **99**
tribes of, 16
Israelites, (children of Israel), 16, invasion, 19
Israeli, air strike on Iraq nuclear reactor, 97, 98
    bombardment of Beirut, 101, 102
    forces invade Lebanon, 101, **97**,
    Ministry of Religious Affairs, 98
    Olympic athletes, **83**
Israeli-Egyptian Peace Treaty, 1979, 88

J

Jabaliya, refugee camp, 108
Jabotinsky, Vladimir, Russian Zionist, 40, **40**, 41, 53
Jenin, 74
    Israeli troops withdrawn from, 130
Jericho, 75, 120
    battle, 17
    early community, 15
Jericho, Israeli missile, 80
Jerusalem, 74
    British capture, 1917, 30
    British withdrawal from, 1948, 48
    captured by Crusaders, 1099, 27
    divided, 1948-67, **54**
    holy city to three religions, 27
    new Jewish suburbs, **99**, **136**
    Old City, 67, 75, 76
    street scene, 1990s, **139**
    studied by archeologists, 28
Jesus, of Nazareth, 24, 25
Jewish,
    agency, 36, 37, 47, 48
    Ashkenazi, 56

Picture Credits